Laying the Children's Ghosts to Rest

Laying the Children's Ghosts to Rest

Canada's Home Children in the West

Sean Arthur Joyce

Library and Archives Canada Cataloguing in Publication
Joyce, Sean Arthur, 1959-, author

Laying the children's ghosts to rest : Canada's home children in the West / Sean Arthur Joyce.

Includes bibliographical references and index.
ISBN-978-1-926710-27-3 (pbk.)

1. Home children (Canadian immigrants) – Canada, Western. 2. British Canadians – Canada, Western – History. 3. Child labour – Canada, Western – History. 4. Joyce, Sean Arthur, 1959- – Family. I. Title.

HV887.C3J69   2014   305.23086'94509712   C2013-906983-6

Edited by Don Kerr.
Designed and typeset by Donald Ward.
Cover design by Tania Wolk, Go Giraffe Go.
Cover photographs: British immigrant children from Dr. Barnardo's Homes at landing stage, St. John, New Brunswick (used with permission, Library and Archives Canada), and photograph of Gladys Martin (collection of the author).

The publishers gratefully acknowledge the assistance of the Saskatchewan Arts Board, The Canada Council for the Arts, and the Cultural Industries Development Fund (Saskatchewan Department of Culture, Youth & Recreation) in the production of this book.

MIX
Paper from
responsible sources
FSC   FSC® C103214
www.fsc.org

Acknowledgements

THERE ARE SO MANY TO THANK for helping me along the path of what has turned out to be one of the biggest quests of my life. First, last, and always, thanks are due Anne Champagne — as great a partner in life as anyone could wish for, without whom, etc. etc. etc., and whose insights at critical points in the writing have been invaluable.

Many others proved themselves allies — unexpected and otherwise — for overcoming threshold guardians or just generally providing support: my parents Art and Dianne Joyce; Brian and Joan Joyce; Ivy Sucee; Lori Oschefsky; John Sayers; Pat Rogers; Perry Snow; MP for BC Southern Interior Alex Atamanenko; Oliver Cosgrove; Joey Catanzaro; Patrick Dunae; Ron Smith; Professor Margaret McNay; Enid Hunt; Charlene Alexander; Home Children activists and researchers in the UK, Australia, and Canada; volunteers and staff with BC, Ontario, and UK historical societies and archives who helped with research and supported my talks about Home Children in BC; all those authors who have courageously written on the topic; and most certainly all those courageous Home Children and their descendants who kindly consented to be interviewed, and their families.

Thanks are due *Acumen Literary Journal* (UK) for first publishing a short version of *Laying the Children's Ghosts to Rest*, "Introduction," and the poem, "The Man Without Stories," in its January 2011 edition.

I'm grateful to the Columbia Basin Trust (CBT) through the Columbia Kootenay Cultural Alliance (CKCA) for a Major Project Grant (Heritage), which sustained me through a major portion of writing this book.

I am indebted to Anne Champagne for her many insights at critical points in the writing of the conclusion.

Contents

Laying the Children's Ghosts to Rest

There walk, as yet, no ghosts of lovers in Canadian lanes. For it is possible, at a pinch, to do without gods. But one misses the dead.

So said the young English poet Rupert Brooke upon visiting Canada in 1913. Of course, it was a naïve assessment: it would have been more correct to say there were yet no *British* ghosts. Plenty of First Nations ghosts had their spirits imbued in the landscape, and in ever greater numbers since the coming of Europeans, guns, and smallpox. But it leads to the question: are we a people who have lost our ghosts? Or are we in fact haunted by them, but can't remember their names? On February 24, 2010, British Prime Minister Gordon Brown raised the spectre of thousands of child ghosts who inhabit our Canadian landscape. Ghosts whose names until now have been mostly stricken from our history.

On that day Brown issued a long overdue public apology to the thousands of children who were shipped to the colonies from the 1860s to as late as 1967, in the case of Australian child emigrants. Some 130,000 children were scooped up from the mean streets of empire to be used as slave labour, mostly on Canadian farms and Australian work projects. It's estimated that about 100,000 of these were sent to Canada. Today by official government estimates there may be four million descendants of what were derisively known as "Home Children." That's about one in eight Canadians. Yet not once in all my years of public schooling did I learn this fact. What was even more shocking to me was learning in my middle age that I am one of those descendants.

My father used to wonder aloud why his father, my grandfather Cyril William Joyce, came to Canada as a lad of 16. "It just wasn't like him to do something adventurous like that," he says. "When I asked him why, he'd just say, 'Oh, it seemed the thing to do at the time.'" Yet my grandfather seldom spoke of his family, and took what knowledge he had of them to his grave. I used to wonder if there had been some terrible family rift, or if something awful had happened that he refused to talk about.

About all we knew about Cyril was that he grew up in London, England and had arrived in Canada in 1926 on his own. We knew Cyril had been sponsored for emigration by the Church of England, but not why. We had no idea what ship he'd sailed on, or what port he sailed from. Cyril spoke only of the backbreaking work of life on a northern Alberta farm, when he spoke about his past at all, which was rare. He was a man of medium stature and slight build, more suited to office work than the rigours of farming. Although I later learned an uncle from England occasionally wrote him letters, Cyril made little effort to re-establish contact with the family. It was as if he was trying to erase his own past. I wondered: what could make anyone want to do that? In 2007 I decided it was time to find out. It began with discovering one of the least known aspects of Canadian history.

1. Heeding the Ghosts of "Gutter Children"

Gutter children poem
Take them away! Take them away!
Out of the gutter, the ooze, and slime,
Where the little vermin paddle and crawl
Till they grow and ripen into crime.

Take them away! Take them away!
The boys from the gallows, the girls from worse;
They'll prove a blessing to other lands —
Here, if they linger, they'll prove a curse.

— from *The Departure of the Innocents*, Rev. J. W. Horsley,
Our Waifs & Strays magazine, August 1887

Like it or not, children / family is everything we are. . . .
— Sean Arthur Joyce, *Requiem*

WITH THE ADVENT OF MECHANIZATION during the Industrial Revolution, the agrarian and cottage-based industry of Britain was wiped out virtually overnight. Thousands of British workers were suddenly unemployed. Families flooded into the cities, where — even with the new factories — there was still not enough work for everyone. The parish relief system established under the Poor Laws dating back to Elizabethan times was overwhelmed. Poverty and disease in British cities became endemic — the shame of Empire. Children were literally dying in the gutter. During the 1866 cholera epidemic in London's East End, 5,000 people died in that city alone. It's estimated that there were 30,000 destitute children in London during this period. Even today, London's East End has the fifth highest level of unemployment in Britain and seven out of 10 children there are from low-income families.

In one of history's fascinating confluences, Annie Macpherson, Thomas John Barnardo, and Salvation Army founder William Booth all found themselves doing relief work in the East End during that fateful period. What they saw there would motivate them to devote their lives to the aid of poor children. Macpherson and Barnardo began by creating "ragged schools" to get poor children off the streets. These schools were so named due to the appearance of the children, who literally turned up on their doorsteps in filthy rags. As early as 1844, a Ragged Schools Union had been established with the patronage of the seventh Earl of Shaftesbury.[1] At least it would help children get some nourishing meals throughout the course of a day. Up to this point in British history an education was mostly the prerogative of the wealthy or the church.[2]

But with the rise of evangelical Christian movements during the mid-1800s, reformers sought to ensure that poor children received more than merely a secular education. Both Macpherson and Barnardo were fervent Christians and saw it as their mission to teach "gutter children" moral values. Partly this was due to the prevailing notion that poverty was an indication of moral failure on the part of parents. It was a "blame the victim" mentality that was buttressed both by the British class system and the church doctrine of inherent sinfulness. However, an effort was also made in Macpherson and Barnardo's ragged schools to provide basic literacy and skills training that could lead to employment. Barnardo's first ragged school was opened in 1867, the year after the epidemic, while Macpherson's Home of Industry opened at Bethnal Green, a borough of East London, in early 1869. It was only a modest step up: the boys might learn to repair shoes while the girls would receive training in domestic skills.[3]

The only other alternative available to poor families during this period was the workhouse, an institution run more like a prison than a soup kitchen. The great Victorian novelist Charles Dickens spent a brief period in a boot-blacking factory as a boy, an experience that led him to satirize British workhouses and orphanages throughout his writing career. Many of the poor preferred to risk death outside the workhouse than endure conditions within. Writing in *Oliver Twist* of the Poor Law Board that administered these institutions, Dickens' wit is at its most wickedly satirical: "The members of this board were very sage, deep, philosophical men. . . . So, they established the rule, that all poor people should have the alternative (for they would compel nobody, not they), of being starved by a gradual process in the house, or by a quick one out of it. With this view, they contracted with the water works to lay on an unlimited supply of water; and with the corn-factor to supply periodically small quantities of oatmeal; and issued three meals of thin gruel a day, with an onion twice a week, and half a roll on Sundays."[4]

Dickens was only barely exaggerating. For the poor, Dickens' London offered a choice of "the devil or the deep blue sea," with conditions outside the workhouse just as squalid and hopeless: "A dirtier or more wretched place he had never seen. The street was very narrow and muddy, and the air was impregnated with filthy odours. There were a good many small shops; but the only stock in trade appeared to be heaps of children, who, even at that time of night, were crawling in and out at the doors, or screaming from the inside. The sole places that seemed to prosper amid the general blight of the place, were the public houses. . . . Covered ways and yards, which here and there diverged from the main street, disclosed little knots of houses, where drunken men and women were positively wallowing in filth. . . ."[5]

Ideologically driven changes to the Poor Law regulations during the early 19th century had led to a system that had little to offer the poor. As Dickens indicated, by the time he published *Oliver Twist*, the workhouse had become a nightmarish legend. Assistance to the poor under the Old Poor Law (1601) was offered either as indoor relief (inside a workhouse), or outside a workhouse in the form of money, food, and clothing. Relief for those too ill or old to work was in the form of items of clothing or food — "the parish loaf" — also known as "outdoor relief." Some of the elderly were accommodated in almshouses, which were usually private charitable institutions. Able-bodied beggars who refused work were often placed in "houses of correction" — i.e., prisons. The workhouse system came into its own as a national system of dealing with poverty in the 17th century. Its primary motivation was to relieve the financial burden of middle-class landowners who supported poor relief through parish taxes. The first workhouses were opened at Abingdon in 1631, and Exeter in 1652.[6]

A government survey done in 1776 revealed that there were more than 1,800 workhouses in England and Wales, in roughly one in seven parishes. The Society for Promoting Christian Knowledge had published a directory of workhouses since 1725, listing only 126 establishments. The Society was an avid supporter of the workhouse system. The growth in workhouses was spurred by the Workhouse Test Act of 1723, requiring anyone seeking poor relief to do so within the confines of the workhouse, in return for a set amount of unpaid labour. It was designed to deter irresponsible claims on parish poor relief. Further relief for the ratepayers came with the 1782 Relief of the Poor Act sponsored by Thomas Gilbert, a land agent and MP. Known as Gilbert's Act, it allowed parishes to form unions, thereby combining resources that allowed for the building and maintenance of workhouses.[7]

But it was hardly "relief" for the poor. Poor Law authorities hit an all-time low in their cost-cutting zeal when cases were reported of husbands being forced to sell their wives to avoid them becoming a financial burden on the parish.[8] Fifty years later Dickens satirized this in *Oliver Twist,* caustically noting that the workhouse authorities "kindly undertook to divorce poor married people. . . and instead of compelling a man to support his family, as they had heretofore done, took his family away from him, and made him a bachelor! . . . The relief was inseparable from the workhouse and the gruel, and that frightened people."[9]

But even these attempts to penny-pinch on the backs of the poor were soon seen as inadequate. Upper-class intellectuals like Thomas Robert Malthus and others of similar mindset saw this system as badly — as in expensively — run, and an "inducement to laziness." An 1832 Royal Commission into the Operation of the Poor Laws sought to redress these deficiencies. The result of the Commission was the Poor Law Amendment Act, which was heavily influenced by Malthusian doctrine. This doctrine proposed that because population is subject to exponential growth, it will always outstrip the ability of a country to feed its people. The result is "surplus population," whose numbers should therefore be reduced either by policy or attrition. The Poor Law amendment sought to make indoor relief in workhouses as unpleasant as possible — a deterrent to those who were supposedly shirking work. The truth was that even with the new factories there weren't enough jobs for all.

By the 1830s, most parishes had at least one workhouse, and their dismal conditions were a threat to physical and mental health. Strangely enough, one of the first attempts to quantify the conditions of poor relief in Britain came from a member of the aristocracy, Sir Frederick Morton Eden. His three-volume work *The State of the Poor* (1797) was undertaken "from motives both of benevolence and personal curiosity, to investigate their conditions in various parts of the kingdom." Eden wanted to provide a factual basis for the political debate on what to do about the poor, which had been dominated by political economists like Malthus applying abstract theories to a very real human problem. Eden reported that the typical workhouse was a dark, filthy place with "small windows, low rooms and dark staircases . . . surrounded by a high wall that gives it the appearance of a prison. . . ." Sleeping wards crammed 8–10 beds in each room, with mattresses of wool or cotton that retained odours and fostered vermin. "No regular account is kept of births and deaths, but when smallpox, measles or malignant fevers make their appearance in the house, the mortality is very great."[10] Early attempts to ban all forms of outdoor relief failed until the 1840s, when the workhouse became a poor family's primary option. Although never passed by Parliament, the amendment was administered as law by Poor Law commissioners.

Oliver Twist was published in 1838; by the time Dr. Barnardo and Annie Macpherson began their relief work 30 years later, the slum conditions in Britain's cities hadn't improved much. The filthy, desperate conditions of poor children, many of them roving in street gangs very much like Fagin's in *Oliver Twist*, confirmed these two philanthropists in their life's work. For all their faults, it was the Christians, not the British government or aristocracy, who were there to catch those falling through the cracks in the Poor Law system. Reverend Andrew Mearns, secretary of the London Congregational Union, took it upon himself to do his own investigation of the living conditions of the poor. The result was his report, *The Bitter Cry of Outcast London: An Inquiry into the Condition of the Abject Poor*, widely published as a penny pamphlet in 1883.

Mearns pulled no punches, calling London's poor districts "pestilential human rookeries. . .where tens of thousands are crowded together amidst horrors which call to mind what we have heard of the middle passage of the slave ship."[11]

Yet Mearns was encouraged that the Christian churches seemed to be actively responding to the challenge. "But it has, as yet, only imperfectly realized and fulfilled its mission to the poor. Until recently it has contented itself with sustaining some outside organizations, which have charged themselves with this special function, or what is worse, has left the matter to individuals or to little bands of Christians having no organization."[12] He criticized what he saw as only a haphazard approach of administering relief to the poor. But with highly motivated individuals like Dr. Barnardo, Macpherson, Booth, and others, this was about to change.

Mearns' work was followed by Seebohm Rowntree, who was inspired by the work of his father Joseph Rowntree and another wealthy industrialist, Charles Booth, in studying the conditions of the poor. Unlike the political economists who studied the problem from a distance, Seebohm — like Mearns — went directly to the slums, this time in York. His two-year study resulted in the report, *Poverty — A Study of Town Life*, published in 1901. What made his approach revolutionary was that — unlike the Christian philanthropists or the Malthusian adherents — he saw poverty as an *economic*, not a moral issue. As head of employee relations at the family firm, he introduced reforms that included a raise in wages and democratic workers' councils. Rowntree's later works, *The Human Needs of Labour* (1918) and *The Human Factor in Business* (1921) argued for a government-mandated minimum wage. Charles Booth concluded from his studies of poverty in London that the state should take responsibility for the poor and he proposed the concept of old age pensions. "Seebohm argued that employers who refused to pay decent wages should be put out of business as their existence was bad for the 'nation's economy and humanity.'"[13]

MEANWHILE, FOR THOSE WORKING on the front lines of abject poverty, it didn't take a skilled novelist's pen or a reformer's zeal to bring the reality brutally home. Historian Kenneth Bagnell sets the scene, in the fall of 1867 while Annie Macpherson is working in Bethnal Green. Perhaps hearing the din of children's voices, she is led up a rickety set of stairs to a cramped attic room. The dingy attic is crowded with more than 30 small girls, "their arms thin as broomsticks, at work making matchboxes. Each child received three farthings, less than one penny, for making a gross of boxes. . . ." The girls were mostly between the ages of eight and 10, though some were even younger. "On a table was a loaf of bread. When the children were so hungry they could not go on, they were given a slice. They paid for it out of their earnings." For Macpherson it was a life-altering experience.[14]

Barnardo was fond of telling the story of young Jim Jarvis, who had lingered one day after his ragged school lessons. When told it was time to go home, Jarvis responded, likely in a Cockney drawl: "Ain't got no home t'go to, sir." Barnardo asked him where he slept the previous night and was told the boy had found a disused donkey cart lined with straw. Barnardo asked if there were more boys like him and was told, "Oh, yes sir! 'eaps of 'em! More'n I could count!" From there the boy led him to the back alleys and hiding places of children to prove his point. Barnardo thus "discovered" hundreds of boys and girls sleeping on roofs and in gutters, carefully avoiding policemen who might send them to the dreaded workhouse.[15]

Or so the story goes. As Bagnell has pointed out, it seems unlikely Barnardo would need to be led by the hand to make such a discovery, given that he had already seen first-hand the destitution in the East End. But it made a convenient story that acquired the status of legend and helped finance his work, leading to the acquisition of his first children's home at Stepney Causeway in 1870. Macpherson's story of the little matchbox girls may be just as apocryphal, but she had already established four children's homes in London by this time. Still, both stories — based on observable conditions — made it obvious that something more than ragged schools, orphanages, and workhouses were needed. Even Stepney Causeway would soon fill to capacity with poor boys who had nowhere else to go. This became painfully apparent when Barnardo was forced one night to turn away an 11-year-old lad named John Somers, known as "Carrot Top" for his flaming red hair. A few days later the boy was found dead of exposure, exhaustion, and lack of food. Barnardo decided that from then on, no child would be turned away. He had a sign installed above the entrance to Stepney Causeway: "No destitute child ever refused admission." But the problem of overcrowding remained, begging for a solution.[16]

That solution presented itself almost simultaneously to both Annie Macpherson and Maria Rye, an upper middle-class social reformer whose initial efforts had been directed at improving the status of working women. The solution: emigrate some of the children to the British colonies of Canada, Australia, and New Zealand. This would serve a dual purpose: to keep the colonies British (white) and provide a source of cheap labour for colonists in desperate need of a workforce to help develop farms and new infrastructure. Poor children had been forcibly emigrated as far back as 1618, when 100 London "street urchins" were sent to the new colony of Virginia. In 1740 Scottish businessmen and magistrates colluded in a scheme to kidnap 500 children and export them to America. But these were isolated incidents compared to what 19th century Christian philanthropists were contemplating. The irony is that the concept of child emigration was concurrent with an age of reform in British social policy. Aristocratic reformer Lord Shaftesbury had campaigned to restrict child labour in British factories, while Charles Booth and the Rowntree family worked to change perceptions of the poor and even to introduce radical new social welfare policies.[17]

Maria Rye had founded the Female Middle Class Emigration Society in 1861 to transport young women to New Zealand, Australia, and Canada. Encouraged by Lord Shaftesbury, she turned her attention to rescuing poor children. Some of them may have wished Rye had passed them over. Contemporary accounts of her methods reveal a woman with little feeling for children and a very harsh concept of discipline. She brought the first shipload of 68 children to Canada in autumn 1869, having first received enthusiastic support on both sides of the Atlantic. They were brought to a receiving home she had been able to purchase in Niagara-on-the-Lake through fundraising done in London. From there the children were dispersed to work on various farms in the Ontario countryside, establishing a pattern that would endure for the next 70 years. Macpherson followed with her first contingent of 100 boys in May 1870.[18]

Before long, other philanthropists would follow in Rye and Macpherson's footsteps over the "golden bridge" to new opportunities across the sea. These included Salvation Army founder William Booth; Father Richard Seddon of the Catholic "Crusade of Rescue"; Scottish philanthropist William Quarrier, who was based in Glasgow and sent children to Canada with Macpherson's parties; John Middlemore, whose homes emigrated children mostly to Canada's Maritime provinces; JWC Fegan of Fegan's Homes; Robert Rudolf of the Church of England Waifs and Strays Society; Reverend Thomas Bowman Stephenson, who established the National Children's Homes; and many more.[19]

Annie Macpherson had published her "little matchbox girls" story in London newspapers, greatly prospering her fundraising efforts. It was she who coined the phrase "the golden bridge" later used to great effect by Thomas Barnardo: "We who labour here are tired of relieving misery from hand to mouth, and also heartsick of seeing hundreds of families pining away for want of work, when over on the shores of Ontario the cry is heard, 'Come over and we will help you.' We are waiting to seek out the worthy . . . we will see to their being properly started on the Canadian shores if you will give us the power to make *a golden bridge across the Atlantic*"[20] (emphasis added). Given the chronic unemployment in Britain at the time, it's hard to comprehend why agencies like Macpherson's didn't emigrate whole families together. But in fact one of the arguments made to funders of Rye's emigration scheme was financial: it would take far less to pay for a child's fare to Canada than it would to continue maintaining that child in an orphanage. And still less than emigrating a child's entire family, presumably.

Thomas Barnardo himself would become the most efficient exporter of poor children to Canada, ultimately contributing some 30,000 of the 100,000 sent here from Britain. Barnardo also made his argument on fiscal grounds, chastising the British government for its initial reluctance to support child emigration, at "half the annual cost that is already being incurred in maintaining the same children in England...."[21] He had begun by including small numbers with some of Annie Macpherson's emigration parties, eventually totalling about 900 children.[22] But by 1882 Barnardo had decided to make it a cornerstone of his childcare policy:

> Well-planned and wisely conducted child-emigration, especially to Canada, contains within its bosom the truest solution of some of the mother country's most perplexing problems, and the supply of our Colonies' most urgent needs. . . . First, it relieves the overcrowded centres of city life and the congested labour markets at home, while, at the same time, it lessens in a remarkable manner the burdens of taxation. Second, it supplies what the Colonies are most in want of — an increase of the English-speaking population. . . . Third, it confers upon the children themselves unspeakable blessings. . . . The change at the young and formative period of their lives . . . gives to each child whose character is good, and who is successfully absorbed into the colonial population, such an immediate prospect of an independent existence upon a higher plane as could hardly have been imagined as within its reach.[23]

According to Barnardo's version of history, young Jim Jarvis was among his first party of emigrants in 1882.[24]

Thomas Barnardo is today probably the most famous of the 19th century child philanthropists, and possibly the most controversial.

I find it telling that only one of his arguments for emigration had anything to do with the welfare of the child. To some extent, it's understandable that, given the sheer numbers crowding in on children's homes, he coined the phrase, "An ever-open entrance to the Homes demands an ever-open exit."[25] But what began as a charitable impulse on Barnardo's part seems to have gradually become an end unto itself. And with so many agencies becoming involved, as historian Roy Parker explains, there was "intense competition between the child-saving agencies for prestige, financial support and popular acclaim. By the end of the century rivalry was probably at its peak." The pressure to increase the size of emigration parties was felt by Stepney Home manager Adam Fowler in 1905, who wrote Barnardo to state that he could not reach the goal of 450 children in the next party.[26]

By design or default, at some point the financial imperative of running a massive childcare organization seems to have taken over. In addition to raising money to run the homes, children had to be equipped with a kit of clothing and basic supplies for emigration — the Barnardo's trunks being the most famous examples — and ship fares had to be paid. Already by 1872 Britain's Local Government Board (LGB), successor to the Poor Law Board, was alarmed at the price being charged by Maria Rye for emigration — £12 per head, compared to Macpherson's £6.6, the adult fare from Liverpool to Canada. Children under age eight sailed at half price, and since boys and girls as young as four had been emigrated, it seemed Rye was earning a handsome profit. When the LGB sent its inspector Andrew Doyle to Canada in 1875 to check up on the work of Macpherson and Rye, his final report noted "a clear gain of £5 per head upon every pauper child taken by these ladies to Canada."[27] When Barnardo began his program of child emigration in 1882, he explained to his financial supporters that, "For the sum of nine pounds, I can now fully equip, outfit, and pay all expenses connected with the emigration of a boy or girl to any part of Ontario." Often the children were required to pay back the cost of their passage from England.[28]

This is where Christian charity started to go off the rails, as Parker notes: "the subsidy arrangements and deals with the shipping companies, together with the lure of free or cheap land in Canada," made it irresistible to the more unscrupulous child emigration agents.[29] The growing demand for child workers overseas put pressure on officials and churchwardens to bend the rules — and in some cases exert their influence to make new laws to their benefit. For one thing, most poor parents were unable to read the agreements they were made to sign with childcare organizations. For another, in British society at that time children were not generally viewed as having any rights. So when some parents objected to the practice of emigrating their children, steps had to be taken.

But as Parker explains, "during the second half of the 1880s there was an orchestrated campaign to curtail the rights of parents who were regarded as irresponsible or who were considered . . . a threat to their children's well-being."[30] At first the campaign concentrated on the right to keep children under the care of relief agencies until age 18 — the law stated they had to be released at 16. The tide turned against parental rights in 1889, when the Prevention of Cruelty to Children Act was introduced, partly prompted by several high profile court cases brought against Dr. Barnardo by families seeking the return of their children. Traditionally, under English law a parent's — in particular a father's — rights over children were supreme. While removing children from abusive parents was a laudable goal, the legislation was broad enough to allow substantial loopholes for childcare organizations seeking custody. Some even called it "Barnardo's Law." It allowed children to be placed in the care of "fit persons" without ever defining that term. Nor did it stipulate whether corporate bodies like Barnardo's could be designated "fit persons."

Once taken from their families, children were essentially branded "orphans," regardless of whether a parent survived or not. Although parents could occasionally visit their children in the homes, some were shocked to discover that what they had considered a temporary placement had become permanent. Or worse

— that their children had been shipped overseas. As Parker observes, "once a child had been committed . . . they were . . . treated on a par with other children in its care and considered for emigration," frequently without obtaining parental consent. Only the Local Government Board made an effort to obtain consent from the children themselves.[31] Historian Gail Corbett notes that by 1892 each admission of a child to a Barnardo's Home was accompanied by the signing of the "Canada Clause," allowing them to be emigrated at any time without having to consult the parents.[32] Most would never see their children again.

A Private Member's Bill in 1893 proposed a clause protecting children against "unjustifiable emigration," which was adopted into the Prevention of Cruelty to Children Act. But it proved ineffectual and was mostly ignored under the chorus of complaints from childcare agencies.[33] There were tragic cases of broken-hearted parents trying desperately to have their children returned from overseas, all to no avail. Once emigrated, it was considered a *fait accompli*. The practice came to be described by Barnardo as "philanthropic abductions."[34]

In Australia many children were sent to live in institutions run by the Catholic order known as the Christian Brothers.[35] These were little more than child labour camps where children were used to build roads, schools, and other infrastructure. English social worker Margaret Humphreys has made it a mission through her Child Migrants Trust in Nottingham to reunite as many Australian child migrants as possible with their families in Britain. Her amazing story is featured in the 2010 film *Oranges and Sunshine*, based on her book *Empty Cradles*. Thanks to Humphreys' work, for many the healing process has begun, the laying to rest of old, anguished family ghosts.

Compared to the institutionalized abuse many Australian child immigrants suffered, British Home Children at least stood a chance of a happier life in Canada. But it was a crapshoot at best. Once children were placed with farmers, they were entirely at their mercy. More responsible agencies like Macpherson's and

Barnardo's did have staff assigned to follow up on a child's living conditions. But they underestimated peoples' capacity for duplicity: many stories are told of these children being threatened not to say anything critical of their farm home. Yet they might be sleeping in a barn, or made to go barefoot in winter. Often those who were routinely beaten had to get help from neighbours or ministers to be removed from the home. Partly the problem was due to the sheer vastness of the country — the province of Ontario alone, where most of the children were sent, was an immense territory to monitor. This made any regular system of visitation a great practical difficulty and potentially expensive. Added to that were the easy pitfalls of expediency and indifference.

The famous Doyle report of 1875 had actually been prompted by reports received from Allerdale Grainger, who had written the LGB in Islington at various times throughout 1874 complaining about Maria Rye. Aside from pointing out Rye's financial interest in the emigration scheme, he reported that her discipline of children amounted to outright abuse. "He described in particular the case of Annie Thompson, aged 10, who, he claimed, had been placed in solitary confinement and given only bread and water for several days on being returned to Rye's Home at Niagara," notes Parker. "Rye, he contended, had also beaten the child with the back of a brush and, when she escaped, had allowed her to 're-main out all night during one of the coldest nights in a Canadian winter.' Fortunately, the girl had been sheltered at a nearby house where she had sought refuge." As Grainger pointed out, the system of obtaining character references for host families was inherently flawed, since few people wanted to give bad reports of their neighbours.[36]

Doyle was an experienced inspector of institutions run by the Poor Law Board. In England, Ireland, Wales, and Scotland, monitoring of workhouses and children's homes was routine. His plan for the summer of 1874 was to visit Macpherson's distributing homes in Knowlton, Quebec; Belleville and Galt, Ontario; and Rye's home at Niagara. From there he planned to visit 400 children dispersed amongst families in Ontario farms and villages — a massive task.[37] Doyle's experience had taught him to be wary of the false fronts often presented by adults and he made an attempt to interview children apart from their host families. Interestingly, a report he had filed regarding rural placement of children in Swansea, Wales, in January 1874 would echo what he was to find in Ontario, with many children "placed in lonely districts far away from any existing schools; they have a long walk to go over rough and hilly roads; they are often scantily clad . . . [and] *they have no advocate to tell of what they endure.*"[38]

Doyle was naturally a product of his time and so was careful in his final report, delivered in January 1875, to emphasize that Rye and Macpherson were well motivated and doing good work on behalf of former "street Arabs." Sensibly, he cautioned against judging the entire emigration scheme based on a few tragic cases. But in practice, the system fell far short of the promised benefits. Maria Rye made no effort at all to check up on her charges, beyond asking friends to look in on her girls from time to time. "She took the view that no news was good news," writes Bagnell. "As a result, large numbers of Miss Rye's girls were never heard from again; what happened to them is left to the imagination of history."[39]

Annie Macpherson, by contrast, seemed to genuinely care about children. She established a system of visitation based on volunteers but simply lacked the resources. Doyle praised Macpherson's considerable energy and dedication to the cause, but found her visitations mostly ineffectual. His report revealed that Home Children had no legal protection from ill treatment or harsh working conditions. Consequently, contracts signed by farmers stipulating a minimum of school attendance were unenforceable. As a result, few of them made it past the eighth grade, if they made it that far. Often the children were lost track of due to constantly being shifted from one home to another. Younger children were often returned to the distributing homes because of their inability to cope with heavy farm work. The result was a repeating cycle of rejection that left deep emotional scars. In Rye's care it usually also meant physical punishment. Barnardo realized the limitations of younger children for work and any of his wards aged five and under were "boarded out" in foster homes. A few of these, such as Leslie Vivian Rogers, were lucky enough to be accepted — if not quite adopted — as family members.[40]

Doyle concluded that the system could not continue in its present form. To that end he met with Prime Minister Alexander Mackenzie and Canadian immigration agent Edward Jenkins, advising them that no more children should be sent until a responsible system of inspections was established. He was particularly hard on Rye, stating that no poor children should be placed in her care, period. Unfortunately, his advice fell on deaf ears in Canada. In Britain it resulted in the LGB placing a moratorium on child emigration that lasted until 1883. This of course didn't prevent private agencies such as Barnardo's from emigrating children to Canada. And although Barnardo's had a conscientious visitation program, it was not immune to the abuses and pitfalls noted above.[41]

The Ontario government finally established a child welfare agency charged with oversight of child immigrants during the 1890s. This was largely a response to exposés published in the Toronto *Globe* by journalist John Joseph "JJ" Kelso, reporting on child prostitution in that city. Although an ambitious journalist, Kelso had a social conscience, following up his articles with the formation of the Children's Aid Society in 1891. When the government passed its first bill to protect children in 1893, he was in the Parliamentary gallery cheering it on. Within weeks Premier Oliver Mowat asked Kelso to serve in the newly created post of Secretary of Neglected and Dependent Children. Kelso abandoned a promising career at the *Globe* to accept the position, beginning a 40-year career that, in Bagnell's words, "would further the welfare of children in Canada in ways unmatched by any man or woman in the country's history." Kelso's department would fall prey to the usual vagaries of politics, leaving it frequently short of funding. Still, a

Canadian government agency had finally taken responsibility for looking in on the country's littlest immigrants.[42]

While Kelso ran the Ontario government's new agency, his counterpart in the federal Immigration Department was George Bogue Smart, Inspector of British Immigrant Children. Smart had worked for Molson's Bank prior to joining the Immigration Branch in 1899 to head up the Interior Department, which had oversight of British child immigrants.[43] He seems to have taken his job to heart, as his many detailed reports and letters to children's homes attest. Writing of his initial inspection of the new Elizabeth Rye Home opened in Toronto by the Church of England Waifs and Strays Society in October 1924, Smart notes, "I impressed upon those in charge of the work the importance of frequent, careful and systematic oversight of the girls under their care and when they place in service in Toronto."[44]

This was no easy task in a country the size of Canada. As Smart himself acknowledged in his year-end report for 1906, "To adequately appreciate the labour necessary, and the amount of travel . . . one has only to bear in mind the fact that the children are scattered through nearly every county in the provinces of Ontario, Quebec, Nova Scotia, [and] New Brunswick," while adding that in the Western provinces, children could be "distant from each other a hundred or more miles." Based on extant records, it seems unlikely the staff allocated to Smart's department was equal to the task.[45]

A colleague of Smart's, writing to him early in 1924 about Church of England girls' accommodations, makes it clear that the Immigration Department had no desire to interfere with the child immigration work. "On account of the Home having recently opened and having many things to deal with in starting, it seemed only fair to them to be careful not to upset the girls' mistresses by a rigid inspection at this juncture and incur the risk of the Society losing good placements for their girls." Yet certain standards were now expected of the homes placing out children as indentured workers. "It should I think be the duty of every Home when placing a child to inform the mistress that the child's room, wardrobe and terms of indenture shall be open to Government inspection." This inspector seems to have taken a personal interest in the children. "I have always felt that it was perfectly right to let the children know that the Government takes a personal interest and would be glad to hear from them. With reference to the suggestion that it is not the duty of an Inspector to inquire into the health of the girls; this has always been an important part of my inspections, as it is in finding out about the girl herself. . . ."[46] Given their limited resources, how much Smart and his inspectors were able to meet this admirable goal is open to debate.

Yet even as societal attitudes were beginning to shift away from child immigration during the 1920s, Smart was on record as a supporter. His 1912–13 report stressed it as "a work of real value to Great Britain, a distinct blessing to the children, and a source of material development to the overseas Dominion — a truly Imperial work."[47] As historian Joy Parr concludes, Smart had made frequent trips to Britain to attend conferences held by public child rescue organizations and shared their viewpoint toward the work. He "acknowledged only those flaws in the policy which could be overcome through more stringent regulation."[48]

It would take until 1925 for the Canadian government to raise the minimum age for child immigrants unaccompanied by parents to 14. In Britain it took until 1933 for the issue of the mutual consent of parents and children to be legislated, with the passage of the Children and Young Persons Act.[49] The Act was prompted in part by two factors: new developments in the field of psychology and social policy; and a growing unease with child labour, particularly in Britain. This unease found its form in the Bondfield Commission led by British Member of Parliament Margaret Bondfield, beginning in September 1924. The commission travelled across Canada, visiting distributing homes, immigration officials and as many children as they could reach. Their conclusion at the end of such an exhausting task was that "while they generally approved the work and believed that a child's prospects were better in Canada than in England, children should only go out when they were of working age." In Britain that corresponded to the school leaving age of 14. Significantly, the commission observed that, "the comparative helplessness of the child makes this form of migration the most liable to abuse."[50]

The timing was serendipitous and not a little tragic: two "homeboys" on Canadian farms earlier that year had committed suicide. For social progressives, this confluence of events was exactly the justification they needed for reform. Labour MP, JS Woodsworth — a founding member of the Co-operative Commonwealth Federation (CCF) — put it succinctly in a House of Commons debate: "We are bringing these children into Canada in the guise of philanthropy and turning them into cheap labourers." Charlotte Whitton, Director of the Canadian Welfare Council (originally the Canadian Council on Child Welfare), fully seized the historic moment while addressing a national conference of the Imperial Order of the Daughters of Empire (IODE). Whitton couldn't help but reflect the prevailing prejudices of the day, with the public's concern that Britain not be allowed to dump "British trash" on Canadian soil. Yet it went beyond that — thinking was beginning to change. Children were gradually being seen less as chattel and more as human beings with feelings and needs. "Why are so many children being brought to Canada?" Whitton demanded. "The only fair inference is that juvenile immigrants are being sought for placements in homes and conditions which the Canadian authorities will not accept for our own children." She challenged the government for allowing children aged 10–13 to be brought into the country as labourers. Like Woodsworth, she concluded that it amounted to "cheap labour that approaches perilously near a form of slavery." It was largely pressure from the Council that had resulted in the 1925 legislation limiting immigration of children unaccompanied by parents to age 14. Unfortunately, it was only haphazardly enforced.[51]

By this time even some of the sending agencies were having second thoughts about emigrating young children from Britain.

In his September 1925 report on the Elizabeth Rye Home, Smart notes a visit of inspection by Reverend Rowland W. Connor, sent from London. According to Smart, the Waifs and Strays Society had dispatched Connor to "report upon the activities of this Home, with the view of deciding upon the future policy to be followed in respect to the migration of girls by them." Connor was not impressed with the situation. He found that the girls' mistresses (employers) were perhaps "not as considerate to the girls as they should be, and were inclined to find fault, which was frequently based on matters which might be considered trivial." Connor told Smart he would be recommending that "if the work is to be continued, no girls under the age of 17 years should be sent out, as there are in his opinion advantages just as good for their girls in the Old Country as in Canada." Enforcement of the new laws would be irregular, but the tide had turned and could not be turned back.[52]

For British child immigrants Canada was hardly the "land of milk and honey" they had been promised. Little did they know it would be their own hard labour that would produce that milk and honey. And because few were allowed enough time to attend school, their working careers as adults would be mostly as unskilled or skilled labourers. Very few would gain access to the education required to enter the professional class. The boys were sought for labour on farms in Ontario, the Maritimes, or Quebec, and to a lesser extent in the West. The girls were earmarked for domestic service in both urban and rural settings. In remote farm households, this left them vulnerable to sexual abuse. We have first-hand testimony thanks to social worker Phyllis Harrison, who placed ads in the late 1960s and early '70s asking for grown Home Children to write her about their experiences. The anecdotes Harrison received demonstrate just how varied a response to hardship exists within the human frame. And they give us memories that range from pleasant but hardworking days on Canadian farms to a living hell of neglect and abuse.

Some families would be decent and try to give the children a truly new start — generally those few who adopted child immigrants as infants. In the early years children as young as four or five were emigrated, though these were typically placed in foster homes until they were old enough to work. But many farm families would use Home Children like pack animals. "The day started at four in the morning with the help staggering out to the barn to begin the chores — milking one hundred cows by hand," William Donaldson of Chipman, New Brunswick wrote Harrison. "The barn work was usually done by six o'clock and breakfast was at seven. After breakfast we went down to the slaughterhouse to kill two or three head of beef or pork. . . . The help would be fortunate to be in bed by ten at night."[53] "You did not get out to play with other boys and girls," recalled Joseph Betts of Belleville, Ontario. "It was all work."[54]

The wholesome, if hardworking, farm life agreed with some Home Children. Ellen (Keatly) Higgins recalls her life as a girl working on the Baillie farm, a family of Scots living near Pictou, Nova Scotia. "With all the cold and hard work I enjoyed life. I will say that there was always plenty to eat. They killed a pig and beef animal for winter meat. Mrs. Baillie had a spinning wheel brought from Scotland. She spun wool from the sheep. . . . We had leather boots and to make them waterproof we greased them often with melted tallow or fat."[55] Colin Perry of London, Ontario wrote: "I had been placed on a dairy farm with the Arnold McPherson family with wages of $10 a month and board. Mrs. McPherson was 23 years old and a real gem. I had certainly come to a fine place and I stayed there for two years. Any time we were not busy Arnold would tell me to go to the house and help Jenny. I did dishes, churned cream, washed floors, painted, babysat — and loved every minute of it. The barn was close to the house and it was wonderful to smell fresh bread and coffee in the morning."[56]

"On Saturday I would hurry and get the work done and after the farmer and his family went to town I would wander across the field," James J. Crookes of Kingston, Ontario wrote Harrison. "I thought it was wonderful to see the lovely trees and birds and rabbits. It was just like being born again." It was a rare moment of peace. Crookes was forced to sleep in an unheated attic and was beaten when he complained. When his term of service was up, he had to contact the RCMP when he learned the farmer was unwilling or unable to pay him. His sponsor, the Church of England, proved unresponsive when he went to them for help.[57] The extreme poverty of many farmers made this an all-too-common experience for Home Children. Although a condition of their placement on the farm, childcare agencies often failed to hold employers accountable for wages.

Added to the work was the stigma these children felt as a result of Canadians' attitudes toward them. As Joseph Betts mentioned, not only was there no time for play but many farm families deliberately kept Home Children away from the other children, as if fearing moral contamination. One former "homeboy," Harold Dodham, interviewed by journalist Jane Cole Hamilton for the *Toronto Star* in the 1980s, recalled references to "scum of the earth," "should have been drowned on landing," and "guttersnipes." "That last word was used about them quite matter-of-factly in a *Globe and Mail* editorial," notes Hamilton.[58]

Even if the living conditions weren't poor, the anxiety of separation from parents and siblings crowded in. "There were times when I was so lonely I sat down and cried," Crookes recalled. "I hadn't known what it was like until then not to be loved. I was cursed like a slave not knowing what to do to please and I tried so hard." For many Home Children this intense loneliness, coupled with abuse, would cast a shadow over the rest of their lives. "At this farm I was given to understand that an orphan was the lowest type of person on earth just about," Michael Driscoll wrote Phyllis Harrison, "and the insults I had to take even at age 10 or 11 have always stayed with me. It's only the bruises on the outside that I don't feel anymore. I was horse-whipped, kicked and belted around until I got so hard I could no longer feel it."[59]

According to Perry Snow, a psychologist and the son of a "homeboy," one of the major psychological effects on these children was a chronic loss of identity and self-worth. His father, Frederick Snow, was sponsored for emigration by the Church of England's Waifs and Strays Society. He arrived in 1925, the year before my grandfather Cyril Joyce. Fred spent most of his adult life trying to track down his records, since he had been sent without even a birth certificate. He had been taken into foster care in England as a toddler and had little memory of his parents or family. Like many child immigrants and their descendants, Fred had a burning need to know "who his people are." But the church treated his records as if they were sealed, or simply claimed they were missing. Perry Snow would have to take up his father's quest after his death — it took the threat of legal action to finally get Fred's records. "They underestimated the strength of needing to know who you are," he wrote in his memoir, *Neither Waif Nor Stray: The Search For a Stolen Identity*. "No one should live their life without knowing who they are and to whom they belong."[60]

Certainly from my father's descriptions of growing up with Cyril, my grandfather seemed to be a man without a presence — a living ghost who mechanically made the daily rounds from home to work and back again. According to Margaret Humphreys, founder of the Child Migrants Trust, loss of identity is a common emotion reported by many child immigrants, as if a giant hole had opened in their psyches. Reporting on her interviews with Canadian Home Children, she wrote: "Their own children — the next generation — now adults themselves, would ask me about their parents. 'You know, the one thing Dad would never give us was information about his childhood. . . .' The longing and pain and hurt had never gone away, even though they were grandparents now. How sad to be 70 years old and not know who you really are."[61]

Thankfully Fred Snow married and — by being a loving husband and father — stopped the cycle of abuse before it infected another generation. Yet, like my grandfather, he seldom spoke of his experiences, even with his wife and children. Because of the harsh stigma suffered by Home Children in Canada, this was a common response. Shame is a powerful silencer, but it doesn't stop the pain. As a general rule, says family systems psychologist John Bradshaw, what is left undone by the parents must be worked out by the children. "Genetic predispositions often coincide with family dynamics, and a child may take on unresolved feelings of sadness that have come from previous generations," Bradshaw explains. For this reason, "depression and anxiety often persists across generations."[62]

Perry Snow is a living example — an echo chamber for his father's unexpressed angst — the angst of being without family identity, or a sense of connection in the world. "Your identity allows you to value yourself as a unique person of some worth," he writes. "How would you feel about yourself if you believed you were an orphaned, abandoned, unwanted and illegitimate nobody?"[63]

2. Tracking the Family Ghost

> Let the living heal the dead.
> — Sean Arthur Joyce
> *Conversations with Crow*[64]

ALTHOUGH I GREW UP IN A MIDDLE-CLASS Canadian family during the prosperous era of the 1960s and early '70s, I always felt out of place. I felt alien compared to the other kids — a feeling many child immigrants shared. Obviously children with an artistic temperament often feel this way, and the "old school," quasi-military approach to education still used during my public school years made it all the more difficult. Being the kid with glasses, the "bookworm," the one last picked for baseball or hockey teams — all contributed to the feeling of being an outsider. Growing up in the "instant" mill town of Mackenzie in northern BC didn't help. Anyone with a greater interest in books than hockey was immediately suspect — a target for assault. Yet it struck me as more than mere coincidence that, like my grandfather, I left home at age 15 — he was 16 when he was shipped to Canada. Unlike him, however, I had a choice.

Cyril left us no clues to his past — not a single anecdote or cherished family story to pass along. Somehow he began to reach out to me a decade after his death. A sudden, nagging need to know bloomed inside me. It struck me that in an entire collection of poetry I'd written during the '90s called *The House of Childhood*, there was nothing about Cyril nor any of the Joyces. Who was he? Why did he come to Canada? How is it that he speaks to me more in death than in life? It soon became apparent from talking with my father Arthur Cyril Joyce that he didn't have any answers either. The question of why Cyril had come to Canada has nagged at Dad all his life. Gentle efforts to pry it out of Cyril were met mostly with silence. Like the Tuatha Dé Danaan of Irish legend, Cyril Joyce may as well have dropped into existence from the air, minus the magic powers.

When I contacted my Uncle Rob Joyce, Cyril's son by his second marriage, he had no answers, either. Rob could recall few details about his father. It wasn't a promising start. Cyril seems to have spoken rarely, even with his own sons. The stereotypical — but real — image of the working man who comes home from work at five o'clock, reads his newspaper before dinner, eats, reads for awhile more and then turns in to bed. A ghostly presence in his own home. No photos survive of Cyril and his new family growing up in Canada. Even letters were read and then disposed of in the Joyce household. Except for one brief trip with Rob as a teenager to London, Cyril never had any more contact with the country of his birth or with his family there. It's as if he were trying to erase his own footsteps, his own past. I wondered: what could make a man want to erase a fundamental part of his own identity? What could make him act as if his family didn't exist? Questions that would drive me on, deeper into the past, seeking answers.

What I learned in the course of my research was that the Joyces had descended from a family going back nearly 500 years in County Dorset, working as tenant millers at White Mill in the lovely dales of southern England. White Mill is situated on the River Stour and it's estimated there have been grain mills at this site for about a millennium. It's not hard to see why: the Stour here is broad but placid, with plenty of water for driving the massive wheels needed to power millstones. It's also not hard to see why our family would remain there generation after generation. The scene is reminiscent of a painting by Constable: the whispering shush of willows, the river a steady stream of life teeming with fish and birds, the brick structure of the mill tucked into the riverbank as if it had grown there — a natural part of the landscape.

While the American Revolution is gearing up to tear a colony from the crown of King George III, a humble man named John Joyce is resident miller at White Mill. His family has been in the Dorset area some 250 years. But by the late 1700s, the mill is in desperate need of refurbishing. Its waterwheel and stone superstructure remains serviceable but the mill itself needs rebuilding. John Joyce convinces aristocratic landowner Henry Bankes to invest £370 for the project, to be paid back at £20 per year. The new brick structure is completed and a date stone inscribed 1776, the year American Independence is declared.[65] But for John Joyce, it's a different kind of independence — one that will enable him to feed his family. With his wife Prudence he will raise eight children at the mill. Prudence dies July 19, 1796 and John marries Mary Howard Collins Small three years later. With Mary a new line of Joyces is born through their son George Small Joyce, who brings a further 13 children into the world. Among them is Septimus Joyce, born 1832. His cousin Thomas Davis Joyce, born in 1841, will grow up to become the last miller at White Mill as modern steam technology makes the stately, elegant water mill obsolete.[66]

While Thomas Davis Joyce and his family remain at the mill, Septimus and his kin seem to have a penchant for accountancy. Septimus grows up at nearby Blandford Forum but his work as an accountant takes him to the Isle of Wight and Bristol at different times during his career. Many of his sons will take up the family business, but not George Ochiltree Joyce. George proved to be the missing link to Cyril I had been searching for. George is the only one of five sons and three daughters to leave the pastoral hedges and dales of Dorset for the city life of London. Records catch up with him when he marries Nelly Firman, a railway stationmaster's daughter who lived in North London. The marriage certificate lists him as a "commercial traveller," British parlance for travelling salesman, selling women's corsets and other sundries. He and Nelly had started a family in East Ham, deep in London's poorest quarters, where my grandfather Cyril and his siblings were born.

What did Nelly feel the day she saw George Joyce step off a train from Dorsetshire at her father's station? Did she see a young, hopeful face, scrubbed bright with the vitality of a country childhood, ready for a challenge, a new beginning? Was George himself on the run from what he decided was a dead-end, even though his uncles and siblings all went into the family business, keeping other people's accounts? Had he faced down his father and shrugged off the weight of family custom to forge his own fate? Once again, Cyril's silence about his father leaves room only for speculation and educated guesses.

The detective work of genealogy helps fill in the gaps. Much can be learned or deduced from simple documents such as birth and marriage certificates. Photographs provide other clues, though typically more speculative. My Dad has inherited only three photos of his grandparents. In one of the photographs, George and Nelly are strolling down the avenue in their Sunday finest while an admiring crowd of ladies watches. Nelly wears a jacket with a large fur collar and George a crisp suit. Was that the moment that made George's severance with his father's dull trade somehow worth it? Whether the Joyces were enjoying their salad days before misfortune struck, or merely maintaining appearances, is impossible to know.

But then in another photograph, George is standing beside Cyril in the back garden, with its cubicle-like brick garden wall. A grinning young Cyril appears to be about 10 years old. George looks haggard, used-up. Born April 6, 1868, George would have been about 52 at the time the photo was taken (Cyril was born in 1910). Yet at 52 George could be mistaken for 72, his hair sparse and grey, his face lined and sallow, with no trace of a smile. How many mouths can a salesman's income feed? How many miles did he pound the cobblestones in those shoes? And how many joints by then had begun to ache with each brisk step on the pavement? What creeping infirmity of health caused him to lie awake nights, wondering how much longer he could keep it up? Did he question his choice to strike out from Dorset and start this new life? And did he finally snap, deciding to abandon Nelly and Cyril? If so, he unwittingly set in motion a whole new set of fates. Or did he pitch into death with the suddenness of a bull under the blade, after the life had long since gone out of him? The truth is, we don't know. As with so many descendants of child immigrants, the details of our family past are muddled or lost altogether.

Fortunately, British literature provides a rich source of material that helps shed light on what George's life as a salesman might have been like in the early part of the 20th century. In his between-the-wars novel *Coming Up for Air*, George Orwell writes of the "commercial traveller's" experience:

> They keep you on a string by hinting that perhaps there'll be a salaried job going in three months' time, and when you get fed up there's always some other poor devil ready to take over. Naturally it wasn't long before I had an on-commission job; in fact I had quite a number in rapid succession. Thank God, I never came down to peddling vacuum cleaners or dictionaries. But I travelled in cutlery, in soap powder, in a line of patent corkscrews, tin-openers, and similar gadgets, and finally in a line of office accessories — paper clips, carbon paper, typewriter ribbons, and so forth. I didn't do so badly either. . . . But I never came anywhere near making a decent living. You can't, in jobs like that — and, of course, you aren't meant to.[67]

Orwell's character George Bowling describes the dreary lifestyle lived by travelling salesmen. Having had some of these low-end jobs myself, it's hard not to hear my great grandfather George Joyce speaking in these lines:

> It was a queer time. The cross-country journeys, the godless places you fetched up in, suburbs of Midland towns that you'd never hear of in a hundred normal lifetimes. The ghastly bed-and-breakfast houses where the sheets always smell faintly of slops and the fried egg at breakfast has a yolk paler than a lemon. And the other poor devils of salesmen that you're always meeting, middle-aged fathers of families in moth-eaten overcoats and bowler hats, who honestly believe that sooner or later trade will turn the corner and they'll jack their earnings up to five quid a week. And the traipsing from shop to shop, and the arguments with shopkeepers who don't want to listen, and the standing back and making yourself small when a customer comes in.... There are chaps who can't even walk into a shop and open their bag of samples without screwing themselves up as though they were going over the top.[68]

Then the Joyce family is plunged into crisis. George is gone — whether cut short by an early death or doing the classic "gone for a smoke and never came back," we don't know. All we know is that George disappears from the records without a trace — no death certificate, no burial records, nothing. The older children by now had left home but that still left Nelly alone to care for Cyril and possibly his older sister Hilda. Nelly had already raised five children in cramped East End row housing — cold, dirty brick monuments to Victorian social planning. She was probably feeling as worn out as George. And as a railway stationmaster's daughter her options were limited. Lacking higher education, she would be limited to doing laundry, cooking, and cleaning at minimal wages.

With 14 being the British school leaving age, adolescents were expected to be working by 16. But in 1920s East Ham, jobs would have been scarce. It's not hard to understand why Nelly would have turned to the Church of England for help once her husband was gone. British newspapers had always been keen supporters of emigration to the colonies, and in particular of Dr. Barnardo's work sending poor children to Canada. She may have read about the farms on the Canadian prairies, and a vast province named Alberta. Conveniently, the Church of England's Council for Empire Settlement had only just been established in 1925, offering paid passage to Canada.

STARTING IN 1871, Edward and Robert Rudolf had been conducting Sunday school services in the church's St. Ann's Parish in London's South Lambeth district and noticed that many needy children were unable to enter orphanages. "One day in 1881 two brothers who attended the Sunday school suddenly stopped coming," explains an online history of The Children's Society. "They were later found in a neglected state begging for food from workers at a local gasworks. Their father had died, leaving their mother with seven children to look after. She was unable to support the boys, but she did not want the family to go into a workhouse. The boys had to fend for themselves." It was an all-too-common situation for Britain's working poor. The Rudolf brothers tried to find a Church of England home for the boys but none would take them without payment. As with Macpherson, Barnardo, Booth, and others before them, the brothers realized something more was needed. Adopting a popular catchphrase of the era referring to London's poor street children, they established the Waifs and Strays Society.[69]

Maria Rye, who had already been emigrating children to Canada for a decade, advised the Rudolf brothers to consider helping girls, since, in her opinion, "they need the help a thousandfold more than the boys." The Waifs and Strays Society regulations stipulated that children admitted to their homes must have lost both parents and "shall have no relatives or friends able to maintain it," unlike Barnardo's Homes' more all-inclusive policy. The first girls sent to Canada by the Waifs and Strays Society came through Rye's agency, with some of the boys being sent to Knowlton, Quebec. By 1885, enough funds had been raised to purchase a home in Sherbrooke, Quebec, dubbed the Gibb's Home in honour of a major benefactor. The Rudolf brothers seem to have taken Rye's advice to heart, since a majority of the Waifs and Strays Society homes established in Britain by 1886 were for girls.[70]

"Compared with the other large agencies, the Church of England sent few children to Canada," explains Marjorie Kohli, with an annual peak of 144 children arriving in 1901. And this even though Maria Rye had turned over her work and distributing centre, Our Western Home at Niagara-on-the-Lake, to the Waifs and Strays Society upon her retirement in November 1896. Both Gibb's Home and Our Western Home were regularly visited by George Bogue Smart, who noted in his 1913–14 report that, "There is a marked improvement in the terms under which their wards are indentured, and the same good system should be noted in regard to supervision of the children." Clearly it was a step up from Rye's regime.[71]

Still, as with other agencies involved with child immigration, the Waifs and Strays Society was no less subject to lapses and abuses, as Frederick Snow's story makes plain. But by the time Nelly is considering Cyril for emigration, a new Church of England scheme has entered the scene — the Empire Settlement Program — prompted in part by the First World War, which had slowed Canadian immigration nearly to a halt. Canada had lost 67,000 men with a further 173,000 wounded, many of whom would be unable to return to full-time work. Working together to remedy the sudden shortage of agricultural workers in Canada, the Canadian and British governments reached an agreement leading to passage of the Empire Settlement Act in 1922. Unlike the majority of emigration programs sponsored by churches and relief agencies, the Act sought to provide aid to entire families. Some 130,000 people received state subsidies for travel to Canada during the inter-war years.[72]

The Church of England responded slowly at first. The minutes for a conference held at Lambeth Palace, London July 23, 1929 reported that the Empire Settlement Program had initially met with a lukewarm reception from church officials. "Four years ago when the Church of England Council of Empire Settlement was established not a few — clergy and laymen — said that migration was an 'economic subject' and as such no concern of the church," wrote Sir Wyndham Deedes, a retired Brigadier General active in social work. "Opinions have changed! At the conference just held not a dissentient [sic] voice was raised." Deedes went on to point out that much of Britain in 1929 was still unaware of the church's work helping families to emigrate through this program. He notes receiving an appeal from the governor of one of the Australian states for more British immigrants. Deedes supports the cause with an appeal to British nationalism: "Need any churchman hesitate to place such an ideal before the rising generation of the public schools and the universities? Let this be for young men an "acid test" of their patriotism. . . ."[73]

The church's role, Deedes explains, is to promote emigration to the colonies by rekindling enthusiasm in a public exhausted by war. His rhetoric makes the connection between church and state crystal clear: "The spirit of 'divine discontent' that scorns to accept the easy, that yearns to essay the hard — that spirit which moved the great Elizabethans and some hundred years later urged Scott and his companions to the South Pole — that is the spirit in which men and nations alone found great world Empires but 'tis the spirit also through which men and nations find their souls."[74]

But the church is a victim of bad timing. Part of the rationale for sending people out of the country is Britain's postwar economic slump. But with the worldwide financial crash of 1929 and its aftermath, that justification soon evaporates. Meanwhile the British government's efforts through the Empire Settlement Act had met with limited success in Canada. The country's economy was barely more robust and Canadian officials were wary of attempts to dump the unemployed here. Many British immigrants lacked farming experience and ended up drifting into the cities, returning to Britain or emigrating to the US. Now, with the onset of the Great Depression, Canada's wide-open door to immigrants once again slammed shut.[75]

Still, it's significant in the history of child immigration that a church- and government-sponsored program provided assistance for *entire families* to emigrate together. In response to a public presentation I gave on the Home Children, a man asked me: "Don't you have *anything* good to say about the subject? What would *you* have done?" I answered that, if it had been up to me, I'd have emigrated whole families from the beginning. Poor parents of children sent overseas weren't likely to do any better at home, given economic conditions. Of course, things are seldom that simple. The situation was complicated by resistance from Canadian trade unions, who saw indentured child labourers as competition for jobs. Added to that was reluctance on the part of Canadian officials to sponsor wholesale immigration, particularly for those viewed as among the "undesirable" classes.

CYRIL WAS AMONG 160 OTHER YOUNG PEOPLE who were sent to Canada by the Council of Empire Settlement between November 1925 and the first quarter of 1927. This was to be the program's "experimental" trial period. Council of Empire Settlement annual reports note that 1,156 people were assisted to emigrate during this period, with most of these individuals being sent to Australia. Although broken down by country of destination, the report does not similarly break it down to indicate how many children and adults this represented. It's not hard to imagine Nelly's reasoning: at least in Canada Cyril might stand a chance. If he were to stay in East Ham, his prospects were bleak.

By comparison with those prospects, the Council of Empire Settlement offered children between the ages of 14 and 19 passage to one of the colonies, covering the cost of tickets, an "outfit for overseas," the required medical examination, incidental expenses such as dental treatment, and "landing money" to meet the Canadian government's requirement that immigrants have at least some cash.[76] The children were to be paid a stipend by farmers for their work, saved up until they reached legal age. They were to be allowed to attend school. And with land cheap and struggling Canadian farmers desperate for labour, Cyril could do very well for himself as a young man. Nelly couldn't have known that many Canadian farmers were themselves too poor to pay their child labourers. By 1934 the Council reported, "new problems in the case of boys still in aftercare developed due to lowered wages, inability of farmers to pay wages earned and consequent discouragement and more frequent returns to the hostels for replacement. . . ."[77] Cyril was sailing into an uncertain future at best.

Canadian customs records show Cyril travelling from Liverpool on the CPR steamship *SS Montclare*, arriving at Montreal July 31, 1926, with his destination the Anglican hostel in Edmonton. He travelled with three other boys, Laurence Sachs (age 16), John Dollery (16) and Thomas Jones (12), and Ellen Burns, listed as a "companion." The only name for next of kin on the customs form is Cyril's mother Nelly. They arrive in Canada with all of three or four pounds Sterling each in their pockets — probably just enough to meet Canadian customs regulations. Typically, little time was wasted getting the boys to the distributing homes — in this case a system of hostels operated by the church. After landing at Montreal, Cyril travels by rail to the Anglican hostel in Edmonton. From there he is sent to work on various farms north of the city near Clyde and Westlock. The report cards used to grade child immigrants' performance show that he was moved three or four times to different farms. Given his slight physique, it's likely he simply wasn't up to the heavy labour, as with many poor children who grew up malnourished. Many younger boys suffered the same upheavals. Collapsing either physically or emotionally under the workload and isolation, they were repeatedly returned to the receiving homes.

Naturally, official church documents maintain an upbeat picture of the success of their "waifs and strays" program. A report from 1934 related the story of another 15-year-old lad, sent to Canada in 1929, through a letter from his father:

I have always felt very much indebted to your Council for their preliminary assistance and the very great help that your Hostel at Edmonton has been to my son. He has been treated very kindly during the past years, particularly on his arrival, which meant so much to him and his parents, and also whenever he changed his employment or took a short holiday. He had nowhere else to go, and knowing that he could always fall back on the Hostel has indeed been a blessing to him and a great relief to us, besides he became friendly with the Superintendent and his wife on account of their kind treatment to him. He has never been out of work, summer or winter, beyond a few days during change of employment, which is entirely on account of your helpful organization.[78]

As is often the case, it's the individuals in an organization who make the difference, just as generations of "Barnardo boys" would nurture fond recollections of John Hobday and his wife. The Hobdays were responsible for the management of Barnardo's Toronto home in the post-WW I years when child immigration was getting back on its feet. One can only imagine what it must have been like to be a young boy or girl arriving in a strange, immense country, delivered into the hands of strangers. The mingled hope, fear, anxiety, and expectation of these young ones needed the soothing of caring adults. Countless letters written to the Toronto distributing home over the years testified to the fact that in the Hobday's care that's just what they got. "To me, he was the epitome of kindness and understanding of youngsters in my circumstances," wrote Albert Wayling.[79] Common to many letters to the home are passages like this one from George Evans about a year after his arrival in Canada in 1928: "I am just fine in health and hope you are the same. Remember me to Mrs. Hobday and your son."[80] Evans requests an address to write to another Barnardo's staffer, Ernest Nunn, who worked as an inspector, often travelling to remote farms to visit the children.

It's not hard to imagine a slow blue flame eating away what love was left for his mother in Cyril's heart. Just a few years short of legal age and he had absolutely no say in his own future. He would emigrate to Canada whether he wanted to or not, as thousands had before and would continue to do after him. In fairness to Nelly, her options were only slightly west of "between the devil and the deep blue sea." Still, Cyril never spoke of his mother or his British relatives. It was as if they had been stricken from his "Book of Life."

Cyril comes of age in 1929 — an extreme case of bad timing. He's free at last, but set free in an era of intense hardship. The Great Depression had hit the Prairie provinces hard and survival for farmers there was even more of a life and death struggle than usual. Farms were being erased in a cloud of dust and bankruptcies. The Council of Empire Settlement reports in 1934 that with the economic crash, "immigration has practically ceased," causing a shift in church resources to welfare work. "Much more has had to be done for persons in all parts of Canada — families desiring to return to England whose relatives could support them; families in Canada desiring to bring out some member of their family but lacking funds; families in the West, in the dried-out area [likely referring to Alberta and Saskatchewan], needing advice as to where to secure clothing; expectant mothers needing advice and assistance; unmarried mothers to plan for; families in the Old Land seeking news of missing husbands and sons; invalids assisted to return to the Old Land; many soldiers and their dependents helped and advised." The writer of the report stresses the church's responsibility for the 5,000 people sent to Canada by the program, "2,000 of whom are young boys."[81]

My step-grandfather, John Herbert Brown, recalls seeing Cyril working on farms in northern Alberta, including the Maynard homestead in Clyde. The Maynards had a young daughter named Marjorie, as sweet and naïve a farm girl as could be imagined. Cyril had made friends with her brother "Bud," a musician who played piano for local dance bands, and had taken up the drums. At a time when money was scarce, barn dances were the sole form of entertainment in rural Alberta, and enjoyed with great zest. There at last one could see something more than pigs, chickens and cattle, buckets of horseshit and stook after stook of curing hay. Beautiful young Canadian women, each wearing their one decent dress, would have been a blessed sight for weary young men like Cyril. Never mind that most of the clothes even for "Sunday best" had to be mended and held together with thread from flour sacks. With music and dance, the sweat and dirt melted away, if only for a few hours. To see the young girls whirl and stumble laughingly past while the band played another waltz, polka or schottische, ah. . . .

Before long Cyril proposes to Marjorie, still a gangly, awkward farm girl. After the modest ceremony they return to their first home — a converted chicken shack. Their bliss will not last. Alberta's farmers must endure hot dry summers and bitterly cold winters. No one has two dimes to rub together. But the crops, such as they are, must still be got in. By the mid-'30s many farm communities are suffering a high rate of attrition as more and more families leave to find work in the cities. Not long after Cyril marries Marjorie (my grandmother), about 1936, they pack up the chickens, cattle, and her parents and move everything in a railway boxcar to the West Kootenay region of southeastern BC. On the shores of Kootenay Lake, pristine and shimmering in the sun, the side of a mountain could be had for a dollar an acre. And all the sweat and gristle you could muster to clear it of trees and coax out a living. Marjorie's parents settle on a small farm in Balfour, near Nelson. Marjorie would later recall being pleasantly shocked "at how green everything was" there compared to northern Alberta. You could easily grow vegetables and fruit and trade with neighbours for dairy and meat. No one on Kootenay Lake during the Depression had a dime, but no one starved, either.

By the late '30s industrial production is gearing up again for the next World War. When Cyril hears that a mining company called Cominco is calling for men at its smelter in Trail, just south of Nelson, he doesn't hesitate. He soon learns the comforting tick of the time clock marking off his days in a smelter office. My great uncle Bud Maynard also gets a job at the smelter, working in the plant that produces heavy water for the Manhattan Project. Smokestacks loom over the small city of Trail like some brooding god deciding whether to kill people quickly or gradually corrode them to death. But once again the upward arc of hope is shot down like a Spitfire over the English Channel. Cyril finds himself drawn into the party life in his free hours, and soon his marriage to Marjorie is unraveling.

She retreats to her father's farm in Balfour with young Arthur Cyril, my father. He will spend some of the most contented days of his early life there, dressing up as the cowboy he would later become in retirement. Meanwhile his mother is agonizing over what to do about her marriage. Her father, Arthur Maynard, though sympathetic, is bound by the times. "You're a married woman. You have to try to make it work." She tries to go back to Cyril, but it's too late. Cyril has moved on. Fortunately, she will soon meet John Herbert Brown, her future husband of more than 50 years. "Herbie" proves to be the steady, faithful partner she needs. Although more at home with mechanisms of grease and steel than the delicate machinery of emotion, his innate kindness easily makes up for it.

In the meantime, my father will be torn between two families as he grows up. Arthur spends his school year with Cyril and stepmother Rose, who punishes him for the slightest infraction or dirty boot left in a hallway. When Arthur has to leave his mother's country paradise in Balfour at the end of every summer holiday, he cries bitterly. Back in Trail, as a teenager he joins the navy cadets. In the photo taken of him wearing his uniform he is an awkwardly stiff 14-year-old, trying desperately to look tough and strong. Like all children caught in the wake of parents self-absorbed by their own dramas, he understands nothing of what he has been cast into. He only knows he hurts. Once again a family has been shattered. It's something Marjorie will unfairly blame herself for the rest of her life. Then, at age 15, young Arthur has had enough. He explodes at his stepmother one day and is told to leave. His mother and stepfather in nearby Balfour are all too happy to take him in. Arthur is just a year younger than his father Cyril was when sent to Canada by his mother. I too would leave home at age 15. A pattern was beginning to echo down the generations.

Thirty-five years of work at the smelter wipes Cyril to a soft shadow, a quiet, gentle existence barely known even to his wife Rose and my uncle Rob. Cyril's life passed over us like a shadow — less than a shadow — a ghost whose footsteps were erased by his own hand. It's as if he thought his life didn't matter. Yet a photo of him at age 80 shows a smile as radiant as that boy beaming beside his papa in a barren East Ham yard. It's a beautiful portrait that radiates the sheer strength of the human spirit.

WHEN I TOLD MY UNCLE ROB JOYCE about the British PM's apology, he wrote, "It is a great day. I wish we could be reading this with Dad now; that would have made it even better. I understand Dad better now than I ever did, and why he was sad at times for reasons I never knew. An understanding that, like the British government's apology has come, sadly, much too late."

But better late than never. Australian Prime Minister Kevin Rudd was the first head of state to offer a national apology on November 16, 2009. "We come together today to deal with an ugly chapter in our nation's history," said Rudd in his address in the Great Hall, Parliament House:

> And we come together today to offer our nation's apology. To say to you, the Forgotten Australians, and those who were sent to our shores as children without your consent, that we are sorry. Sorry that as children you were taken from your families and placed in institutions where so often you were abused. Sorry for the tragedy, the absolute tragedy, of childhoods lost. Sorry for all these injustices to you, as children, who were placed in our care. We acknowledge the particular pain of children shipped to Australia as child migrants — robbed of your families, robbed of your homeland, *regarded not as innocent children but regarded instead as a source of child*

labour. For these failures to offer proper care to the powerless, the voiceless and the most vulnerable, we say sorry (emphasis added).[82]

Thanks to the work of British social worker Margaret Humphreys, Australia took the lead in healing this wound in its collective psyche. The Australian government provided her with a staff person and an office in Australia and later awarded Humphreys the Order of Australia for her work reuniting child immigrants with their families.

Next came Prime Minister Gordon Brown's apology on February 24, 2010, and the establishment of a £6 million fund to help child immigrants re-establish contact with their families in Britain:

> To all those former child migrants and their families, to those here with us today and those across the world — to each and every one — I say today that we are truly sorry. They were let down. We are sorry that they were allowed to be sent away at the time they were most vulnerable. We are sorry that instead of caring for them, this country turned its back, and we are sorry that the voices of these children were not always heard and their cries for help not always heeded. We are sorry that it has taken so long for this important day to come, and for the full and unconditional apology that is justly deserved to be given.[83]

Brown went on to acknowledge the work done by Humphreys and her Child Migrants Trust in raising awareness and campaigning for justice. Among the seven Canadian former child immigrants given invitations to the apology was former Fairbridge Farm School resident Roddy McKay. "It was an honour and I felt Prime Minister Gordon Brown was very sincere with the apology. I was a bit irritated as all the speakers emphasized the hardships suffered by the Australian child migrants. Other than the Prime Minister, who did include Canada, New Zealand, South Africa and Tasmania, there was no mention of the distress endured by so many of Canada's child migrants. As happened to many other Fairbridgians, I was separated from my brothers and sister in 1939, and over all those years, I received absolutely no assistance in my search from the government or Fairbridge." A sad irony, since by far the majority of child immigrants were sent to Canada.[84]

Meanwhile, Canadian Immigration Minister Jason Kenney said the Conservative government had no plans to apologize. "Canadians don't expect their government to apologize for every sad event in our history," Kenney told reporters. "We have laid out some criteria for that, and the reality is we haven't seen a demand or an expectation for that." Kenney claimed that the experience for Canadian child immigrants was different than the Australians, without qualifying that statement. He also failed to comment on the disparity between this decision and formal government apologies made to Japanese-Canadians interned during World War II and for the Native residential school scandal.[85]

For any Canadian government to disavow responsibility for the Home Children is evasive at best, disingenuous at worst. As historian Roy Parker explains, "Subsidies were paid by the federal government and by some of the provincial governments," and critics of child emigration complained about the large sums being spent on the various programs.[86] Clearly, the Canadian government was deeply invested in the scheme, because farms were chronically short of both workers and cash. What the governments of both Britain and Canada failed to spend much money on was monitoring the children once they disappeared into the Canadian hinterland. It was a system begging to be abused. The provincial government of Ontario at least made an effort thanks to the agency formed under JJ Kelso's oversight. The federal government, on the other hand, did little to enforce measures designed to protect child immigrants, often looking the other way while agencies like Barnardo's and Fairbridge continued shipping children to Canada even during dangerous wartime conditions.

The Health Committee of the British House of Commons was

appointed in 1997 to examine the issue of the welfare of former British child migrants, taking testimony from nearly 250 elderly former child migrants. "The committee also visited Australia and New Zealand and heard directly from 200 of those who had been sent there as children," explains Parker. Although the committee focused on the re-establishment of post-WW II child emigration schemes — primarily to Australia and New Zealand — its conclusions are applicable to the entire history of child emigration. "It is now an inescapable conclusion that the re-establishment of these emigration schemes in 1947, largely by the voluntary children's societies, was a grave wrong, especially in the light of what was, by then, understood about child development. That has now been acknowledged by all concerned: apologies have been offered and the magnitude of the hurt that was perpetrated recognized." The Chief Executive of Barnardo's at the time admitted: "It was barbaric; it was dreadful. We look back on it in our organization with shock and horror."[87]

Shock and horror is certainly the appropriate response to the many cases of British Home Children who died at the hands of their hosts from neglect and severe brutality. Take the case of George Everett Green, a "Barnardo boy" whose journey across the "golden bridge" to Canada ended in a life cut brutally short. In May 1895 he was sent to work on a 40-hectare farm owned by Helen Findlay in Ontario's Keppel Township, near Owen Sound. The teenaged George may have been what we would today call "learning disabled" but what was then known as "slow" or "simple." Still, this gave Findlay no right to make the terrified boy spend the night with the pigs for not getting his work done. Nor did he deserve to be kicked, punched, hit with sticks and fed barely enough to keep alive. His body was found covered with sores and bruises and showed evidence of malnutrition. The coroner, Dr. Allan Cameron, said upon his inspection of George's quarters on the Findlay farm that in 40 years of medical practice — including working the slums of Glasgow — he had never seen such squalid, filthy conditions. George had been made to sleep on two planks with a hole cut in the centre as a toilet and straw beneath. Findlay was charged with manslaughter but spent only one year in prison. George was just 17 when he died — his last lonely moments wracked with pain, sickness, and terror.[88]

Although George Green's tragedy is probably the most famous case of abuse leading to death, it is far from the only one. A more recent case that has come to light is that of Arnold Walsh, who was sent in July 1905 to work for James Kelly of Masson, Quebec. Kelly had a substantial property but despite his wealth, Arnold was forced to live and sleep in the barn. He froze to death by February 1906 and was buried in a box too small for his crumpled body. The autopsy showed he had been prodded with a pitchfork, was undernourished, poorly clothed, bruised, had severely frost-bitten hands and feet, and a fractured skull. Arnold lay on a bed of manure in his coffin. He was 15 years old. James Kelly was found guilty of manslaughter on January 19, 1907 and sentenced to seven years in the penitentiary at St. Vincent de Paul. Unlike Findlay's sentence, the punishment was at least beginning to fit the crime. Meanwhile neither Green nor Walsh were given the dignity of a marked grave.[89]

Green's case prompted much agonizing in the press of the day over the whole question of child immigration. The *Winnipeg Free Press* of November 29, 1895 even came to the conclusion that, "the whole system of shipping the waifs and strays of old world big cities to Canada is reprehensible. But it is doubly so when the Government at Ottawa takes public money to subsidize the professional philanthropists who collect and dispatch them hither."[90] Clearly the press had no problem recognizing the government's complicity in child immigration. Sadly most of the outrage focused on the importation of the "blind . . . lame and scrofulous," rather than on the terrible tragedy of children torn from their families and homeland or mercilessly killed as Green and other boys had been. Not to mention those driven to suicide from sheer despair. But public outrage has a way of dying down quickly once the issue fades from the news. The importation of children from

Britain for use as indentured labourers would continue for many decades yet.

SUFFERING IS IMPOSSIBLE TO QUANTIFY, but its reach is long — echoing down the generations. How many of these exported children have had to live with the emotional scars of being unwanted — in the words of 19th century social revisionists, the "residuum" of society?[91] As historian Kenneth Bagnell concluded, "the act of uprooting children and sending them, alone, across the ocean to work in a strange land . . . must be regarded as one of the most Draconian measures in the entire history of children in English-speaking society. Its impact on the life of a sensitive child — even one who was placed in reasonable circumstances — is difficult to measure, sometimes even difficult to imagine."[92]

For the families of child immigrants, it's not difficult to imagine at all. The psychological repercussions continue to this day. As the 1997 British Health Committee explained in its final report, far from helping poor children adjust more smoothly to society, many of the child immigrants suffered lifelong problems with various aspects of socialization. "The consequences of child migration for many include difficulties in forming or maintaining relationships; fear of closeness and sharing emotions; a need to be understood; psychiatric disorders including many attempts at suicide and alcoholism; and feeling socially handicapped. We have also heard accounts of inability to accept authority or hold down a job, a propensity to itinerant lifestyles." Indeed, the committee reported that 46 percent of women and 42 percent of men they interviewed said they had suffered significant emotional problems. That's far from the happy picture painted by 19th century child emigration enthusiasts.[93]

Canadians have accepted the view that our vast landscape is a shaping factor in the national character, a trope well embroidered by our great writers. It's not unusual for families to be spread out across the entire country. Yet it may be that the Canadian Home

Child experience has had just as powerful an effect in forming our national character. In analyzing the letters received by Phyllis Harrison in her book *The Home Children*, academic Roy Parker forms an interesting conclusion: "Hardly any of the people had stayed in one place until they were 18. Unhappiness, the end of a short-term engagement, being considered 'unsatisfactory,' running away or being removed because of ill-treatment, all contributed to this history of unsettlement. Indeed, a pattern of 'moving around' and restlessness, particularly among the boys, was liable to continue into adult life. In the 1930s the Depression increased this trend as work was sought throughout the country and in the United States."[94]

We are walking history. Like it or not — believe it or not — we carry its burdens. As individuals or as a nation, we either lay the ghosts of family past to rest or remain haunted by them — and pass them on to our children to deal with. The psychic dislocation of abandonment echoes down the generations like a gunshot, a bullet tearing through the heart.

It seems to have fallen to me to heal the wound I inherited, the same as if it had happened to me. And so Cyril comes full circle in the footsteps of a grandson he barely knew. Home again — at last. Despite being wrenched from his family roots in England, he accomplished the most simple yet profound achievement for an "orphaned" child — a home, and roots as a Canadian. "Ancestors are calling out to me in dreams / Howling for me to right their wrongs. . . ." I once wrote in a poem.[95] The elders of the Native American Siksika/Sauk Blackfoot Nation say there is great healing power in the acknowledgement of past wrongs, and that healing goes both forward and backward in time. The children's ghosts are waiting. Let the healing begin.

The one who started it all: Cyril William Joyce, the author's grand-father, about age 12, in East London. Joyce family collection.

THE LAST PORTRAIT OF DR. BARNARDO.

Yours in the Children's Cause
Thos. J. Barnardo.

Dr. Thomas John Barnardo, whose organizaton became the largest of all the "child-saving" agencies. Barnardo's was responsible for emigrating 30,000 of the 100,000 children sent to Canada. Barnardo's.

Not everyone was impressed with the emigration solution. On the eve of child emigration, Victorian cartoonist George Cruikshank revealed the prevailing attitude toward "gutter children."

OUR "GUTTER CHILDREN."
BY
GEORGE CRUIKSHANK.

OUR GUTTER CHILDREN.

TECHNICAL TRAINING
CARPENTERS' SHOP

Dr Barnardos Homes
18 & 26 Stepney Causeway
London E.1

Just one of the many workshops operated by boys in Barnardo's Homes in England. Boys were trained in carpentry, bootmaking, tinsmithing, baking, and printing. Ivy Sucee collection.

Charles Dickens was the first popular writer to satirize the conditions in British orphanages and workhouses — 35 years before child emigration began. Public domain.

CHAPTER 2

Annie Macpherson
and the Little Matchbox Makers

1. MATCHBOX MAKERS AND A FEISTY EVANGELIST

FEBRUARY, 1900. Nine-year-old Elizabeth Emma Thompson and her sister, seven-year-old Caroline Maud, are shivering on the doorstep of Annie Macpherson's Home of Industry in East London. The moist air is made doubly frigid by a stiff winter wind. They huddle close to their father, James Thompson, as he uses the brass knocker to rap on the towering door. To Elizabeth and Caroline, it may as well be the great black maw of a beast that could open at any moment and swallow them whole. They've heard their father and grandmother talking in hushed tones about Macpherson's "Little Matchbox Makers" and how the determined Scotswoman had begun her great work providing homes for destitute children 30 years earlier.

But to the girls it all seems remote, confusing. What does it have to do with them? All they know for certain is that their mother died in childbirth,[1] leaving them in the care of their father and a grandmother whose age was steadily wearing her down. James had been suffering from recurrent bouts of bronchitis, leaving him unable to work much of the time. Porridge had become their mainstay, with bits of bacon mixed in on a good day. On a bad day they learned not to ask what was in the "stir-about" ladled out to them for dinner. Elizabeth and Caroline had eavesdropped on the hushed conferences through their thin bedroom wall but could only pick up on bits and pieces of the conversation.

"We can't continue like this," their father would say. "At this rate I'll be the ruination of this family."

"Come now, ye've done your best, dearie," their grandmother would reassure him. "Were I twenty years younger, I'd do far better meself, fillin' the hole left by their mother."

"Aye, but ye aren't now, are ye? I cannot ask of ye what I cannot do myself, not at this time of your life."

There had been many such evening conferences in the Thompson household leading up to this moment, shivering in the cold and damp of a London winter. The girls had become used to hearing their father's coughing fits — usually worse at night — and including him in their prayers. But God had other things on his mind, it seemed, and James' condition grew worse. Finally, the day of decision could be put off no longer.

A girl about Elizabeth's age opens the great door. "Miss Macpherson be 'spectin' you." She curtsies and swings the door wide. "This way, if you please," she says, motioning down a long hallway. They follow the girl to a tall oak door. There is a small bench in the hallway outside Macpherson's office. "You girls be welcome to wait here." Caroline begins to cry, tugging ferociously at her father's sleeve. "No, papa! Please! Don't leave us 'ere!" James tries to comfort her but it's no use. He gestures at Elizabeth for help. "It's alright, papa only needs to see Miss Macpherson. He'll be back soon." Caroline sets up a determined wail, tears wetting her cheeks. Elizabeth tries to comfort her little sister but can barely keep from crying herself. The girl from the home, seeing that Caroline won't be placated, raps three times before gently pushing open the door and disappearing inside.

Soon she returns. "Miss Macpherson says though usually she prefers to speak with you in private, in this case she will make an exception, sir. Please come in."

The room retains its Victorian air of muted opulence, dark wood paneling with ornate sconces and wainscoting. But otherwise it is furnished very plainly, with a large desk at its centre and a few armchairs of cracking leather. A single tall window partially shuttered in aging velvet draperies allows the pale winter light to creep inside.

Macpherson is seated at the desk and has been busily writing but sets her pen aside as James enters with the girls. Her clothing is as Spartan as her surroundings — a simple black dress with white collar and cuffs. Her graying chestnut hair is drawn into a tight bun, revealing a face of fine if not quite beautiful features. She looks over James and the two girls with warm, clear eyes and a smile that suggests both welcome and a no-nonsense attitude. Although age and a heavy workload have rounded her features, her face is surprisingly unlined for someone nearly 70 years old. She rises from her chair to extend a handshake to James, then in turn to Elizabeth and Caroline, warmly but lightly grasping little hands. She motions for them to be seated. Elizabeth takes an armchair but Caroline crawls into her father's lap.

Macpherson is gracious but wastes no time. "Such pretty girls! A credit to your papa, I'm sure. Now then, Mr. Thompson, I have here your letter, explaining your situation. Having spent most of my life in the service of families such as yours, I can well imagine the difficulty you face raising two girls without their mother." She casts a sympathetic glance at the girls. Elizabeth returns her look but Caroline buries her head in James' chest.

"My late father, God bless him, was also named James and like myself a devoted servant of the Lord. How well I remember his sermons, reminding us that our Heavenly Father is far more than an avenging angel upon the wicked. Indeed, he has given us charge of his little ones, just as Jesus said, 'Suffer the little children to come unto me.'" Turning to Elizabeth, who remains captivated by this austere yet charismatic woman, she continues. "Jesus himself teaches us that his Father loves all children. He delights in seeing them at play and in prayer."[2]

Uncertain where this is leading, James Thompson coughs. "Indeed, ma'am."

"In your letter you say you are qualified as an engine fitter, but unable to continue caring for your children, as you are suffering from chronic bronchitis. The girls have a grandmother living at home but she is too elderly to care for them should you —" Macpherson clears her throat, catching herself. She now concentrates a compassionate gaze on James. "You realize of course that once the girls come under my care, they must remain so until the age of majority?"

There is a long silence while he considers. "Certainly, ma'am."

Macpherson smiles broadly. "Good. Naturally, we shall do our utmost for the girls to see that they are given every opportunity."

"I — I hear that many are sent to Canada."

"Indeed — many thousands of our waifs have found a new and better life there. Emigration for these children is a golden bridge of opportunity stretching from Britannia's shores to the New World. An opportunity few will find — where did you say you reside?" She shuffles some papers. "Ah, yes — Hoxton, East London. Very near Bethnal Green, where our work began 30 years ago. A district of sad prospects, truly."[3]

"Aye, I have little doubt of that," says James.

"In fact, we have a group of children scheduled to leave for Montreal next month!" She looks again at Elizabeth. "Wouldn't you like to have a fine new home in Canada, on a farm, with all the food you can eat, fresh from the milk cow, and fine warm clothes for winter?" The blood suddenly drains from James' face, leaving it white as a Canadian snowdrift.

Now it's Elizabeth's turn to cry, though she does so softly. She is after all the older sister and must set an example. Too late — Caroline picks up on her sister's tears and adds to the onslaught with another loud wail. James gently reproves her. "Now Carrie, you must behave for Miss Macpherson here. She is only offering to help us." Caroline subsides but now there are two small, streaked faces staring at Macpherson from across the great desk.

Her composure remains unruffled. She rises from her chair and walks around the desk, offering a handkerchief. Elizabeth submits to having her cheeks wiped but Caroline only buries her head deeper in the folds of her father's coat. Elizabeth, determined to be strong, stops crying. Her face becomes pale, inscrutable — suddenly far older than her 12 years.[4]

February–April 1900. The girls have barely had time to adjust to the shock of being removed from their family home. A few months spent in the Home of Industry has left Carrie doubly dependent on her big sister. After the cramped confines of home, with its peeling wallpaper and the musty odours exuded by old buildings, the Macpherson home seems gigantic, antiseptic, and frightening. Although Macpherson's humanizing touch has done much to make the place more inviting, its origins as the warehouse at 60 Commercial Street hang in the air like a ghost. During the cholera epidemic of 1866 it had been used as an emergency hospital and many had died there. Some said it was haunted by the spirits of dead mothers, fathers, and children and would never be used again. Yet under Macpherson's guidance and the generous financial support of Mr. RC Morgan and the readers of *The Revival* way back in 1868, water and gas lines had been installed on every floor and everything scrubbed to sparkling. No children would live in squalor and filth here.[5]

It had been *The Revival* that had helped Macpherson change the course of history in London's East End, providing a regular venue for her to appeal for donations. Her now famous booklet *The Little Matchbox-Makers* had struck the first sparks to set the nation alight with her passion to save destitute children. Miss Clara M. Lowe, daughter of Sir Hudson Lowe (Governor of St. Helena during Napoleon's captivity) and a dedicated relief worker in the East End, had introduced Macpherson to the child slavery being practiced there.[6]

"It was high up a winding stair, in an attic in a narrow lane, that the first group of pale-faced little matchbox-makers were found," Macpherson wrote in *The Little Matchbox-Makers:*

They were hired by the woman who rented the room; the children received just three farthings for making a gross of boxes; 288 pieces of wood in each gross had to be bent, sanded, and covered with paper. The wood and paper were furnished to the woman, and she received twopence-halfpenny per gross, but had to pay the children and provide paste and the firing to dry the work.

Every possible spot, on the bed, under the bed, was strewn with the drying boxes. A loaf of bread and a knife stood on the table ready for these little ones to be supplied with a slice in exchange for their hard-earned farthings. This touching scene gave a lasting impression of childhood's sorrows; never a moment for school or play, but ceaseless toil from light till dark. Even the nursling, scarce out of its mother's arms, sits pasting the sand-papers on the boxes, for this early practice is considered necessary to produce quick fingering in days to come. Children from eight to ten years of age are generally the swiftest box-makers. . . .

I have seen a woman whose thumb was worn to the bone, caused by the friction of putting on the sand-papers, and tiny children who could not speak plainly, with fingers raw and blistered from the same cause. The other day I took upon my knees a little girl of four years old. Her mother said the child had earned her own living ever since she was three. The infant now makes several hundred boxes every day of her life, and her earnings suffice to pay the rent of the miserable room which the family inhabits. The poor little woman, as might be expected, is grave and sad beyond her years; she has none of a child's vivacity, she does not seem to know what play means. . . . She has never been beyond the dingy street in which she was born. She has never so much as seen a tree, or a daisy, or a blade of grass. A poor, sickly little thing, and yet a sweet, obedient child; the deadly pallor of her face proclaiming unmistakably that she will soon be mercifully taken away to a better world, where at last the weary little fingers shall be at rest.[7]

Annie Macpherson's niece Lilian Birt writes eloquently of the events that first motivated her aunt to launch into her life's work. Macpherson had gained some notoriety for her missionary work among the coprolite diggers at Eversden, north of London in Cambridgeshire, during the early 1860s. Coprolite is fossilized feces that had been discovered some 40 years earlier on Dorset's "Jurassic coast" by fossil hunter Mary Anning. In 1842 the Reverend John Stevens Henslow, a professor of Botany at St. John's College, Cambridge, patented a process for reducing coprolites with sulphuric acid to extract their phosphate content for use as fertilizer. This soon led to mining coprolites on an industrial scale, causing an influx of workers in areas such as Felixstowe in Suffolk and Eversden in Cambridgeshire.[8] Many of these people were migrant, illiterate workers with a strong taste for liquor. It was here Macpherson first heard her call to action in the work of saving souls.

Raised in a Quaker household exposed to her father James' compassionate sermons as a little girl, Macpherson was already primed for a life of Christian service when the evangelical revival swept through Britain in 1859.[9] Hearing revivalist preacher Reginald Radcliffe speak quickened her purpose in life, "to bring souls into God's Kingdom." Her innate drive led her to establish in Eversden "clubs, coffee-rooms, evening classes, prayer meetings and mission services . . . not only in the evenings but at the dinner hour, in barns if no other place was available, or in the open fields." Yet despite her obvious ability as a speaker, Christian doctrine did not yet allow women to preach in church, though she spoke often in public. She was assisted in the evangelizing work by her brother-in-law Joseph Merry and her sister Rachel Merry. But it was clear Annie was the driving force. "The whole countryside was soon aroused and influenced, while village life was transformed," wrote her contemporary Reverend Frank M. Smith. "Her personality was more than magnetic. How we all loved her. . . ."[10]

Given the times, Macpherson's family life had been a rare one of nurturing — an ideal preparation for her later work with poor children. In addition to her father's example was her mother, who took two orphans into the family circle. "The quick-witted girls did not fail to notice the equal footing enjoyed by the stranger children and the tenderness with which they were treated," wrote Lilian Birt in her 1913 book, *The Children's Home-Finder*. "Little did their mother know what she was doing when she took the orphans to her bosom. She only thought to make a happy home and a bright future for the hapless pair, but in effect she was preparing a home and a hearty welcome for thousands of the poorest children on God's earth." When James Macpherson died in 1851, Annie took charge of her mother's care and of younger siblings Rachel and Louisa. A brother "ran away to sea and was never heard of more," Birt recalled. "This sorrow kept their hearts ever tender to all wanderers, enabling them to see in every lost boy their beloved brother."[11]

Annie Macpherson moved to London with her mother in 1865, attracted by the charismatic Radcliffe, who since 1860 had been preaching at London's Shoreditch Theatre of the need to "Feed the lambs in the East of London." His sermons had activated many other public-spirited Christian ladies. Among them were the aristocrat Lady Rowley and her cousin Miss Clara Lowe, who first showed Macpherson "the courts and alleys where work was most needed, and set her to work visiting and distributing tracts from house to house and assisting with the Mothers' Meetings they had gathered in various small rooms." It may well have been Clara Lowe who led Annie Macpherson to that room full of little matchbox-makers.[12]

Already by the time she encountered these ragged child slaves, Macpherson had found plenty in London's East End to arouse her sense of compassion. While we have plenty of historians' accounts of the cholera epidemic of 1866–67, Lilian Birt writes with the freshness of an eyewitness, based on the journals of Macpherson herself:

At that period the East End was a gloomy district of over a million people, who dwelt in indescribable slums and worked incredibly long hours for starvation pay. Since the industrial revolution of the early nineteenth century, thousands who had previously gained their living in the country in cottage industries or agricultural labour had been swept into the vortex of city life. Neither municipalities nor employers of labour had taken sufficient steps to provide decent accommodation for the ever-increasing town population. Wherever old dwellings were pulled down, lofty warehouses took their place, and the congestion became yet more acute. The building of the Great Eastern Railway's Goods Station displaced thousands of poor from their dwellings, for whom no provision was made.

The people sought relief from the crushing misery of their lives in drink and vicious courses, or the excitement of crime. No railways had then been constructed by which visitors could cross London from the north and west to the east. Consumption was rife, and swept away whole families underfed and shockingly housed. Smallpox was very common. Miss Macpherson visited one room where a man's eight children were all suffering from it, while in the same room he himself was weaving white chenille fringe of an expensive description for sale in West End shops. Nothing was being done for the children in the way of isolation or medical treatment, except that the father had rubbed some oil on their faces because he had been told that was good for smallpox.

The mortality among children was frightful. Indeed we find in Annie Macpherson's journal the following sentences: "We can but be deeply thankful that in parts of the East End *four out of every five infants die before they reach their fifth year*, because the other side of the picture among the living ones is so black, so awful, so crushing in its dreadful realities."[13]

Within a year of moving her mother to London, Annie Macpherson would receive her baptism of fire: the cholera epidemic. A veritable army of volunteers, including Macpherson, Thomas J. Barnardo, Clara Lowe, and many others, would discover firsthand the consequences of overcrowding, poor sanitation, lack of clean water, and a social hierarchy that left the poor to fend for themselves with next to no resources. Lilian Birt cites Lowe's description of events during the summer of 1866: "In the first week of July there were fourteen cases, in the third week 346 fatal cases occurred, 308 of which were in the East End. In the second week of August there were 1,407 deaths."[14] The roster of fatalities would grow to 4,000 in the East End by November that year. Social workers and health authorities alike were yet to realize the role unclean water played as a disease carrier. The East London Water Company had been drawing unfiltered water from the River Lea, "in dangerous proximity to sewers, cuts and canals."[15]

One can only imagine the sense of helplessness and horror Macpherson and other well-intentioned evangelists would have felt, trying to drain this ocean of misery with teaspoons. "In one house, from which the mother had just been buried, the children had been removed to a woodshed for safety," writes Birt:

> One child lay dying on a poor pallet, and when this child breathed its last another sickened and took its place, but for want of bedding and covering he had not been undressed for days. A blanket was borrowed, and in this he was carried to the Hospital to die. Upstairs an aged man of seventy-five was sinking fast. In one corner lay the dead body of his daughter; by his side sat his helpless wife. She had been in the Hospital with a broken leg, but had been removed to make room for cholera patients. In the next room a young widow was almost hopelessly watching her only child, and beside her sat her paralysed mother, for whose support she received from the Parish a shilling and a loaf weekly. . . . The cries for "Water, water! My child, my baby!" were heart-rending.[16]

It was scenes like these that made Macpherson and Dr. Barnardo realize that if any souls were to be saved for the Christian cause here, their bodies would need saving first. Both began opening "ragged schools" that provided at least one meal per day for children attending. "It was the sight of children such as these that roused all her intense mother nature, and made Annie Macpherson resolve to give herself to the work of rescuing these helpless ones from the wretchedness to which they seemed doomed," Birt recalls. "She began holding classes at night to teach them, providing a meal as inducement to come in. Sometimes she held an auction of second-hand clothing which the poor mothers would buy for their children; or give lectures on the use of soap and water, selling penny towels." The dominant philosophy of the day still affected even this compassionate woman's outlook, however: "She said that her aim was not to pauperise [sic] by giving anything that the poor could be induced to work for or to buy."[17]

Over the next three years Macpherson's work continually expanded as she opened homes that came to be known as "Revival Homes," after the magazine through which she appealed for support. Her first home was for boys under 10 years old, followed shortly by a home for girls. One little girl taken into the shelter was excited to find that she had a bed all to herself. "I always slept with eight in a bed; four at the top and four at the bottom."[18] A third home was soon opened for boys 10–13 years of age; here they were taught to read and write as well as basic skills such as tailoring and shoemaking. By the time a fourth home had been opened, it was obvious that still more was needed.

What seemed to the Macpherson sisters an answer to prayer appeared in the form of the former warehouse at 60 Commercial Road. It became their largest home to date, the Home of Industry, opened in February 1869. It was ground zero in Poverty Row. Lilian Birt wrote that, "Over 3,000 thieves lived around the quarters of the Home of Industry when Miss Macpherson began her work there. Even the police did not dare to venture singly down these streets...."[19] There were beds for 120 or up to 200 in an emergency, with plenty of large rooms for classes or workshops and a large kitchen on the top floor. Some of the children had suffered the ravages of the cholera epidemic. "Tonight how your hearts would have rejoiced to have seen me and my happy hundreds of little toiling children in our new schoolroom at the Home of Industry,"

Macpherson wrote upon its opening. "One whispered, 'It was here my mother died of cholera.' Another, 'Oh! I was in this ward before, so ill of black cholera.'"[20]

Ironically, Macpherson employed some of her little wards as matchbox-makers in the Home. "By this arrangement Miss Macpherson secured an hour and a half in the day to feed and educate them, paying them for the time as if they were working, instead of holding classes in the evenings, when they were so exhausted as to fall asleep over their lessons," explains Birt. She concludes on an appropriately irate note: "This is how Christian England treated her widows and fatherless children forty-five years ago!"[21]

The Home of Industry attracted another soon-to-be mover and shaker in the child emigration movement. "Dr. TJ Barnardo in early days used to come to drill the boys, and gathered much inspiration from Annie Macpherson. The Home became a training school for Christian workers. . . ."[22]

2. Macpherson's "Golden Bridge" to Canada

By 1869 Macpherson had decided that "emigration [is] the only remedy for chronic pauperism in the East of London," to quote the title of a pamphlet she and Ellen Logan published that year. Lilian Birt provides some economic context: the cholera epidemic of 1866 had been followed by an economic slump that left even more people out of work:

> After the cholera came the winter of 1866, with a most serious financial crisis. Work was hardly to be found; people who once could and did charitably assist the poor were reduced to penury themselves. . . . In 1869 matters seemed worse than in 1867–8. Labouring men entreated to be sent to some place, no matter in what part of the world, where a man might earn his living and support his family. Annie Macpherson became convinced that the real remedy lay in

emigration. Not only were those who went out benefited to an immeasurable extent, but they left behind elbow-room and less eager competition for the bit of work or charitable dole.[23]

Birt writes that Macpherson's Revival Homes and the Home of Industry were already "filled to overflowing with fatherless children," and the economic depression meant that older boys in the homes had few employment prospects. Macpherson may have got the idea to emigrate the children from the Reverend Styleman Herring, who had been sending whole families abroad. The pamphlet she and Logan published contained the now famous appeal: "We who labour here are tired of relieving misery from hand to mouth, and also heart-sick of seeing hundreds of families pining away for want of work, when from the shores of Ontario the cry is heard, 'Come over and we will help you.'" An emigration fund was opened at the Home of Industry to send selected families to Canada and according to Birt some 500 people were sent — apparently families — in the summer of 1869.[24]

But Macpherson's public relations masterstroke was in creating a slogan that would be the envy of advertising agencies today. "We are waiting to seek out the worthy, not yet on the parish list, but who soon must be; we will see to their being properly started and received on the Canadian shores, *if you will give us the power to make a golden bridge across the Atlantic*"[25] (emphasis added). This theme would later be further embroidered by Dr. Barnardo, who would use it to great effect in his own work. Meanwhile Annie Macpherson not only accompanied her first group of 100 boys in 1870 but assisted Dr. Barnardo to send a small group of boys to Canada that year:

You will be glad to hear that all your boys seem to have got comfortable places, and I trust they are doing well. The behaviour of the boys on board and on the journey afterwards was most excellent with very few exceptions, and all in the country were well pleased with the well-trained appearance

of the boys, and seemed fully to appreciate the religious influences with which they had been surrounded, and which
actuates the conduct of so many of them. This is a very fine
country, with splendid openings for those who will work and
put their hands to anything for the first six months.[26]

Another child emigration pioneer was Maria Rye, though she
seemed more motivated by economics than by missionary zeal. She
would later be condemned by Poor Law Board inspector Andrew
Doyle in 1875. Yet doubts about her work were voiced as far back
as 1868 by William Dixon, a Canadian immigration agent based in
Britain. According to historians Roger Kershaw and Janet Sacks,
"He called Rye a 'passenger agent of the sharpest description,' explaining his rationale: 'She appeals to the public through the press
for contributions to aid her in assisting poor girls to emigrate. . . .
She then applies to the registry offices for girls and asks them how
much money they can raise towards the price of a passage . . . she
also applies to the unions of factory towns and . . . *the guardians
pay all the expenses.* If the girls have two pounds and Miss Rye's
subscriptions come in freely she supplements what is required, re-
taining what she considers reasonable . . . *it is a profitable business*"
(emphasis added).[27]

Tellingly, Rye's speech in 1870 before the National Association
for the Promotion of Social Science, chaired by Lord Shaftesbury,
focused on the economic argument. "Noting that in London alone
there were more than 10,000 children in the workhouse and another 46,000 on outdoor relief, she revealed that she could take
girls to Canada for £10 a head," write Kershaw and Sacks. In a
lecture to the Liverpool Literary and Philosophical Society, Dr.
Hayward pointed out that Rye had already saved Liverpool ratepayers £5,000, "which would have been the cost of maintaining the
children she had taken to Canada from eight years of age to 18."[28]

Rye met with at least some opposition to her fundraising efforts
for the 1869 party she emigrated to Canada. Political cartoonist
George Cruikshank "replied by publishing a pamphlet denoun-

cing her plan," note Kershaw and Sacks. Entitled *Our Gutter Children*, it depicted street children "being carted away like rubbish, their pitiful cries overridden by voices of authority and a Maria Rye-like figure which proclaimed, 'I'll drive off to pitch the little dears aboard of a ship and take them thousands of miles away from their native land so that they may never see any of their relatives again.'" Cruikshank cut to the heart of the matter — the permanent separation of poor British children from both their homeland and their families.[29]

But Cruikshank's dissenting view was still by far the minority in the 1870s, though not all Poor Law guardians were enthused about child emigration as a solution to their problems. As Manchester historian Andrew Simpson writes, "From the outset there were those in the 1870s who raised doubts about the safety of the children in Canada on remote farms and homes, which despite promises and assurance never went away."[30] Once again, however, these conscientious voices would find themselves drowned out by the chorus of child emigration supporters. Britain was not yet ready to face the shadow side of its class system.

It would take a gradual shift in societal views and the development of the nascent field of psychology in the early 20th century before serious opposition arose. "Speaking at a meeting of the (Manchester) Guardians in 1910," notes Simpson, "Catherine Garrett had said, 'They were not fighting particular cases *but the general principle* of sending out children to another country to live and *to be employed there under conditions which were illegal in their own land*. In some cases children of seven were being sent out by boards of Guardians' (emphasis added). And laying aside the principle," explains Simpson, "it was the simple exploitation of the young people in their care that drove William Skivington to hammer away at the issues from 1907 onwards." Skivington pointed out that these children, once in Canada, "were sent to work for their livelihood at an age which would not be tolerated in this country," and that, "for children from seven years of age the conditions denoted forced labour, not voluntary or free; that being employed or hired work they were robbed of their childhood and of the opportunity of a sound education. . . ." He concluded that, "emigration of young children for working purposes savoured of traffic in child labour." As Simpson notes, Skivington, Garrett, and a few others "argued that the children in their care should be given vocational training to set themselves off on a productive life in Britain. . . . Sadly they were still in a minority and every attempt to reverse the policy was defeated."[31]

Annie Macpherson seems to have had her hands quite full without resorting to Maria Rye's tactic of skimming child emigrants from the Poor Law Unions. But the Thompson sisters who were taken into Macpherson's care in 1900 would find that the "golden bridge" of opportunity in Canada was a hard road indeed.

3. The Thompson Sisters
in the Land of Opportunity

May, 1900. The brand-new steamship *SS Tunisian*[32] is easing its way seaward from the Liverpool docks amid the usual blare of ship's horns. Included in the ship's manifest are 55 children bound for Canada,[33] taken from various homes and orphanages in England and emigrated under the auspices of Annie Macpherson. Among them are Elizabeth and Caroline Thompson. Lizzie must now step fully into her role of Big Sister, and Carrie clutches her hand desperately anywhere they go on the ship, as if she might fly off into the air if she let go. The ship's crew are invariably polite and helpful, eager to assist the children by giving them little "jobs" to do to help the time pass more smoothly. But the mighty Atlantic is a temperamental body of water at the best of times and its weather can turn on a dime from pleasant to hellish.

Barnardo's Canadian agent Alfred de Brissac Owen writes in the agency's *Ups & Downs* newsletter of a boatload of children sent to Canada in March 1900 by Barnardo's on the *SS Cam-*

broman. It's a fascinating insight into the journey the Thompson sisters and their companions must make. Following a stormy, miserable crossing, the ship puts into Halifax first, where a contingent bound for Manitoba is disembarked. From there the balance of the party proceeded to Portland where they landed two days later. "The United States officials — quarantine, alien, and customs — dealt graciously with us," Owen wrote, "and the Grand Trunk (Railway) representatives at Portland . . . gave us every facility for the entraining of the party, and sent us forward by a fast special that covered the distance to Toronto in twenty hours, enabling us to reach our destination on the morning of the 12th."[34]

Owen offers a vivid first-hand account of the process the children went through once cleared of Canadian Customs. No time was wasted getting them from their ports of arrival to the distribution homes and from there to placements with farmers and others in need of child labourers. Describing the Barnardo's home in Toronto on Jarvis Street, Owen explains, "At the Home it was a case of quickly come, quickly go, and 48 hours sufficed to leave the premises well nigh again emptied. Seventy-nine little lads have been placed in foster homes, where their maintenance will be paid for until they are old enough to take situations. The rest have gone out to support themselves henceforward by the sweat of the face, and to contribute by their labour to the upbuilding of the wealth and progress of the Dominion."[35]

By the time the Thompson sisters arrived in Ontario, Macpherson had moved her receiving home from Galt (now Cambridge) to Stratford. Annie Macpherson's sister Rachel and her husband Joseph Merry had been managing the receiving home in Stratford since its opening in 1883. Following Rachel's death in 1892, their son William Merry took over management.[36] The house at 51 Avon Street must have seemed like something out of a storybook to the boys and girls arriving there on their way to farms throughout Perth County. Its imposing square towers topped with spire-like railings would have reminded them of architecture back home in England, although more reminiscent of an upper-class mansion than a country cottage.[37] The home was nicely situated on the outskirts of Stratford, surrounded by lush countryside.

The emigration parties usually arrived between March and June. Thanks to the writing of Ellen Bilbrough, who managed the Marchmont Home in Belleville, and Annie Macpherson's niece Lilian Birt, we have a vivid picture of what it would have been like for children like Elizabeth and Caroline Thompson arriving at any of the three Canadian distributing homes during this period. Writing of the scene at Marchmont, Bilbrough recalled:

> One conveyance after another drives up and is fastened under the shady maple trees, while the farmer and his wife are shown into a good-sized parlour. There we refer to his previously sent in application and see his letter of recommendation, and being satisfied that it will be a good home in which to place one of our charges proceed to call in from the garden, field or playground, some half dozen boys of age and size required. . . . (W)hen the choice is made . . . the happy little fellow is sent for his possessions, while the different arrangements as to wages, clothing, schooling etc., are attended to, and written down in the page allotted to each child's history in the report book. Soon the little man returns, his earthly all contained in the white canvas bag. After a hearty shake of the hand, a promise soon to come and see him, and an earnest reminder to write to his friends, he jumps into his new master's democrat and drives off among the deafening cheers of his companions who have gathered round the veranda to bid farewell. . . .[38]

But hidden amongst the rousing cheers was bound to be disappointment and tears at being last picked. Farmers naturally prefer older boys and girls capable of shouldering the hard labour required of them. Younger or smaller boys often find themselves left behind or moved often from farm to farm. Lilian Birt offers a glimpse into this emotional dynamic in her account of children arriving at the Knowlton, Quebec distribution home in April 1877:

> Occasionally during the first days of our distribution work there would be a hue and cry from the children, "A farmer's coming! Oh, let him have me, Mrs. Birt!" "No, let him have me. I want to be a farmer and earn my own living." On bringing in about half a dozen and letting the farmer speak to them, it was very funny to see these dear children stretch themselves up to their greatest height; and, if I relaxed and permitted any freedom, the scene would become trying with beseeching voices saying, "Take me, sir, I'll be such a good boy." I have seen both men and women weep, and reply, "My dears, my heart is big enough to take you all, but my house ain't." And when the choice was made it would take a little time for the rest to get over a feeling of intense disappointment at not being the distinguished chosen one. . . .[39]

No wonder the farmers and their wives were moved to tears. As further inducement these scenes often featured a recital or impromptu concert by the children. "What can you sing boys? *Sweet Bye-and-Bye, Safe in the Arms of Jesus, What a Captain, Pull for the Shore*," writes Bilbrough. "We select one, the lads sing it heartily; meanwhile the farmer is studying the different countenances, and after a little conversation chooses one. The others go away rather disappointed." Macpherson's Homes had made an effort to establish a screening process for applicant farmers, who applied to the distribution homes, "giving at least two references from the community. These were often from neighbours, but mostly from clergy of the local churches," Bilbrough explains.[40] But in practice this provided no guarantees of fair treatment.

The other heartbreak for thousands of these children was being separated from siblings, often the only companions they had in the world. Neither Bilbrough nor Birt wrote of these wrenching separations. Elizabeth Thompson is just nine years old when she arrives in Canada and Caroline only seven. Brothers and sisters just like them had clung together on the difficult Atlantic crossing and been awestruck by the pristine Canadian landscape, only to be split apart soon after they arrived at the distributing home.

From the Stratford home Elizabeth is placed with Joseph Mc-Cracken of Donegal, in the heart of Ontario's prime agricultural district, Perth County. But Caroline is placed on a different farm, with the George Patterson family in Brunner, Ontario. Although only 18 kilometres apart, for two young girls dependent on adults for transport it might as well have been an ocean away. Siblings are encouraged to write each other, but visits are generally rare. The records show no trace of Elizabeth's grief over her separation from Caroline. This is where history often fails us — giving us facts and figures but seldom the emotional lives behind the scenes. Elizabeth is reported as "well and happy" in August 1900.[41] The same stock phrase had been used of Caroline in July 1900, though it appears she is of a more fragile constitution. The June 1901 report notes that she has "improved in health and had a good home with Mrs. Patterson who took great care of her."[42]

July 1901. Records kept by the Macpherson's Homes suggest that Elizabeth is indeed one of the lucky ones. She is affectionately known by the McCrackens as "Lizzie." The family is allowing her to get at least some schooling, where she is "making good progress." As with almost all Home Children, she must rise early to pump water from the well and have breakfast on the table by the time the family rises for the day's farm work in the wee hours of the morning. In July 1902, she is reported as "making good progress in every way," and said to be "truthful and obedient." These stock phrases appear often in such reports, making it difficult to read between the lines. By June of the following year, "Lizzie" is noted to have "grown a great deal but still small for her age. She seemed happy and contented and her foster parents, Mr. and Mrs. McCracken, spoke highly of her. She did very well at school."[43]

Caroline's reports could almost be carbon copies of those written of her sister Elizabeth. By July 1902 she is reported as "getting along nicely, was willing, helpful, and seemed quite happy," but her health continues to be a little shaky. In June 1903 the records show her as "improving and well-liked."[44]

The annual reports on the two girls reveal that Macpherson's Homes are living up to their commitment to visit each child once per year. Bilbrough explains that among the protocols governing the Homes is that, "after the children are placed in homes, our influence and care must not cease; as far as practicable they should be visited annually, complaints attended to, arrangements as to wages, clothing, schooling faithfully carried out; advice and loving counsel given, and friendly feeling kept up."[45] Among the early visitors working for Macpherson's Homes in Canada were Leslie Thom and George Roberts, covering a vast territory. Just a few years before the Thompson sisters' arrival, in 1894, the Reverend Robert Wallace had explained to the First Ontario Conference on Child Saving in Toronto that, "As far as the Marchmont Home, *three visitors are in the field this year traveling, covering a territory from Owen Sound to Montreal*" (emphasis added.)[46] With a workload like that their reports would have to be brief.

And in fact it was this aspect of the program that came under heavy fire by Local Government Board (successor to Britain's Poor Law Board) Inspector Andrew Doyle in his 1875 report on child immigration to Canada. While praising Annie Macpherson and Ellen Bilbrough for their energy and devotion to the cause, it was obvious to Doyle they lacked the resources to do a thorough follow-up on the children. Doyle argued, according to historian Kenneth Bagnell, that "there was a crucial difference between the kind of casual visit her workers made and the kind of careful inspection that was required. 'The visits,' he said, 'do not constitute the sort of inspection that is of much use, having a good deal more the character of visits from friends and guests of the employers than of an impartial inquiry into the conditions and treatment of the children.' As a result of this superficial gesture, he had encountered numerous cases, not just of missing children, but of abused children, boys and girls who complained of mistreatment that was all too often merely confirmed by their masters." Maria Rye, by contrast, made no secret of the fact that she made no effort to follow up on the children. Doyle concluded that, "no pauper children should be placed in her care for shipment to Canada."[47]

December 1903. Lizzie has come down with swollen tonsils and is returned to the Marchmont Home in Belleville, "where she was to have had an operation recommended by the doctor. Mr. and Mrs. McCracken wanted her back." The records fall silent on the question of whether she was returned to the McCrackens. The next time we hear of her — in May 1904 — she is being moved to British Columbia accompanied by a Mrs. Gillespie, probably a volunteer with Macpherson's. She is allowed to visit her sister Caroline before leaving. Elizabeth is headed for a farm at Enderby, BC, in the lush north Okanagan valley. The name of the family she is placed with is not noted. As per the usual contract between farmers and Macpherson's Homes, she will be given room and board, some time off for schooling, and a stipend to be paid out when she comes of age. Two years later, in January 1906, the report notes, "Elizabeth wrote a bright letter, saying she was very comfortable, and had a nice Christmas with many presents." Once again, if this single sentence is anything to go by, it appears she has landed with another kind family.[48]

Caroline writes the Macpherson's Homes a letter in January 1905. Mrs. Patterson tells the Home that, "it would break her heart to part with her and that she (is) a very affectionate child." But it appears that won't happen for some time yet — Caroline will stay with her a few more years before going out on her own. The June 1906 report notes that she likes her home and is "well-clothed." By 1907 the Macpherson's Homes visitor notes that she is considered "one of the family," yet another stock phrase whose basis in reality is difficult to determine.[49]

Enderby, BC, 1910. Now that she is 19, Elizabeth is too old to be called "Lizzie," a child's nickname, and prefers the more adult "Lilly" amongst her friends. She finds work at a local café and soon learns to be quick on her feet. Though she may not know him personally, she has doubtless heard of Vernon's Joe Harwood — another former Home Child who arrived in Canada with Barnardo's in 1889. Harwood had made his way west, working in Calgary for a time before moving to the BC Interior to settle in the newly developing town, starting up a fast-expanding cartage and delivery service. (See Chapter 6: "Joe's Story.")

One day a young man named George Deptford is seated in one of the booths in the café where Elizabeth works. His oil-stained overalls suggest either a mechanic or railway worker. She betrays her nervousness at first, chattering about local gossip. But the growing attraction is mutual. Soon George is timing his meals at the café to coincide with Elizabeth's shift. Gradually she pieces together his story from the snatches of conversation they are able to share. Born in Tottenham, England in 1889, George had arrived in Canada as a young lad not yet 20 years old. As with many young men seeking opportunities, he had heard and responded to the "Call of the West." Just a year earlier, in 1909, he made his way to Field, BC, in the shadow of the snow-capped Rockies of the Rogers Pass. He was hired there as a wiper with the Canadian Pacific Railway (CPR). Elizabeth is impressed — the CPR is a good source of reliable jobs.[50]

"May not sound like much just now, but good workers can go a long way with the CPR — and I don't mean just the travel," he chuckles. "A lot of the older guys I know on the line working as engineers started off in my job."

A marriage proposal isn't long in coming. George's work with the CPR settles him in Revelstoke, BC and they are married there September 20, 1911. The last entry in the Macpherson's Homes records is made in 1912 when Elizabeth is 21, where it's noted that "she is married and starting a family." A report on Caroline the same year notes that she has been "working for herself and had been doing so for the last four years," or since she was 15. When she finally leaves the Patterson household, she is sent to Revelstoke and later ends up working in the kitchen of a large farm in Yakima, Washington. She writes her final letter to the Macpherson's Homes in December 1940 from Chelan, Washington. She has married Edward Wells and the couple has adopted a daughter named Marjorie.[51]

April 9, 1912. George and Elizabeth welcome their first child, Helen May, into the world with the help of Dr. Sutherland. During this era many births occur at home and regular house calls by physicians are a lifeline in small rural communities. The Deptfords will have another seven children: Norman, Eva, James, Lillian, Florence, Beatrice, and Georgina. Beatrice is born October 1914, on the cusp of the Great War's outbreak. As if stricken to the bone by the shadow of the largest war in human history, she will die of spinal meningitis at eight years of age, on July 9, 1923. "Only a week before the little girl . . . was enjoying the outing with her fellow Sunday School scholars," notes the obituary in the *Revelstoke Review*. "Soon after she was under treatment at the Queen Victoria Hospital and though all possible was done for her there, she expired on Wednesday last." When her daughter Georgina is born three months later, Elizabeth must learn to balance both joy and sorrow. Georgina contracts scarlet fever as a young girl, leaving her deaf. She is later sent to a special school in Vancouver, where she will make her home as an adult.[52]

November 11, 1918. Elizabeth bustles into the bedroom of her daughter Helen, obviously flustered with excitement. Helen has been ill and confined to bed.

"Quickly! Get on your dressing gown and come downstairs with me!"

"What, what mama?"

"Quickly! You'll see, but hurry!"

They hustle downstairs and Elizabeth takes Helen's coat from the hallway closet, making sure to bundle her up. A Revelstoke winter can be bitingly cold. The front door is swung open and at first all Helen sees is the brilliant, clear winter sky causing the snow to glisten on the glaciers surrounding the town. She looks up at her mother, wondering at the look in her eyes. Then, at the stroke of 11 a.m., the town erupts with bells ringing, locomotive horns blaring, and a few cars bleating. "The Armistice has been signed! The Great War is over at last," Elizabeth explains. Tears stream down her face, just one among millions whose relief goes up in a great sigh as the joyful scene is repeated across the world.[53]

Families everywhere can now turn from the anxious expectation of receiving death notices to the joy of receiving home the survivors. Among them is Elizabeth's brother James Thompson, who arrives a few months later in Revelstoke with his bride Sarah, returning from his posting in England. It's the first time Elizabeth has seen her brother since she and Caroline were sent to Canada nearly 20 years before. As a war veteran, James has no trouble landing a job with the CPR and before long the couple is able to buy a house on Seventh Street near Selkirk school, where they will raise their own family. Elizabeth's daughter Helen May (later Edwards) later writes a memoir that demonstrates a deft hand for evoking the past:

> One by one the Deptford children started school in the Selkirk school only three blocks away. There they met the many neighbour children with whom they would grow up. Phyllis Lapworth, Lulu and Craig Rutherford, Hazel Hanna, the four Briar girls, the Southwells and the Altenhovens. Most all their fathers were CPR employees (firemen and engineers). Mrs. Southwell and Lil became very friendly and often picked huckleberries together, either up Mt. Revelstoke or out east of town.[54]

Life in Revelstoke during the early part of the 20th century is idyllic for the Deptford family — in total contrast to the impoverished conditions that had brought Elizabeth and Caroline to Canada as Home Children. The Canadian West is expanding fast and Revelstoke is a critical juncture on the Trans-Canada CPR line. George is obviously a dedicated, reliable worker who soon earns promotion. Already by 1913 he had earned the rank of locomotive engineer.[55]

Our growing family soon needed more rooms so we moved to a two-story building with seven rooms on Second Street. We especially enjoyed a huge crabapple tree, not only for the shade but also for the delicious jelly Mom made. We were all well fed with her bread, buns, Irish stew, dumplings, pies, Christmas cakes and mincemeat pies. She made mincemeat English style. She taught us well, including steak and kidney pie. Mom loved her little garden and six chickens and, as usual for her, taught us about seeds and watering. And the chickens needed their warm bran mash every day they produced eggs. No wonder those eggs were special and the vegetables were so good and always fresh throughout the summer and fall.

Bregalissi's store was just a half block away, so very convenient, and we visited often, such lovely people. The Pradolinis lived in their castle home across the avenue. Charlie Sing called often with his full, horse-drawn wagonload of fresh vegetables from his own farm. Christmastime was special, a Chinese lily, grown in water, sitting on rocks. And silk stockings from China for our growing girls. Gallicano's bread was always a treat and always delivered as needed. Mr. Campbell kept us supplied with his excellent quality milk in glass bottles. The cream tops were always there and nearly always froze in winter. The cream would push up about two to three inches with its cap still on. Mom often got extra for a special treat of ice cream. We all took turns turning the crank and watching the cream freeze.[56]

George and Elizabeth Deptford keep themselves busy on the local social scene as members of the Fireman's Lodge, Lady Firemen's Lodge, Masonic Lodge, Oddfellows Lodge and Pythian Sisters. Elizabeth cuts an attractive figure at the Lady Fireman's fancy dress balls. The couple is active in the local Anglican Church and the children are sent there for Sunday school. "Then there was bowling, inside and outside, and the children had their exercises and swimming lessons in the YMCA building just behind our house. With no transportation except Jim's bicycle, there was always hiking and swimming in Williamson Lake, a few miles south of town," recalls Helen. "And in huckleberry season, Mom got us up at four a.m., packed a lunch for us and we climbed Mt. Revelstoke to pick all day. We also met our share of bears and lost berries when we ran all the way home!"[57]

During this era the ethos of "spare the rod and spoil the child" still held sway. According to Helen, her parents were "strict disciplinarians, and we obeyed or be spanked, and we all had our turns. I grew up to be a very serious student; good training at home kept us all in check." But the dominant impression Helen recalls is of scrumptious meals shared by the family in traditional English fashion. "The Sunday meal was roast beef and Yorkshire pudding, with apple pie for dessert. Dad always gave his special prayer of thanksgiving."[58]

Illness strikes any family and the Deptfords were no exception. Helen notes in her memoir that both Norman and James came down with polio, putting the house under quarantine. "No school, no home deliveries, except to the gate only (we had no phone), and no visitors but the doctor. Jim recovered quite well and quickly but Norman suffered on for some time." Through it all Elizabeth was a devoted mother and George a supportive father. "During all these difficult days, Mom stayed upstairs with the boys and Dad stayed home downstairs with the rest of us doing the cooking, cleaning, laundry and everything else needed."[59]

Revelstoke is the very picture of rural splendour, nestled in the crook of the Columbia River between the Selkirk mountain ranges. But its location leaves it vulnerable to avalanches in the winter. Elizabeth's sons Norman and James followed in their father's footsteps as CPR employees. "And in those days of deep snow and heavy ice buildup we heard many stories of tragedies that befell our neighbours and friends with the CPR, especially through the Rogers Pass," Helen recalled. "Heavy loss of life from slides coming down on trains from both sides of the valleys. Norman just missed one tragedy himself. . . ."[60]

George Deptford continued to be rewarded for his hard work, working as fireman in 1933 on the Royal Scot when the famous train passed through the Rogers Pass, and again in 1939 on the occasion of the visit of King George VI. He rises to engineer of the pilot train by the time of the visit of Princess Elizabeth and the Duke of Edinburgh to Canada in 1951, during the Revelstoke-Kamloops leg of the tour. George retires in 1953 but is in failing health. He dies at home in Revelstoke on December 3, 1956.[61]

With the passing of George, one circle began to close even as the Deptford children's lives rippled out in wider circles. In later years Caroline and Elizabeth are reunited again, apparently living together for a time in Washington. Georgina and her family are living in Vancouver and Elizabeth takes advantage of her lifetime CPR pass to visit her often. Even into her 80s she still climbs the steep slopes near Revelstoke to go huckleberry picking. Elizabeth spends her final years in Vernon, where she passes away on August 6, 1984 at the age of 92. She is buried in Revelstoke next to her husband — a world away from the poverty of her London childhood.[62]

Helen May Deptford marries Philip Edwards of Revelstoke in 1933, starting family life in the depths of the Great Depression. Initially the Edwards family tries homesteading on the Arrow Lakes at Fauquier, "more or less camping," writes their daughter Helen, "while neighbours helped build a log house." The West Kootenay region had developed a thriving fruit industry — particularly on the West Arm of Kootenay Lake — in the early years of the 20th century. But the decimation of the local workforce during World War I and persistent pests like the cherry worm causes the industry to crash in the postwar years. Still, the Edwards thought it was worth a try. They were disappointed. When a maintenance job comes available at the Connaught Tunnel in the Rogers Pass, Phil leaps at the chance. In 1943 he is transferred to the CPR machine shops in Winnipeg, but the family find the city not to their liking and return to BC two years later, in May 1945. "Mom and Dad saw for themselves how people were led to believe a good living could be made growing fruit. [They] eventually just cried when they were charged more to ship the produce than it was worth. But at least they could grow enough to feed the family on the land. A few chickens, a cow, geese and what more could a person want?"[63]

It was the very dream that had inspired generations of Canadian farmers, and the philanthropists who sent generations of Home Children to Canada. But no dream comes without its shock of reality. In the post WW II era Phil Edwards finds himself following work with his family in tow — doing everything from picking cherries to firefighting. The family spends two years at Sheep Creek before ending up in Salmo, BC, where Phil finally lands a decent job at the Can-Ex mine. "Bit by bit they were able to furnish their home with furnishings found in families' basements," recalls their daughter Helen. "They were not fussy."[64] If it's true that most people stay in the economic class they're born into, then her mother, the daughter of a Home Child, stays true to form. Despite the glossy promises of child emigration, most descendants of Home Children will find themselves working in manual labour occupations the same as if they'd remained in Britain. It will take another generation for Elizabeth Deptford's descendants to begin rising above the humble origins of so many Home Children.

4. Filling in the Gaps of History

For Elizabeth Deptford at least, Annie Macpherson's dream of giving her immigrant children a new and better life in Canada proved a reality. But as always, reality is far from simple or straightforward. Generations of Home Children would go to their graves without sharing their experience with their own children. Annie Macpherson and Lilian Birt, probably acting from a protective instinct, did their best to shelter newly arriving boys and girls from the negative views of them often found in the Canadian press. "Mrs. Birt has studiously endeavoured to keep the record of the children in Canada clear and free of stain or reproach. After a child is once admitted to the Home *no reference is allowed to be made to its past history.* As few details as possible that are in any way prejudicial are passed on to Canada" (emphasis added).[65] Yet this policy had the unintentional effect of obscuring from child emigrants the details of their own family past — critical elements of self identity. This was compounded with the passage of time and the inevitable decline of memory.

"If only she'd had no bitterness or regrets," Elizabeth's grand-daughter Helen May (Edwards) Dickey writes, "we may have learned of some happy memories of childhood friends and games they played, what her family — cousins too — were like. Did she remember her mother?"[66] If she did, she seems never to have spoken of her — a common reaction amongst Home Children. As historian Roy Parker notes, this is hardly surprising, given the stigma child immigrants were faced with in Canada. "This is how one woman, arriving in Canada in 1913 explained it: 'You weren't considered as good as the rest of the kids, because you had no home of your own and no parents. . . . You don't know what this does to you. I have never got over it.'"[67]

To the end of her life, Elizabeth Deptford felt bitter about her father's decision to put her and her sister into Macpherson's care. There is simply no cure for a child's feelings of rejection or aban-donment. Even with a stable, loving marriage, many children and a degree of material security, emotional wounds linger. A child will typically blame herself for family problems but will nevertheless feel deeply hurt if they are taken away from the family. Helen writes that her Aunt Florence spent time with Elizabeth in her later years in Vernon, trying to soothe the bitterness. "Mom was always bitter with her Dad for sending her and Carrie away on the orphan boat," wrote Florence Deptford. "But in her later years, we had a good talk and I told her that he did it for a good reason. They had a better chance in the colonies than in London. She forgave him."[68] James Thompson was, after all — like so many parents of British Home Children — a victim of his own poor health and circumstances. Elizabeth and Caroline, however, were among the lucky ones. For thousands of Home Children the promised "better life" consisted of a childhood of brutally hard work, often subject to abuse.

Victorian society did a poor job of discerning between causes and effects when it came to social problems, and tended to blame the victims. The terms "vicious" and "depraved" were often used in connection with poor parents dealing with chronic unemployment and alcoholism. The evangelical revival of the 1860s was driven by a strong moral imperative to reform the ills of society. Even well-meaning Christian philanthropists saw no hubris in taking children away from their families. Dr. Barnardo's term "philanthropic abduction" was as much a rationalization as an oxymoron. There was also a strong belief that the "evil influences of the city" could be remedied by sending children to live and work in the countryside. About the time Elizabeth Deptford is having her first children, Lilian Birt is writing her book *The Children's Home-Finder*. She notes that at that time the consensus was still that farm life was a better option for destitute children than being raised in an institution. "Apart from the absence of blood-relationship, which nothing on earth can fully make up to them, the children thus placed out in families are better off, are happier, and are receiving a better training for life's duties than thousands of children in their own homes."[69]

It's interesting that Birt acknowledges that the "absence of blood relationship" cannot be compensated for. Yet she goes on to reiterate the rationale for emigrating children — more a statement of belief than of actual experience. Even with the system of inspections established by Annie Macpherson, Barnardo's and the Ontario government, abuses clearly were going on. The killing of George Everett Green in 1895 should have been a clear warning signal that in these remote locations anything could happen to children who were left alone and undefended.

Birt in 1913 argues that even more than 40 years on, the situation in Britain's cities is still abysmal. "The housing problem is still acute in the large cities, and equally in country villages, leading to the depopulation of our countryside. There is constantly present a large amount of unemployment. There are about half a million workmen belonging to the principal trades registered as "unemployed" throughout the year, but these are the aristocracy of labour. For a large number of our slum population we have had to invent the word "unemployable": untrained to any skilled labour, unused to steady work of any kind ... their children are those who fall to charitable societies to take care of from the cradle to the grave." Birt backs up her argument with statistics: "The Guardians under Local Government Board direction have 71,000 children living in institutions entirely under their control, and 182,000 more on outrelief; many of the latter are very sadly neglected and not getting a fair chance in life. These numbers are those receiving relief on one day, 1st January, only — above half a million (500,000) children receive Poor Law relief at some time or other throughout the year."[70]

Posing the question, "Is the work still necessary?" Birt notes that the population of Britain is increasing by one million every three years, further limiting opportunities in a poor labour market. Perhaps unaware of the irony, she quotes a wealthy aristocrat, the 15th Earl of Derby, Sir Edward Henry Stanley: "We are and we must be an emigrating country. We shall always have men enough left at home; and even if emigration were to go the length of checking the increase here, which it almost certainly will not, surely it is better to have 35 million human beings leading useful and intelligent lives, rather than 45 million struggling painfully for a bare subsistence."[71] Sir Stanley takes no note of the fact that most Home Children will still continue to "struggle for a bare subsistence" in Canada. Only a few will gain access to the higher education that will enable them to ascend the economic ladder. (See Chapter 7: "Leslie Vivian Rogers — A Scholar and a Gentleman.")

As historian Andrew Simpson notes of the Manchester Poor Law Board of Guardians, there were from the earliest days of child emigration those who objected to the practice, but these were drowned by a vocal majority. Then in the first decade of the 20th century, "a small band of socialist Guardians on the Chorlton Union argued the case against sending children from our workhouse to Canada, citing evidence and making a principled stand.

They pointed to the long hours and lack of schooling that was the lot of many of the children, which as they argued, contravened our own child protection laws and above all was an abrogation of our duty *to solve the problem here in Britain.*" (emphasis added)[72]

Elizabeth (Thompson) Deptford and family, circa 1937. Back: Helen May (mother of Helen Dickey), Norman, Eva, James. Middle: George Frederick Deptford, Lillian, Florence, Elizabeth Emma (Thompson), and Georgina (centre front). Helen Dickey collection.

Elizabeth (centre) and Caroline with their father James Thompson and their younger brother James Jr. about the time the girls were admitted to Barnardo's care. Helen (Deptford) Dickey collection.

CHAPTER 3

The Roberts Brothers —
Bridge of Gold, Bridge of Straw

29 ALFRED STREET, BRISTOL, 1892. It's late in the evening, the pale light from gas lamps reflecting on the cobblestones outside the Duddridge home. It's a working-class neighbourhood, so the brick row houses are sturdy but unattractive. Several families must share a lavatory, housed in dingy sheds built in narrow courtyards adjoining the housing blocks. There is no running water and a constant problem with rats and mice. Quarters meant to comfortably house a few people are routinely crammed with a dozen or more.

Lavinia Roberts answers an insistent rapping on the door. Her heart races, wondering if it might be a policeman again. She eases the door open a crack, but before she can ask who it is, it's flung open. Her husband Fred Roberts stands swaying in the doorframe, reeking of booze. "Damn ye!" he screams. "Found ye at last!" Lavinia's mother Elizabeth covers her mouth in fear — she had hoped and prayed that such scenes were finally a thing of the past.

"Ere, what's the problem?" It's the steady voice of Lavinia's father William, stepping up behind her. At 57 he's well past his prime but decades of work as a stonemason have given him a sturdy physique. She practically swoons backward into him for support.

"You stay out of this!" bellows Fred, jabbing a finger in his direction. "This woman is me own lawfully wedded wife, and I'll have 'er, by God!"

William steps protectively in front of Lavinia, who is visibly shaking. "Just as you had 'er before, Fred? Treated like an old mule for knockin' about?"

"She's taken my children from me!"

"Well, ye had the other children and couldn't keep them, either. Don't get me wrong, Fred, I like a tipple as much as the next man, but ye've half crawled inside the keg."

Lavinia catches her breath. "You have such talent, Fred — to let it go to waste — "

"Shut yer hole!" Fred lunges forward, fist raised.

William blocks him, holding him at arm's length. "That'll be quite enough of ye, now."

Fred staggers backward, nearly falling. "Damn you, Lavinia! Breaking up our home, goin' with any bloke in long pants!"

Lavinia gasps. "You know that's not true!"

"Fred, we've been over the barrel and round the barnyard on this one," William insists. "Ye know Lavinia has been faithful. She's done naught but work fingers to the bone sewing and serving the gentlewomen o' Bristol to keep your wee mites fed."

But by now Fred is practically foaming. "Liar! You're all liars! I'll burn your house out, and all o' ye for keepin' 'er from me!"

Now it's William's turn to burn red with anger. "Ah, ye will, will ye? We'll see about that. Shall I call for a copper, then? T'wouldn't be the first time, now, would it?"

Fred's face blanches at the mention of police. With a kind of enraged whimper he staggers backwards, moving crookedly away from the doorstep. William fills the doorframe, watching until the shambling form finally melts into shadow. He closes the door firmly. The storm passed, Lavinia's control dissolves in a wash of tears. Her mother strokes her cheek, her hair. "There, there, dear."

Her father places a comforting hand on her shoulder. "I think the time has come, Lavinia. We oughter swear out a complaint against him. Ye heard his threat. He could well do't."

"We can't put the children at risk, now he's found us," her mother agrees.[1]

LAVINIA TAKES HER FAMILY'S ADVICE and swears out a complaint against her husband. The local magistrate issues a writ and Fred is "bound over to keep the peace." That will likely mean he is headed for the workhouse, that hell on earth that even the poorest of the poor avoid like the plague. She can't help thinking back on happier days in Liverpool, when their first child Frederick Jr. was born 11 years ago. Her husband's skill as a watchmaker had become almost legendary, leading some to describe him as a man of "genius." He was a respected man and with such a specialized skill it had seemed a fine foundation for the marriage. Under Prime Minister Gladstone, England had enjoyed a boom period during the early 1880s, so it seemed a good time to start a family.[2]

But by the time Lavinia's other children had been born — including her youngest sons William George on September 16, 1886 and Walter Henry on February 22, 1889 — the economy was sliding into the depression of the 1890s. Fred's business had slumped, and he slid with it into the numbing comfort of the bottle. The burden of supporting five children had fallen more and more to Lavinia. Although skilled in needlework, during tough times such a skill wasn't enough to feed a large family. Lavinia took to working as a sick nurse and finally as a domestic servant. But despite the long hours of hard work, it still wasn't enough.

For Fred what had begun as a crutch had developed into full-blown alcoholism, stoking his paranoia and insecurity. His drunken temper gradually became more and more violent. When Lavinia becomes pregnant with their fifth child, she fears for its safety. It had taken her weeks to pluck up her courage but finally in September 1890 she leaves him. She flees Liverpool with her 10-year-old daughter, Ada Lavinia, to return to her father's house in Bristol. Fred's deepening collapse solves the problem of what to do with the boys. Before long he brings Frederick Jr., Walter and William to stay with his sister in Bristol, Mrs. Barton. It also gives him an excuse to track down Lavinia. But Frederick's sister has 11 children of her own to feed on a milk-seller's wage and quarters are cramped. Lavinia's parents also have their hands full. Her four brothers, although all working, are still living in the Duddridge home — the eldest 21, the youngest 14.[3] Still, they generously take in Lavinia and her daughter. Her youngest, Florence Minnie, is born in April 1891. Within a year she must be boarded out with another family. It costs Lavinia four shillings a week out of her meager annual income of £18.[4]

April 2, 1893. Lavinia receives news from Toxteth Park Workhouse, Liverpool that her husband has died of pneumonia.[5] The British workhouse system is run more like a prison than a relief agency, and persons convicted of lesser crimes are often committed to the workhouse instead of prison. Workhouse yards are surrounded by high brick walls, men and women are segregated — even spouses — and children kept separate in another ward. Children are given basic training in trades such as baking, tailoring, and shoemaking, but the list of rules is onerous and infractions severely punished. Adults are treated as virtual slaves, working a 12-hour day picking oakum or breaking rocks. Most of them are continuously confined to the workhouse grounds except for church services the first Thursday of each month. The massive Toxteth Park Workhouse houses up to 700 inmates, kept in line by the enforcement of a strict set of rules. Punishment is by solitary confinement for up to 24 hours with only bread, rice, or potatoes for meals. Lavinia can't help but feel saddened — it's a bleak, miserable death for her husband.[6]

Following Frederick Sr.'s death, his sister can no longer care for the boys, but she offers to keep Frederick Jr., as he is old enough to be of help to the family. By now Barnardo's Homes are well known throughout England and Lavinia decides it's time to get help. On one of her rare days off, she steels her courage and makes her way to the home. Though spring is on its way the streets of Bristol seem particularly grey on this day. When she arrives at the Barnardo's Home she is quietly ushered into a small office, where she is met warmly by Miss Parsons. Though young and attractive, she bears a serious air, as Lavinia has seen with many evangelicals. Explaining her situation, the accumulated stress of recent weeks makes it difficult for her not to weep. But dabbing her eyes with a handkerchief, she carries on.

"You must understand, Miss Parsons, I do my best for my children. I don't seek charity but for a last resort. I'm at my wit's end."

"I do understand, Mrs. Roberts. After all, what can one do on £18 per year? And with five little mouths to feed."

Lavinia smiles weakly, relieved. "I'm so glad you understand."

Parsons reaches across the desk, lightly patting the back of Lavinia's hand. "Of course. First, we must do a full assessment for Walter and William, but I have every confidence they will be received by Dr. Barnardo's Homes. We provide clothing, healthy meals, education, and once the boys are old enough, training in a trade. We have training shops for tailors, bootmakers, bakers, carpenters, and wheelwrights. The girls are given the best of domestic training. Best of all, Mrs. Roberts, is the security of knowing your boys will be off the streets, where evil influences may soon overtake them. It is truly the Lord's work."

"But you're sure the Home will accept my boys?"

"No destitute child is ever refused, to quote the good Doctor," assures Miss Parsons.

Lavinia finds herself flinching. "Well, I'm not sure I would call them *destitute*."

"Naturally, I meant no slight to your character as a mother, Mrs. Roberts. We understand that circumstances beyond our control often force one to seek help." Parsons opens a drawer in her desk, pulling out a form and sliding it toward Lavinia. "This is our standard contract. Please read it carefully and when you are ready, sign it."

Lavinia scans the document, a little nervous about her ability to understand such contracts. But two words in bold print catch her eye: "Canada Clause." A quick reading of the clause causes her blood pressure to rise.

"Do you mean to tell me that you will send my boys across an ocean to Canada?"

Parsons smiles, her serious demeanour thawing. "It's the standard contract, Mrs. Roberts. It means that Dr. Barnardo's Homes reserves the right to emigrate children in its care at any time to Canada. It's the golden bridge to a wonderful land of new opportunity, such as they might never see here at home. Once you sign, you are implying your consent for emigration."

"But I am to be consulted of such a thing even if I sign, am I not?"

Miss Parsons' smile becomes thin, forced. "In your case, I should think so. You seem to bear an excellent character from all I see here in your application."

Lavinia's mood hardens. "Do you mean to say that if Dr. Barnardo's judged my character less than sterling that I might not be consulted?"

"I suspect you have little to concern yourself over."

"You're being evasive, Miss Parsons."

"Dr. Barnardo runs our organization to the highest of Christian standards, Mrs. Roberts. So long as you meet those standards, you have nothing to fear for yourself or your children. Once the contract is signed their ultimate disposal rests with us."

"Disposal?" Lavinia probes Miss Parsons deeply, but the young woman seems unshakeable. What she is not being told is that in cases where a parent admitting children is judged to be morally inferior for some reason they are unlikely to be consulted or even informed of a child's emigration to Canada. In the worst cases, after-sailing notices are only sent to the parents after the child has been overseas for some months.[7] It will take Lavinia much soul-searching to bring herself to sign the Canada Clause. What if the Barnardo's staff takes her reluctance as a sign of an unfit parent? Will she know when her boys are being emigrated? And if they are, will she ever see them again?

June 27, 1893. Lavinia is back in Miss Parson's office, clutching the shoulders of little Walter, four, and six-year-old William, known to the family as "Willie." The boys cling bashfully to their mother's skirts. She's made a special effort to dress them in good clothing — dark sailor's tunics with bows, white shorts, new socks and shoes. She may be poor but she has her pride. Parsons seems unusually light and cheerful.

"Trust me, Mrs. Roberts, you've done the right thing. The boys will be well cared for. We shall encourage the boys to write you letters once they have learned their alphabet."

Parsons' glib assurance does little to ease the anguish Lavinia is feeling. Even now she must fight the urge to flee with the boys' hands gripped tightly in her own. The room seems off-kilter, as if she were suffering vertigo and about to collapse. But she has determined to keep her composure for the boys' sake. She kneels down to their eye level, swallowing the lump of grief in her throat. "Now darlings, Mama has found you a nice place to live, with lots of other boys to play with. Read your Bible and be good boys for me. Willie, you must look after your little brother now — promise me?" Willie dutifully nods, unsure what this will mean.

She will spend many nights crying herself to sleep in the weeks to come.

PRIOR TO ADMISSION THE ROBERTS BROTHERS are examined by the Barnardo's medical officer. Although at some children's homes this could mean disqualification if a child is found to be "mentally or physically unsound," Barnardo's Homes had adopted a more humane approach. Medical exams are more a means of streaming children into the appropriate home — even Dr. Barnardo's "crippled" kids are cared for in a special home where they learn to make crutches and medical appliances. From his early days at the Stepney Causeway home he had provided a 30-bed infirmary for his "little wounded soldiers." This is a revolutionary idea at a time when the disabled are considered even more disposable than the poor. As Barnardo's historian June Rose writes, "before Acts of Parliament prohibited child labour, little bodies twisted and maimed by machines, or climbing boys badly burned by chimney-sweeping, were a common sight in city streets. Very badly deformed children with large labels tied round their necks were sent into the streets to beg or exhibited at sideshows."[8]

Dr. Barnardo is also highly sensitive to inflammatory reports in the Canadian press that Britain is dumping its "inferior stock" in Canada, a concern shared by immigration authorities. But Walter and William Roberts are both healthy and robust at the time of their admission. "Both boys are strong little fellows," writes Barnardo's medical officer. Perhaps an offhand testament to their mother's strength of character, he adds that, "They are easy to lead but will not be driven." Everything from their hair and eye colour and complexion, to their weight, height, and chest measures is carefully noted. As if keeping one eye on Canadian immigration regulations, the doctor even notes that William has a "few spots on [his] right side."[9] Their admission photos show a blond-haired William, and Walter with a mop of curly brown hair, the innocence of lambs in their bright eyes. William looks at the camera with a slightly hurt, puzzled look while his younger brother is wide-eyed, open — too young to know what to make of it. Posed together, they lean close to each other as if inseparable. If they hadn't been so well dressed by their mother they would have made adorable poster children for Barnardo's.

July 28, 1893. With even the best of intentions, in an organization as massive as Barnardo's, odd decisions are sometimes made that have the potential to cause great emotional distress. The Roberts brothers are sent from Bristol to the famous home at Stepney Causeway for the first few weeks following their admission. But then four-year-old Walter is moved without his older brother to Sheppard House at 182 Grove Road, East London. Suddenly stripped of both his mother and his closest sibling, he too will cry himself to sleep in the darkness of a strange ward. His brother arrives at the home a week later, on August 3. No mention is made in the records of the reason for temporarily separating them.[10]

Life at the Stepney Home for the Roberts brothers must seem like a case of "from the frying pan into the fire." The massive, impersonal buildings at Stepney are uninviting from the outside, and only slightly less so inside. Wards filled with rambunctious boys, many of them hardened by street life, are confusing and terrifying for the younger boys. Discipline is strict, bringing both relief from the chaos and a burden of its own. "We weren't physically abused," recalled Barnardo boy Ed Cousins in his later years. "But not once can I remember any affection being shown. You had to accept a way of life so foreign, so disciplined."[11]

January 20, 1894. The Roberts brothers are sent via Southampton to Teighmore Home on Jersey in the Channel Islands. Dr. Barnardo had opened the home in 1879 as a means of providing a home for the youngest and most frail of his boys in the London facilities. The property had been gifted to Barnardo's by Lady Cairns' niece, Mrs. McNeil, part of the organization's ongoing patronage by royalty.[12] Dr. Barnardo writes with obvious satisfaction of his latest facility in one of his many public letters. "My object in opening a home in Jersey was twofold — first, to relieve the London Institution of children who are so very young (their ages ranging between four and nine years) that their admixture with older boys was undesirable; and secondly, to secure for these small mites of humanity the fresh air, sea breezes, abundant milk, and delightful scenery of Gorey, Jersey."[13]

Barnardo paints an idyllic picture of Teighmore Home. Situated near the top of Daisy Hill, the home is 10 minutes' walk from the little railway station at Gorey, "and about eight minutes from one of the most beautiful prospects in the whole island," with its own private beach in Grouville Bay. Presiding over the bay crowded with fishermen's cottages is the old castle on Mount Orgeuil. "No wonder if a poor East Londoner, whose general outlook in Stepney, Limehouse or Ratcliff is enlivened only by chimney pots and red tiles . . . may well fancy himself transported to fairyland when gazing for the first time upon the Jersey view!"[14]

Once again Dr. Barnardo takes pains to counter the impression that he is introducing moral or physical disease to the local populace. "It has got abroad — how I cannot imagine — that our Home at Jersey is intended as a convalescent home, and I fancy some of my neighbours there . . . have been somewhat alarmed lest disease should be imported through our means. . . . All the boys who are sent there are most carefully examined before leaving London, and are not dismissed unless in good health, sound in body and mind, and fit for the journey." He invites Jersey islanders to visit the home and see for themselves. Always with one eye on the flow of donations, he is quick to credit the islanders for their generosity. "Imagine my delight when a few days ago I received from a lady resident in Jersey £20, the sum necessary to support two little boys at Teighmore for a whole year! Would it not be a delightful method of manifesting the practical benevolence of the people in Jersey if every one of my 70 boys were provided for in a similar way by others?"[15]

But for the Roberts brothers the quaint island scenery and financial overhead for their new home is probably the least of their concerns. The island is 160 kilometres from London — a world as distant as the moon to two little boys. And despite Dr. Barnardo's assurances to the islanders, William is somewhat of a frail — though healthy — child compared to Walter. He will get little nurturing at Teighmore Home; this is no holiday camp. The regime is distinctly military in model. One boy is assigned bugler duty, up at dawn to play *Reveille* and then outside again at twilight to blow the *Last Post*. As at Stepney, discipline here is strict. If a boy wets his bed he is made to wear his dirty sheet over his head and clean all the chamber pots. Even toilet use is regimented to certain times of the day, and one toilet serves between 70–100 boys. After using the toilet the boys are assembled and their trousers inspected. Anyone found with dirty underwear is thrashed with a cane.[16]

Ed Cousins recalls his arrival at Teighmore and the shock of the new regime he would endure for three years. "I felt very lonely when I went on the boat from Southampton. At the home in Jersey, the Superintendent, Captain G., assembled all the new boys in a small yard. Then he made a little speech, telling us what we had to expect. He dismissed us into the play yard, but we weren't moving fast enough, so he produced a cane and proceeded to whack us on the knees to drive us faster. The next three years were torment. Only one boy ever ran away. When he was brought back we were all assembled in the yard in a circle and the boy was placed naked in the centre and his arms outstretched. The Captain whacked him as hard as he could on the buttocks. Afterwards he had to jump into a cold bath with iodine in it because he was bleeding so badly. I never thought of running away after that but I often thought of suicide. . . ."[17]

The food at Teighmore Home leaves much to be desired. Portions are small and the quality poor. When important visitors to the home arrive, the staff spares no effort, putting on a lavish show of fine food. The Roberts brothers and many of the other boys on these occasions can often be found outside after meals, vomiting. Their stomachs are simply not used to such large portions of rich food.[18]

Lavinia Roberts is getting a second chance at happiness — she marries John Browning at Farnham, Surrey in 1895. Within a year they will begin a new family, when Clara May Browning is born, followed by Dorothy Hilda "Queenie" Browning in 1897. Sadly, Browning seems to have taken no interest in adopting Lavinia's other children.[19] It's not hard to imagine the Sophie's Choice she must have faced. Continue as a single mother in Victorian England, her work prospects limited to menial wages, or marry a man who can help support her despite his lack of interest in her other children. Her ethical conundrum doesn't stop there. Does she write Walter and William on Jersey to tell them the news and risk their heartbreak? Or let the news pass unreported, and spare them the angst? Lavinia may feel she has little choice. She has made an effort to keep in contact with the boys. But Barnardo's is seldom known for returning children to their parents, even in the best of cases. "They are mine now," he is known to say.

March 26, 1900. It has been six grueling years for Walter and William at Teighmore Home. Barnardo's has decided they are old enough to move on. Now 11 and 13, they are transported back to the Stepney Home in anticipation of their emigration to Canada with a large group scheduled to leave March 31[st.] They will cross the Atlantic on the *SS Cambroman*, a converted cargo ship not known for her creature comforts. The ship is described by Barnardo's Canadian manager Alfred Owen as "a staunch and smart if not a very steady vessel." Serving the Liverpool to Portland, Maine route, her capacity is 1,275 passengers, all in third class or "steerage" accommodations.[20] For this journey, the *Cambroman* is slated to make port at Halifax before proceeding to Portland. There are 265 in this contingent from Barnardo's, including the Roberts brothers and two other boys from the Teighmore Home, and a family of six whose passage has been paid by two sons who had gone ahead of them to Canada. Forty of the older boys are destined for Barnardo's Farm Home in Russell, Manitoba. About the same number of the youngest girls and boys are destined for boarding out in foster homes in the Muskoka region of Ontario. The rest are bound for farms throughout the province.[21]

Owen writes eloquently if a little despairingly of the Atlantic crossing. "A pleasant passage we had not, being favoured with but one solitary fine day during the voyage from Liverpool to Portland. Sometimes it rained, sometimes it snowed; always it blew. The skies glowered over our heads, the seas rose in their might against us from beneath. We were generally shut down in darkness, gloom, stench and sickness; water pouring down upon us always and everywhere, in spite of hatches and tarpaulins that availed only to exclude the escape of foul air and the entrance of fresh." The scene below decks during the rough crossing resembles a casualty station on a battlefield, with boys of all ages retching from seasickness. It's a scene Walter will recall with a shudder to the end of his days. Ever eager to put a positive spin on the story for public consumption, Owen concludes: "Despite it all, however, we came up smiling in the end and landed as healthy and jolly a party as anyone could wish to see."[22]

April 9, 1900. After one of the worst ocean crossings in recent memory, the *Cambroman* docks at Halifax. The 70 boys bound for

Manitoba disembark to be processed through the immigration sheds. The *Cambroman* proceeds to Portland, Maine where the rest of the Barnardo's contingent will disembark for Toronto. The Roberts brothers are destined for the Winnipeg distribution home at 115 Pacific Avenue along with about 30 other boys.[23] The Manitoba contingent is met by Edmund Struthers, manager of the Farm Home.[24] Struthers takes charge of the boys on the long train ride to the prairies. Even with stern discipline, boys will be boys, and their excitement at seeing this new country on the other side of the "golden bridge" can't be suppressed. After the confinement and nausea of the Atlantic journey, pent-up energy is finally released. Boys' faces are pressed against the windows of the day carriage specially provided by the Canadian Pacific Railway. "Watch out for cowboys and Indians!" "And buffalo!" they shout. "That's bison, boys," corrects Struthers with a chuckle.[25]

The boys arrive at the Winnipeg home on April 13. After staying only one night, the Roberts brothers are sent by themselves on the train to their first placements near Yorkton, Assinaboia territory (Saskatchewan) — a 450-kilometre journey.[26] Eleven-year-old Walter, though two years younger than William, is taller and has a more robust physique. Barnardo's has placed him with Charles Henry Lakey of Mulock. When they arrive at the train station, no one is there to greet them. The chill of winter lingers in the spring air, remnants of snow clinging to the vast stretches of prairie fields. The boys huddle for warmth, thankful at least they have been kept together — for now. But they know they are going to different farms. It's the first time in their lives they are facing the prospect of being apart. The frostbitten prairie with its seemingly endless sky, so beautiful in the light of morning, seems utterly empty.

Growing colder and tired of waiting, Walter and William begin walking into the town. They are looking into a store window display when a wagon rolls up beside them. A gruff-looking farmer jumps down. The boys watch him warily. Will he offer help or harm? "Which one of you is Walter Roberts?" he grunts. Walter raises his hand, as he has been taught to do at Barnardo's when his name is called. Without warning, the man seizes Walter by the armpits and lifts him into the wagon. He leaps back up and clucks his tongue, urging the horses onward. William wants to shout out, "Wait! We haven't said goodbye!" but the sudden departure has left him speechless, choking back tears. Walter turns to wave at his brother standing alone in the street, but Lakey grabs his arm, wrenching him to face front. William is bound for Theodore, a small outpost just 42 kilometres further northwest, where he will work for Herbert J. Gregory. He re-boards the train alone, staring sadly out the window that until today had been a panorama of sheer wonder.[27]

When they arrive at the Lakey farm, Walter is told to unhitch the wagon, remove the reins and tend to the horses. The boy has had no such training. Gamely he sets about trying to figure out how to disconnect the confusing harness. Lakey stomps back out of his house 20 minutes later. When he sees that Walter is still groping hopelessly with the reins, he explodes. Lakey grabs the boy, pulls out his belt and begins thrashing him. Walter is strong for his age but still the tears come. After being told to chop kindling for the woodstove, he is told he will share a bed with the dog by the stove. The dog looks at him forlornly, knowing all too well the impact of Lakey's hand and boot.[28]

The boys had been instructed by Mr. Struthers that they should write the Winnipeg home as soon as possible after their arrival on the farm to report on their situation. Walter is torn by his loyalty to Barnardo's and his fast-growing dread of Lakey. If he tells the truth, will he make Barnardo's look bad? Will Lakey punish him even more? If he pretends all is well, will Lakey go easy on him? In the end he opts for the latter option. Lakey has made it quite clear he will punish the boy severely if a negative report is made. Walter writes a cheerful postcard to the Winnipeg home saying that he has a "nice home" and is glad he came. But even this won't stem the tide of Lakey's violent rages.[29]

Barnardo's gets its first hint that all is not well with Lakey when he sends his indenture contract for Walter with a note stating that "at present it is impossible for the boy to attend school." Although contrary to the general articles of the contract, David White, the manager at the Winnipeg home, decides to let this go. After all, Lakey has agreed to most of the terms — board, lodging, clothing, and necessities plus $125 for the period of Walter's service. Lakey writes that the boy is "good tempered and willing" and he likes him very much.[30]

January 1901. Lakey writes the Winnipeg home asking for Walter's removal, claiming that the boy won't work during his absence. White answers the letter while noting in his report for Barnardo's that Lakey's complaints are minor. "We are writing to boy's brother asking him to get a situation for boy and we hope to arrange his transfer in a few days," White assures him. But as yet no details of Lakey's violence toward the boy emerge. Meanwhile, William has been lucky — his placement at the Gregory farm is working out well. He writes in February that he is settling in happily. "Health good," notes White on the record. "Reports very cheerfully of himself. Has learned to ride well and seems to be happy and thriving."[31]

March 1901. White notes in his records that he has received a telegram from Struthers, asking who signed the certificate and application form sent in by Lakey. He demands full details of the case. Struthers' concern is prompted by a letter from EH Watson of Yorkton, who has raised the alarm about Lakey. Watson writes to complain of Barnardo's placing Walter with the man, who "half-starves" and abuses the boy terribly. "He is overworked and punished out of reason. He is used as well as some men use dumb animals and unless he is taken away soon there will be nothing to take away but bones." Watson recommends Walter be removed immediately from the farm, calling Lakey a "treacherous rascal." So treacherous, in fact, that Watson requests that Barnardo's not disclose who has written the letter.[32]

One Sunday in December 1900 Walter had been forced by Lakey to go to Sunday school during a blizzard. Walter had walked several miles to the church to discover that it was closed and had to return home again in the blizzard. His big toe on his right foot was badly frozen, his other toes and fingers frozen less severely. When he got home he questioned Lakey about sending him out in such a severe storm. Lakey said he knew the church would be closed, but wanted to be rid of Walter for a few hours. Besides, he said, the exercise was good for the boy. Meanwhile the skin on Walter's big toe sloughed off, leaving the bone exposed. Lakey had done nothing to ease his distress nor did he take Walter to a doctor. Instead Walter was forced to continue his usual chores. The excruciating pain of the toe, combined with malnutrition, left him dangerously weakened, barely able to work. This only made Lakey's rages and attacks worsen.[33]

Adding insult to injury, Walter is not given adequate clothing to protect him from the Manitoba winter. He is forced to wrap himself in "gunnysacks" from grain shipped to the farm. One day in late March, two men delivering grain are gently teasing Walter. They whirl him around to see which brand of grain he's wearing *this* day, causing him to faint. Walter has a high fever from an infection caused by Lakey ramming a dirty pitchfork into his thigh during one of his rages. Realizing instantly that the boy is in serious danger, they report the situation to the police. One of these men is likely the EH Watson who also wrote Barnardo's Winnipeg home to report the abuse. Constable C. Junger of the North West Mounted Police is dispatched to investigate. Junger takes him into protective custody, getting him immediately to hospital, where the infected toe is amputated by Dr. TA Patrick. The constable writes the Winnipeg home March 26th, informing White that he has boarded Walter at a local hotel.[34]

Constable Junger charges Lakey with assault and recruits the help of John McDonald of nearby Theodore, who promises to look after Walter until after the trial. The constable writes Winnipeg to ask if the boy's medical treatment expense will be covered, "as if not, subscription will have to be taken up." White writes Constable Junger, instructing him to send Walter to the Winnipeg home, enclosing a train ticket. Incredibly, a letter is also sent to Struthers at the Farm Home in Russell, asking him if the character of Lakey is "at all favourable." The grisly facts of Walter's abuse have yet to penetrate the crust of disbelief at Barnardo's.[35]

Barnardo's only employs five visiting agents, "through whose spectacles we have to look," to watch their children throughout all of Ontario, Manitoba, and Assinaboia (Saskatchewan). After the initial visit by Mitchell upon Walter's placement at the Lakey farm in April 1900, no further visits had been made prior to the discovery of his ill treatment a year later. "We have had to 'hustle' to keep ourselves up to the mark in the Visiting Department," notes an editorial in the *Ups & Downs* newsletter, "and our energies have been so far taxed that if the coming year brings us anything like as large an increase in our number as last, we foresee the necessity for a permanent addition to our Visiting Staff."[36]

Constable Junger writes March 31st that he is sending Walter to the home as instructed, and encloses his report. He notes that the two men who had reported Walter's condition to him had wanted to send the boy back to Winnipeg earlier but that Junger had intervened to send him to a doctor first:

He has since stayed with me at the hotel where I am living and has been properly treated during that time. The case against Lakey came up last Friday and the evidence for the prosecution is so very strong, and enough to warrant the magistrate's committing the prisoner CH Lakey for trial at the next sitting of the Supreme Court in Yorkton on May the 6th. The information was amended and Lakey is charged under Section 262 of the Criminal Code and I am almost sure he will be convicted when he comes up before the judge. As the boy is the main witness he will have to come up to Yorkton and give evidence at the trial in May, but he will be notified and duly subpoenaed. Mr. Lakey is known as a bad character and a great deal of satisfaction is felt here that he has been committed to stand his trial. There are several men in the community who will take the boy and whom I know will treat him well. . .[37]

While Walter is recovering from frostbite and his leg wound in Winnipeg General Hospital he is visited by none other than Barnardo's Canadian Superintendent Alfred Owen, who travels from Toronto to see him. "The little boy Walter H. Roberts has undoubtedly had a hard place," he notes in his report, "and although the man we sent him to had been well-recommended to us and we had every reason to believe that the place was a good one, the boy was treated with a good deal of harshness, and was chastised for trifling neglect in his work in a manner that was altogether unjustifiable." But then he concludes that Walter, "has almost recovered and *does not look by any means the worse for his experiences*" (emphasis added). Whether due to the institutional blind spot that seems characteristic of Barnardo's in such cases or an attempt to rally the spirit of the British "stiff upper lip" it is impossible to say. Certainly, Owen's comments beg the question of whether Lakey's references were ever checked.[38]

By April, William has heard of Walter's predicament and writes to ask for his address in Winnipeg. Struthers receives a letter from RW Parsons of Yorkton, informing him that the Crown Prosecutor has taken charge of the case. The prosecutor subpoenas medical records from Dr. Halpenny, who had treated Walter at Winnipeg General. His report is grisly reading. "Great toe of right foot had been frozen last December, had not received any treatment and the end had partly sloughed off, leaving the bone exposed." Walter is discharged from Winnipeg General and returned to the home on Pacific Avenue.[39]

Lakey attempts to ward off the inevitable, writing a pleading letter to the Winnipeg home, claiming he had "done everything in his power for the lad and was about to send him to the Home for treatment" when Constable Junger arrived to arrest him. He claims the infected wound on Walter's thigh was where he "accidentally 'pricked' him with a fork." While admitting to having punished the boy for his "filthiness and laziness," he claims to have kept Walter "well fed and clothed," despite the gunnysacks. He begs the home not to prosecute.[40]

May 5, 1901. Walter leaves Winnipeg for Yorkton where he is to present evidence at court. Struthers joins him at Millwood, Manitoba to accompany him during the trial. It emerges that Walter had written his older brother Frederick in Wales on April 1st, describing Lakey as "harsh and inconsiderate." He had made the boy work all through Christmas day. "If I don't get my work done he flogs me till I can't stand and when I am hurt a lot, I cry out, 'You will kill me,' and he says, 'I want to kill you.'" Frederick had passed the letter on to Barnardo's, awaiting their response before contacting police. White had written Owen in Toronto but by then the deliverymen had already contacted the Yorkton NWMP. Owen had written Frederick a letter dated April 26, confirming that the boy's accusations about Lakey were true.

"I want to kill you." It's damning testimony, but in a court of law, *intent* to harm can't be prosecuted. Still, there's plenty of physical evidence to convict Lakey of assault with intent to cause bodily harm. The judge orders him to pay a fine of $55 or spend eight months in jail. Walter is granted witness fees and his travel expenses to Yorkton, amounting to $12. Struthers takes Walter to stay at the Farm Home until a new placement can be found. Once they arrive in Russell, Struthers "appropriates" the payment given Walter by the court. At least they don't make him pay for his lodgings at the hotel or his hospital bills.[41]

June 1901. In typical fashion Barnardo's wastes no time finding a new placement for Walter, this time with considerably more attention to the farmer's references. He is placed with Richard Tibbotts of Foxwarren, just 33 kilometres south of the Russell Farm Home but over 200 kilometres from Theodore, where William is living with the Gregorys. It seems that Struthers is taking a personal interest in Walter, keeping him close to make regular visitation easier. On June 24, Tibbotts writes the Winnipeg home, enclosing his signed indenture agreement for a period of up to five years. Upon finishing his indenture Walter will receive $100. He notes that he "likes Roberts very well so far." Just six months later — in November — Struthers visits Walter on the Tibbotts farm. It's rare for most Barnardo children to receive visits more than once per year.[42]

"The regular and systematic visitation of all children placed out has been one of the strongest planks in the platform of Dr. Barnardo's immigration enterprise," the editor of *Ups & Downs* had written the year the Roberts brothers arrived in Canada. "From the earliest commencement of his Canadian work he has insisted that every child in a foster home or situation shall be personally visited *at least once in each year* without notice or intimation to the employer or foster parent, so that by personal inspection and observation we may be assured that the boy or girl is being kindly and properly treated, and that causes of complaint may be ascertained and investigated." The writer admits, however, that it's not "the only sure means of protecting children against ill-usage. . . ." To this end, the federal government had appointed George Bogue Smart as Inspector of British Immigrant Children and Receiving Homes in 1900. However, it seems he had his hands more than full, since his presence was yet to be felt in Manitoba and Saskatchewan. Barnardo's wrote approvingly of his appointment, noting it as an "eminently right and wise step on the part of the government." But Smart's minimal staff means he is mostly kept busy inspecting immigration sheds and receiving homes.[43]

Owen himself takes an ongoing interest in the Roberts brothers. In December he notes in a report on William that his health is good and conduct "satisfactory." He adds that William is "growing fast and overcoming his deafness. Has a comfortable happy home that he evidently appreciates." The deafness Owen refers to was incurred during the difficult crossing on the *Cambroman*, during which William had an ear infection leading to hearing loss.[44]

In March 1902 the *Ups & Downs* newsletter features a report by Struthers, in which he mentions that the farm is now connected by telephone to the distributing home in Winnipeg. "[T]he two offices are connected by wire — telephone to the Farm to the railway station at Russell, five miles; telegraph to the general telegraph office of the Canadian Pacific in Main Street, Winnipeg, 223 miles; and telephone to our Pacific Avenue office, so that in an interval of three minutes a reasonable message can be transmitted between Dr. Barnardo's town house and his interesting country seat in the extreme northwestern corner of the Province, and a reply returned thereto during a like space of time. It was only at the beginning of January this year that, through the indulgence of our General Superintendent Mr. Owen, who ordered the city connection, we were enabled to perform these wonders...." One wonders whether the Lakey scandal had prompted Owen to press for faster communications.[45]

December 31, 1902. A report is made by Owen noting that Walter, now 13, has "improved and developed remarkably well, is behaving himself very creditably and appreciates his present comfortable, happy, well-ordered home. [He] is developing into a useful little worker, is well fed, clothed and cared for and is happy and thriving in his home." At last! A safe and caring home. Owen is keeping close tabs on the boys. He reports of William that his health is good and he is "doing his best although not very bright. [He] is treated with every kindness and consideration and is evidently contented and happily settled." That "Willie's" placement with the Gregorys has been a good one is evident by a letter he has published in the April–May issue of *Ups & Downs*: "I'll never wish to go back to England, because there is plenty of work to do and [I] have good wages. We have lots of work to do this winter: there isn't hardly any time to write in the weekday nights." Still, the Gregorys give him time off on Christmas to visit his friend John Black on a neighbouring farm.[46]

The comment "not very bright" occurs in many reports of Home Children and is often a reflection of a farmer's bias toward a child with no experience in farming. For William it probably had more to do with his hearing impairment. Although letters published in *Ups & Downs* may or may not represent the true conditions a child is working under, in William's case it seems accurate. After the disastrous experience with Lakey, Owen is sending inspectors to check up on Walter about every six months, and is apparently satisfied that William too is in a safe home. His visits continue on the regular annual rotation. Barnardo's inspector RA McRae is assigned to Walter's case and sees him again in July 1903.[47]

"Willie" publishes another chatty letter in *Ups & Downs* in its April 1903 edition. He notes that the CPR has recently been adding to its spur lines in this part of Saskatchewan, "so that the farmer won't have to go and take their grain down to Yorkton, 25 miles away. It's killing horses." The winter months have been bitterly cold, with a minus 50 Fahrenheit cold snap over the Christmas holidays. Still, he isn't complaining. "Well, I like the country fine. I thank Dr. Barnardo very much for sending me out to this splendid country. It is a little bit too cold. I got my ears frozen this winter. We look after over 50 head of cattle; most of them I take to the bush; and I chop ice to get water for the cattle out of a big slough. There has been quite a number of wolves round here, and there's a man been round here catching them with his hounds." This alternated with a very wet spring in 1902 and a generally wet growing season. "The creeks were full of water, sometimes running over the banks, the sloughs were full right up till about haying time, and then we had some very dry weather. My employer put in oats, and wheat and barley. We never put very much hay up last fall because it was a job to get at it. Some people thought the grain was never going to ripen, because it was green when it was about time to cut it; but nearly everything was late in ripening. I helped in doing the stooking and loading and pitching it on the stacks. The threshers came round in November and threshed us out. I was one of the band cutters. We got over 1,000 bushels of grain." For Barnardo's, it's the ideal letter, a testament to their success in creating another little farmer.[48]

January 1904. William is progressing toward the end of his indenture, still working for Herbert Gregory. Owen reports that William "continues to satisfy [and] is with excellent people and happy in his home, improving and developing both physically and mentally, becoming useful and takes an interest in his work; [he] can handle a [horse] team in workmanlike style." William will be

18 in September but in a rare exception to Barnardo's rules will be paid his $100 in April. Gregory likes him so much he offers to hire him for another year after his contract expires, with a raise to $110 per year, plus board and lodging. Walter is still with the Tibbotts, in good health, and according to Owen, "is picking up his work in excellent style; a bright, intelligent lad; [he] has fairly comfortable home although his surroundings are far from luxurious, [and] gives every promise of turning out well in future." Compared to William, whose physique is slight, even frail at times, Walter has "grown considerably the past year."[49]

The business of negotiating the indenture contracts, by Barnardo's own admission, is a tricky one. "The task of appraising values in drawing up agreements is always one of the most perplexing and critical that falls to our lot," notes an article in the July 2, 1900 *Ups & Downs*. "We are called upon to fix a fair wage for the services of boys for a period in advance, generally of from three to five years, and while this would be a comparatively simple matter if boys would only grow and develop in some uniform ratio, it becomes a very much less easy operation when we have to consider that while some boys are backward and slow in growth, others shoot up in a year or two to almost a man's strength and capability." The writer could be describing the Roberts brothers — William, small and slight, and the more sturdy Walter. "To be sure, the agreement is not a hard-and-fast contract, but can be terminated on either side by a month's notice; but we never like to depart from the original bargain if we can avoid it."[50]

A long overdue reunion occurs at Christmas, when the brothers see each other for the first time since their arrival in Canada four years ago. Their long separation is ending at last.[51]

January 1905. William is now a young man on his own, known as Bill. He has changed employers and is working for RS Reed of Springside, Saskatchewan. Upon completion of his indenture contract in April — five months before his 18th birthday — he is granted Dr. Barnardo's medal for good conduct. He has saved his money and even managed a donation to Barnardo's Homes. A note in Owen's report calls him a "thoroughly well conducted lad, a credit to the Homes." William is just one of more than 200 lads who will receive a Barnardo's medal during 1905. The medals are designed "as a means of personally encouraging his boys in good conduct and faithful service...having earned a satisfactory character from their employers" during a long term of service. It's also a way of discouraging frequent changes of employer.[52]

McRae has been replaced as Barnardo's inspector by a Mr. Tarbox, who will continue to keep a close eye on Walter. His inspection reveals "a manly, intelligent lad and very useful to [his] employer. Not a first class home. Employer kind but far from well-off. Boy will be able to get a good place in the neighbourhood at fair wages at expiration of his agreement."[53]

Tarbox had reported in September 1904 that Tibbotts' financial circumstances are poor. Early in 1905 he writes Tibbotts, reminding him that the boy's indenture contract expires on April 1st, "when $100 becomes due . . . and after which time boy will be left to make his own arrangements." By March, Walter has been moved to another farm in Foxwarren, this time with William Pizzey. Throughout the year Barnardo's hounds Tibbotts for the payment of Walter's remittance. Tibbotts, obviously a responsible man, writes in March that although he can't pay the full $100 at present, he will pay half of it now and the balance on December 1st. A flurry of letters between the Winnipeg home and Tibbotts during April and May keeps up the pressure. Not all "Barnardo boys" will receive such diligent treatment — Walter's ordeal with Lakey has cast a long shadow over Barnardo's in Canada. Walter himself is more generous, only writing in June asking for $20 to buy a pocket watch and chain. Tibbotts manages to pay out the final $50 that month — six months ahead of schedule.[54]

In September, Walter is sent the Barnardo's Silver Medal from the Toronto office. Whether due to the pressures of farm work or to ambivalence, he waits until November to write a letter of thanks for the medal. Is it awarded to him for his good conduct? Or due to guilt on the part of Barnardo's staffers who didn't check Lakey's references, subjecting Walter to a near-death experience? As he is only 16 and therefore still a ward of Barnardo's, he must write the homes to ask for $12 to buy new winter clothing. He is told that he will receive his $100 for a year's service to Mr. Pizzey. Barnardo's sends him an invitation to join a party of boys visiting England but he declines. Walter is more interested in reuniting with his brother, who hopes to join him in Foxwarren if he can find work.[55] In November Walter writes Owen to inform him that he intends to spend Christmas with Bill again this year.[56]

January 29, 1906. William's health has taken a turn for the worse. The alarm is raised by a Mr. Davis, secretary of the Winnipeg home, who notes that a letter from Lavinia had been passed through Owen to him from Barnardo's in London. William had written his mother complaining of indigestion and catarrh — an unpleasant build-up of mucus often caused by flu. The damage to his ears on the Atlantic crossing has left him particularly susceptible. "The mother seems to think that the lad's work does not suit him," notes the secretary. The Roberts brothers' files are red-flagged so an immediate follow-up report is ordered. However, now that "Bill" is 18, he's basically on his own, although Barnardo's typically tracks their wards until age 21.[57]

William has been working for the Reed family in Springside, Saskatchewan, near Yorkton. Reference is made to Tarbox's last visitation report in September 1904, who reported him to be "in good health, well clothed and well trained. Says that he has a good home with kindly people. No mention was made in this report, or in any previous one, regarding his having suffered from catarrh in the head. . . ." A visit by McRae in July 1904, however, had remarked upon William's "small stature." "Unfortunately last year Mr. Tarbox was not able to see the boy himself when on his visiting rounds, but elicited information from a Mr. Ball in the Yorkton District that the lad was still with Mr. Reed, in the enjoyment of good health and doing well."[58]

William writes the Winnipeg office to inform them that he has changed his employer and is now working for the Reese family in

Theodore for $160 per year. The secretary notes that, "when Mr. Tarbox is next at Theodore, which I expect will be about the 16th February, I shall get him to endeavour to see the boy personally and to report specially in this case." Meanwhile William sends $20 to be forwarded to his mother. As promised, Tarbox visits the Reese farm in February but apparently finds William in good health. A collective sigh of relief passes through the chain of command at Barnardo's Canada. They do not need another scandal. To the contrary, William has so impressed the Gregorys that they have written asking for "another boy like Roberts, who was such a kind and truthful little fellow." Proving that the feelings are mutual, he continues to visit the family long after his contract has expired.[59]

September 12, 1906. Independence at last! William writes the Winnipeg home that he and Walter have made an agreement to buy a farm from Reed for $1,000. The Roberts brothers will work the quarter section while continuing to earn money at other farms to pay for the land.[60] The brothers will soon be able to put to the test the great promise of the "golden bridge" not just in Canada but in the "golden West." With nearly 20 years of bringing boys and girls to the farms of Ontario and western Quebec, Barnardo's had begun in 1900 pitching the need for help in Canada's "North-West," Manitoba and Saskatchewan. "[O]n the prairie lands of the North-West . . . our lads can aspire to rise beyond the position of labourers and have a grand opportunity of establishing themselves on farms of their own, where . . . they may hope in a few years to reach independence and prosperity. Everywhere men are to be met who came to the country with little or no capital, but today have fine farms, good buildings, teams of horses, bands of cattle and sheep that they can count by scores. . ."[61]

For boys like the Roberts brothers, coming from such a marginal existence in Bristol, it's a tantalizing dream. But the reality is much harsher. Most boys will do well to have saved up $150 from their years of service with Barnardo's. In the early 1900s, the minimum required for shelter, seed, stock, and implements on government grant land would be $500. By 1907 that amount is closer to $1,000. It's a recipe for bitter disappointment for all but the strongest and most determined.[62]

November 1909. By 1908 the Roberts brothers manage to till about 20 hectares of land for cultivating in their quarter section. Struthers continues to check on Walter, who turns 20 in February. He becomes known in the district as an excellent dairyman and good at repairing farm machinery. William had been visited by Tarbox in February 1908 and is noted again for having "the highest of characters." One report from this period records that although William is now working his own farm, already he has thoughts of selling. Farming is not for the small of stature or frail of health. It only takes a couple of bad harvest seasons to push marginal farmers like the Roberts brothers over the brink. For Barnardo boys whose only capital is earned from the sweat of their brows, the "golden bridge" can quickly become a bridge of straw.[63]

The Roberts brothers "graduate" from Barnardo's into the adult world at a time of great turmoil. Within five years they will see the outbreak of "the war to end all wars," and with it the global pandemic of the Spanish Flu. Walter marries Edith Yeatman — 10 years his junior — in 1917 and they will eventually have five children. Ironically, it's not the more frail William but Walter who is laid low by the flu outbreak in 1918–19. Willie helps Edith nurse Walter back to health with the assistance of quinine pills.[64] This flu will kill more people than the war, with between 20–40 million deaths worldwide — the worst pandemic in history. A particularly virulent strain, the virus often kills people within hours of contracting it. Even farmers working in the fields of Alberta wear masks in hopes of avoiding the disease. Although most flu viruses tend to take down the elderly or very young, the Spanish Flu targets those in the prime of life, between ages 20–40. Walter is 29, and one of the lucky survivors.[65]

In October 1924 Walter moves his family to Trail, BC, just months after his youngest, Frederick William, is born. Once there he sets up a dairy farm in nearby Glenmerry, where the couple's fifth child, Phillip, is born. In its drive to become all things to all people — or just to corner the local markets — the Consolidated Mining and Smelting Company ("Cominco") in Trail sets up its own dairy in 1928. Walter soon finds he can't compete with the corporate giant. He is forced to close his dairy and go to work for Cominco in the lead refinery.[66] The Roberts family moves to the mountain community of Rossland, just nine kilometres from Trail. With no dairy to direct his energies to, Walter cultivates a garden — a habit hard to give up for many Barnardo boys raised on farms. Rossland had been established in the 1890s with the onset of the Kootenay mining boom. The LeRoi mining claim had set off a local gold rush when it was first discovered in 1890 by two prospectors traveling the Dewdney Trail.[67]

Walter and Edith separate in 1934. His younger sister Minnie had been living in India, where their brother Frederick is prospering as a jeweler. After the collapse of a brief, disastrous marriage, she had emigrated to Canada in 1926 to live in Toronto, where Lavinia had moved after the war with her daughters Ada and May. Walter — needing help caring for his children — travels by train to Toronto to ask Minnie if she will consider coming to live with them. He promises to pay her a small wage and she agrees to move to Rossland. While in Toronto Walter visits his mother. One can imagine the scene: the anxious searching through the crowd at the train platform, the unspoken thrill of recognition as he sees her for the first time in decades. Lavinia, eyes rimmed with tears, afraid what her son will think of her yet overjoyed to see him again at last. And Walter nervously fumbling his words as he embraces her awkwardly, unsure of his own feelings toward her after all this time.

William meanwhile is drawn to the US, where he visits his half-sister Queenie Browning in Los Angeles. She has married into wealth, and photos from the period show her dressed in furs and posing beside airplanes. The California sun is enticing and he picks up odd jobs to prolong his stay. A job as an electrician's helper takes him to Chicago, but the "windy city" can't hold him for long. His old employer, Mr. Reed, continues to show his concern for William, writing often. Eventually Willie makes his way back to Theodore, where he meets Esther Knutson Nurembacher, a widow with one son. They marry but the couple will have no children of their own. William continues farming and is well liked by the community. He is known as a kind but quiet man.[68]

Fortunately for Walter he is employed at Cominco during the tenure of its president Selwyn G. Blaylock. While most company presidents are union busting to keep wages down, Blaylock shares a sense of solidarity with his employees. He had begun work in the mining industry as a metallurgist and through sheer brilliance at his craft had managed to rise through the ranks. In his own words, when it came to dealing with labour negotiations, he "preferred the carrot to the stick," and built the success of Cominco on "honest work and honest dealing." He refused to fire a man as long as he was willing to do a good day's work. When he has his Tudor-style mansion built on the shores of Kootenay Lake near Nelson in 1935, he advises the men, "It's hard times, there isn't much work, so just take your time and do a good job." To undercut the formation of a union at the Trail smelter, he offers steady employment, good wages, and decent benefits. Often he meets with workers' representatives personally. During the difficult Depression years, Blaylock refuses to lay anyone off but must reduce everyone's hours. Walter will struggle to feed five children and pay a small wage to his sister Minnie for her work as a house mother.[69]

But eventually Walter's work at the Cominco smelter in Trail takes its toll on his health. Safety standards during this early period in the company's history are woefully inadequate, and many men employed at the smelter end up with lead poisoning. Walter is among them. On July 11, 1938 he succumbs, dying at just 49. The company is not eager to admit to the lead poisoning, so the death certificate lists the cause as "hemorrhaging ulcers." Some time afterward Edith Roberts is remarried to Rudolf Lidstrom and the couple settles in Ymir, BC, near Nelson. Minnie continues to live in the house in Rossland, caring for Fred, now 14, and Phil, 11. They visit Edith a few times a year but Rudolf has no car so visits are sporadic. A bitter custody battle ensues and eventually Edith is granted custody of her sons. By this time their eldest child Violet is a young married woman, while Lavinia, 19, and Lorne, 16, are no longer living at home. For Walter it's been a short, sharp life wracked repeatedly by severe shocks to the system — the neglect and abuse of Lakey as a child, the Spanish Flu of his early married life and the lead poisoning that killed him at an early age.[70]

The Roberts brothers' long road together has come to an end. William survives another 12 years, but then falls ill in September 1950. He is sent to Regina for medical treatment but dies about a week before his 64th birthday. Esther writes Minnie from Theodore enclosing photos of his funeral.[71]

THROUGHOUT THEIR DIFFICULT LIVES, William and Walter maintained a close bond. It was evident from the moment the Barnardo's photographer captured them together upon admission to the homes. Although siblings were often allowed to live in the same Barnardo's Home, once they were sent to Canada, all bets were off. Brothers or sisters could find themselves suddenly wrenched apart and separated by hundreds of kilometres. At a time of limited mobility for most families and a still-developing road system in many provinces, such a separation may as well have been to another planet. Not all siblings were able to reconnect as children or even as adults. As Joseph Betts, who arrived at Marchmont Home in Belleville, Ontario in 1927 explains, "when I came over here I left three sisters behind in England. I have never heard from them and cannot seem to get track of them,"[72] a common experience for Home Children. For many this vast country had a way of swallowing them up. The experience of being shifted from farm to farm often led to an equally unsettled adulthood — moving from place to place, province to province, in search of work. In this respect the Roberts brothers were lucky — placed on farms sometimes as close as 30 kilometres, they were able to reconnect as the end of their indentures grew closer.

But with the onset of the Great Depression funds for travel would have become scarce, once again creating a separation between the brothers. "Walter and Bill were close when they were young but, after they married and had families and additional expenses and responsibilities we don't think that they were able to see each other very often," says Ruth Roberts, wife of Walter's fourth child Fred. "Travelling was expensive and travelling to visit was a luxury few people could afford then. It was just not usually done. Walter was a good letter-writer so they could have remained connected through letters. In Trail at that time mail was delivered twice a day and sorted locally so it was possible to send a letter to another Trail person in the morning's mail and receive a reply in the afternoon's mail."[73]

Ruth Roberts speculates whether the serious nature Walter displayed in life was a result of having the spontaneity drummed out of him in his years at Barnardo's.

> I have been thinking about the two photos we have of Walter and Bill taken at Barnardo's. In the first 1893 photo, Bill at age 7 can be identified as the same child as in the 1900, age 13 photo — same personality [and] characteristics, just older. Walter on the other hand has greatly changed; in the photo aged 4 he is a happy, friendly, eager-looking child who likes to have fun while I find it difficult to find any of these characteristics in 11 years and 1 month old Walter as here he looks much, much older than 11; he looks reserved, staid and as if having fun is far from his mind. He looks like a young adult. What did Barnardo's do to that child to create such a change? They must have chastised this boy often to create such a change. Bill, most likely, was not a child who got into mischief or misbehaved so he would not have been chastised as Walter probably was. He would not have had his spirit broken. Then Lakey added to Walter's change and undoubtedly broke his spirit further.[74]

Still, Walter and Bill carved out lives for themselves. Listen to Ruth about Walter's love of music and his engineering skill: "He built a dumb-waiter in the kitchen of the house in Rossland so that the perishable food — meat, milk, butter, cheese, etc. could be moved easily between the warm/hot kitchen and the cooler basement. He was quite ingenious — like his son, Fred. He enjoyed playing his organ and singing hymns. It was said he could get a tune out of any musical instrument. Minnie would join him when she lived with them. Edith probably sang the hymns, also, as she, too, was very musical."[75]

Fred recalls his father being "rather strict at times," in keeping with the general approach to child raising in the 1930s. Yet it was clear that Walter's children meant everything to him. When Edith and Walter separated he was adamant that the children should stay with him. "He talked to them, made a big bobsled and wooden toys which he then painted," writes Ruth. "He took them huckleberry picking every summer and, after the boys were older — Fred was given a BB gun for his 12th birthday — took them out to shoot gophers. Fred said they actually shot very few gophers as they usually ducked back into their holes but it was pleasant to be out with their father." The three boys — Fred, Phil and Lorne — would meet their father in downtown Rossland as he arrived on the bus from the smelter so they could walk home with him. Often feeling too unwell to eat his lunch, he would share the remnants with his boys.[76]

Dr. Barnardo's legacy of Christian devotion lived on in many of his protégés. And like Barnardo, for some this meant an unorthodox approach to Christianity.

Walter was quite religious and spent two evenings per week attending religious meetings which were held in the members' homes. These church members rotated hosting these meetings and also having the itinerant preacher, who arrived about four times per year, stay with them for anywhere from one to several meetings. At other meetings a layperson would conduct the meetings. Walter's children had to attend these meetings but Edith never did, as she was not religious, although her parents belonged to "The Truth" as this religion was known, and it was at meetings at her parents' house where she met Walter. So, that was one big difference between them there. Walter spent quite a bit of time reading his Bible; that probably gave him comfort while living with Charles Lakey. . . .[77]

You can imagine the comfort a Bible would be to a kid who feels he is utterly alone in the world. He will seize naturally upon the transcendent passages, "The Lord is my shepherd, I shall not want. He leadeth me to lie down in green pastures. . . ." He will also naturally *not* read the passages in Leviticus about slaughtering whole villages in the name of the Lord. Nearly every boy or girl sent to this country by these agencies came with a Bible. Ironically, the very thing that brings them comfort also reinforces the hierarchy that keeps them in their place. Picture a lonely Walter or Willie in a shabby, almost lightless room, miles from anywhere, in the freezing Canadian winter, thumbing the pages by candlelight.

Put yourself in these boys' place: dragging furrows into a Prairie horizon behind a team of horses, wondering when you'll see anyone else besides your boss on the farm. If he has children, they will go to school, but you likely won't. When there's time you'll get to go to Sunday school. Socializing with the neighbouring kids is frowned on. So you won't be getting many dance invitations. And when you're 8 or 12 or 16 years old, an indenture contract lasting until legal age is a lifetime. If there's a more complete definition of loneliness I'm at a loss to describe it. No wonder that treasure chest — their steamer trunks — stayed with many of them their entire lives. It contained not only all their worldly goods but treasures of priceless value: a copy of the Bible inscribed by Dr. Barnardo and *Pilgrim's Progress* — the keys to another world.[78] Many boys and girls sent by Barnardo's also got a copy of *The Traveller's Guide — From Death to Life*, a compendium of spiritual guidance.

And then, one blustery afternoon when your spirit is as grey and limp as the day, a lonely figure appears on the horizon — the visiting agent coming to see you.

"I went through more than I ever want to go through again," recalled a Barnardo boy who was sent to Rapid City, Manitoba at age 13 in 1901 — about the same time as Walter Roberts. "I know myself that I often looked forward to the time for the man from the Homes to come, Mr. White, but when he did come I used to be too scared to say anything for fear that I got more after Mr. White was gone, although I must say Mr. White done all he could. . . . I would not want them to get any things on the Homes as the Homes had been good to me for that. I have often said I would like to have my time over again in the Homes in England but not here." [79]

And besides monsters like Lakey there were decent caring folks like the Gregorys and the Reeds, who gave Willie Roberts a home. For years after he completed his indenture with the Gregorys he would come back to visit them. He seems to have kept in touch with the Reeds, too. Sadly, William Roberts hasn't left us a cache of letters from this period of his life. If he did it would be the prairie, male equivalent of Anne of Green Gables. No wonder that story resonates with Canadians. But others who had positive experiences did write about it. Joseph Betts wrote of coming to Canada to be with a couple who really did treat him like family. "I was with them from the time I was 17 years old and called them Mom and Dad and their two daughters were the same as sisters to me. He worked just the same as I did, he would not give me a job he would not do himself. . . . I owe them an awful lot and I miss them very much now that they are gone. I try to make it up by looking after their graves and putting flowers and wreaths out for them. They were wonderful people and I shall never forget them and what they did for me." [80]

Barnardo's admission photographs of William (left) and Walter Roberts. Thousands of children were photographed by Barnardo's. Fred and Ruth Roberts collection.

Walter Roberts as a young man. Fred and Ruth Roberts collection.

Lavinia (Duddridge) Roberts: one of thousands of mothers facing the loss of their children to child emigration. Fred and Ruth Roberts collection.

CHAPTER 4

From Pillar to Post —
The Story of Gladys Martin

1. In the Shadow of World War

APRIL 24, 1915. Britain is huddled beneath steel-grey war clouds, menaced by the German zeppelin attacks on London in January. In February, Germany had set up its blockade, attempting to isolate the British Isles and cut off the flow of supplies into the country. The British government had responded in March with its own blockade, but things are not going well on the battlegrounds of Europe. Germany's military might is slowly but surely forcing the Russians out of Poland. On April 22, a dark shadow had fallen over humanity: the use of poison gas on the battlefield as the second battle of Ypres erupted, killing 6,000 troops within 10 minutes of their exposure to the chlorine gas. At such times in history, families everywhere question the wisdom of bringing children into this world.[1]

For seven-year-old Gladys Irene Martin and her four-year-old sister Louisa, the war probably seems distant and incomprehensible.[2] Yet their own lives have been eclipsed by a shadow every bit as shattering to their world in the poor quarters of Bristol. Their father Lavington Frederick Martin, 56, has been failing in health for some time. His marriage to Elizabeth Martin has collapsed as she succumbs to the dissolution of alcohol. Unable to control her addiction, her life spirals out of control, leaving her sick husband to cope with Gladys, her siblings Percival, Louisa, and Enid, just two years old. Lavington Martin's options are slim. As a railway porter his wages — when he can work — are insufficient to support himself and four children. He decides to approach the Bristol Union, the local chapter for parish relief, for help.

2. Bristol: A Tradition of Philanthropy

Although seriously disadvantaged, the Martin family lives in a city with a strong history of philanthropy, both public and private. In response to the recurrent cholera epidemics that had so devastated working-class Bristol during the early part of the 19th century, Prussian-born Christian zealot George Müller had established day schools for the poor in 1834. Established under the aegis of the Scriptural Knowledge Institution (SKI) in partnership with Scottish evangelist Henry Craik, the objectives were less purely humanitarian than they were evangelical. The SKI's mission statement as reported in its first annual report was to "put the children of poor persons to such Day-schools, in order that they may be truly instructed in the ways of God, besides learning those things which are necessary for this life."[3]

Within a year of establishing SKI, Müller founded the first of his Orphan Homes, using his family home on Wilson Street in the St. Paul's area of Bristol to house 30 girls. This soon expanded to three more houses on the same street housing up to 130 children. By the 1840s he had acquired land on Ashley Down, just outside the city, and in 1849 Müller opened an orphanage with room for 300. He was assisted in his relief work by his wife Mary Groves Müller. The couple had already lost three children to death — two of them stillborn. A son, Elijah, born in March 1834, lived only 15 months. A daughter, Lydia, was born in 1832 and survived to adulthood.[4] These losses likely gave the Müllers a unique compassion for poor families who had lost parents or children to poverty and disease. Combined with the Christian injunction to care for the poor, these personal losses likely provided powerful motivation. By 1870 there was a total of five houses at Ashley Down, housing more than 2,000 children. Müller's continental background meant that he also had a high regard for secular education so long as it was part of a curriculum steeped in Christian doctrine. The Müllers were accused at one point of "robbing factories, mills and mines of labour" by *over*-educating their Orphan Homes children. In 1885 the grade point average of his children based on six subjects was over 90 percent. Müller boasted that all his funds had come as a direct result of prayer and for this reason he avoided fundraising campaigns.[5]

About the time the Müllers are planning their expanded Orphans Homes at Ashley Down in 1846, social reformer Mary Carpenter establishes the St. James Ragged School.[6] Carpenter, the daughter of a Unitarian minister, becomes instrumental in lobbying for progressive changes to British educational legislation. She is a supporter of women's suffrage and campaigns for female access to higher education. When she establishes the Red Lodge Reformatory at Bristol, she takes the unusual step of making it an all-girls institution. The school is funded by the widow of the poet Lord Byron. Unusually for the Victorian era, Carpenter's guiding principle is that, "Love must be the ruling sentiment of all who attempt to influence and guide these children," a truly visionary approach for the times.[7]

Meanwhile in the public sphere the Bristol and Barton Regis Board of Guardians had their hands just as full. The unsanitary conditions typical of early to mid-19th century England meant that Bristol like other British cities was regularly swept by cholera epidemics — in 1832, 1848–49, and 1866. Disease typically hit the poor the hardest, fragmenting families and creating a steady supply of orphans needing care. The crisis was compounded by an exponential growth in population for this busy port city — from 68,000 in 1801 to 266,000 in 1881. As was the case with the rapid growth of London's population during the Industrial Revolution, working-class accommodations could not be built fast enough to meet demand. Added to that was the pressure from Irish immigrants arriving in Bristol and Liverpool seeking work. The result was overcrowded, chaotic neighbourhoods — ideal conditions for alcoholism, prostitution, crime, the fast spread of disease, and homelessness. By the time of the 1866–67 London cholera epidemic — likely caused by contaminated water supplies to the East End — Bristol's public waterworks, begun in 1846, had been extended to cover the entire city using piped mains. A network of sewer mains was begun in 1850, further improving sanitary conditions.[8]

Mary Carpenter — like her better-known counterpart Thomas Barnardo some 20 years later — realized early that if destitute children were to benefit from schooling they would also need to be properly fed. Unlike many of her contemporaries, who seemed focused on a triage approach to poverty, Carpenter was interested in prevention. She saw that the poor, due to their limited options, were all too easily tipped into a life of crime. Yet it was clear to her that sending minors to prison for stealing a loaf of bread was hardly the solution. "They must as far as possible be brought to feel themselves a part of society, regarded by it with no unkind feeling, but rather, having been outcasts, welcomed into it with Christian love."[9] Her "reformatories" would thus be designed to deter children from crime by providing them with education and practical skills. Carpenter's extensive writing on the topic highlighted the need for what she called "feeding industrial schools."[10]

Agnes Beddoe, who had worked with Carpenter in just such a school as well as in Carpenter's Home for Working Girls, founded the Bristol Emigration Society in 1882. In part this was a response to free passage to Australia being offered to families at this time. By the 1880s, overcrowding in orphanages and workhouses had become chronic, so emigration was seized upon as the logical solution. Beddoe was assisted by Mark Whitwell and Margaret Forster, who was appointed the Society's agent. According to historian Marjorie Kohli, the Society began emigrating children to

Canada from local orphanages, industrial schools, workhouses, and reformatories by 1886. "The Society had no Canadian home but placed children through the immigration agent at Saint John, New Brunswick," the province where many of its wards would later be settled. Annie Macpherson's Marchmont Home in Belleville, Ontario served as a distributing home for the Society and still other children in their care were sent to Montreal and Winnipeg.[11] Forster and Whitwell often accompanied the children on their arduous Atlantic crossing, though Forster apparently liked to travel first class. When the Society began using the ships of the Allan Line later in the century, Liverpool became the point of departure. But the Society suffered from poor organization and no attempt was made to follow up on children placed in Canadian situations. Some children were placed on ships without an escort and no attempt was made to establish its own distributing homes in Canada.[12]

By 1910 the Society had ceased its work. Meanwhile the Bristol and Barton Regis Board of Guardians had already been emigrating children, starting with the first boatloads of children sent under the supervision of Annie Macpherson and Maria Rye in 1869–70. When Local Government Board Inspector Andrew Doyle made his famous report on the placement of children in Canada in 1875, Bristol's Board of Guardians acted on his recommendation to stop sending wards of public institutions. The board would not resume child emigration until 1883, when it felt that sufficient regulations had been passed to ensure proper supervision. This included medical examinations prior to departure, proper recordkeeping, and the signing of indenture contracts with Canadian farmers. The Bristol and Barton Regis Board were also to be kept informed of the name and address of the farmer caring for the child.[13]

By the time little Gladys and her sister Louisa are taken into care by the Bristol Union in 1915, the redoubtable Dr. Barnardo had already passed on. But his legacy had survived intact, despite the privations of war. Through the magazine *Night and Day*, Barnardo's made regular appeals for funds, since "grim-visaged war has stolen the children's bread." Records for 1915 show the organization caring for 7,480 children in various homes and training schools throughout Britain. Nearly as many new applications for help — 6,228 — were received that year, many of them war orphans. By year's end, Barnardo's would receive a stunning 82,126 applications for admission to their care.[14]

3. The Girls' Village Home at Barkingside

July 4, 1916. Founder's Day at the Girls Village Home, Barkingside. The 25-hectare village grounds look like a dream compared to the cramped quarters Gladys and Louisa had known in Bristol. The 68 Tudor-style cottages are arranged with Victorian precision in a long rectangle surrounding a central green, by now lushly grown up with lawns, flowers, and gently swaying trees. Each cottage can house up to 20 girls. More like a private estate than a village, thousands of girls had passed through its gates since its inception in July 1876. Yet like a village, it has its own church, hospital, steam laundry, nursery, and school. Although babies are cared for in the village's Queen Victoria House and Babies' Wing, Dr. Barnardo's policy is to get them "boarded out" to suitable families as soon as possible.[15]

As with the story of Jim Jarvis, the "waif" who was said to have shown Dr. Barnardo the extent of juvenile homelessness in London, it was apparently a little girl named Martha who prompted the good doctor's desire to establish a girls' home. The 11-year-old had been fending for herself on the streets of London when she showed up on Barnardo's doorstep at Stepney Causeway during the winter of 1872. But until his marriage to Sara Louise "Syrie" Elmslie in June 1873, he had been unable to offer the same assistance to girls as he had to boys. Whether the marriage was based on love or strategic thinking we may never know. Syrie was the only daughter of the influential William Elmslie, Chairman of Lloyd's Bank. The wedding was held at the 6,000-seat Metropolitan Tabernacle, Newington Causeway. Upon their return from the honeymoon, Lord Shaftesbury presented Mrs. Barnardo with a silver tea service. But by far the most generous gift came from Sir John Sands, Chairman of the London Stock Exchange, who offered the Barnardos Mossford Lodge, a palatial house at Cranbrook Road, Barkingside, Ilford. At that time Barkingside was still in the country.[16]

Mossford Lodge was placed at their disposal, rent-free, for a 15-year term. Dr. Barnardo lost no time in renovating the lodge for use as a girls' home. By 1874 accommodation for 12 girls was ready, but within a year this number grew to 54. Syrie took charge of Mossford Lodge with the assistance of other good Christian ladies, but it quickly proved beyond her capabilities. And with the growing need, the lodge became overcrowded, too much like a workhouse barracks. Soon the solution presented itself to Dr. Barnardo: a "garden village" on property surrounding the lodge, with plenty of room for homely cottages and play areas.[17]

Barnardo's vision got off to a rocky start when he learned that a Roman Catholic sisterhood had plans to buy the very land he had his eyes on for the village. Writing another of his typically fervent and eloquently worded pleas in *The Christian*, he rallied the evangelical community to his cause with funds to purchase five hectares. His father-in-law William Elmslie came through with money for another five hectares. But now at least £10,000 would be needed to build the first 13 cottages. Money for the first cottage showed up serendipitously during a train ride to Oxford, when Dr. Barnardo met a supporter of his work who had recently lost a young daughter. By 1875, enough had been raised to build the first baker's dozen of cottages. His high society connections came through for him when Lord Aberdeen laid the foundation stone for the first cottage, and again on July 9, 1876 when the newly completed cottages were opened in a ceremony presided over by Lord Cairns, the Lord Chancellor. Cairns had been detained by parliamentary duties but managed to arrive just as Ira Sankey was singing the hymn *Rescue the Perishing*. *Sankey's Hymn Book* would later accompany every Barnardo's child to Canada. By 1887 another 19 cottages had been built. The Girls Village Home had become a reality.[18]

FOR GLADYS AND HER LITTLE SISTER LOUISA, their first year at Barkingside has been an odyssey. A year in a child's life can seem an eternity, especially when faced with major changes. Getting used to the regimented lifestyle at Barkingside has not been easy but is gradually becoming routine. Each of the cottages has a name and Gladys Martin is lodged in Billiter Cottage. The day starts early, with preschoolers rising at 6 a.m. and school-age girls at 6:30. Breakfast is at 7 a.m., followed by prayers. Lunch is at 12:45 p.m., high tea at 5:30, again followed by prayers. Gladys and Louisa, like other girls under age 10, are in bed by 6:30 p.m. The younger girls look with envy upon the older girls — up to age 14 they can stay up 'til 8 p.m. and once finished their school years 'til 9 p.m.! All but the youngest girls are expected to work in the laundry and kitchens. The list of rules is onerous — a probably futile attempt to control childish energies. "Talking is strictly forbidden in the bedrooms both morning and evening," states one regulation.[19]

In 1886 Dr. Barnardo had written a mission statement to guide the staff in charge of his homes. Among the aims listed was to "bring up the said child carefully, kindly and in all respects as one of *my family*." This had to be balanced against both fallible human nature and the sheer scale of operations like Barkingside. The matrons who supervise the girls can be fierce in one cottage and kind in another. But they demand respect and any lack of it is punished, often severely. No small task, directing the chaotic energies of over 1,000 girls in various stages of development. At the same time, once children are admitted to Barnardo's care, in his view they "belong" to him. His 1886 manifesto stated that his policy is "not to enter into any correspondence with any person who may claim relationship." Visits by relatives and friends are carefully screened and controlled.[20]

The matrons or "cottage mothers" must adhere to a strict regime, although they had from 2–5 p.m. off daily (except on weekends), "after which time they must be in their cottages, except on their evening off." Their Sunday duties include teaching Bible classes from 4–5 p.m., and they are to take their cottage girls for walks on Saturdays, weather permitting.[21] Gladys Martin discovers to her dismay that her cottage mother has a harsh concept of discipline. Like many young girls and boys, the sudden immersion into a new and strange way of life, with its many rules, causes great stress. Bedwetting becomes a common problem but Victorian thinking singles out the unfortunate result rather than the underlying cause. When Gladys wets her underpants, her cottage mother makes her wear them on her head in front of the other girls as they jeer and taunt. Cottage discipline extends to eating habits: the girls are required to eat everything on their plate. When Gladys refuses to eat lentil soup, she is served the same bowl of soup meal after meal until she eats it.[22]

For these disadvantaged girls the gates at Barkingside must have seemed a portal to another world. And all the more so on Founder's Day — honouring the good doctor himself on his birthday.[23] The program of festivities is an exciting break in the routine, and a chance to attract high-profile donors to the cause. Special trains are scheduled to bring visitors from London. The Barnardo's Boys' Brass Band plays throughout the day, songs both patriotic and spiritual wafting over the lawns. The Girls Village Home choir raises more than 300 voices in song for the delight of visitors, many of whom are aristocracy, prominent businessmen, and politicians. The younger girls like Gladys and Louisa are drilled in the Maypole dance, its colourful streamers a visual echo of the bright ribbons in their hair. Older girls proudly display the products of their training in needlework, sewing, and cooking exhibits. A procession of "children and young people trained and in training as useful citizens of the Empire," shows the entire range of ages from infancy to late teens. For Gladys and Louisa and the rest of the girls, it's a dazzling afternoon, a fun-filled reprieve from their daily regime.[24]

Another highlight in the Martin sisters' lives is a lady visitor from Ilford, Miss Alice Whiteman, who takes a special interest in Gladys. It may be from Whiteman that the girls learn they have a maternal aunt, Louisa Canopli, living in Canada. While Whiteman is allowed and even encouraged to visit the girls, no communication is allowed with their family. Like the mother and father they no longer know, their Aunt Louisa remains impossibly distant, unknown to them — more an idea than a blood tie. Though Dr. Barnardo had been dead for a decade by the time Gladys and Louisa arrived at Barkingside in 1915, they are, after all, "Barnardo's girls," part of his still-growing "family." As the war years drag heavily on, austerity hits even the Girls Village Home, and Founder's Day celebrations are postponed until war's end.

With the manic worldwide celebrations of Armistice Day on November 11, 1918, the world is launched into a new era. The 1920s are to become a time of great social progress. The decade will see the return to the political agenda of the women's suffrage movement, and with it their right to vote across the Western hemisphere. The war years have also revolutionized women's work. Women are now entering the professions and helping shape postwar policy, particularly as regards social work. In Canada, Ontario feminist Charlotte Whitton pushes for the abolition of child immigration, forcing the government to limit the age of unaccompanied minors to 14 and older. On the west coast, Laura Holland will revolutionize childcare in British Columbia as that province's Superintendent of Neglected Children.[25] Though she champions the foster care system first envisioned by Dr. Barnardo decades earlier, ironically this would mean the death knell for institutions such as his Girls Village Home.

For Barnardo's too there is a changing of the guard, if not exactly of its philosophy. Sometime during 1920 the Girls Village Home at Barkingside receives two new governors, Anne MacNaughton and Beatrice Picton-Turberville. They seem to be equally infused with a desire to innovate, at least within the bounds of a patriarchal system very much consistent with Dr. Barnardo's intent.

The lady governors introduce to the village home the Girl Guide movement along with more crafts classes, club activities, folk dancing, and outside competition with other local girls' clubs. The lady governors may be broad-minded in their attempt to involve the girls more fully in life beyond the Barnardo's bubble, but lenient they certainly aren't. The list of rules they draw up is as rigid and unbending as ever. Girls are required to be accompanied by a matron when leaving the village home. One rule even stated, "No girls may go outside The Village gates without hats on." Another one, unlikely to have had much success, is, "Girls should not ask silly questions why." It's a curious mixture of caring and curbing.[26]

For Gladys and Louisa, too, 1920 will mark a new era. Though they may have been unaware of it at the time of their admission, Barnardo's Canada Clause will change their fates forever. On February 23, 1920 Alice Whiteman writes the village governors: "I hear that my little friend, Gladys Irene Martin of Billiter Cottage, is going to Canada very shortly, and I should like to see her again before she goes." Unlike many parents of Barnardo's children, Miss Whiteman had been given the courtesy of a before-sailing notice. This too was Barnardo's policy in cases where parents were considered "disreputable." "To avoid confrontation and evade relatives' raiding attempts on travelling parties, Barnardo staff decided it 'best and quite simple just to take no notice' of letters enquiring about emigration plans," writes historian Joy Parr.[27]

Whiteman asks to visit Gladys Irene on the 25th, a request that is granted.[28] A contingent of children is being prepared for their journey on the *SS Sicilian*, scheduled to depart London for St. John on March 11.[29] Gladys and Louisa are on the list of passengers. Miss Whiteman writes the governor's office, "I wish to visit Gladys Irene Martin in Billiter Cottage on the 10th March as she is going to Canada this week and I should very much like to say goodbye to her."[30] Perhaps Miss Whiteman helps the girls pack their Barnardo trunks, making sure to include the required books: a Bible, a copy of John Bunyan's *Pilgrim's Progress*, and *Sankey's Hymn Book*. She folds their socks, underwear and other clothing neatly, chattering to them about their "great adventure."

Not all the girls are convinced. Prior to the war, Village Governor Godfrey had appealed to the executive committee in London, pointing out that many of the girls were unhappy about being emigrated to Canada. But by then emigration had become a cornerstone of Barnardo's policy. Although they noted that parental objections "should not be disregarded," the executive focused its efforts on convincing parents and children alike of the fantastic benefits awaiting Barnardo's wards across "the golden bridge."[31]

4. Crossing to a New World

March 11, 1920. Gladys and Louisa cling to each other, feeling lost in the crowd of children and adults waving from the decks of the *Sicilian*. Gladys is 12 now so she must be the stoic one, the older sister. Her coppery red hair and pale grey eyes mark her out as the rebel, not someone to be messed with. But even her resolve cracks from time to time with a tear skating down her cheek, a tear she is careful to brush away before Louisa, now 9, can see it.

It's the first postwar shipload of Barnardo's children, supervised on the journey by the new managers of the Toronto home, John and Rose Hobday and their assistant Ernest Nunn. The contingent from the Girls Village Home is to be joined by a group of boys from Boys' Garden City at Woodford, Goldings. "On Thursday 11th March we left our cottages at the Boys' Garden City and lined up at 8:30 a.m. waiting for the motor buses which were to take us to the Surrey commercial docks," writes a boy correspondent for Barnardo's newsletter *Ups & Downs*. "We boarded the buses and were given three very hearty cheers by our old Woodford friends."[32] The journey starts out well enough, with the usual fanfare and congratulatory speeches given the children by Dr. Barnardo's successor William Baker. "Then he taught us a short prayer, and after that the news came that we were to go on board the ship."[33] After posing on deck for newspaper photographers, a tug pulls the *Sicil-*

ian into the Thames. The ship sails early the next morning for Le Havre in France to pick up cargo. "Owing to so much cargo being on deck, we had to remain below, and played draughts, alma, snap and dominoes, and later on we had a fine gramophone." By Saturday the 13th they are on their way for St. John.[34]

The Atlantic during the spring months can be a daunting expanse to cross. The St. Lawrence Seaway during the early part of the year is still mostly ice-bound so the wintertime port of call for many child migrants is Portland, Maine or St. John, New Brunswick. Advances in steamship technology have made the ships far more comfortable but they are still at the mercy of the elements. The *Ups & Downs* correspondent writes of the boat "rocking dreadfully and waves broke right over the ship."[35] The chaos of seasickness below decks amongst 200 children and their handlers can barely be imagined. But an article in *Ups & Downs* describing a similar journey in March 1900 offers a lucid picture: "if any misanthrope is curious to contemplate the most abject despair of which the human soul is capable, and to witness the extremest [sic] depth of mortal misery, he should live and move amongst the party during, say, the first two days after leaving the Irish coast. The sick and wounded after a battle is the only similitude that will compare to those rows and heaps of hopeless, helpless, apparently lifeless sufferers, lost to every sense but that of a horrible and awful aching void within, that insists periodically on being still further voided."[36]

Fortunately the weather breaks and the children are kept to a busy schedule to keep their minds off their weak stomachs.

We had many forms of entertainment when we were feeling better . . . and we had several concerts, and there were some nice singers among the girls. A boy named Weston danced the sword dance, which was one of the best pieces of the concerts. Many of the girls and boys sang and recited. One of the stewards entertained us with some conjuring tricks. . . . Then on deck we had many interesting sports and games such as blindfold boxing and blindfold fencing. A good set of boxing gloves were very popular. We had three Sundays at sea, and on the second Sunday it was rather rough again, but we had a nice service conducted by Mr. Hobday. He then told us the Prince of Wales had sent us a wireless message, which gave us great pleasure. Some evenings Mr. Nunn gave us object lessons. . . . On the third Sunday three lady missionaries on the steamer came and told us about their work amongst the Indians. When we were well we had plenty to eat, and the stewards were very attentive and clever in carrying several cups of tea at a time balanced on top of each other. [37]

The children are amazed to see both whales and dolphins at sea, something they would likely only have read about in books before.

Most days on the voyage we found that the sea was as smooth as a sheet of glass and . . . instead of the great waves dashing against her as before, there was only a gentle lapping sound. Later on we had fog, and some nights the Captain had to stay on the bridge all the time. The hooter went off at regular intervals to warn other ships of our position so as to avoid a collision. We were now getting to the end of our journey, so we had kit inspection and discovered that at last we were in sight of land, which showed some parts covered with snow. At last we were paraded on deck to go ashore, and the Captain came to say goodbye to us.[38]

The correspondent skips the boring part of the story — being processed through Canadian Immigration at St. John. The girls have their group photo taken on the ramp leading to the immigration sheds. It will become an iconic image of child immigration: about 125 girls and their women chaperones standing on the dock, dressed all alike in their wool overcoats, long scarves and tams, the youngest about 10 and the oldest probably 17. Photographic technology too has advanced, so luckily the girls don't have to stand for long in the freezing Atlantic gale.

> We then got onto the train, where the YWCA and YMCA secretaries distributed games, apples, oranges and candies amongst us, and soon we started on our two days' and two nights' journey. Good arrangements had been made for our meals. On Wednesday morning we made ourselves extra smart, for our long journey was to come to an end at Toronto. At six o'clock in the morning the girls reached their destination at Peterborough, when Mr. Hobday gave them an address on the platform to say goodbye and good luck, and then the girls gave three cheers for Mr. and Mrs. Hobday, who had brought us all safely for so many thousands of miles. We boys gave the girls a cheer and went on without them. Toronto was reached at 10 o'clock and then we were driven to the Boys' Home there, and when we reached the Home we were told that shortly we should be learning to work like men for our own living.[39]

In other words, the fun and games are over. As Dr. Barnardo himself put it, "We are not so young and unsophisticated as to imagine that the farmers take our boys for love. . . . The primary object of the farmers in taking a boy is that his services be useful to him."[40]

After such a long, tiring journey, Gladys and Louisa Martin may find it difficult to have much enthusiasm for what lies ahead. It's early in the morning when their train pulls into Peterborough, where it huffs to a halt at the junction of the Cobourg-Peterborough line on George Street just below Conger's Hill, where Barnardo's Hazelbrae Home overlooks the town. In many respects Peterborough is a mirror image of many country towns in England, with substantial brick houses lining leafy streets and the Otonabee River meandering through town. The countryside is lush with gently rolling hills thick with maple trees. Near the Midland Railway station is the castle-like pinnacle of Strathormond, the red brick mansion built in 1892 for wealthy business-man and politician James Kendry. A more appropriate symbol of Victorian opulence could hardly be imagined. From the railway station the girls make their weary way the short walk up Conger's Hill to Hazelbrae, now known as the Margaret Cox Home.[41]

The Martin sisters can be glad they didn't have to go on to Toronto when Alfred Owen was still Barnardo's director in Canada. The Hobdays, it turns out, have been sent to replace Owen to hush up a scandal. Owen had become sexually involved with Barnardo girls, fathering two or more illegitimate children. Details began to emerge in 1912 when CH Black, secretary at the Toronto headquarters, learned that a Barnardo girl had been made pregnant by Owen. "I was slow to attach much weight to it as Mr. Owen had told me that misrepresentations as to his character had been made by certain Barnardo girls and that he had ignored them. . . ." Black's perseverance in investigating the matter resulted in fresh evidence he felt clearly implicated Owen. His efforts created a tense work environment at the Toronto headquarters. In 1916 Black tendered his resignation because he "could not condone the offences and irregularities" he had begun to uncover, including Owen's propensity for encouraging underage Barnardo boys to enlist in the armed forces. Black pressed for a full enquiry but the executive in London pleaded the strains of war on staff resources to avoid sending anyone to Canada. It took until 1919 for Owen to be charged by police with "the criminal offense of cohabiting at the time with a ward of Barnardo's, Maisie Skelton, 'in the guise of his housekeeper.' Mr. Owen made a written confession of guilt but for reasons unknown was never brought to trial." The November 1919 issue of *Ups & Downs* mentions that Owen has resigned, but with no explanation. Owen may well have had John Hobday to thank for escaping conviction. In a private report to the Barnardo's executive Hobday noted making every effort to ensure there was "no grounds for gossip or undue enquiries." Barnardo's cozy relationship with the authorities had once again paid off.[42]

Maisie Skelton, better known as Mafey Skelton, was born May 18, 1900 in Sheffield, England, so named for the day the Siege of Mafeking ended — a British milestone in the Boer War. Skelton's father Fred, a file cutter, had died at 45, leaving her mother to care for four children on a servant's wages. She is admitted to Barnardo's Homes in Sheffield on March 17, 1910 and is boarded out with the Butler family near Stroud, Gloucestershire. After two years with the Butlers she is emigrated to Canada aboard the same ship as Gladys and Louisa Martin — the *Sicilian* — on September 19, 1912, arriving at the Hazelbrae Home in Peterborough on September 30. Mafey is sent to the small farming community of Lifford, some 40 kilometres southwest of Peterborough. At age 18 she can be found working at a telephone office in Toronto, where Barnardo's Canadian headquarters is located.[43]

Barnardo's wards are encouraged to visit the Toronto Home for encouragement or advice and if Mafey had done so she would have met Owen at this time. She next turns up in February 1925, when she travels alone to England and gives birth to a daughter, Mary Minnie Owen. Alfred Owen is recorded as the father. During Owen's frequent trips between Canada and England he is known to stay in apartments for foreigners at Denison Avenue, London. Following Owen's resignation in disgrace it is believed he moved to Kelowna, BC, where he turns up in records listed as a "Provision Merchant (Master)" for the municipality. Incoming passenger records after the birth of Minnie show Mafey's destination as Kelowna. Moving across the country would certainly have been a way to start a new life, and her descendants believe she changed her name. Her subsequent history has thus all but vanished.[44]

April 7, 1920. Miss Whiteman writes the Governor of Girls Village Home asking for the address of Barnardo's homes in Canada so she may continue to correspond with Gladys Martin. She is instructed to write Gladys care of the Margaret Cox Home, formerly known as Hazelbrae.[45] Its curving driveway is lined with trees just beginning to come into full leaf and the broad, open veranda seems to say "welcome." The grand staircase is inviting but its banisters require frequent polishing to preserve the wood. Hazelbrae girls learn early that — unlike the fun and games they enjoyed on the Atlantic crossing — they are here to work. There are chores from morning 'til evening to be done, with time allotted for school and recreation. By now Hazelbrae is reaching the end of its life, so its Victorian splendour is fading. Built by Alexander Smith in 1871–72, Hazelbrae predated the stately Strathormond by at least two decades. Peterborough millionaire George A. Cox, president of Midland Railway, acquired the home in 1883. By the following year, when he learned that Dr. Barnardo was seeking a distribution home in Ontario, he offered the use of Hazelbrae, rent-free. Cox's wife Margaret, a staunch supporter of Barnardo's work, is commemorated by the renaming of the home.[46]

But neither Gladys nor Louisa will spend much time in the grand house crowning Conger's Hill before being placed — separately — in farm homes throughout the Trent Valley. Gladys is given her first farm placement within three weeks. She is sent to work for the Gillespie family in Cannington, 70 kilometres west of Peterborough in the Kawartha Lakes region. Gladys soon gets her first bitter taste of rejection. The Gillespies send her back to Hazelbrae on May 1st as "unsatisfactory," possibly because she is too small to perform their chores. Within a week, on May 8th, Gladys is shipped out again, this time to the Baskin family in Norwood, Ontario — about 32 kilometres northeast of Peterborough.[47]

Gladys doesn't like what she finds in the Baskin house — alcohol. To a young girl whose mother's alcoholism had shattered her family, even its presence must have seemed threatening. She informs the Margaret Cox Home and a visitation agent is sent to Norwood in July to investigate. "I learnt from Mrs. Baskin Senior that her son does take drink but that she has not known him to be intoxicated since he returned from the war some years ago," writes the agent. "Mrs. James Baskin has a nice little home in the village. She is a war bride and says that if she had searched the world over, she could not have found a better husband. Gladys says she has seen Mr. Baskin taking liquor along with other men, but he does not get intoxicated and has always been kind to her." Stymied by a lack of any clear evidence of misconduct in the Baskin household, the agent turns her frustration on Gladys. "This child seems to have a discontented disposition, and is not very willing to help. She does not like looking after children and that is principally what Mrs. Baskin wants her for. The child says she is not happy here but I cannot think she has much to complain about. She has had some scoldings and was slapped for eating a bowlful of preserved cherries." The conclusion? "Gladys will probably be returned in a few months time as Mrs. Baskin will require experience and help. I'm afraid this child will not be easily placed. She would rather be where there are no children."[48]

True to the visiting agent's prediction, by October Gladys is being moved, this time to the Clysdales, a family with three children living in Warsaw. The Barnardo's visitor's report notes that Gladys has a "safe room" and is in good health but is "untruthful" and "not clean," but without specifying what is meant by the latter comment. She has been in the country a little over six months and has already had three placements. For a child, whose need for home stability is a primary requirement of healthy emotional development, this kind of upheaval leads to deep stress. A symptom of this stress often shows itself in enuresis, or bedwetting. Visitor's reports noting "unclean habits," a frequent comment, are likely referring to this condition.[49] As with many younger girls not yet strong enough to keep up with the heavy workload required of them, "Mrs. Clysdale would prefer an older girl," notes one report. Gladys is "not equal to requirements," and on November 16, 1920 is returned to the Margaret Cox Home in Peterborough to await yet another placement. The instability will only get worse as she is transferred from farm to farm another three times over the next year.[50]

As the snows of her first Canadian winter descend, she is transferred to the Hollands family in Bannockburn early in December. But this too is not to last. Mr. Hollands is suffering from an ongoing illness that "necessitates economy," so "they will probably have to part with Gladys." By March 7, 1921, she is moved to the home of Minnie E. Fair in South Monaghan, where Gladys will have her longest stay yet — five months. However, Fair's brother-in-law Robert Thorne seems to have greater need of Gladys and in early August she is transferred to his farm in the same community.[51]

April 19, 1921. Meanwhile, back in England, her youngest sister Enid Ruby Martin, now eight, is admitted to Barnardo's care. Thanks to the ban on correspondence with family members, Enid during the intervening six years has become all but a stranger to Gladys and Louisa. It's unlikely Gladys was informed of Enid's admission to Barnardo's. She will never see Enid again. And by now she has already lost track of Louisa's whereabouts.[52]

March 21, 1922. Barnardo's sends a Miss Smith to visit Gladys at the Thorne farm. Smith provides the most detailed report so far, noting that Gladys has a room to herself and her health is "fairly good, clothes in fair condition, work and behaviour fairly satisfactory." Gladys attends church, Sunday school, and day school regularly, according to the Thornes. But Smith is given "only a fair report of Gladys" when she visits the school. This would hardly be surprising given the workload expected of a British Home Child, leaving time for only sporadic school attendance. "Gladys is staying with Miss M. Fair (sister of Mrs. Thorne) for a few days on account of Mrs. Thorne being ill."[53]

But Gladys is deeply unhappy at the Thorne's. On July 19 she is placed with the Fred Ruddell family in Georgetown, near Brampton. The Ruddells are a kindly family and the result is a dramatic change in Gladys. This time, when a Miss Sharp visits the farm, the report is much improved. Although "very small for her age," she now has "a very tidy appearance." She is "a willing, well-behaved child" who has at last "settled down happily in her new home and promises well." The all-too-common — often meaningless — comment in visitors' reports that Gladys is treated "as one of the family" this time seems to ring true. Sharp describes the Ruddells as having "a very good farm home," with two of their own children, and Mrs. Ruddell pictured as "motherly." Gladys, notes Miss Sharp, is an "intelligent, bright child, and, given an opportunity, Mrs. Ruddell thinks she will make good. She had just baked her first batch of biscuits when I called, and they looked very good. The child seems to take an interest in her work and is fond of the children." It's a refreshing contrast to earlier reports of Gladys as "untruthful" and "very slow," clues that should have alerted Barnardo's visitation agents to a less than happy situation.[54]

Gladys does indeed settle down with the Ruddells. She remains with the family over three years — by far her longest placement yet. Sharp visits the Ruddell farm three more times during this period. Her reports hint that Gladys is still displaying signs of emotional turmoil. A report from January 3, 1923 notes that she is "sulky, bad-tempered. Gladys has an excellent home here, and does not wish to leave, though Mrs. Ruddell has at times thought she would have to return her. The girl however promises to do better." What is sulkiness and what is inarticulate grief in a child? Having been shunted from pillar to post for as long as she can remember, it's not surprising that even in a good home there would be days when she feels out of temper. But Mrs. Ruddell is a patient woman. Despite repeated citations by Miss Sharp for being "not very satisfactory," and even "lazy and disobedient" at times, Gladys is given many second chances. Her "disobedience" may be nothing more than an innate ability to stand up for herself.[55]

As Gladys is being shifted from farm to farm, social reformer Charlotte Whitton is storming the country as the chair of several Child Welfare Conferences. After a brilliant academic career at Queen's University during World War I, Whitton joined the recently formed Canadian Council on Child Welfare. Her campaign to introduce better supervision of juvenile immigrants is reported even in Britain. Under the headline, *Child Slavery in Canada*, the October 10, 1923 *Nottingham Post* accurately predicts that "boy and girl immigrants in future will be more effectively sheltered from exploitation and abuse," as a result of Whitton's efforts. The

Post was reporting on a Child Welfare Conference recently held in Winnipeg, where "one instance reported was of an English lad whose employer made him sleep in a dark cellar. He was beaten and overworked until he became a wreck, and he died alone in the cellar from pneumonia." Many more similar cases could have been cited of children dead from neglect, suicide, or manslaughter. Whitton claimed at the conference that 20 percent of the unwed mothers in Ontario were "young girls brought from the British Isles," openly hinting at the sexual abuse many of them must have suffered. Yet Whitton is a curious mix of progressive and regressive impulses. Her arguments seem motivated as much by the popular concern with "not contaminating the Canadian gene pool" as with protecting those who have no protectors.[56]

While at the Ruddell's, Gladys continues her correspondence with Alice Whiteman. One visitor's report in 1924 notes that Gladys is "very anxious to see her sister Louisa again," and has been writing her letters. But no effort is made by the Margaret Cox Home to help re-establish contact. Gladys will have to wait until she is an adult before she will see her sister again.

Her final report at the Ruddell home notes that she is having trouble with her eyes and has been seen by a doctor, but is otherwise a "big, stout, strong-looking girl." "Gladys has been happy in her home with Mrs. Ruddell," writes the visiting agent on November 21, 1925. Unfortunately, times are tough for the family, and Mrs. Ruddell no longer feels she can afford to pay the girl's wage during the winter months. She has requested a younger girl. Gladys has worked her way up to $12 per month and younger girls are paid less. One can only imagine how crushed Gladys will feel when she finds out she must leave her happy home. On December 1, 1925 she is returned to South Monaghan, where she will once again work for Minnie Fair and the Thorne family. She will not leave with fond memories of her time there.[57]

January 21, 1928. Gladys is transferred to the home of Mrs. Percy Barker in Weston. But deliverance is on the horizon — she has just a year to go until she is 21 and freed from her indenture with Barnardo's. That indenture has had her uprooted from farm to farm, home to home, nearly a dozen times in eight years. Her horizon is about to brighten in another way. While in Toronto one wintry afternoon in January, she bumps into a young Englishman at a streetcar stop. They start chatting while waiting for the trolley and discover an instant affinity. His name is Victor Frederick Fudge and like Gladys he too was born in Bristol. He had emigrated to Canada with his parents, possibly on the suggestion of relatives already living in Weston, and the Fudges had settled in Belleville.[58]

December 3, 1928. Toronto. Things have moved quickly, as they often do in young romance. The final report on Gladys is made on this date: "Gladys came in to do some shopping for her wedding tomorrow to Victor Fudge." Although still only earning a meager $15 a month, she has plenty of clothes and her health is good. She returns her Barnardo's trunk before launching into married life. On December 4, 1928 Gladys and Victor are married in St. Paul's Anglican Church, Toronto. Their wedding is witnessed by John and Rose Hobday.[59]

Gladys writes Rose Hobday, thanking her for Christmas greetings. She informs the "Lady Superintendent" that the couple has found a farm home in the hamlet of Carrying Place — just a few miles from Belleville. Hobday writes back with a congratulatory letter. "I trust all will go well and that this year will be one of happiness and prosperity for you and your husband." But prosperity is a long way off yet. Lack of work forces the couple to move in with Victor's parents. Her next letter is written on December 17 from the Fred Fudge home on Moira Street, Belleville. "I was wondering if you would kindly forward my account from the Toronto Bank of Commerce to the Bank of Commerce in Belleville for me as soon as possible. I have made my home in Belleville and would like to draw some money for our home as we sure need it. We are getting along fine but need a lot of things. . . . Hoping this will be alright."[60]

Rose Hobday seems happy to help out at Christmastime, sending Gladys a money order for $20 on December 18. But Gladys is seeking the balance of her account, saved up since her arrival in

1920. The Lady Superintendent encloses a rather stiffly worded response: "I have been exceedingly surprised to receive your letter making application for money. You do not appear to realize that marriage makes no difference to a Trust Fund. It is still not payable to you until you are 21 years old. As it is Christmas you may like to have a little money and I am therefore sending you $20 but you must not make application for payments from your Trust Fund again. You are married and your husband must provide for you." Gladys has struck at the nerve of a core Barnardo's belief: their wards are to become self-sufficient, not dependent. Yet she is only asking for money she has already earned at great effort.[61]

Gladys writes the Lady Superintendent the next day. She thanks Hobday for her consideration, but explains that the couple is in dire straits.

> I certainly was not in favour of spending my money. But . . . my husband hasn't much money. He stayed in Toronto for a long time. And he was looking and enquiring for a job for us all the time. Well, we heard of a man here in Belleville that would hire us if we came here and when we got here another man had seen him first so he took him. There are two more jobs in sight here but we will not know for sure until Saturday. Hanging around Toronto with no money coming in soon runs off with what a person has. We certainly are trying our utmost to get work; we are both very willing. We have had ads in the papers hoping to get work. If you know of a place would you kindly let us know please. It sure is a bad time around Christmas.

As Gladys closes the letter, her Barnardo's training kicks in: "I am sure very thankful to you for looking after my money as I know it is all for my own good. Wishing you a Merry Christmas and a bright and happy New Year." Fortunately Gladys' 21st birthday is just around the corner, in March 1929. She receives $290.23 — the full balance of her earnings for eight years' work — in early May.[62]

Victor and Gladys have the misfortune of starting their family at a very difficult time in history. By late October 1929 — not even a year after their marriage — the stock market crash has sent shudders through the entire economy of the Western world. Meanwhile, Nature takes her course. The first child, George Percival, is born to the Fudges in 1930. Gladys stays on good terms with Barnardo's, sending news of her family at regular intervals to be published in the official newsletter, *Ups & Downs*. Their wedding picture is printed in the August 5, 1930 edition. An announcement in the April 5, 1932 issue heralds the birth of daughter Jeanette Irene Louise. The edition features a front-page editorial celebrating "The Migration Jubilee Year." "From 1882 to 1932 this migration work has proved to be one of the most wonderful enterprises undertaken by the Barnardo Homes. Thirty thousand youngsters have followed in the footsteps of that pioneer party — an average of six hundred per annum over a period of 50 years — and not two percent of these young Empire builders have failed to make good in the very best sense of the word." But with the onset of the Great Depression, the reality is very different. Thousands of these former Barnardo's children are facing a very uncertain future.[63]

Young George Percival Fudge's photo will appear in *Ups & Downs* at least twice, along with birth notices and photos of his siblings. Three more children are born to the family during the decade: Charles Austin Burges Fudge in 1934, Harold Edward Scott Fudge in 1935, and Annie Irene in 1938. Continuing in the Barnardo's tradition of royal patronage, the June 1936 edition announces that King Edward VIII will succeed King George V as royal patron. With Hitler's rise to power in Germany, political tension escalates throughout the '30s, making another war inevitable. Already in 1938 Britain's government is seeing the warning signs and organizes the evacuation of children from London. *Ups & Downs* reports in its December edition that 1,500 children have been evacuated from Barnardo's facilities within two days and boarded out in the West of England. It's a dress rehearsal for what will follow in less than a year.[64]

5. Searching for a Lost Brother

For Gladys Fudge as a young bride, more than just feeding her growing family has begun to prey on her mind. Besides leaving behind her younger sister Enid, she and Louisa had also left behind a brother, Percy. She writes the Public Assistance Committee in Bristol in April 1935 asking if they might help locate him. The committee refers the request to Rose Hobday in Toronto. A flurry of letters ensues in the search for Percy. Hobday writes PT Kirkpatrick at Barnardo's head office in Stepney Causeway, London, explaining that the boy was last known to be in care of the Bristol Poor Law Union, "and while they do not definitely state that Percy was placed in Dr. Barnardo's Homes, they infer it by telling her to write there for information from their records." The Canadian Immigration Department gets involved in the hunt, writing Bristol in May. Then, early in June, a break — the Bristol committee discovers in its files that Percy had been discharged from the Children's Homes to "Mr. Hillier of Dr. Barnardo's Home, Bristol, on the 19th March, 1915, and it was then understood that arrangements had been made by him for the boy to be admitted to the Sutcliffe Industrial School, Bath." Though hopeful, the letter comes with a shock: "I may add that the mother, who bore a very unsatisfactory character, died at Southmead Hospital on the 20th December, 1923." Gladys had never been told. She would have been 15 and working for the Ruddells at the time.[65]

The Canadian Immigration Department takes the enquiry seriously, writing Superintendent JH Roberts of Barnardo's Homes, Clifton, Bristol to ask if he can trace Percy. The flurry of letters continues. Finally on June 28, 1935, Superintendent James Sullivan of the Sutcliffe Boys' Home at Bath writes Roberts. "To reply to your enquiry re: Percy Martin I have to inform you that it is recorded in my Committee's minutes that this boy was drowned whilst on summer holidays at Burnham in August 1918 and that the parents were duly informed." Roberts writes Stepney Causeway the same day with the news. "It seems a little strange that the parents never informed the girl of the loss of her brother," he muses.[66]

July 1, 1935. Gladys is reading a letter from the Immigration Department with the news of her brother's death. The news had filtered its way through the chain of agencies, finally landing on Rose Hobday's desk in Toronto. Though she and her brother had been separated for 17 years, Gladys can't help feeling deeply grieved. In one blow, she has lost both her mother and brother. Barnardo's wall of silence had done little to help the situation.[67]

Perhaps hoping to soften the blow, Rose Hobday writes Stepney Causeway on July 15 asking for the last known address of Gladys' family, as "she is now very anxious to get in touch with them." Gladys must now wait anxiously for several months while the enquiry works its way through the system. In October, James Sullivan informs Barnardo's that he is unable to trace their address, but provides a few more details: "Occupation of parent (father): Railway Porter. Residence not given. (Local, I believe.) Cause of application: Mother in prison for neglecting the children." (Here "prison" is likely synonymous with the workhouse.) But then Roberts writes from Bristol with a lead. "Although repeated enquiries have been made for the relations of this girl without success, I accidentally fell in touch with those who can enlighten us on this problem. Whilst in Bedminster this week, and near what was Berkeley Square, but is now nearly demolished, I stopped at a greengrocer's shop, seeing an elderly lady standing in the doorway. I asked if she had known many of the people who lived in the houses and told her I was seeking the relations of Gladys Martin who used to live there many years ago. She remembered them and advised me to visit Mrs. Smith of Langdon Park, nearby, as she felt sure she would be able to tell me about the family, as she had been nursing Mrs. Mills who had been ill for two years and died recently." Roberts notes the address of the Mills family and of Maud Martin, a worker with the Salvation Army (but apparently no relation). "I would suggest that Gladys get in touch with Mr. Mills, from whom I think she will get all the news she desires."[68]

If Gladys made any effort to contact the Mills, no letters survive to prove it. During the 1940s Gladys will bear two more children: Ernest Carl in 1940 and Gordon Douglas in 1942. "From the frying pan to the fire" perhaps best describes the situation for the Fudge family as wartime restrictions kick in and Canadians are asked to tighten their belts. After a decade of economic depression it's a wonder they had a notch left to tighten.

Barnardo's will face the same threat as any other British citizen living in London during the war: the nightly bombing raids of the Blitz. The December 1941 *Ups & Downs* reports that the Stepney Causeway headquarters had already been bombed eight times. The Girls Village Home, where Gladys spent her formative years, is damaged by bombing raids. Many other Barnardo's Homes across Britain, including the boys' home at Goldings, are also bombed. By 1941 there are 3,356 "Barnardo Boys and Girls" serving in the armed forces, with more to come. Of these, 500 are from Canada. Casualties noted are 29 deaths in the British Navy and merchant marine. The war is busily making more orphans for Barnardo's to care for — 519 children are admitted as a result of the bombings. Many thousands more will be traumatized as they are uprooted from their homes and families and rushed off to remote parts of the British Isles.

6. Epilogue: Repercussions

It's a testament to the power of the maternal bond that even when a mother has been seriously negligent, her children often still revere her memory. Such was the case with Gladys. "My mother used to say, 'You lose your best friend when you lose your mother,'" says her daughter Irene. Matrons hired by child-care organizations like Barnardo's were seldom of a character to fill that void. Many had probably been victims of neglect and abuse themselves while growing up, and not a few of them came from orphanages.

Unlike many Canadians who felt ashamed of their past as Home Children, Gladys told her children some of her experiences as a "Barnardo girl." It may be her refusal to quietly submit to abuse that earned her so many negative reports from visitation agents. But Gladys was determined not to become another faceless "woman without stories." She told her children many stories of abuse on the farms to which she was indentured. In one instance, a fair was coming to town and her host family told her she could go. You can imagine the excitement — a fair! Colourful tents full of exotic acts, animals, and toys! Maybe even a ferris wheel and rides! Just the thing to take the sting out of her endless hours of domestic drudgery. On the morning of the fair, Gladys got up even earlier than usual to get her chores done. As she hurried back to the house to get ready, she saw the family car driving off without her. "I was young when Mom told us this story and I can still remember crying myself to sleep," recalls Irene. At one of the farm homes, she was taunted by the daughter of the family who boasted that she was going to become a schoolteacher while Gladys "would never amount to anything."[69]

Despite the rosy promises of "the golden bridge" to Canada, where all of the old class distinctions of Britain were supposed to have fallen away, the Home Children found themselves at the bottom of a new social hierarchy. Historian Joy Parr argues that the indenture contracts signed by farmers were a double-edged sword. On one hand, they protected the child by stipulating wages and basic requirements. On the other, they reinforced their status as hired hands, "cast in a distinctive status, as a servant of the household separate from the siblings of the family." This "destroyed the illusion, the warm and welcome illusion of being 'like family,' which every child immigrant must have at some time entertained."[70]

It also made a mockery of the standard notation on visitation reports, "Treated as one of the family." At one of her farm placements, Gladys was told of an impending visit by the Barnardo's inspector and given a better room, which she was to pretend was her own. "Now, you're happy here, remember?" she was coached.

When the inspector arrived, the woman said to her, "Well, what could you possibly have to complain about? You have your own room, with a window to look out of and a nice bed. Lots of girls don't have as much." But it was a façade — one that frequently fooled visitation agents.[71]

Gladys also told her children of her beatings. As was so often the case, she was warned not to tell the visiting agent or she would face more beatings later. But finally she couldn't take it anymore. When the lady visitor from Barnardo's arrived, Gladys pulled off her shirt to show her the welts on her back. "She was removed from that house only to be treated the same at many other homes," Irene writes.[72] Fortunately for Gladys, she was placed on farms within reasonable traveling distance of the Peterborough distributing home. Had she been on one of the more remote farms, she might have had to wait up to a year to be removed from an abusive situation.[73] Physical punishment in Barnardo's Homes was forbidden, and against the law in Canada except for "moderate chastisement" of servants. But in the back country, where no one was watching, the law meant little, and "the moderating influences of blood ties were absent." Parr adds that even in Barnardo's Homes, evidence exists of excessive punishment for nine percent of boys and 15 percent of girls. "The Homes were good to us but the discipline was out of this bleeding world," recalled Vernon Nelson.[74] The percentage would be much higher once the children got to the farms.[75]

As is often the case with those who have suffered want, Gladys would grow up to become a generous person. The skills she learned at the Girls Village Home stayed with her — she was constantly knitting for someone or doing some form of needlework. "Her hands were never idle," Irene recalls. Her sister Jeanette tells a story of the "Dirty Thirties," when hunger reared its ugly head over millions of people. One afternoon a "hobo" arrived on the steps of the Fudge home, asking for food. "Well, mister, I have a lot of little mouths to feed, but I'll see if I can find a little something for you." Although Gladys had just finished canning cherries to put away for winter stock, she gladly opened a jar, cut him a four-inch slice of homemade bread and buttered it. "I know what it's like to be hungry," she told him.[76]

Gladys spoke seldom of her family to her children. The tragic story of Percy's drowning would not surface until 2000, when Irene received her records from Barnardo's Aftercare Services. "I remember when my mother got the telegram that her father had died," Jeanette recalls. It was 1939 and Lavington Frederick Martin was 80. As a little girl of eight she seemed not to know that she might have had a grandfather living somewhere. "I remember thinking the man who delivered it was another hobo, only better dressed, and I remember the yellow paper. We had a radio on at the time and when Mom sat down to read the telegram, she switched off the radio. As she read the telegram she started to cry and I asked her why."

"My father has died."

"Your father? Where is he?"

"In England."

"Why didn't he come to see you?"

"He didn't have the money, I guess."[77]

The old adage, "the apple doesn't fall far from the tree" proved to be true in Louisa's case. Unlike Gladys, who became a strict teetotaler and refused to allow alcohol in her house, Irene recalls her Aunt Louisa as a party girl, a *bon vivant* much like her mother Elizabeth. Louisa had a flair for performance and worked as a chorus girl. It's precisely the profile that Barnardo used as justification for taking children away from such parents in one of his "philanthropic abductions." But Irene recalls her Aunt Louisa with fondness, as a colourful, enlivening character. "I liked her; she loved to party, wear nice clothes and she liked to drink." But for Gladys, Louisa may have been too much of a reminder of the mother whose dissipation had landed them in Barnardo's in the first place. "They kept in contact but they weren't really buddy-buddy because they were so different."[78]

The distant relationship of the two sisters echoed down into their children. Irene recalls not getting to know her cousins while growing up. When an article was published about the family's Home Child past in an Oshawa newspaper a few years ago, Louisa's granddaughter contacted Jeanette. As a result there was a meeting with second cousins they didn't know they had. One daughter of Louisa's has chosen not to renew family ties. "I think like her mother, Louisa, she is ashamed of having anything to do with being a BHC [British Home Child]," says Irene.[79]

Despite the harsh punishment meted out to her as a child, Gladys made a conscious effort not to do the same to her own children. "I recall my Mom calling us kids to help with washing the dishes," says Jeanette. "'Harold! Charles! Jean! George! Gordon! Ernest! Irene!' she'd shout. 'Who's going to come here and help your mother with the dishes?' We'd all find some sly argument for why it should be the other kid. 'Upstairs, all of you!' she'd say. 'I'm coming up with the belt!'" But Jeanette says the strapping never materialized, nor does she recall Gladys ever hitting any of them. Yet she had shown them the marks on her body where she had been beaten as a girl.[80]

Gladys resisted the urge to physically punish her children. Yet the ghosts of her past occasionally asserted themselves in her speech. The experience of verbal abuse was common to Home Children so it's not surprising they repeated the habit in times of stress. Whether due to these lapses or to her latent emotional angst, the children picked up on the turmoil and were affected in different ways. As mentioned in the Introduction, family systems psychologists know that this angst is often passed down the line subliminally, expressed as depression, alcoholism, drug abuse and other dysfunctions. The nascent field of epigenetics asserts that there is even a genetic component to intergenerational trauma. The Fudge family has seen several lives marred by tragedy. Irene speaks of her older brothers as having had "a terrible life; they took it out on their families [and] they both died being very bitter and unhappy."[81]

Young adults have a way of becoming absorbed with their own lives, and family history often takes a back seat until later years. Gladys' stories of growing up as an indentured servant on Ontario farms gradually faded into the background. That is, until 2000, when Irene decided it was time to write Barnardo's for her mother's records. Gladys had passed away in 1985 from pancreatic cancer at the age of 77. Irene was rewarded with a thick file of reports and letters from the Barnardo's archives, and a pleasant surprise: "Enid was emigrated to New South Wales in Australia on 19 April 1921," wrote Aftercare Officer Karen Fletcher. "Now to the very important piece of information I have for you. In 1990, Enid's daughter contacted Aftercare through Barnardo's Australian Office to request information about her mother's childhood. My point in mentioning this is to ask whether you would like to make contact with your cousin. . . ."[82]

Did she indeed! Irene was put in contact with her cousin Gai Fugar and learned that her mother Enid had worked at a sheep station cooking and cleaning for a family. The remote outback stations would have seemed just as distant from civilization as the backcountry farms of Ontario — suffused with loneliness for a Home Child. And for a child without parental protection, a long way off from any help should she need it. From there Enid had gone to Sydney to work but her experiences as an indentured servant were deeply unsettling. Enid died never knowing she had siblings living in Canada.

Irene's siblings had been averse to her research at first. "Why would you want to drag all that stuff up again?" Jeanette recalls herself thinking. "Why open that can of worms?"[83] But the discovery of not one but four long-lost cousins — Owen, Gai, Chris, and Susan — turned the tables for her. In 2002, Irene and Jeanette flew to Australia to surprise Gai for her 60th birthday. What they learned of Enid's life was a sad echo of what had happened to Gladys and Louisa. "My mother was sad her whole life," Gai told Australian reporter Jodie Duffy. "She had no love, she never belonged to anybody. She was very bitter until the day she died."[84]

When the invitation came for the unveiling of the commemorative Home Children stamp in Ottawa in 2010, siblings George, Jeanette, Gordon, and Irene attended, along with other families.

For George, who was 80 that year, the trip was made all the more challenging by recovery from recent heart surgery. Immigration Minister Jason Kenney didn't even bother to show up. Jeanette says the ceremony was strictly stage managed, with no time for any of the Home Children families to speak about their experiences. "It's as if they wanted to make sure nothing negative was said about it," she recalls. The extent of the "ceremony" was a huge image of the stamp projected onto a wall.[85] "I always felt that if the Natives got their apology for the residential schools the Home Children should too," adds Irene. "I wrote to [Prime Minister] Harper and [Governor-General] Michaëlle Jean asking: When are you going to apologize? I said we want an apology, we need more than a stamp."[86]

With the knowledge available to us now, Irene wonders if it could have been different for her family. "Because of the way my mother was brought up she didn't know how to love. Reading all her letters helped us understand where she was coming from, why she was so bitter. Quite often when she was frustrated and didn't know what to do she would revert to the way she was treated. We all wished we had known this while she was still alive."[87]

A shipload of Barnardo's girls arriving in St. John, New Brunswick, 1920. Gladys and Louisa Martin are in the front row, fourth and fifth from left. Library and Archives Canada #PA-041785.

Gladys Martin, about age 10, in a photo taken by Barnardo's. An "old soul" seems to peer out from this child's eyes. Irene (Fudge) Campbell collection.

CHAPTER 5

George's Story —
Welcome to the Hard World

July 24, 1909. William Baker leans over his desk, reading the handwritten notes left there by his secretary. The office is well appointed, with walnut paneling and brass fittings giving it the characteristic richness of a Victorian business establishment. Except that in his mind — and despite the increasing numbers on Barnardo's Homes ledgers — this is no business. Unless it be considered the business of caring for God's lost little sheep — the "waifs and strays" of Empire. "Better a philanthropic abduction for these boys and girls than that they should remain in the darkness of spiritual poverty," Baker muses.

The office at Stepney Causeway had been outfitted by his mentor, the renowned Dr. Thomas John Barnardo. At the time of his death in 1905 there were nearly 9,000 children under his care in 96 homes across the UK, and the numbers continue to grow. Many of these desperately poor children will soon be sent to the colonies. As Dr. Barnardo had said, the children were being sent across a "golden bridge" to new lands of opportunity — far more than they could expect if they remained in the slums of London, Manchester, Edinburgh, or Dublin. Baker can still recall as if it were yesterday hearing one of Dr. Barnardo's classic speeches, upon returning from his first visit to Canada in 1884. "Very soon now several hundred children per year will be sent across the Golden Bridge, that marvelous structure which spans the ocean with its Highway of Hope, one pier of which rests amid the gloom of Darkest England and the other set among the glorious plains and limitless possibilities of our Colonial Empire."[1]

Baker turns to the case at hand — a certain George Evans, age one year, one month, son of Emily Sarah Evans, age 23. Reading the caseworker's report, Baker can't help but sigh. It was all too typical. Little George had been born in Evesham Workhouse May 31, 1908, his case brought to the attention of Barnardo's Homes by the Reverend HW Wood of Norton Vicarage, Evesham, Worchester. Reverend Wood had heard of Emily Evans' difficulties. "George is the mother's second illegitimate child," notes the caseworker's flowing, careful script. "The mother, in a letter, stated that her mother died nearly five years ago, and that she has not a very good father. According to the same letter, the father of the elder child (George's half-sister) promised her marriage as soon as he could get a home together, but died before he could fulfill his promise. It appears that for two months he contributed 2s/6d per week towards the child's maintenance. George's father . . . absconded before the child was born, and has not been heard of since."[2]

"The mother is at present living with her father, who, however, does not want her at home. She is working in some market gardens at present, where her average weekly earnings are about 7 shillings. She will lose this employment in the winter, and, as the grandfather would not then continue to keep her and the children, the only prospect before them would have been that of the Union. It was hoped that if we took George off her hands she would be able to go into service, and board out the half-sister, Emily."[3]

Baker recalled visiting Evesham, a pretty village nestled in a bend of the River Avon, lush with greenness. He recalls being struck by its market square, with its quaint mix of Tudor and Victorian shops and houses, presided over by the majestic Lichfield bell tower, survivor of Henry VIII's dissolution of the monasteries. It was all that was left of the once proud Evesham Abbey, founded by Saint Egwin, third Bishop of Worcester in 701 AD. Local legend had it that the location of the abbey was inspired by a local swineherd named Eof, to whom the Virgin Mary appeared in a vision. In fact it's likely the 8th century Saxon Minster Church of Evesham Abbey was founded on an even earlier church, as was the case everywhere in Britain. Following the Norman Conquest, the Abbey appeared in that great Rosetta Stone of imperial inventory, the Domesday Book of 1086. The Normans were clever enough not to destroy everything in sight and the Abbey was renovated and extended by them. The influx of tradesmen helped add to the primarily agrarian local economy. Regular flooding by the Avon ensured the fertility of the soil and the village's reputation for fine quality fruit and vegetables. Baker had enjoyed buying his food for the day at the farmer's market, and had picked up a postcard with a print of a fine drawing of the square by Edmund Hort New.[4]

Reading the carefully scribed report on the infant George Evans, Baker can't help but reflect on the child's misfortune. It's a misfortune not uncommon for poor country folk whose luck has taken a turn for the worse. His grandfather Thomas Evans, now 52, is a shepherd — an idyllic life in this pastoral setting but one doomed to poverty. Two of his uncles work in the dark purgatories of coal mines — his uncle George in a mine east of Birmingham at a place called Hinckley. But the whereabouts of his uncle Aaron Evans is not known. Another uncle, Jack, works as a carrier's assistant in Blackwell, Worcestershire; while his youngest uncle is still a boy of 14, working with his grandfather Thomas on the farm. Little George's aunties aren't much better off. Aunt Rhoda, 16, earns only £9 per year working as a domestic servant not far from Evesham at Hawington. And Annie Evans is still a girl of 10, living with grandfather Thomas. "Hmmm," mumbles Baker, "not much in the way of prospects there." It only takes a single misfortune — in this case the death of George's grandmother and the abandonment by his father — to pitch a family like the Evans into disaster.[5]

"Well at least the medical report certifies that the boy is in good health," Baker tells himself. "The poor child has come to us by God's graces." In this he heartily agrees with the caseworker's notes implying that had George ended up in the Evesham Union Workhouse, he would have been far worse off than as a ward of Barnardo's Homes. Although like Dr. Barnardo, Baker has little time for fiction, he had to admit Charles Dickens' novels held a portrayal of the workhouse only slightly more bleak than reality. Reverend Wood's parish had seen little improvement in wages since 1797, when Sir Frederic Morton Eden's survey of the district revealed that the common labourer was only earning 1s/4d per day.[6] Poor relief had only recently become fully centralized. To provide an organized system of assisting the working poor, the Evesham Poor Law Union had been formed on April 7, 1836, its board of guardians representing Evesham's 32 parishes.[7]

The local Poor Law Union is a product of the New Poor Law Act of 1834, which sought to lower the financial burden of poor relief, largely by creating a severe workhouse regime that discouraged entry. The Act was influenced by the theories of Robert Malthus, who formulated the concept of "surplus population" and the need to reduce it. One goal of the workhouse was thus to discourage breeding amongst the poor classes, hence the gender segregation in workhouses. Victorian-era revivalist preachers grafted onto Malthusian ideas the old Biblical concept of humanity's innate sinfulness, implying that the poor were "depraved." In fact, poor relief costs had soared largely due to the unemployment following the Napoleonic wars, crop failures, and the jarring transformation from a craft and agrarian-based society to factory-based industrial capitalism. Steam technology was displacing the need for human labour faster than it could create general prosperity.[8]

Rescuing the poor from their "depraved" influences — a lack of religious instruction at home, one or more alcoholic parents, and a general lack of education — became the focus of social reformers and Poor Law boards alike. The New Poor Law discouraged (but thankfully could not entirely prevent) "outdoor relief," meaning any parish relief outside the workhouse. Some Poor Law authorities ran their workhouses like factories, benefiting by the low-cost labour of its inmates. While some were employed grinding bones to create fertilizer or picking oakum using a large metal spike, some of the labour — such as crushing rocks — seemed purely punitive. No wonder the poor referred to the workhouse as "the spike."

The Evesham Union Workhouse was built in 1837 on the south bank of the River Avon at Little Hampton, based on the cruciform designs of architect Sampson Kempthorne, locally adapted by John Plowman of Oxford. The walled-in design of this workhouse complex was designed to keep the different subgroups of the poor segregated, with open areas like prison exercise yards. Baker recalls bristling at Dickens' description in *Oliver Twist* of the workhouse diet as a subsistence of "three meals of thin gruel a day. . . ." In fact the diet varied greatly from parish to parish, depending on the generosity of the local Poor Law board.[9]

But to the New Poor Law commissioners, the new workhouses were seen as a triumph. In their eyes, workhouses predating the 1830s had been little more than large almshouses, "in which the young are trained in idleness, ignorance, and vice; the able-bodied maintained in sluggish sensual indolence; the aged and more respectable exposed to all the misery that is incident to dwelling in such a society." One assistant commissioner may not have realized the irony in his comment that the new workhouses would be something "the pauper would feel it was utterly impossible to contend against."[10]

BE THAT AS IT MAY, Baker realizes, he must live in the present. And that means making a decision about the infant George Evans. After all, there are scores of new cases coming into Barnardo's weekly and they must be dealt with quickly. A quick scan of the register for Barnardo's Babies' Castle at Hawkhurst, Kent, reveals that at 120 infants it has reached its capacity. Besides, Babies' Castle is generally reserved for those infants too weak or sickly to board out.[11] Baker decides to place little George in the Girl's

Village Home at Barkingside, Ilford, for a few days until he can be boarded out with a family capable of caring for a one-year-old. Barkingside will be too brief a sojourn to make a lasting impression on the infant's memory, even with its village square of cottages and whispering greens. He is there barely two weeks, from July 26 'til August 9, 1909, when the Clapp family at 23 Alston Road, Ipswich agrees to take him.[12]

It's a little too soon to send George to Barnardo's latest facility, Boy's Garden City, at Woodford, Essex. Baker smiles to himself, staring at the photo of Dr. Barnardo on one corner of his desk. The doctor casts a formidable shadow, but the Woodford acquisition is a respectable addition to the Barnardo's Homes legacy, alongside its pioneering Barkingside facility that by now has grown to house nearly 1,500 girls. It was Dr. Barnardo's attempt to humanize British workhouses and orphanages. Still, Baker often wonders whether Barkingside or Woodford could possibly replace the family environment these children had lost.[13]

"Success breeds success," Baker muses, thankful that his mentor's reputation has smoothed the way for further expansion. When Gwynne House at Woodford Bridge was offered to the organization with an option of purchasing it within three years for £6,000, Baker had leapt at the offer. It was a fine, rambling old building with extensive offices, surrounded by 16 hectares of land — less than the village-sized space of Barkingside's 24 hectares but still ample. The goal was to accommodate 900 boys in 30 cottages in a complex that would include a church, playground, school, sanatorium, and isolation hospital. For Baker, 1909 will remain a magical year. He will always cherish the memory of standing proudly among the dignitaries when Boy's Garden City was officially opened by Her Royal Highness the Duchess of Albany. Although not a fanciful man, Baker could almost feel Dr. Barnardo's slight but powerful presence, standing approvingly at his shoulder.[14]

A GRIEVING "MA" CLAPP sits at her kitchen table in her modest Ipswich home. Even the hollyhocks seem to be leaning toward the back window, trying to see what the matter is. When her husband comes home and shuffles out of his work boots he finds her still weeping softly. "What's the matter, Ma? What's happened?" She waves a half-crumpled letter at him. He plucks it gently from her hand and sees the letterhead: Barnardo's Homes, Stepney Causeway, London. "They're taking our George away," she sputters, her eyes red.

Clapp does his best to read the letter, reading not being his strong suit. The letter, written in impersonal, officious tones, simply states that, as per Barnardo's policy, boys reaching the age of 13 must be removed from their foster homes to begin trades training. George will be transferred to Boy's Garden City, where he will be given training as a bootmaker. Clapp does his best to comfort his wife, shaking his head sadly as he stares out into the garden. "Well Ma, they did tell us when we took the boy this might happen," he reminds her. But by now the "boarding out" agreement they'd signed has become barely a dim memory.[15] The Clapps already had two children of their own and had generously opened their home to George. Now their foster son is being snatched away after 12 years, as if he were nothing but a blossom to snip or a hedge to be trimmed. For George it means being robbed of the only family he's ever known.

The couple had given themselves a day or so to recover from the shock before telling George. The boy rages in a most uncharacteristic manner before collapsing into tears and refusing dinner. Ma Clapp spends the evening at his bedside, stroking his hair and trying to soften the blow, telling the lies we tell children when we can't comprehend an overwhelming injustice. "It's for the best, Georgie. Pa and I can't do much more for you." She later confesses to her husband to nearly choking on her own words.

May 11, 1921. George leaves the Clapps, bound for Boy's Garden City, where he will live for two years. At age 15 he is transferred again to William Baker Technical School (WBTS), Golding,

Hertford — known by the boys as Goldings — to complete his training. He seems to be moving on a descending scale — from a loving foster home, to the simulated village atmosphere of Boy's Garden City, to the massive technical school at Goldings, with its cold brick façade daring the world to penetrate its secrets. Often the jarring changes are wrought by Barnardo's in May — the month of George's birthday. His transfer to Boy's Garden City — tearing him away from the Clapps — occurs in May 1921, and he is removed from there to Goldings on May 5, 1924. Then he is bounced back to Boy's Garden City just over two weeks later, on May 21. One can only wonder at Barnardo's rationale, bouncing him from place to place after a long settled life with caring foster parents.[16]

A report from the technical school dated October 13, 1927 notes that he has received three years and four months of training at Goldings. But under "character and disposition" is written simply, "Good; needs careful handling." Had his grief swelled into rage, suddenly making him a "problem child"? A reference letter written by a Barnardo's secretary and dated July 5, 1928, chronicles George's history in Barnardo's Homes. It notes that, "for the last four years he has been receiving training in our Bootmaker's Shop at our William Baker Technical School. During the whole time he has been in these Homes, he has borne an excellent character." By this time, George has turned 19 and, although having been "placed in a situation on the 7th of May last as a bootmaker . . . is desirous of emigrating to Canada."[17]

If George is embittered by his experiences at Goldings, he could be forgiven. The institution is "run with a rod of iron," as one of his fellow inmates puts it. "Healthy bodies mean healthy minds," the instructors continually harangued. In fact it's as much a quasi-military college as a boys' technical school, complete with marching, incessant physical training, and cold showers to kill any newly budding sexual appetite. Some boys are given a private "pep talk" by the Governor upon leaving, warning them to beware of "loose women, gambling and drink." Most boys raised in a strict environ-

Laying the Children's Ghosts to Rest   169

ment like Barnardo's barely know what these are. Their options are limited to learning shoemaking, tinsmithing, carpentry, printing, and gardening. Woe to the creative soul caught in the technical school's web of iron, crushing the life out of the more sensitive boys. George recalled one of his dorm mates, a slight lad named Tommy, who was simply not cut out for technical work. He ruined every exercise in carpentry shop and bootmakers' shop before they found him a job washing dishes in the kitchen. The poor boy was continually excoriated for his "stupidity" and told he'd amount to nothing useful. It's a wonder he didn't kill himself, George often thought. He wouldn't be the first boy there who'd succumbed to suicide, nor the last.[18]

Tommy had found a listening ear in George and after lights out each night they talked, softly so as not to attract the wrath of the warders. Tommy used to say at least the kitchen got him off the incessant marching but the cook was a tough taskmaster. Every dish had to be wiped dry. Tommy learned to dread the cook's inspection of his work, which consisted of holding a pot or bowl upside down. If a single drop of water fell out, he was smacked across the back of the head with a wooden spoon — once for each drop. "Guess I went from the frying pan to the fire," Tommy used to joke, but in a tone of such sadness George had to hold back tears. Other times Tommy laughed about the army of cockroaches that lived in the kitchen. But George knew it was false bravado.[19]

It's the sense of camaraderie that kept George and Tommy and the other boys going. Being a member of one of the six "houses" that comprised the population of Goldings provided the semblance, if not the substance, of family. And if you had the luck to be the kind of boy with a natural aptitude for trades and a regimented lifestyle, you could do all right. Letters appeared regularly in the *Guild Messenger* from former "Goldonians" whose training at William Baker had served them well in their working lives. Many in future years will recall their time — and many of the staff — at Goldings with fondness. But for George and Tommy, they will always shudder at the memory of housemaster and drill instructor Joe Patch. He was known for patrolling the dining room with his Alsatian hound, ready to punish the smallest infraction with a hard slap.[20]

Despite getting a job in July 1928, George is readmitted to Goldings in September — just months after his reference letter had been written. Clearly, George is conflicted, unable to settle. Not to worry — Barnardo's has just the solution — emigration to Canada. George has had enough of England anyway. He's a young man now. It's time to leave.[21]

September 21, 1928. George is in Liverpool, about to board the Canadian Pacific steamship SS Duchess of Bedford, bound for Canada. At just over 180 metres in length, with a beam of 23 metres, two masts and two funnels, the ship's massive silhouette dominates the docks. A true ocean liner, there is accommodation for over 1,500 passengers — 580 cabin, 480 tourist and 510 in third class, where he will be bunking. The ship had only just been christened on January 24, 1928 by Mrs. Stanley Baldwin, wife of the British Prime Minister. Her maiden voyage had been in June, from Liverpool to Quebec and Montreal. On her second voyage she set a new record of six days, nine and a half hours from Liverpool to Montreal. George can't help feeling excited at the prospect of a record speed journey in a state-of-the-art ocean liner. Regular blasts from her horn seem to be a cry of urgency, and he's ready — itching for a change.[22]

For a young man who's grown up in a modest foster home and the Spartan surroundings of a boy's home and technical school, the SS Duchess of Bedford is like walking into a dream. The guests crowd into the main lounge in the evenings to enjoy concerts by the orchestra, with a diverse and cosmopolitan selection of music. An evening program could range from Offenbach to Mozart's Marriage of Figaro to corny popular songs like I Love the Moon, ending with rousing renditions of God Save the King and The Star Spangled Banner. Comedian Charlie Olden gives George a much-needed belly laugh or two.[23] He feels like a fish out of water, with his rough English tweed jacket in a sea of dinner jackets and elegant dresses. Still, it's an exhilarating glimpse into a world he'd barely imagined was possible. But the sidelong glances he's thrown make it clear — he's stepping outside his class. He drifts outside to the deck railings, watching moonlight splashing in the ship's wake. There, he is in a class of his own, with no one to compare or criticize.

September 27, 1928. George is given little time to savour the new sights, sounds, and smells of Quebec City when the ship lands. He has his Canadian Pacific Railway ticket for Winnipeg and the schedule is arranged so as to waste little time getting him to his first job placement. The stately 17th century spires and masses of brick and stone remind him of England, not entirely a welcome sight, but strangely comforting somehow. As the train journey clicks off the seemingly endless miles it takes to cross Ontario, George is struck by the first splashes of autumn colour daubing forests with red and gold. It's hard to believe a country could be so vast — so beautiful, unspoiled. His first stop will be the Toronto receiving home on Jarvis Street, where he will meet John and Rose Hobday.

The resignation of former Superintendent Alfred Owen in 1919 left Barnardo's Canadian branch in a precarious state. Warfare in the Atlantic shipping lanes had seriously hindered child emigration entirely. Barnardo's headquarters at 214 Farley Avenue had been emptied and sold. One of John Hobday's first jobs had been to find new facilities. He is assisted by his wife Rose, known to Barnardo boys and girls as "Lady Superintendent." The impressive Victorian mansion at 538 Jarvis Street fits the bill admirably — it's comfortable, spacious and somewhat less institutional than the Farley Avenue facility. Still slender in his 40s, Hobday is an Anglican of liberal humanitarian persuasion. In Britain his skill and personality had won him the position of assistant general secretary of London's Central YMCA. Like her husband, Rose Hobday is known for her genial nature. Although most Barnardo boys who pass through the Toronto receiving home will only be there at most a few nights on their way to placements, fond lifelong impressions will be made by the Hobdays.[24]

As George resumes his train journey westward, the countryside levels out from the rolling hills and maple forests into the "big sky country" of the Prairies. He wonders if he could possibly be in the same world, much less the same country. Never has he seen a sky so huge, its early evening indigo so vividly tainted with orange it appears aglow with embers.

His first evening at the Winnipeg distribution home at 75 Bannerman Avenue is spent mostly listening to the effusive house manager, Edmund Struthers, over dinner. Although the farm school at Russell is no longer in operation, Struthers boasts about the many farm placements he has found for Barnardo boys coming west. With his waistcoat and fob watch and cheap cigar belching out smoke, George is reminded of pictures he has seen of Dr. Barnardo himself. Struthers has already lined up a job for him at a place called Ribstone, Alberta, a tiny farm community some 280 kilometres east of Edmonton, straddling the Saskatchewan border. Actually, Struthers can hardly take the credit. The Winnipeg distribution home has been greatly assisted by the Hudson's Bay Company Overseas Settlement Branch, which had advised him of the Ribstone placement for George in a letter dated October 16, 1928.[25]

September 1929. Though his encounter with the Hobdays had been brief, George's impression of them is lasting. He writes John Hobday from his placement in Ribstone, Alberta on September 22, 1929: "Dear Sir. You will be surprised to hear from me. I am at my second job and like it very much; have been here nine months. We have been very busy lately with the hay; there is not much grain around here. I am just fine in health and hope you are the same. Remember me to Mrs. Hobday and your son. Please send me Mr. Nun's address. I think this is all for now and would [like to] hear from you. Thanking you for helping me on, I remain yours truly, George Evans. P.S. Please excuse bad writing."[26]

The "Mr. Nun" George writes of is Ernest Nunn, an orphan whose life goal had been to work for Barnardo's. He had worked for a child rescue organization in Dublin and when the opportunity for an interview with the doctor himself arose in 1895, Nunn jumped at the chance. Dr. Barnardo could only offer him a job as night watchman at Stepney Causeway but it was enough. Then in 1903 Nunn accompanied one of the first shiploads of boys bound for the Russell, Manitoba Farm Home. By 1920, he had moved to Canada to supervise the shipments of children arriving from Britain. He made an effort to visit as many as possible of the thousands of children scattered throughout Ontario's vast countryside. Many would later recall him arriving at a homestead by horse and buggy and his quiet, kind manner as he interviewed them to make sure they were being treated fairly.[27]

FROM THIS POINT ON, George's tracks grow steadily fainter, as if buried in the accumulating snows of a Prairie winter. One wonders what use a bootmaker would have been to a farmer living in a remote part of Alberta. But by George's letter it appears he was content with the work, and as long as one had a strong back, bringing in the hay didn't require much training. As with Cyril William Joyce, who had arrived in Alberta just a couple of years earlier, George had the misfortune to begin his working career just as the economy plunged into the Great Depression. The Prairie provinces were hit particularly hard, due in part to cultivation practices that had resulted in dust storms during drought periods. Many would be forced to leave for other parts of Canada where there might be a hope of getting work.

In the meantime, George was not quite as alone in the world as he may have thought. His foster parents the Clapps are anxious to re-establish contact and begin as early as 1929 to seek him out. Mrs. Clapp writes the Winnipeg distributing home on January 3, 1929. "I have been informed to write to you, asking if you will kindly let me know the address of George Evans. He was supposed to have gone out to Canada last autumn and I have not heard from him. He knows my address. He left me at the age of 14 years old. And after a time went to Goldings to learn the boot trade, which he did. But it did not turn out successful. I should be very glad if you would let me know his address."[28]

To his credit, Struthers wastes no time trying to pass along Mrs. Clapp's letter, which had been copied to the Hudson's Bay Company Overseas Settlement Branch. In a letter dated January 18, 1929 Struthers writes to George care of LL Pound at Ribstone. "I hope all is well with you and I am now writing you a few lines to let you know that your old friend Mrs. Clapp, who gives her address as 38 Nansen Road, Ipswich, Suffolk, England, would be very pleased if you would drop her a few lines, letting her know how everything is moving in your part of the world. I know you are likely too busy to communicate with the writer but a short message which you could write on a card would be gratefully received." Struthers, however, underestimates the relationship between George and Mrs. Clapp, calling her a "friend," while in her letter she notes that George is her "foster son."[29]

July 24, 1935. The Clapp family once again tries to contact George through Barnardo's, this time because Mrs. Clapp has died. Their letters are all returned by the postmaster. Barnardo's tries to contact George, writing his employer, Mr. Kinney of Three Hills, Alberta, and the postmaster. But by now George has already moved on. "I understand he worked for you some time, but may now have gone elsewhere," writes Barnardo's staff. "Any news of his whereabouts you can send me in enclosed stamped envelope will be very much appreciated." A photo had somehow been passed along to George showing Mr. and Mrs. Clapp with son Vic, daughter-in-law Ena and a grandchild just three weeks old. On the back of the picture is the date it was taken: August 1934, with the notation: "The last photo of poor Mother, she was not well then." Another photo taken in 1935 shows Vic standing by Mrs. Clapp's grave.[30]

An agent from the Hudson's Bay Company Overseas Settlement Branch responds to the Clapp family on August 2, 1935: "In further reference to your enquiry about George, I wrote to Mr. Kinney, his former employer at Three Hills, Alberta, who has written today to say that he left him on the 15th February last, to take up work in a box factory in Calgary, Alberta. George has never written since. We will keep your enquiry in mind."[31]

Ma and Pa Clapp would have been happy to know that George had married Grace Margaret McCulloch in 1936, while working at a coal mine in Coleman, Alberta. George tells his bride that he is 25 years old, although he is actually 27. In fact, he doesn't know his own birthdate. Their three sons are all born in Coleman — John Robert "Jack," born August 29, 1936; Ronald James, born September 15, 1938; and David George, born September 29, 1940.[32] It's unknown whether George was able to contact the Clapps, though he seems to have contacted Ena during the war.

September 28, 1940. George enlists in the Canadian Armed Forces at Coleman, Alberta. While stationed for training at Montreal, he writes the Barnardo's Home in Toronto. But by now the home has been closed, with the last shipment of children arriving on July 8, 1939.[33] Britain had set up the Children's Overseas Reception Board (CORB) in anticipation of removing British children to safer shores, but the sinking of the SS *City of Benares* on September 17, 1940 had scuttled the program. The ship had on board 90 children bound for Canada. A German U-boat torpedo struck the ship on the port side below the cabins where many of the children were quartered. The attack claimed the lives of 134 of the 197 passengers — including 70 children — as well as 131 of the 200-member crew.[34]

The letter answering George was likely written by George Black, who had set up an Aftercare office at 466 Briar Hill Avenue in Toronto.[35] "We were pleased to have a letter from you after such a long time, and are most interested to see that you have enlisted in His Majesty's Forces. I wonder what unit you are in? Do let us know in the enclosed envelope." George has apparently asked after someone named Mary but the letter leaves a blank where her last name should be. As with George himself, Mary has moved on. "Mrs. Hobday tells me that she has not heard from Mary for some time and the last letter we sent to her was returned, so we do not know where she is living now." Black urges George to visit the London headquarters of Barnardo's when he is posted over-seas, but braces him for the wartime scene: "You will be sorry to know that they have been through a very trying time, having been bombed three or four times and suffering a great deal of damage — all the large stores of clothing, food, toys, literature, etc. being destroyed. Mercifully however no one was hurt. It always cheers them up so much to see one of their 'Old' Boys from Canada."[36]

The next time we hear from George, he is writing from Ballater, Aberdeenshire, in Scotland, some 65 kilometres inland from the east coast city of Aberdeen. George is serving with the forestry unit in Scotland, where he will spend the duration of the war. With shipping lanes to Britain severely restricted, a need arises for more timber to support the coal mines, a vital part of the war effort. The wood is used as "pit props," structural support for the mines. George's experience in the coalfields of southern Alberta has given him the experience needed to know how to build such props. And Canadians have a reputation as first-class lumberjacks.[37]

On November 9, 1939 British Secretary of State for Domin-ion Affairs had sent a telegram to Newfoundland Governor Sir Humphrey Walwyn seeking 2,000 men "capable of good work with axe and hand saw" to be sent to Britain to work in its forests. Newfoundland's Commissioner of Natural Resources responded by sending out a call for volunteers by radio broadcast on Novem-ber 17. Although the British government had suggested making the unit a civilian corps, the Newfoundland government passed the Newfoundland Forestry Act, authorizing the formation of the Newfoundland Overseas Forestry Unit (NOFU). The British gov-ernment was scrambling to get enough timber supply, so to get the men started they sent them to the Scottish Lowlands to live in two deserted army camps.[38]

By spring 1940 the NOFU foresters had completed building the Glenmuick Camp in Pannanich Wood near the River Dee. Although only a remnant of the great Caledon Forest, it's a setting worthy of the great forests of Western Canada, with massive Cal-edonian Pine soaring to 120 metres. The Newfoundland lumberjacks build cabins in a clearing at Dalmochie in true Canadian style, using rough-hewn logs draft-proofed with moss. When completed, the camp consists of a cookhouse, a recreation hut and three bunkhouses, each sleeping 20 men. Terraced into the mountainside is a second row of bunkhouses, a washroom, staff room, and office, and smaller buildings for tools and stores. Although the setting is rustic, the camp is built to modern standards of hygiene. Clean water is piped in from a reservoir, with wastewater treated in an irrigation plant below the camp. To service the horses used in logging, stables and a blacksmith shop are added. Like the Newfoundlanders, George is paid $2 a day for his labour, of which $1 is to be sent home to family.[39]

May 25, 1943. George has been asked by the military authorities to supply them with a birth certificate. He's beginning to wonder if he has any relatives in England, not having seen any of them since he was an infant. George writes Barnardo's London office from the camp at Ballater, seeking information. "Dear Sirs. I am writing to you wondering if you can give me any information about my past such as age, birthplace and if I have any relations. I am an old 'Barnardo boy' having been boarded out at Mrs. Clapp's, 23 Alston Road, Ipswich." Like many child immigrants sent to Canada, he lacks even a birth certificate, and thinks he is two years younger. George relates his chronology with Barnardo's, including his emigration to Canada in September 1928. "While at Aboyne recently I talked to a lady who was with the Barnardo's Band and this lady kindly advised me to write to you and thought you would be able and only too pleased to give me any information possible," he concludes hopefully. "While in Canada I made several donations to Jarvis Street. Thanking you in anticipation, I am Yours Very Sincerely, George Evans."[40]

Barnardo's London office promptly sends a reply from its CEO TF Tucker, who says that he has no information but will search the records.[41] George writes back on June 6 from the camp at Ballater. "I received with appreciation your letter and although I am disappointed at the absence of information; I have still some hopes that I happened to have some relatives some place. One of the main things I would like to know is my age; at present I am going as 33 on May 31st but my foster sister at Ipswich says I must be older than that. I hope you can give me something definite on this subject." He promises to send Barnardo's a small donation after payday but reminds them that, "a soldier's pay is not very high and at present it practically takes all for cigarettes and toilet accessories."[42]

June 10, 1943. A watershed moment for any Home Child — George learns that he does indeed have relatives living in England. Barnardo's writes him a letter announcing that they have located his personal history files, "which confirm that you were born on the 31st May 1908 in Evesham Institution. We do not know anything of your father, but we see your mother's name was stated to be Emily Sarah Evans, and at the time of your admission her address was 52 Norton near Evesham, but this was of course in July 1909 and since then we have no further news. You had a half sister, aged three, and she was with your mother. Your grandfather Thomas Evans aged 52, was also at the same address." The letter goes on to list his relatives at the time of his admission to Barnardo's Homes, including uncles, aunts, and grandparents.[43]

It's not known whether George spent any of his leaves during the war trying to locate his birth family. The passage of nearly 35 years has likely scattered them across the English countryside, though probably not far from Evesham. The letter writer from Barnardo's is unable to give him more up-to-date information and wishes George luck tracing his family. He is so broke it takes him several months to come up with the cash for his birth certificate. It is finally sent to him with a letter dated November 12, noting that the balance from his contribution has been used to enroll him as a member of the Barnardo "Old Boys" Club.[44]

His marriage to Grace McCulloch will become yet another casualty of war. Grace had learned that while George was in Scotland he'd been with another woman. The marriage to Grace had been rocky from the start. She had been barely more than a child bride when she married him at age 17. Marrying during the Great Depression hadn't helped matters. George had spent most of his time either looking for work or working away from home. Grace will later realize that of the nine years of their marriage, only about two had actually been spent together. Although sporadic attempts are made to save the marriage, within a year or two of the end of the war, it, too, is over. For George it's an ironic situation for a former child immigrant with no ties to his family of origin. And a bone-crusher of a choice to have to make: return to his Canadian family or divorce Grace and remain with his wartime lover Dorothy and her two children. He chooses the latter, though they never marry.[45]

January 16, 1951. Hillcrest, Alberta, 10 a.m. George slips on a blue wool overcoat and rubber overshoes, absent-mindedly taking his grey tweed cap from its hook. He empties a box of shells into his coat pocket, leaving the box on Dorothy's sewing machine. She'd come to Canada to be with him after the war and found herself in the foothills of southern Alberta coal country. The softly rolling hills stretching eastward from the mountains are a white ocean in wintertime, threatening to swallow a lonely soul whole. The postwar economy is still some years away from booming and George has found himself out of work again.

"I'm headed over to Coleman to see if they're hiring at the International Mine," he shouts out, one hand already on the doorknob.

"Alright, dear. Can you get a lift from Hank?"

"Nah, it's only six miles. I can walk."

"Will I see you at suppertime?"

A pause. "Maybe." Before the discussion can go any further, George quickly slams the door behind him.

The winter dark falls fast and early. Dinnertime comes, but no sign of George. Dorothy feels more than just the bite of winter cold. A nagging worry nips at her consciousness, a worry she puts down with a stoic shrug. "He must have got himself a job, and has been put to work right away on the afternoon shift."

The next morning, when she goes to her sewing machine to

repair a hem, she discovers the empty box of shells and realizes that George has taken the .22-calibre rifle. "Maybe Daddy's gone hunting," her daughter Christina chirps hopefully.

"Yes, perhaps he's gone rabbit hunting again," she says, reassuring herself as much as her daughter. "No use calling police now," she tells herself.

But once again when evening falls George has not returned. The reassurance of the morning has given way to barely suppressed panic. She phones the local RCMP detachment.

"Blairmore RCMP detachment, Sergeant Charles Hetherington speaking. How can I help you?"

"My — my, oh dear, I don't know how to say this. My husband George Evans left home yesterday morning on his way to Coleman and hasn't come home yet."

"What was the purpose of his trip?" asks Sergeant Hetherington.

"He told me he was hoping to get a job at the International Mine."

"Hmm. Not sure they're hiring lately. But I'll check there first to see if George applied for work. If that doesn't pan out, we'll get a search party out at first light. Was he walking or driving?"

"He said he was going to walk."

"Hmm. Makes it a bit more complicated. He may have got lost in the snow. But don't worry, Mrs. Evans, we'll do our best."

"Oh, thank you Sergeant."

The International Mines lead turns up nothing. Complicating matters further for the RCMP search party, a bitter cold front settles in. Still, Sergeant Hetherington and his constables do their best, covering an extensive area. But George is not found.[46]

May 12, 1951. Three boys are out looking for horses that have gone astray. Brothers Leonard and George Beaver and Al Wood Bohmer are enjoying the fresh lilt of spring air and the stimulation of an afternoon's adventure. They are just a half kilometre from Hillcrest, about 15 metres off the old cemetery road, when one of the boys spots something odd — what appears to be a jumble of clothing beneath a secluded clump of trees. But when they get closer, the innocence of their day is shattered. They are standing over the badly decomposed body of a man.[47]

The boys race home to telephone the Blairmore RCMP. Before long police and Coroner Dr. DJ Liesemer of Coleman arrive to cordon off the site. A neighbour of George's from Hillcrest identifies his body. It's clear that the rifle had been fired. Dr. Liesemer and Sergeant Hetherington exchange nervous glances. This could mean suicide, but declaring such as the cause of death is every coroner's worst nightmare.

"At all costs, we must keep such speculations out of the public eye," says the coroner.

"Agreed," Sergeant Hetherington responds. "Will this mean an inquest?"

"Yes I think so. Even then we must be careful what we say, especially to the press. We have the widow and her children to consider. This will come as a terrible shock."

"Think this could be a hunting accident?" asks the sergeant, looking dubious. He is fully aware that George is a war veteran with military training in the use of weapons. An accident seems highly unlikely.

Dr. Liesemer avoids his glance. "Doubtful. Let's hope so. At this stage of decomposition it's hard to say, one way or the other. But doubtful."

George was just 43 at the time of his death. He died much as he had come into the world — a solitary figure in a landscape emptied of human contact.

THE REAL TRAGEDY of George Evans and of many Canadian child immigrants like him is that they were doubly robbed of family. George left this world never having known his mother or any of his other English relatives. Yet having any real connection with his own children was just as elusive. During the mid-1980s journalist Jane Cole Hamilton published an article in the *Toronto Star* based on interviews with elderly Home Children. Among them were men who found that their experiences in British orphanages and Canadian foster homes left an indelible mark on their emotional lives. "There was no affection," remembers James Rook. "No one ever touched me or gave me a hug. That was the hardest thing." This void of human warmth persisted into adulthood, even after marriage. "I never knew what love was," said Harold, "until I met my wife. It was difficult learning to love, because I just couldn't figure out what it was all about." Hamilton notes that it was no picnic for their wives, either. "Ken's wife Marge didn't find it easy being married to a man who'd been frozen into himself as a child. A man who had never in his life been given a present, and who didn't know where to start in the intricate give and take of marriage."[48]

Sadly, the frozen landscape of the Alberta winter in which George Evans died seems to have been reflected in his inner landscape. Dave Evans recalls of his parents that, "It was not a good marriage. My father often left for long periods of time. He was overseas for four years. When he came back the marriage ended in divorce. They tried for a while but just could not make things work. Later my mother learned he had another woman in England. He was a troubled man that no one could reach."[49]

This emotional deprivation echoes down the generations. Descendants often tell a tale of families wracked by emotional distance, depression and even second-generation suicides. This is the story the "official" version of Canadian history does not tell. Most stories of the Home Children focus on their "unique contribution to the building of our nation," concentrating on their hardiness. As researcher Andrew N. Morrison discovered when he interviewed Canadian Home Children, cultural conditioning and innate character has much to do with such resilience. Recent discoveries in the field of Early Childhood Education and epigenetics confirms that resilience is partly a function of the kind of treatment received during the critical birth to age five period. "You see, this stuff is generational," one respondent told Morrison. "I don't know if people understand this or not. Trauma does not go away, abuse does not go away. You get a successful life, you can have families, but those things are passed on."[50]

Coming from a culture that still held to traditional views of children as wholly subject to the authority of adults, many orphanage children and child immigrants were taught to simply "buck up and shut up." As adults they may have acknowledged having a difficult or painful childhood but felt the best way to cope was simply to get on with life. Some of Morrison's respondents even said they felt that childhood adversity strengthened them as adults.

Unfortunately, this was hardly the case for all of them, as George's story illustrates. As one descendant of a child immigrant told Morrison, "in my family, there's an awful lot of people that suffer from depression. . . . And I often wondered, Andrew, if it has anything to do with the attitude that my grandfather had. He didn't trust people particularly. . . . I think his soul was injured and it never recovered."[51]

George and Grace, with sons David and Ron, probably soon after George joined the Canadian Army in 1940. Dave and Janet Evans collection.

CHAPTER 6

Joe's Story —
A Barnardo's Poster Boy in the West

NOVEMBER 14, 1890. Young Joe Harwood sits in a police cell, his foot tapping uncontrollably. From time to time he runs his fingers through his hair in an attempt to calm himself. Just two weeks ago he'd celebrated his 20th birthday in modest fashion at the Fleming farm. Now he finds himself here, his mind spinning, his young life already flashing before his clenched eyes. *What have I done? Dear God, what have I done?*

Joe thinks of the day he first went to Barnardo's soup kitchen in London at the Youths Labour House. It hardly seems possible that wasn't even two years ago. Not a farthing in his pocket, like so many of the other boys. Some of them his age but many of them as young as 13 — the age he'd left Hertford's Greycoat Free School to go to work.[1] And both older and younger boys had been chatting excitedly about going to Canada where a young man with hard work could become rich. It was a far cry from the spartan surroundings of this soup kitchen with its bare benches and tables, and the street-worn clothes draped from their bodies.

What would Father and Mother think of me now? With 11 children to feed, honest John had laboured at the same job as a grocer's carman for 20 years, earning a measly 20 shillings a week. Rent took four shillings a week. By the time Joe had turned 13, more hungry babies were being born to the cramped Harwood cottage at 53 Porthill, Hertford.[2] It was time to start earning some money to help supplement the family's meagre income. *Poor Mother, she always looked as if it took every ounce of her will to keep going.* His eldest brother Frederick had started work early, too. There was little choice.[3]

But something in Joe couldn't settle down like his father, John. He'd been so excited to learn that Father had found him a position as pageboy with Dr. Spall in Hammersmith. He was fired from that job — a blow that had hit him hard at 13. Then it had been Mr. Maffia the Hertford silversmith. Joe soon learned that "errand boy" or "pageboy" was a short step away from "slave." After eight months he'd had enough. He took another job as pageboy with the Reverend Mr. Jackson at Waltham Cross. That had lasted nine months before he couldn't take it anymore. Was it boredom this time? The Reverend could be a colossal bore at times. This time when he left he told no one, not even his parents. The great metropolis of London seemed to draw him in, promising a new start.[4]

But his new start was not to be — yet. He had no better success in the great city of Empire than he had in Hertford. Word got back to Father and Mother that he was sleeping in a common lodging house, a place where sailors, hopeless drunks, and loose women shouted at all hours, wept, moaned, and shrieked like damned souls. His father may be poor working class but he wasn't having Joe living in those conditions. John scraped together the train fare to bring Joe home. *I thought that might be it then,* Joe muses, *my new start. But no.* Father had found him a position with Mr. Hardman, the butcher. He was aptly named. Who wouldn't become hard, earning a living by slaughtering animals day in and day out? What does that do to a soul? But the man was impossible, the work disgusting. Soon he was off for lighter work as a pantry boy at Simmonds Hotel, Brook Street, Grosvenor Square. That fell apart in only a month when he got on the wrong side of the head waiter. Another job as steward's boy waited at the Prince of Wales Hotel in Scarborough. *Oi! Such posh digs, these hotels! But not for the likes of me.* It was almost worse than the butcher shop, having to kowtow to rich folk all the time. Knowing he was eating stewed potatoes and onion while the posh folk ate three-course meals on bone china in the next room. Yet again he'd clashed with the staff and lost his job by the end of the season. *I used to wonder when my life would get started.*[5]

He decided the call of the open air was just the ticket. Followed the roving crowds of itinerant workers hop picking, fruit picking, following the seasons.[6] There at least he could enjoy the camaraderie of field workers, the lunchtime brotherhood as meals were unwrapped from handkerchiefs. Best of all, there were no bosses to chew down his neck if he slowed up a bit. It was all piecework, paid by the bushel. He'd grown stronger with each year, better able to handle the work. He loved the gentle green bosom of the English countryside. Problem was, the pay was still miniscule. *At this rate, mate, I'll be grinding 'til I'm 70 before I can afford to marry,* Joe remembers thinking.

So he'd ended up in London again when picking season ended, not a shilling to his name. Found another job doing errands but yet again things didn't work out. Managed to live hand-to-mouth on those mean streets a couple of months before winter really hit home. A younger boy he'd met on the streets told him about Dr. Barnardo's and his soup kitchen at the Youths Labour House.

"'Ere, you oughter see the Doctor, lad."

"Doctor? I ain't got no money for a doctor."

"Cor, mate — I mean Doctor Barnardo's Homes — no child refused. Three squares a day and a cot at night. Clean sheets — imagine that, mate! They works you pretty hard, but ain't it better than going on the tramp?"

The boys had to listen to one of Barnardo's staff talking over their meals. While most of the boys slurped and ate like emaciated strays, Joe recalls being fascinated by the man's sermon. Not the religious part — he could get that any Sunday in any parish church. It was what he said about Dr. Barnardo's grand vision of rescuing the waifs of Empire, turning them into well-trained, useful citizens. It plucked at the guilt he had for being so unlike his steady father. And it gave him hope that here might be his new start. When the man spoke of sending "the select of our flock" to Canada, something in him knew this was it — this was indeed his new start at last. By the end of the speech he'd queued with the other boys, eager to sign up.[7]

And before he knew it he was standing with a large group of boys on the docks at Liverpool, staring up at the impressive steamship *SS Vancouver*, his Barnardo's trunk at his side. A date he'll never forget: June 23, 1889.[8] Just six months after checking into Youths Labour House. Some boys had to wait years for this, until they'd grown up enough, though many on this journey were still far younger than his 18 years. Joe recalls being struck by the small but riveting figure of Dr. Barnardo in his slick top hat, spats on his polished shoes, cane, and a fine summer suit. Like himself, the Doctor was barely over five feet tall, yet when he spoke it was with the voice of a giant, a man possessed of the Holy Spirit. He'd actually forgotten most of the speech now but at the time it was like nothing he'd ever heard before from any minister in any church. When the Doctor had concluded with, "Work hard, my lads, be honest and truthful as good Christians ought, and a credit to your British blood," Joe had been among the loudest sending up a parting cheer. "God bless you! God bless you, Sir!"

The journey across the Atlantic had been much like any other, starting with the excitement and mystery of the ship, the jovial faces of captain and crew. But when the heavy weather set in, Joe was recruited to help with the younger boys, who tended to suffer more terribly from seasickness. Partly that meant keeping them busy — playing games, singing songs, running laps — anything to distract them from their uneasy stomachs. He chuckles, remembering them. *Poor little blighters, never even seen a steamship before, much less lived on one for nearly two weeks.*

Joe smiles as he remembers first setting foot on the docks at Quebec. There was Mr. Struthers, ready to take the older boys with him on the train to the Farm Home in Manitoba. Much taller than Dr. Barnardo, he seemed the perfect character for the job of Farm Home manager — solidly built, with a forthright, open manner and a ready smile shining through that elegant beard. Instead of the Doctor's silk top hat Struthers wore a more understated but still neat Homburg and a tweed suit. His hair was thick compared to Dr. Barnardo's thinning pate — the very picture of health, nourished on farm food. *Dear God, what have I done? Is this how I've repaid this fine gentleman?*

Joe couldn't believe how long it took to get to the Farm Home at Russell, Manitoba. If he'd been on a train in Britain they'd long since have reached the far north of Scotland. Yet the Canadian landscape rolled on and on, mile after mile, day after day. Ontario alone was massive and took two days to cross. Its lushly wooded, gently undulating hills reminded him of the English countryside. And then the gradual levelling of landscape as the prairies rolled into view from the train windows. By the time they got to Yorkton to get off the train and travel the rest of the distance by horse team, the land had flattened entirely. It was as if the horizon had no end. Joe Harwood might as well have been on the moon, the landscape was so strange.

At first the novelty of his new situation agreed with him. Not so much the chores around the farm — this was heavy work, starting before sun-up and only winding down after sunset. And he felt a natural affinity for the horses, these gentle yet powerful creatures so willing to do man's work. The other boys — really young men — could be cruel at times, especially to anyone the least bit different. But Joe had already worked with all kinds of rough and tough characters. That was no problem. Gradually he felt the old disaffection creeping in. *What is it with me? Why can't I settle? Has God placed some canker in my soul?*

Of course he knew the Farm Home was never meant to be a place to settle. It was Dr. Barnardo's springboard for launching new farmers into the Canadian West. But when he discovered what it actually cost to get started as a farmer, even here, where the Canadian government was letting young men have land on favourable terms, it rankled. Some boys had worked for years and only managed to save up $150. Yet ten times that was needed to get enough land and the basic equipment to set the first furrow in the ground. He never minded working, but this just seemed impossible. Night after night in his bunk he'd festered, the promise of the "golden bridge" seeming as elusive as a gold sovereign in a London gutter.

It had started small, with just a single tool, stashed in a pile of empty barrels behind a shed. *My savings account, I used to tell myself,* Joe recalls. Then one night the sudden stab of lantern light as the watchman caught him tucking away another implement. Quickly he'd explained himself and to his surprise, the night watchman was sympathetic. Told him a couple of the other boys had been doing the same. Only now Joe spent his exhausted nights itching with guilt, pricked by fear of being caught. Then when he left Russell to put his newfound Canadian farming skills into practice on the Fleming farm, he'd realized how impossible it would be to carry off all those tools without being noticed. *Come back for them another day*, he promised himself. And when Mrs. Fleming innocently wrote the Winnipeg Home for Joe's winter clothes, the jig was up. Within two weeks of his birthday, Mr. Struthers had sent a constable round to pick him up.[9]

And now here he sits on this hard bunk in a Canadian prairie jail made of planks, his foot still tapping the floor as if independent of his body. *How could I have been so stupid? So ungrateful to Dr. Barnardo? To Mr. Struthers? What was it the minister in Russell used to say about the Devil's temptations? Why, oh why did I give in?* An image of his father John, his weary mother Annie speeds his foot's nervous tempo, his face flushing in shame. *How could I do it? How could I shame them like this? Father, who's worked so hard for so little. Mother, whose life has wasted away caring for us.*

Afraid he'll break into tears, Joe scans the bare cell desperately for distraction. Nothing but a tiny patch of prairie sky outside the single barred window. He's already offered prayers, begging for a second chance, just one avenue of redemption in the seething metropolis of sin he's landed in. Then he remembers that tattered copy of *Ups & Downs*, Barnardo's Canadian newsletter, tucked into his jacket. He turns to the letters section, always crammed with glowing copy from Barnardo boys who are now men making their way successfully in the world. Though he never suspected for a moment they weren't genuine, they all read nearly the same: "Just wanted to let you know I got a good job helping with the dairy herd here. . . . Lost a few calves to wolves last winter. Never thought I'd see such cold but I like the work well enough. Hoping to save up for my first quarter section. Meantime here's a dollar toward the Old Boys fund with thanks to the Doctor and all his helpers for keeping up God's work."[10]

Joe looks up again at the barred window. He knows what a dollar is worth in labour. Some Barnardo boys were lucky if they made $25 a year over and above room and board. He knows what it takes for a kid from Hertford, Glasgow, Liverpool, or Dublin to part with a dollar. What it takes to earn that "buck," as the Canadians say. Yet here is a Barnardo boy sending some of the sweat of his brow to repay the good Doctor's kindness. Even as the poor lad nurtures hopes of buying his own farmland one day. *Maybe, just maybe there's still a chance for me*, Joe muses. *With enough hard work and the right opportunities. . . . Maybe Canada is my new start after all.*

Fortunately, Struthers is a kind man. After spending only one night in jail, Joe is released without being charged. He walks out with head held high, ready to begin again.

March 24, 1893. Clouds of dust plume behind wagons rattling along the streets of the newly bustling frontier town of Calgary, causing men to cough and women to breathe into handkerchiefs. The disastrous fire of November 1886 had caused city officials to pass an ordinance requiring all downtown buildings to be built of sandstone, lending an air of elegance to the fast-growing city.[11] Joe Harwood is hurrying along the boardwalk when he spots a gentleman he recognizes from four years ago when he arrived in Canada. The man is well dressed, with a bowler hat and long overcoat. At the same moment, the gentleman recognizes him and takes the initiative.

"Joseph Harwood, isn't it?" He extends a gloved hand.

"Yes — I'm sorry, I do know you, sir, but — "

"Watkins. How are you, my boy? I hadn't heard since you left the Farm Home."

"Yes, of course, Mr. Watkins. I'm well, very well, thank you. I'm married now and have a small house here."

"Ah, delightful! And who is your lady wife then?"

"Mary Bioletti. Our first anniversary will be June 21st of this year. As fine a helpmate as could be asked for, sir."

"Wonderful. You have plenty of work then?"

"Yes, sir. Plenty — the place is booming, as you can see. You've heard of Burns Meats? Well I've worked for Mr. Patrick Burns here. Worked on CPR construction gangs between here and Edmonton too."

"Fine, fine." Watkins pauses as if considering his next words. "You haven't written the Home for some time, Struthers tells me."

"Ah, no Mr. Watkins. Been very busy working."

"Shall I write him then on your behalf?"

"If you like. Please tell him I'm happily married and have my own little home."

"I shall indeed, my boy, I shall indeed. Well, good day to you."[12]

With a tip of his bowler Watkins turns to cross the street. Joe shuffles on, feeling a pang of guilt. Why hadn't he written yet? Three years had gone by since that terrible night in jail. It was true, he had been busy working. But it was nothing to write home about — working for a livery stable doing deliveries, working as a plasterer in the many new homes being built, even delivering messages. Anything to keep food on the table. Joe is so buried in thought he nearly crashes into a woman wrapped in a beaver collar. "Pardon me, ma'am." He tips his hat to her politely.

Truth is, I'm still an odd jobber, Joe muses. *Just like I was in England. What can I possibly report to Barnardo's compared to the successes of other Old Boys?*

Still, Watkins' reminder has pricked his conscience. Success or no success, he should write Barnardo's Winnipeg office and let them know how he's doing. Night after night he tries to write the letter, but finds himself unable to summon the words. *What can I possibly say? I have so little to report.* Finally in April of 1894 — a year after his encounter with Watkins — he forces out a few terse lines: "I am pleased to say I am in good health. I am married, working in Calgary plastering. There is plenty of work here."[13]

Joe Harwood's time is yet to come, though far sooner than he thinks.

March 3, 1896. Joe sits down by lamplight at the end of a long hard day working at the stable. He has great news to tell Barnardo's — at last. "I am now living at Vernon in the Okanagan Valley of British Columbia and am working as a market gardener and doing odd jobs. I have a lot in the city and a line on 10 acres that I intend to buy as soon as I can save the money. Land is cheap out here and things are moving fast. Will keep you posted."[14]

For Barnardo's this letter comes as a kind of détente in their chilly relations with Joe Harwood following the Farm Home incident. On March 26 they dispatch a cheery letter from the Winnipeg office asking Joe to provide details of his career to date for possible inclusion in *Ups & Downs*. It's just the chance he's been waiting for to begin making good with Barnardo's. By May 25 they have a letter from him detailing his exploits to date. But sadly it doesn't make the cut. As if confirming his suspicions that he simply isn't successful enough yet, his letter does not appear in the newsletter. Or he may merely have fallen victim to the editor's impersonal blue pencil. But Joe remains undaunted. If success means working harder, then so be it. Here in the Okanagan Valley there are opportunities dripping from every bush. The City of Vernon had only just been incorporated on December 31, 1892, and the city fathers are anxious for development to move ahead quickly.[15]

JOE'S TIMING COULDN'T HAVE BEEN BETTER. The Canadian West — widely promoted as the "Last Best West" — is only just being opened up in the 1880s with the help of federal government land grants. At that time the three Prairie provinces are still known as the North West Territories. With the completion of the national railway in 1885 at Craigellachie, near Revelstoke, British Columbia it is at last to be fully opened to European settlement. Barnardo's training farm at Russell, Manitoba — 360 kilometres northwest of Winnipeg — is designed to help open up the Canadian West with a steady supply of well-trained young farmers of British stock. The first shipment of boys arrived at the Farm Home on April 15, 1888, a year before Joe's arrival in Canada. For many of these British émigrés, their first exposure to a Manitoba winter will be a severe shock to the system. Farm manager Edmund Amos Struthers noted of that first winter in 1888 that the boys had "proved their pluck and suitability in a most encouraging degree."[16]

As with all of Dr. Barnardo's building projects, the Russell Farm Home had taken some years to become reality after the initial purchase of property in 1881. During his first visit to Canada in 1884, Dr. Barnardo negotiated with the Manitoba government and the North West Railway for land grants to bring the property up to the size he felt was necessary — 4,030 hectares. He also took time that autumn to visit another new acquisition — the Hazelbrae distribution home in Peterborough, Ontario. By the time of his second visit to Canada in 1887, construction at Russell was underway. The farmhouse, built in 1887–88, housed 100 boys, with offices, laundry, bathrooms, hospital, store, and kitchen. Other buildings included a cottage for farm manager Struthers, a large barn, a stable for 45 cows, two stables for horses, a feeding shed and two piggeries accommodating 300 hogs. Water was pumped by windmills with a reliable source in the Assiniboine River, which meandered through part of the farm.

Besides a garden of some 20 acres, explains British Home Children Canada:

> Also on these grounds was a creamery. In the summer season wagons were sent through some 200 square miles collecting milk and cream from the farmers for manufacture into but-

ter. A trained and certified butter-maker was kept in constant employ of the farm. The boys drafted for the Manitoba Farm were sent out from England under the agreement to work on the farm for one year for a wage, with the average term lasting about 8 months before the boys were placed out. They were awakened at 5 a.m. with a bugle, with an hour and a half break midday, and worked till 6 p.m. A short prayer service was conducted twice during the day, by the house master in the morning and by the manager before retiring in the evening. On Sundays a full service was provided by a clergyman from Russell.[17]

The Farm Home also featured a well-stocked library. Whatever their faults, 19th century evangelists like Dr. Barnardo placed a high premium on literacy. Christmas concerts and amateur dramatics were performed by the boys — a highlight of the year for hard-working Manitoba farmers with few options for entertainment.[18] Barnardo's Winnipeg branch office serves as a distribution point and way station for young Brits hoping to make their futures in farming:

We beg to remind those who intend joining the excursions that most of the special trains leave Toronto during the afternoon of the days advertised, and as in most cases they will have time to spare in the city, they will be cordially welcomed at the Home during their stay, while on their arrival at Winnipeg we shall be pleased to have them make their headquarters at the Home until they can settle where to locate. 115 Pacific Avenue is about seven minutes' walk from the station, and they will find Mr. White able and willing to give them full information and reliable advice for the direction of their movements, and a talk with him will probably prove very useful to any of the newcomers. A letter of introduction to Mr. White, while not in the least necessary to secure his good offices, will be gladly given or sent to anyone on application.[19]

Barnardo's partners with the CPR and Grand Trunk railways to promote settlement in Canada's newly opening "North West." Opportunities in the Prairie provinces are regularly promoted in *Ups & Downs*:

> We anticipate that a good many of our bigger lads will avail themselves of the extremely low rates offered to take a trip to the golden West. We strongly advise their doing so, and to make their minds up to stay there. As mere farm labourers the difference in wages between the East and West is perhaps not sufficiently high at the present time to offer any special inducement, but on the prairie lands of the North-West, as we have so often pointed out, our lads can aspire to rise beyond the position of labourers and have a grand opportunity of establishing themselves on farms of their own, where, under ordinary circumstances, they may hope in a few years to reach independence and prosperity. . . . Everywhere men are to be met who came to the country with little or no capital, but to-day have farms, good buildings, teams of horses, bands of cattle and sheep that they can count by scores, in some cases by hundreds.[20]

It's precisely these kinds of dispatches that draw young men like Joe Harwood "Westward Ho!" But it's no easy path to wealth for the labouring class. In what he will later recall as "a tough time," Joe works on a farm near Brandon, Manitoba and in Moosomin, near Qu'Appelle, Saskatchewan driving oxen and then in railway construction near Regina.[21] Letters from Barnardo boys printed in *Ups & Downs* capture a flavour of the country that Harwood worked in, including the Qu'Appelle Valley. Alfred Hanwell writes that, "I would rather be in the valley than on the prairie. If you talk to people on the prairie about a storm they tell you, you don't know what a storm is in the valley. There is a lot of bush and trees, and in the summer there are cherries, which make nice jam. The climate up here is very cold but dry, and with plenty of clothing I can stand it alright; windy days are bad. I thank you for getting me such a nice place and getting me so near my brother."[22]

Many of the farming families in Saskatchewan are of German descent, including those of the Mennonite faith and Russian Doukhobors. "I am situated with German people," writes William H. Harding. "They are very good to me and my food is just the same as they have themselves. My master has 384 acres of land. He has been in this country 25 years now." Harding's master writes to say of Harding that, "So far I am very much satisfied with him, just as if he is my own child." German farmer John Posehn writes of Barnardo boy Edward Bishop that he is "a brave boy. . .very kind to the children, and that is worth quite a bit." Bishop had written that he had learned to speak German just as well as his master, who gave him "a very good home." A young lad named Charlie Brown had written Barnardo's that he could "write German, read German, talk German high or low," and that he has "lots to eat, drink and sleep." In characteristic fashion, the German diet is rich and satisfying to a fast-growing boy. "There is no cake or pie or preserves like in Ontario; here is better. A fellow never would get strong from that; but he gets strong from buttermilk, thick milk, sour milk and potatoes. That is what a fellow needs if he wants to be a German boy."[23]

JUNE 20, 1898. Joe writes Edmund Struthers, the first time he has addressed the Farm Home manager since being released from jail. It's a poignant moment for Joe. This time he has something truly exciting to report — he is now the owner of his own express and delivery service. It's exactly the kind of success story Barnardo's uses to great advantage in promoting its work in the pages of *Ups & Downs*. Joe checks the post office anxiously over the coming months, hoping to see his letter in its pages.

Finally the January 1899 issue arrives. As if alluding obliquely to Joe's trouble with the Farm Home, the *Ups & Downs* editor notes that, "Harwood, without doubt, has had his Ups & Downs, not only in the Home, but after going out to a situation, and I can believe he many a time was tempted to look back in the furrow."[24] The "never look back" adage is one assiduously promoted by Barnardo's. The farming metaphor may be apt, but Joe has moved on to the livery and hauling business. One can hear him addressing Struthers as a son speaks to a father — it's the chance he's been waiting for, both to prove himself and make amends:

Dear Sir. In answer to your kind and welcome letter, I was very glad to receive it. It made me feel very thankful that the Doctor and his helpers had so much interest in me. Although so many years have passed, I have not forgotten, and cannot forget, those who had my interests to their heart. It often comes before me as a picture just as real as if it was only yesterday. It does not seem long since I first saw you at Quebec. I shall never forget the way in which you cherished us all. I long to see the Home and your face again, so that I can show you that I do appreciate everything that has been done for me. I often feel that in the Home was the making of me morally and spiritually. I often pray that God may bless the institution, and I hope some day to show my gratitude by helping the cause along.

You understand that I have bought out an express business, and it has taken out all the cash I had, and I have had lots of other expense [sic] to get things in shape. . . . I have got opposition on the road, but with the old motto that we had in the Home, "Grit, Go and Gumption," and doing to all men as they should do to me, I feel that a share of the trade is mine. I hope to work up a business that will surprise myself. I am under no obligations to anyone, only to God, who has spared me and helps me by His Grace, to do that which is right.[25]

Joe proudly relates that he is the owner of "a frame house 20 feet square," a garden, and a large stable. His next comments reflect the tenuous background of many working class English families: "So you see by having no rent to pay I have no one that can come and tell me to get out. What I have got I have had to work hard for; but I thank God for my health and wealth. . . ." He concludes his letter by noting that the *Ups & Downs* newsletter, with its relentless optimism, "does me good every time I see it and my wife thinks that it is the best paper that comes into the house." He keeps private his more personal attachment to the newsletter.[26]

By 1900 *Ups & Downs* could report that the prairie provinces have "attracted great numbers of farmers' sons and farm hands from Ontario and the older provinces and depleted the usual sources of farm labour." The result was a demand too large for Barnardo's to keep up with. "We have now nearly 800 youngsters in the West who have been placed out from the Winnipeg Home since its opening in November 1896. Most of our little lads in the West are engaged, or indentured, for four years, to receive board, lodging and clothing and a hundred dollars in cash, payable at the end of the term."[27]

May 1902. Harwood writes Barnardo's again, noting that *Ups & Downs* "does me and my wife good; I feel myself connected and interested as much and more than ever I did in my life." Joe's hard work is paying dividends. "I am gaining ground with my business; I have six horses working, running a light and heavy rig. I am thankful to say that I have good health and strength, and family are doing well. Sometimes I come across boys who have been through its doors. Like myself, they have never lost the lessons and the manliness that was put in them while in the Homes. I hope some day that you, Sir, will be able to give me a call. I am sure you would enjoy the trip down the Okanagan Valley, as it is the garden of British Columbia. We can grow everything but oranges."[28]

The *Ups & Downs* editor had hinted at the darker side to Joe's experiences on the prairies. Now he expresses wistfulness for the farm school run by Struthers. "I hope some day to be able to visit the Farm Home. Though years have rolled on since I was there, I feel a longing to see it again. I hope to have a good summer's work this summer and make the business twice as big. I feel that I owe the Institution a good deal, and hope some day to make it practical; but I am anxious to get a heavy truck and heavy team, so that I will be able to take everything that comes along. I must conclude with thanking you for your great kindness to me and the bridge that carried me over."[29]

December 4, 1903. Joe is seated in the office of Mr. E. Davis, Secretary for Barnardo's Winnipeg branch. He's grinning ear to ear as Davis writes in the record book: "Joseph Harwood called this day en route to England to visit his friends. He is married with five children (boys), sole owner of express wagons, drays, etc. Has a five-year contract from Dominion Express Company and CPR; also runs stage. Reports himself well and doing well. $700 invested in stocks and also has considerable real estate. His business, property, etc. is assessed at $8,000." By December 30 he is in Barnardo's London headquarters at Stepney Causeway, sharing the news of his good fortune with staff there. Unlike Walter Roberts or George Evans, for whom Barnardo's "golden bridge" had become a bridge of straw, for Joe Harwood its promise has proven true.[30]

JOE SEEMS TO DISCOVER early an innate genius for public relations in business — to Vernon residents he is known as "Sunshine Joe." He seems to adjust easily to rapidly changing times. Before the advent of refrigerators, he hauls ice for customers. By 1910 his livery business has expanded to 40 horses. His motto is "nothing too big or too small." Then in 1917 Joe takes advantage of a new technology — automobiles — and becomes the first person in Vernon to use a truck for deliveries. Mary is no less a hard worker, doing the books for the family business while raising five sons and two daughters. She is quite capable of driving a team of horses when necessary. Joe's youngest brother Edward Gilbert "Ted" Harwood, hearing of his big brother's success out West, emigrates from England in 1912, arriving in Vernon after a brief stint with the Royal Navy. As a lad of 18 Ted had served with Captain Robert Falcon Scott of Antarctic fame on the HMS *Bulwark*. Another younger brother, Robert, joins the growing Harwood clan in the North Okanagan. Ted works for Joe in his cartage business but soon leaves over a pay dispute. When the family firm celebrates its 50th anniversary on July 15, 1948, "Joe Harwood, cartage, baggage and express" boasts a fleet of 12 modern trucks.[31]

Joe's genial public persona makes him a natural for politics and he takes an early interest in civic affairs. He runs successfully for a seat on the Vernon School Board in 1908, described in a July 1937 *Vernon News* story as "the niche that delighted his heart." Testifying to his popularity with voters, he is re-elected for 28 consecutive years, becoming president of the BC School Trustees Association in 1923. Despite his success, however, his experience as a working class Brit leaves a deep mark. "I could have gone farther, been more successful, if I had only had a better education," Joe tells the *Vernon News* reporter. "And that is why I have always worked as hard as I could in Canada to sponsor education for everybody, and in short, a better deal for the underprivileged." His efforts earn him another nickname — "The Children's Friend." It was said he was the only trustee in the board's history to visit the school nearly every day. He also helps raise $10,000 for a crippled children's hospital in Victoria, BC.[32]

Joe was one of those rare souls who lived to see the fulfillment of his hopes for social change. Canada's public school infrastructure is created largely along the egalitarian lines Joe envisions. This was quite unlike the British system, where a "public school" traditionally meant its opposite — an elite boarding school for the rich. By contrast, Joe lives long enough to see "well-equipped, adequately lighted and heated schools, [where] the Barnardo boy saw the sons and daughters of prosperous people, some of whom stemmed from the British aristocracy, rub shoulders, sharpen pencils and play games, also learn the "Three Rs," with the children of penniless immigrants from other countries, who had come to Canada to seek those very things for which Joe crusaded."[33]

Joe's optimistic disposition gave him an innate advantage that not all British Home Children shared. Human resiliency is a highly individual quality, and varies widely. What damages one person for life may only graze another person's psyche. Arriving in Canada as a young man probably spared Joe the abuses of younger child immigrants. Despite coming from a class system that spat him out into the world with only Barnardo's to offer a helping hand, Joe remains loyal to Empire. He returns to Britain to attend the coronation of George V in 1911 and again in May 1937 for the coronation of George VI. Perhaps the amiable among us truly are blessed by lacking a sense of irony — that these same monarchs perpetuated the very system that had made hundreds of thousands of British children so desperately poor they were exported as indentured servants. But for Joe Harwood his return to the "Old Country" as an old man is a heartfelt journey to his youthful past:[34]

What a thrill it was to be back in England, though it was not the same England that he had left as a boy. But perfect weather made it pleasant. Everyone was smiling. Flowers seemed everywhere. And the delightful countryside brought tears to his eyes as he went on to London, which he had not seen for 29 years. Again he walked in the streets of London he once haunted when he ran away from home, hungry and destitute. Again he looked for the cheap boarding houses in which he had once sought refuge. The streets were there, but to Joe's delight, the boarding houses were gone.[35]

Joe reconnects with his family — a privilege few Barnardo's boys or girls will enjoy. When he arrives at London's Euston Station his brothers John and Frank are there to greet him. "My God they looked good to me," Joe recalls. The Harwood brothers spend two or three days at Leyton, allowing Joe time to rest up from his cross-Atlantic journey. "He started off for Hertford, 'almost afraid' to come to his native town again. But there he was again welcomed by a sister, Kate, and the council invited him to a luncheon," notes the press. Joe attends his hometown church with his niece, "who was not at all ashamed of her rough old uncle." While in London, he also meets his brother Charlie, and the brothers tour Covent Garden, the House of Commons, the Derby, the Royal Navy fleet at Portsmouth, the Isle of Wight, and of course the Coronation events. "An enjoyable weekend down in Kent, with another sister, found that section in all its glory, with the cherry blossoms out."[36]

During his 1937 visit Joe becomes a kind of "poster boy" for the success of the child emigration movement. He is given unprecedented access to Canadian and British immigration officials, three members of the British Cabinet, the Commissioner of the Salvation Army, and members of the aristocracy. All are eager to hear his rags to riches story. They also express interest in his political views. Joe goes on record as an avid supporter of child emigration:

> Pointing to the fact that emigration from the Old Country to Canada is tapering off . . . that the United States is continuing to exert an ever-greater influence on Canadian life, that emigration from mid-European countries has become a very vital factor in the Dominion's growing citizenry, and that particularly in the Pacific Coast neighbourhood the Oriental offers another ever increasing problem, "Joe" was able to stress with forceful emphasis the need for Britain's strengthening its ties with Canada. "And what better way could there be," Joe asked, "than to send out your young British men and women, properly trained, to take their places in a growing country? There is a real need for truly British blood in our technical activities."[37]

In London Joe is welcomed at British Columbia House by Agent-General McAdam — just the first of many dignitaries he will meet on this trip. The Canadian government seems eager to make the most of his success as a Barnardo boy. The Honourable Vincent Massey, Canadian High Commissioner to the UK, arranges an appointment with Lord Henry (Harry) Snell, who is eager to discuss immigration to Canada, "particularly of underprivileged English boys."

Lord Snell is one of those rarities in the British class system — a working-class individual who has risen from the bottom rung of society to the peerage. The son of agricultural workers, he was educated at his village school in Nottinghamshire but had been required to work full-time from the age of 10. From his early years he'd been an assiduous reader and furthered his education while working in London by reading at University College, in particular the works of Thomas Paine, John Ruskin, William Morris, and John Stuart Mill. Combined with his working-class origins, these leading thinkers convinced him to become a socialist. Joining the Independent Labour Party and the Fabian Society, he was elected to a seat in the House of Commons in 1922 and 1929 and was made first Baron Snell in 1931. He gives Joe the grand tour of London's exclusive clubs and sightseeing. Lord Snell has much in common with Joe Harwood — like Joe he left home at age 12, dissatisfied with his lot and eager to better himself.[38]

During his visit Joe spends much of his time visiting Barnardo's institutions. He is given "a royal welcome" when he visits the Barnardo Homes in and around London. He introduces himself as a "Barnardo boy of 50 years' standing." Barnardo's residential care in Britain has reached its height during the 1930s. In 1933, Barnardo's had more than 8,000 children living in 188 homes across the country.[39]

Among the Barnardo institutions Joe visits is Goldings, the massive William Baker Technical Institute in Hertfordshire, capable of housing and training 750 boys. This is no ragged school. The bakeries, wheelwright, shoemaking, and carpentry shops of yesteryear have given way to the new industrial age, teaching boys how to run sophisticated new machines. As Joe delightedly observes, "It was much different when I was a boy." He is also invited to the Girls Village Home at Barkingside. There, too, training has shifted from old school domestic skills to typing, hairdressing, librarian, and other modern trades. The school declares an "Overseas

Meeting Day" where Joe as guest speaker is introduced as an "Old Barnardo Boy." He shares the platform with government ministers from the colonies and other "Old Boys." Joe reminds them of the help they have been given, and the need to pass their good luck on to other unfortunate souls. Joe's penchant for embroidering the truth comes into play in his speech:[40]

> With honesty, willingness to work, and a belief in God, any young man has a simple formula that will be effective. I came [to Canada] unable to read or write, with no money, and nothing made easy for me. The going was tough, but it could have been a lot worse. I've never been on relief, never will be, nor any of my children. I've been able to do something for others and will always continue to try to do so. And I am satisfied.[41]

Clearly Joe has been one of the few lucky ones left unscathed by the Great Depression. Many just like him lost everything. The relief he refers to was a vital support for the millions pitched out of work following the stock market crash of 1929. Joe's optimism is somewhat shy of reality: after seven years of economic chaos, there isn't enough work for Canadians, never mind immigrants — of any nationality.

Joe is an instant hit with both the staff and the boys he meets in the Homes. Barnardo's London Superintendent PT Kirkpatrick writes John Hobday, Canadian Superintendent: "It was a pleasure to meet him when he called at Stepney. He had such a cheery manner, and we appreciate his special sympathy and interest in his efforts on behalf of the Homes." As well they should — Joe has become something of a public relations bonanza for Barnardo's. Canada's signature magazine *Maclean's* publishes an article about Joe written by *Vernon News* editor GJ Rowland in its November 1937 issue. "I can assure you it gave us a thrill," Hobday writes Rowland. A highlight of Joe's trip is having his photograph taken in London with two young Barnardo boys. This photograph will be reprinted widely, in Toronto's *Saturday Night* magazine, the *Vernon News,* and on the cover of the June 1937 *Ups & Downs.*[42]

Back home in Vernon, Joe writes a poignant letter to John Hobday. He thanks him for the copy of *Ups & Downs,* "as it was taken on one of the best days of my tour." Hobday informs him that the two boys on the cover are now in Canada and doing well. Joe is clearly delighted that many Barnardo boys are now writing to him, as if he were a mentor or father figure. While listing his accomplishments in public life, he concludes on a modest note:

> Yet I feel there is no credit coming to me as this was my duty and privilege to follow out that wonderful address given by Dr. Barnardo on the ship *Vancouver.* There are many boys that were in the same party who are the backbone of citizenry west of Toronto. *Thanking God for the opportunity to make good* and never forgetting the bridge and the builders in giving me an opportunity too in life.

He closes with a warm invitation to John and Rose Hobday should they ever come west. Joe's letter is a kind of testament of redemption for that youthful mistake all those years ago. And like those boys who'd written of sending in their hard-won dollars, Joe continued making donations to Barnardo's throughout his life.[43]

But all the high-profile publicity for Barnardo's comes at exactly the wrong time. With double-digit unemployment the order of the day, neither the British nor Canadian governments are sanctioning immigration, for adults or children. For Canada the great era of child immigration is all but over. For Joe, his journey has come full circle.

JOE HARWOOD, BARNARDO BOY AND VERNON PIONEER, dies on May 21, 1950. The *Vernon News* obituary reports his age as 83.[44] In fact, Harwood was born November 2, 1869, making him 81 at the time of his death. Joe is known among his descendants as something of a spinner of tall tales. While claiming that he arrived in Canada only capable of signing his name with "the cross of illiteracy," his eloquent letters to *Ups & Downs* suggest otherwise. A consistent theme in Joe's story as he told it was that he came to Canada as a boy of 12, when in fact he was nearly 19. It's possible he was referring to his age upon first leaving home in England to work. Or he may have fudged his age by one year, since most Barnardo boys were discharged at age 19 as adults. Memory is a highly malleable faculty and all of us are prone to confabulate details of our own past. It's the stuff from which myths are made, and history is not immune to it.

In his obituary the *Vernon News* noted that Joe's "greatest defeat came when a school building program was rejected by the ratepayers . . . and his greatest satisfaction just a few weeks before his death, when one of Vernon's new schools was named in his honour." To this day, Harwood Elementary School in Vernon bears his name.[45]

In a man like Joe Harwood all the elements for success are there — disposition, timing, energy, and adaptability. In Okanagan historian Mabel Johnson's view, he "could have been a prime minister, or a great leader." She describes Joe as "an individualist (with) the type of rugged, kindly, frank personality not too often met. He felt everything keenly."[46]

Still, it seems there was something of the Gemini to Joe Harwood. On the one hand, his image in the press was consistently positive. "His personality is his outstanding characteristic and anyone who has lived here in the past four decades has remembered his smile and hearty greeting," is a fairly typical depiction of Joe in the *Vernon News*.[47] On the other hand, relatives like nephew Vic Harwood remember him hardly smiling at all. It's an impression reinforced by many photographs of Joe. Was there some secret pain he carried but was unable to confide? He certainly was popular with staff and management of the CPR, with whom he had a long association through his cartage business. Vic recalls him being able to "get on a railroad caboose with two or three bottles of whiskey and travel all the way to Montreal." In fact, it appears Joe was known as a hearty drinker. Family stories tell of grandchildren having to bring him home from the local men's club at the end of the day. Perhaps it was his way of coping with the private grief he felt he couldn't share.[48]

This dual aspect to Joe's personality extended to his feelings of patriotism. "He did not talk in a grandiose manner about the land across the seas as 'back home.' Canada, to him, was 'my country.' But at the same time he was intensely loyal," writes Johnson, who recalls Harwood wearing a Union Jack during World War II. It was in tune with the times — Canadians were routinely expected to wear the dual faces of nationalist pride and British Loyalist.[49]

As with anyone who's utterly sure of what they believe, Harwood probably rubbed some the wrong way. But even the *Vernon News* obituary writer, while waffling that Joe "was not the wealthiest or the poorest, the most brilliant or the dullest, the most charitable or the meanest," had to admit "Joe Harwood . . . was perhaps Vernon's *best known* citizen. . . . He had qualities which endeared him to Vernon. . . . To few men are given the gift of friendship to the degree he had. He was on a first name basis with everyone, from the president of the Canadian Pacific Railway, to the janitor at the schools, and equally at home in the company of either." The writer's conclusion? "Vernon is a better place because he was here."[50]

Now that's a legacy to leave behind.

Joe Harwood at the time of his admission to Barnardo's, age 18. Vic and Bev Harwood and Barnardo's collections.

Joe Harwood in his role as school trustee in later years. Vernon and District Museum and Archives.

Success over "the golden bridge": Joe Harwood's livery service, Vernon, BC. Vic and Bev Harwood collection.

An early photo of Mary and Joe Harwood. Vernon and District Museum and Archives.

CHAPTER 7

Leslie Vivian Rogers —
A Scholar and a Gentleman

I. LVR ARRIVES IN NELSON

"ON A WINTER'S DAY . . . a man of firm, confident step approached the Nelson High School on Latimer Street. He glanced up at the snow-covered mountains hemming in the little mining town, then walked up the entrance and into the freshly-oiled hallways. He was Leslie Vivian Rogers, and he had come as the new principal."[1] It was to be a pivotal moment, not only for this dedicated teacher, but for generations of Nelson students who deeply admired his "patience, gentleness and quiet authority."[2]

"What kind of person was LV Rogers? You could easily lose him in a crowd; he was shortish, upright, and spoke quietly, without mannerisms. Usually, he wore grey suits and with those brown shoes, well broken-in and highly polished, hinting that he came from another part of the world. His hair was close-cropped, which became quite stylish with the Second World War crew-cut, and behind the round, magnifying lens glasses which he always wore, the eyes were steady, comprehending. It was a gentle, kindly face. Even so, his thoughts were difficult, if not impossible, to read."[3]

With this eloquent vignette begins Leslie Drew's tribute to Rogers in her booklet *LVR — The Wit and Wisdom of Leslie Vivian Rogers*, published for a Nelson, BC high school reunion in the mid-1980s. Rogers was among that select few of the British Home Children who had become a "poster boy" for the movement — those whose lives can be counted as true success stories. During the early days of Dr. Barnardo's work in London, he was in the habit of promoting his work using before-and-after photographs of destitute children transformed by the training and care they received in his Homes. This led to the creation of poster boys and girls to promote his work, a practice that came under fire in the 1870s. Dr. Barnardo was forced to abandon this approach, which was seen by many as misleading and exploitative of the children.[4]

Rogers spoke proudly of being a "Barnardo boy," who had been sent to Canada at the tender age of five. As journalist Jane Cole Hamilton wrote, "The Barnardo Homes' own records show that at one time the mayors of 14 Canadian cities were ex-Barnardo boys. More than 6,000 joined the Canadian armed forces in World War II. Many . . . were decorated or mentioned in despatches."[5] The cases of Joe Harwood and LV Rogers would have been ideal promotional material for Barnardo's. This picture of success and patriotism can be misleading, however. The reality for most Home Children was very different, with a consistent strain of loneliness, isolation, lack of love, and — all too frequently — abuse. Attempts by Dr. Barnardo and other children's philanthropists to give boys and girls some skills training was well intentioned enough, but often failed to keep abreast of the rapidly changing needs of an industrialized society. Joy Parr's groundbreaking 1980 thesis on child immigration to Canada noted that only 12 out of 105 cases she surveyed could be classed as "occupationally successful" as adults. Admittedly, a small sample, but telling nevertheless.[6]

2. Farmed Out at Age Five

Leslie Vivian Rogers was born November 2, 1886, the son of William L. and Emily (Vivian) Rogers, in either Cornwall or London. While researching her booklet, Drew had written Barnardo's Aftercare services for biographical information on Rogers but was informed that this information is only given to the individual or to a close relative.[7] Because he died without heirs, we may never know the details of his life up to age five. As was often the case with British child immigrants, both parents may have died, or the father died, leaving the mother alone to try raising a child at a time when women had few options for work.

Rogers was placed in the care of Barnardo's and by June 1891 he had been sent to Canada, placed with a family on a farm near Cobourg, Ontario. "One wonders how helpful a smallish boy could have been on a farm at age five," muses Drew. "Did he fetch the wood, carry milk pails, feed the chickens?"[8] Drew's understandable confusion about emigrating a child so young to a remote Canadian farm led her to write Jane Cole Hamilton, asking if this was regular practice. "As for his age, children as young as four have been reported as going to farms on the philosophy that 'even a child of four can feed hens,'" answered Hamilton. "Usually such young ones were adopted rather than used as labour."[9] Hamilton was partly correct: certainly children as young as four were emigrated to Canada, especially in the early years of child immigration. However, very few were ever adopted. It's more likely Rogers had been placed in Barnardo's "boarding out" program, which paid families to care for younger children until they were of an age to work. As Drew accurately surmised, "Barnardo's kept track of him right up to 1913; if he had been adopted surely Barnardo's would have had no reason for noting his 'excellent progress' so many years later."[10]

Dr. Barnardo — along with Rye and Macpherson — had realized within a decade of opening his first "ragged school" for poor children in 1867 that "an ever-open entrance to the Homes demands an ever-open exit."[11] He was well acquainted with Macpherson's child emigration work since she sent her first boatload of 100 children to Canada in May 1870. Barnardo had already sent between 600 and 900 children from his Homes through her agency prior to 1882, when child emigration became a central feature of his operations.[12] Ultimately his organization would send 30,000 children to Canada until child emigration to this country officially ceased with the outbreak of World War II.[13] By the time Rogers is emigrated as a preschooler in 1891, Barnardo's has three centres of operation in Canada: the Hazelbrae distribution home for girls in Peterborough, Ontario; the distribution home for boys on Farley Avenue, Toronto; and the farm school at Russell, Manitoba.

Once Dr. Barnardo's emigration program was well established, he turned his attention to creating a system of foster care for babies and toddlers. "His idea was to board them out in carefully selected homes, and pay for their maintenance as he had done in England, placing them with kindly folk who would in all respects act the part of father and mother toward them," explains Barnardo biographer SE Williams. "This new development quickly took root, and applications for boarded-out children came in such numbers that only a percentage could be entertained." "Boarding out" wasn't entirely a new innovation, although it had never been as widely practiced in England as in Scotland. "Since the 16th century it had been the practice in Scotland to place 'any beggar's bairn' with a respectable family so that the child would grow up to be a sober, industrious citizen," writes Barnardo's historian June Rose. "By the 19th century, the Scots placed orphan or pauper children away from their own parish with small crofters or farmers in the country."[14]

By 1886 Dr. Barnardo had begun to make his foster care program a major branch of his work. In 1887 he hired one of the early British women doctors, Dr. Jane Walker, to oversee the arrangements. Dr. Walker visited foster homes at least every three months, taking care to make only surprise visits. "Within five years he was dealing with well over a thousand children annually in this way," notes Barnardo biographer Gillian Wagner. Leslie Vivian Rogers was one of these children. Yet the choice to board him out in Canada rather than Britain seems questionable. Dr. Barnardo took note of the Scottish precedent, choosing foster parents who were mostly cottagers and working class families "as distant as possible from factories and railway stations."[15] A condition of acceptance for foster parents was that they be devout Christians; irreligious families would not qualify to receive a child. "He chose boys between the ages of five and nine because he believed that it was young children who suffered most from institutional life," notes Rose.[16] Children raised in workhouse conditions had a high rate of recidivism for crime. Dr. Barnardo saw it as his mission to put children back on the high road.

In some respects the "boarding out" program is a precursor to the foster care system adopted by British and Canadian child welfare authorities after World War II. Barnardo's was the first child charity to pay for foster care. Dr. Walker reported that it was actually the most economical means of caring for the youngest children, aside from being a healthier approach to raising destitute children. The agreement that had to be signed by foster families was Dr. Barnardo's typically curious mix of caring and control. On one hand, they were to be "brought up carefully, kindly and in all respects as one of my family, (trained) in habits of truthfulness, obedience, personal cleanliness and industry." The child was to be taken to church regularly and allowed to attend school when of age. On the other hand, no contact was to be allowed with the child's family of birth. Only rarely were visits from family members allowed, and letters were to be forwarded to Dr. Barnardo's office unopened.[17] In principle, a careful checklist was used for screening foster families. In practice, the Canadian branch lacked the staff to do an adequate job. With boys and girls arriving by the hundreds every year, speedy placements were needed to avoid overcrowding distribution homes. At the time of the Doctor's death in 1905, he had over 900 children boarded out in Canadian homes.[18]

Leslie Vivian Rogers seems to have been among the fortunate ones who were sent to a caring family. Leslie Drew was able to determine that he may have been placed with the Roberts family of Alnwick (Haldimand) Township, Ontario, south of Peterborough, and attended high school in Cobourg. Once again, due to lack of records, we must allow for the inevitable confabulation of human memory. Writing in the Nelson High School's commemorative school yearbook on LV Rogers, BC school inspector JB DeLong recalled: "His life story is a very thrilling one. He came to Canada as an orphan when five years of age, and was sent to a rancher a few miles north of Cobourg, Ontario. He attended elementary school in that district. The rancher died and left the ranch to his son. The son had tuberculosis, and told Rogers he was going to leave the ranch to him, and asked him to bring a lawyer to make out the will. The son died before the lawyer arrived. A family in Cobourg was interested in Leslie and asked him to live with them."[19] In fact, Rogers may not have been an orphan. His admittance papers to Queen's University in 1907 noted that his father was deceased, with no mention of his mother.[20]

3. LVR Comes of Age:
Following the Bread Crumb Trail

UNLIKE MOST OF THE HOME CHILDREN sent to Canada, Rogers managed to do well with his education. Obviously a bright child, his life would not be marked out for labour jobs as with so many other child immigrants. As Joy Parr explains, "The young apprentices themselves often complained in adulthood that emigration *ended* rather than expanded their opportunities for schooling. . . . Two-thirds of Barnardo's children aged 9 or younger when they came to Canada received regular schooling, but three-quarters of his emigrants aged 10 to 12 attended irregularly or not at all, and about the same proportion of arrivals aged 13 to 14 never saw the inside of a Canadian schoolroom. The first compulsory school attendance bill was passed in Ontario in 1871, although similar legislation was not in place in Western Canada until half a century later."[21]

Rogers attended the Collegiate Institute in Cobourg but before he could finish school, the Second Boer War erupted. Although only 15 years old, in 1901 Rogers answered the call for men of British origin to fight "for king and country." Because of his age — some who knew him claimed he was the youngest soldier in that war — he was made a drummer boy. He served with the 40th Northumberland Regiment as a member of the 2nd Canadian Mounted Rifles, earning the South African medal with three clasps. "Returning to Canada, he rejoined his old regiment and was speedily promoted to the rank of Colour-Sergeant, and later to a provisional lieutenancy, which he held for three years," noted the *Kelowna Courier* in August 1916.[22] Fellow teacher Derek Tye wrote Leslie Drew that he thought of Rogers every Christmas when the classic *Little Drummer Boy* was played.[23]

Even in the 1980s the breadcrumb trail of Rogers' early years was growing thin for Leslie Drew. In her enquiries with the Township of Haldimand, Drew writes that in her letter to the *Cobourg Star* newspaper, "I did not mention his Barnardo background since I gather the name of Dr. Barnardo produces mixed reactions in Ontario today." If she'd scratched a little deeper in the soil of Home Child history she'd have learned why. Drew further noted "never for a moment thinking one would be refused information on someone who was in their care nearly 100 years ago and who has been dead for 40 years."[24]

In answer to Drew's enquiries, a letter from a former student of Rogers, Clarence Thackeray, confirmed that Rogers had married Eva Jane Roberts in 1908. It was said to have been a "whirlwind courtship." Eva was the youngest daughter of Mr. and Mrs. James Roberts, who lived in the Village of Roseneath, Alnwick Township. Eva was from a family of eight, with three brothers — two of whom were teachers — and four sisters, all of whom married locally and lived their lives in the Cobourg area.[25] Without access to Barnardo's records, it's impossible to trace Rogers' footsteps from age five to 15, but it seems likely he worked for the Roberts family in his teens, perhaps after being transferred from Haldimand to the Roberts' farm near Cobourg. He was said to have "boarded with a family by the name of Manasseh Brown," and to have walked a mile to the school.[26]

Rogers enrolled at Queen's University, Kingston in 1907, graduating with a Bachelor of Arts degree in April 1911, taking honours in political science and completing his teacher training during this period.[27] Again, the exact sequence of events is hard to pin down, but it seems he taught for three years in the Cobourg area prior to enrolling at Queen's.[28] Cobourg native Thackeray had been Rogers' student in a small country school known as Woodvale. He recalls that Rogers "liked to smoke a pipe and he would smoke this pipe while walking to school. He knew us students were aware of him smoking and he would give us boys a lecture on how habit-forming smoking was, and hoped we would never begin."[29] It seems that by the time Rogers began teaching in Nelson he'd abandoned the habit, since none of the many recollections of former students there have mentioned him smoking.

Rogers next moved to Elbow, Saskatchewan — a tiny community 125 kilometres south of Saskatoon — where he taught for three years while doing his second and third year undergrad studies from Queen's. His final year was completed at the university.[30] A teaching opportunity brought Rogers to the West, arriving in Kelowna, BC in August 1911. Compared to Eastern Canada, British Columbia was just getting its public school infrastructure established. Kelowna High School at that time had a total enrolment of 33 pupils; the entire enrolment of BC high schools at the time was only 2,151. By the time he entered the political fray as the local Liberal candidate in August 1916, he had been principal of Kelowna High School since 1912. Barnardo's appears to have monitored his progress right up to 1913.[31]

The *Courier* does its best to downplay Rogers' youthful inexperience in politics compared with the more mature incumbent. He was 30 at the time and already well respected for his ability to articulate the issues of the day. "He is filled with a well-balanced ambition, is a clever debater, a concise and eloquent speaker, and is altogether a credit to the Liberal electors whom he represents, as well as to the Liberal party."[32] Yet in both attempts to gain a constituency seat — in 1916 and 1920 — Rogers failed. Derek Tye, a teacher who worked with Rogers at the Nelson High School recalled, "His brilliance, wit and charm captured a large group of followers — almost enough to win. He lost only by a mere handful of votes."[33] Former student Gerry Priest observes that Rogers' gentle nature ultimately proved him unsuitable for the often brutal game of politics: "Because he was liked and trusted they presumed he would be a good politician. But he had no aggressive appetite for slaughtering an opponent at the polls. The bickering climate of politics would be foreign to him."[34]

Yet it's not hard to see why Rogers was popular enough to be put up as a candidate. He was already a favourite among his students. Former student Janet EV Graham recalls attending Kelowna High School in June 1920. "But, oh! The joy that comforted us when Mr. Rogers entered our classroom. We knew with certainty that he loved us, each and all. Our small class of 14 students all knew the comfort of his arm around our shoulder while he bent over our desk and helped point out the solution to some problem or other. Then there was his happy sense of humour. But my memory of those studious ten months is of his empathy, and his constant loving kindness toward us all." Rogers' gentle approach was visionary at a time when the prevailing approach to education was primarily disciplinarian.[35]

Rogers was raised under the guidance of the Barnardo's system, whose organization maintained the patriarchal system of governance well into the 20th century. Yet his politics were progressive. While running for a seat in the provincial legislature he reminded voters that one of the BC Liberal government's first acts had been to extend the vote to women in 1917 — just a year behind Manitoba. Leslie Drew noted that Mary Ellen Smith had already become the first woman Member of the Legislative Assembly, "and he credited her with helping to create a general awareness that now women were 'co-partners with men in the public affairs of the province.'" Rogers also supported other social reforms such as a minimum wage for women, juvenile courts, and widows' pensions.[36]

Two defeats at the polls were enough for him to realize that his true calling lay in teaching, not politics, and he never entered the political arena again. After teaching at King George High School in Vancouver during the 1920–21 school year, Rogers accepted the post of principal at Nelson High School, starting in 1922. He taught arithmetic, geometry, and French, but was best known as a master teacher of Latin, frequently lacing his lessons with outrageous puns. He never looked back. And from the testimonies of his many students who recalled him with fond memories in later years, we can be glad he didn't.

4. A Man of Exceptional Character

Considering the temper of the times while Rogers served as principal of Nelson High School — a quarter century that spanned the stock market crash of 1929, the ensuing Depression decade, the increasing militancy leading up to the Second World War — his fairness in dealing with students was exceptional. Even while I was attending high school in Kaslo, BC during the mid-1970s, there remained a vestige of the quasi-military discipline that once held sway over Canadian public schools. But by all accounts, this approach would have been alien to Rogers' kind nature. His legacy persisted at the high school in Nelson when I arrived there in 1975 — teachers at LVR Senior Secondary had already abandoned the heavy-handed approach of the past.

Rogers' colleague Derek Tye recalled that he had a "unique" way of conducting staff meetings. "He was never dictatorial. He would, in a most reserved way, introduce the idea of a possible policy change . . . in a way that suggested he had not made up his mind. He would then solicit our 'two bits worth,' allowing us an opportunity to suggest modifications and methods of implementation. We were made to feel that we were making a valuable contribution, whereas, in reality, he undoubtedly knew precisely what he intended to do from the very start." Tye recalls a particularly disagreeable school inspector named HB King, "who had been elevated to be the number one educational dictator," and had made a damning report on Nelson High School despite never actually visiting the school. Rogers wrote a detailed reply to King's critique, showing why NHS was "among the most progressive high schools in the province." The Department of Education was compelled to write Rogers an apology.[37]

When the new Nelson high school was christened LV Rogers High in 1956 — 10 years after Rogers' death — the school yearbook paid him tribute. Former student become principal Gerry Lee spoke of Rogers' teaching as "effortless — the mark of a true artist. How we enjoyed his lessons. . . . With what pleasure we went to the board when he asked 'the lad' to step forward, 'travel light, just take your brains'. . . . I can still see him standing in the hallway looking at us as he came in with that quizzical, slightly humorous look we grew to love so much."[38]

But if he was appreciated by fellow staff at the school, he was just as popular with students, who knew him as "Jolly Rogers" or simply as LVR. Rogers was renowned for his Latin classes, which even in the pre-World War II era was considered a "dead language." Rather than simply pull rank, he used humour to ease students' difficulties learning Latin grammar. "As a student of Mr. Rogers (about 1944)," recalled Gerry Priest, "I suffered considerable frustration with Latin. In a fit of pique I had written on the flyleaf of my textbook: 'Gerald Priest studied this misbegotten gibberish in his misspent youth.' I inadvertently left this book on my desk when I changed classes. Mr. Rogers returned it to me next Latin period. Written underneath my inscription in his handwriting . . . was the following: 'Latin is a buried language / Dead! As dead as dead can be / It put the mighty Romans down / And now it's killing me!'"[39]

Another student recalled Rogers standing by the school's main entrance, ringing the bell. He would greet each student by name and ask how they were doing with sincere interest and a kindly smile.[40] "I remember so well his consideration and kindness," wrote

Mildred Ford Cherry. "I can see him sitting on a corner of the desk, chatting with us."[41] Priest recalled Rogers instilling in his students "sensitivity, perceptiveness, antennae at full scan. Because of his influence we are still aware if we meet another human being with these qualities." In part, this reflected Rogers' mastery of language. "He had used them [words] brilliantly on public platforms at a time when 'oratory' was valued in a communicator. He used them in the classroom to much more lasting effect. The ultimate weapon in his arsenal of words was a marvelous sense of humour."[42]

Former student Jim Fraser recalled that Rogers' understanding of psychology and human nature generally had a way of easing awkward situations. "The philosophy he practiced was to let someone who has made an honest mistake not feel humiliated before his peers. That's how he was able to create a pleasant atmosphere in the school. I can speak from experience. LV let me save face on more than one occasion." Leslie Drew's biography of Rogers, however, leaves an impression of a complex, multi-faceted personality. "He could be blunt and he could be baroque. He could be pragmatic and he could be poetic . . . he was extraordinarily diverse, too original to be predictable."[43]

Rogers seems to have faded into history with his typical modesty. "In his last years, owing to failing health, he was a very private person. He and his wife Eva (they had no children) lived quietly in a downtown apartment, seeing only a few close friends." The war years may have been a nasty reminder of the carnage he'd seen as a young lad in South Africa and then again in World War I. "During the Second World War, Leslie Rogers had little to be cheerful about. He watched some of his lads go off to their deaths, a tragic repetition of what he had seen at Kelowna a generation earlier." Rogers' kindly nature made it impossible for him to condone the hatred stirred up against the Japanese during the war. When a school band arrived at the Nelson High School from Coer d'Alene Idaho, one of its members was a Japanese-American. Shirley Stainton recalls being asked by Rogers to take her into her home as a billet.[44]

Leslie Vivian Rogers died on August 27, 1946. Just 60 years old, Rogers died "at his post," busy making preparations for the new school year when he was struck down by a heart attack. His wife Eva had died a year earlier on May 2, 1945. Their whirlwind romance had lasted nearly 40 years.[45]

Drew speculates on just how much of Rogers' character retained the stamp of Barnardo's from his earliest years. He was in the habit of referring to boys in class as "the lad," or students generally as "urchins," recalled former student Gordon Fleming.[46] "He definitely seems to have taken to heart Barnardo's insistent advice to the young, that they be honest, hard-working Christians," concludes Drew. "And yet, perhaps people other than Barnardo's played a greater role. In being bounced from one foster home to another, he may have acquired a better legacy than the farm. He may have had employers and teachers who, for all the work they laid on him, nonetheless proved kindly and could not only recognize potential in a youngster but encourage it as well. Maybe . . . [he] landed on the right doorsteps in Canada."[47]

LV Rogers poses as the youngest soldier in the Second Boer War (bottom row, third from left). LV Rogers Senior Secondary School collection, Nelson, BC.

A young Leslie Vivian (LV) Rogers, early in his teaching career. LV Rogers Senior Secondary School collection, Nelson, BC.

CHAPTER 8

The Failed Eden —
Fairbridge Farm Schools in BC

1. An Imperialist's Dream

THE OLD NEWSREEL FOOTAGE IS JUMPY, streaked with dust, the images seen through a sepia blur. It's 1939 and in true *Movietone News* style, we're being treated to footage of British children arriving at the Prince of Wales Fairbridge Farm School in Duncan, BC. The title cards are exultant: "Brothers and sisters reunited!" Everyone is dressed in neat sweaters and shorts or skirts as if attending the finest English parochial school. The newsreel progresses through a procession of dignitaries consecrating the school's new chapel — everyone from the Bishop of Columbia to BC Lieutenant-Governor Eric W. Hamber. Much of the film is devoted to a special sports day, at which Fairbridge children win many ribbons. Children are seen running races and laughing in friendly competition with other Vancouver Island school teams.[1]

But other than special sports days, Fairbridge boys and girls only occasionally interact with other students. The Fairbridge Farm School is meant to be all things to all its children — home, school, church, social life, and agricultural college. In this way founder Kingsley Fairbridge had attempted to avoid the pitfalls of other child emigration schemes and institutions. A Rhodes Scholar born in South Africa and raised in Rhodesia, Fairbridge had spent little time in Britain prior to his first visit in 1903 at age 18. His initial exposure to the plight of the British poor had been during that six-month period, when he became acquainted with the work of London's East End church missions. And like many 19th century philanthropists, he was appalled at what he saw — the brawling, drunkenness, and squalor of the poor and the hopelessness of their situation. He began formulating his concept for his farm school shortly after returning to Rhodesia.[2]

Following Cecil Rhodes' death in 1902, the terms of his will stipulated that a fund be established from his financial legacy allowing "young colonists" to study at Oxford. The Fairbridge family had been friends of Rhodes and the elder statesman had taken a liking to young Kingsley. However, his youth had been spent more in the fields developing the family plantation than in school. Still, he was encouraged to return to England to study for an equivalency exam that would qualify him for a Rhodes Scholarship. In 1906 he cashed in his insurance policy to fund his studies. He decided on a roundabout route to England, travelling first to some of the colonies to investigate opportunities for child emigration. His globetrotting journey took him to Australia, New Zealand, and Canada. Travelling second class, he arrived in Vancouver on the RMS *Minerva* on August 30, 1906. From there he traversed southern British Columbia, likely riding a CPR sternwheeler on the Arrow Lakes on his way to Nelson, where he met with Earl Grey, Governor-General of Canada. These early impressions of Western Canada clearly made an impact on the young Fairbridge and would bear fruit in BC nearly 30 years later.[3]

October 19, 1909. Fairbridge pitches his dream to 50 of his colleagues at a meeting of the Oxford Colonial Club.[4] As he rises to address fellow students, dons and other members of the club, he cuts a dashing figure — handsome and immaculately dressed. For a man of 24 he has an ambitious vision: "Now there are in England over 60,000 'dependent' children, orphans or homeless, who are being brought up in institutions, who will be put into small jobs at the age of 12 or 14, jobs for which they become too old at 18. They have no parents, and no one standing in any such relation to them. What have they before them that can be called a future? I saw a street in London — no air, not enough food, children's lives wasting, while the Empire cried aloud for men to till its virgin lands." His colleagues thump the tables to cries of "Hear! Hear!"[5]

In fact, Fairbridge's estimation is low: by the time he addresses the club the number of children under the jurisdiction of Britain's Poor Law is 70–80,000.[6] There have been a number of cases of serious abuse and even deaths reported of Barnardo's wards placed with Canadian farmers, causing many to question the organization's methods. Rather than simply import children into the colonies and then dump them into the hands of fate, Fairbridge has a better plan: the farm school system. "The idea is to have a series of small farms grouped about one central farm, or farm school, the children to be looked after by a staff of men and women skilled in the various branches of agricultural and domestic science," he explains. A primary goal will be the cultivation of children's "health, ability and morality" through the "character-forming qualities of the system."[7]

"It is considered essential that the children shall be brought up to look after themselves in all possible ways," he says, his eyes alight with purpose. "The artificiality that is the hallmark of 'institutions' must be utterly abolished; the children must be in touch with all the needs of daily life; they must begin to do their own cooking, dig their own gardens, grow their own food, and mend their own clothes as soon as these things become possible. Self-reliance, self-help, and self-respect must be the outcome of the farm school system, or the system will have failed in its object." He goes on to speak of how London's East End had both haunted and inspired him. In the blistering heat of a typical South African afternoon, his vision had come: "I saw great Colleges of Agriculture [not workhouses] springing up in every man-hungry corner of Empire. I saw little children shedding the bondage of bitter circumstances, and stretching their legs and minds amid the thousand interests of the farm. I saw unneeded humanity converted to the husbandry of unpeopled acres."[8] This last comment reveals a blind spot typical of the age — the assumption that the colonies where Aboriginal nations had lived for millennia were "unpeopled" and waiting for settlers.

Fairbridge seems to have come by his interest in philanthropy naturally — his great-grandfather, Dr. James William Fairbridge, had been a committee member of the Children's Friend Society. Established by retired naval Captain Edward Pelham Brenton in 1830, its aim was to emigrate destitute children to the colonies, with sufficient training to support themselves. But the Society's original name — the Society for the Suppression of Juvenile Vagrancy — is a clue to the attitudes of the day toward the poor. The Society had created controversy by emigrating children without their parents' consent. A press report in 1839 accused it "not only of transporting the poor children, but of selling them to the Dutch boors at the Cape...."[9]

So Kingsley Fairbridge is entering the field of child emigration late. By 1909 the field had been well cultivated. Barnardo's alone had emigrated 13,500 children to Canada by 1903.[10] And the emphasis placed on "character-building" and morality bears distinct echoes of Dr. Barnardo's vision for his children's training. But by the Edwardian era the Christian revivalists are passing off the scene in Britain and the emphasis for training children is shifting from a religious to an imperial motivation. "In church weeklies . . . and in the publications of the rescue homes charitable Britons were urged to combine their philanthropy with imperialism, the 'love of children with a love of empire,'" notes Joy Parr. The British government was naturally an enthusiastic supporter, and at Imperial Conferences in 1907 and 1911 not just emigration generally but child emigration within the Empire was urged.[11]

Neither was the farm school system a new idea. These had actually first been implemented in Europe with the experiments of Swiss aristocrat Philipp Emanuel von Fellenberg at Hofwyl near Berne in the early 19th century. Many were familiar with the Mettrai Institute in central France where juvenile offenders and pauper children were sent for "reform." Ellinor Close had already attempted to operate a farm school in New Brunswick. "To the idea of the cottage home Mrs. Close added that of the farm home where children would be trained for rural life. Her Ellinor Farm Home . . . had started with nine children in 1906, most of whom had come from the East End of London." An economic downturn in 1907–08 starved it of funds and the Canadian Department of the Interior decided her scheme was too costly to be practical.

Despite all the government-sanctioned imperialist rhetoric, financial support for Fairbridge's child emigration scheme is slow in coming. When his proposals for bringing child migrants into Rhodesia and South Africa are rejected by British authorities, he turns his attention to Canada and Australia. On that October day in 1909 at Oxford, he has an ace up his sleeve: the government of Newfoundland has offered 20,235 hectares (50,000 acres) of uncultivated land for his first farm school in Canada.[12]

When Fairbridge finishes his speech to the Oxford Colonial Club, he is greeted with raucous applause. A motion to form the Child Emigration Society (CES) is unanimously approved. Like his mentor, Rhodes, Fairbridge is an ardent imperialist, and this is reflected in the mission statement adopted by the newly formed society.[13] Its two prime mandates are an interesting blend of the compassionate and the political: "1. To rescue children from damaging conditions — poverty, neglect, antisocial influences, as well as the prospect of deteriorated health, unemployment or blind alley occupations. 2. To train these children in Fairbridge Farm Schools for life and work in the Dominions. The accomplishment of this object has the result of forestalling a waste of children, for the sake of the children themselves, and at the same time valuable and calculable contribution is made to the problem of Empire Settlement." It's a somewhat more distilled version of Fairbridge's appeals for the unification of Anglo-Saxon people throughout the Empire. The Newfoundland land grant fails to materialize, however, so Fairbridge begins negotiations with the Australian government for land.[14]

Fairbridge Farm Schools are conceived along the lines of Barnardo's boys' and girls' villages at Woodford and Barkingside, with a significant difference. Whereas Barnardo's villages are run more as nurseries, training and preparing children for emigration, Fairbridge will take children as young as eight straight from Britain to his farm schools. They will live in the Fairbridge community until age 16 when they will be expected to leave and find jobs. Boys and girls on Fairbridge Farm Schools will live in segregated cottages, 14 or so in each with a "Cottage Mother." "It was Fairbridge's dream to create a rural, village-like environment for the children," note historians Stan Sauerwein and Arthur Bailey. "The girls taken in would receive training in domestic pursuits, and the boys would be trained in manual arts and agriculture. Vocational training was to be supplemented with moral guidance and leavened with recreational pursuits in such a way that the young emigrants would be able to take their places as productive citizens in the host communities."[15]

The children will be paid wages, half of which is held in trust until their 21st birthday. Like the apprenticeship scheme at Barnardo's, these funds provide a "nest egg" to help young men and women get started. Acting as a kind of employment agency, Fairbridge makes an effort to place them in jobs once they come of age. "The aim of the school is to be a home to the children," explained a 1942 Vernon News retrospective on Fairbridge, "and until a child is 21, he or she may come back to the school at any time, just as a boy or girl, finding [themselves] temporarily out of work in ordinary life, might return to the parental roof for the time being."[16]

APRIL 1912. Newlyweds Kingsley Fairbridge and wife Ruby depart for Western Australia on the *Afric*. Ruby is pregnant with their first child. When they arrive on April 15, news of the *Titanic* tragedy is shocking the world. They have just £2,000 to establish the first Fairbridge Farm School and conditions are still primitive. The Fairbridges travel throughout the Perth region looking for a suitable property. They discover the 65-hectare parcel at Pinjarra that had been established as a training farm by Church of England clergyman Reverend H. Freeman in October 1910. Although the venture had received good press coverage in Britain, after signing the lease in July they discover the property is in a state of disrepair. They set to work in the Australian summer heat and by August they are ready to open.[17]

Their timing is hardly fortuitous. Within two years of their arrival, the outbreak of the First World War slows emigration to a trickle due to German attacks on British ships. "At first, the scheme almost failed for lack of sufficient funds," recalled the *Vernon News*. "But after the war of 1914 he visited England twice, and told governments and societies of his work. This time he found listening ears and willing hearts."[18]

But Kingsley Fairbridge has a global vision and Canada still holds great appeal as a base for another farm school. "I have long thought that the Child Emigration Society should establish our second farm school in British Columbia," he wrote in the fall of 1914 to his Oxford friend Colonel Harry Tremaine Logan, a Professor of Classics at the University of British Columbia (UBC). "From what I saw there, you have room for towns of thousands of budding farmers.... Training otherwise homeless youngsters to be fine, upstanding and honourable men and women can in its way be quite as fine as the Parliament House in Victoria." Logan had been present at the meeting of the Oxford Colonial Club in 1909 and is an enthusiastic supporter of the Fairbridge plan.[19]

Fairbridge will not live to see his farm schools expand to BC. Difficulties with financing the Australian farm school at Pinjarra, waffling of government officials over funding, and disagreements with the Fairbridge committee in London force him to return to England in 1922 to resolve the crisis. By then he has been heavily overworked and it begins to take a toll on his health. He suffers repeated bouts of malaria. A major coup had been the striking of an agreement with Barnardo's in July 1923 to supply the farm with children from the Doctor's homes. The long ocean voyages exhaust him further, yet he struggles on, preparing the new farm location north of Pinjarra for its first arrivals. Although he seems to rally in November, by April 1924 he is confined to bed, while planning yet another voyage to England with his family. Upon operating, surgeons realize there is nothing more they can do for him. On July 19 he dies at age 39, with the official cause listed as lymphatic tumour.[20]

The late '20s will be a period of turmoil for the Fairbridge organization, with numerous changes of staff at Pinjarra. Ruby Fairbridge makes a bid for directorship of the farm but is turned down by the London executive. It will take until September 1931 for Kingsley's dream of a BC farm school to germinate, when London committee member Miss LP Leatham proposes a farm in Canada. The offer of a property in BC arises soon afterward from a godparent of Fairbridge children, Miss Jean Bostock, daughter of a former Canadian Minister of Immigration. Both efforts are rebuffed by federal and provincial governments, citing the 1925 regulation banning the immigration of children under 14. Bostock and Leatham join forces and soon acquire an ally in BC businessman FB Pemberton, whose son-in-law, another Rhodes Scholar, "had known and admired Kingsley Fairbridge." The CES is anxious to expand in both Canada and Australia and begins actively pursuing the idea in 1934. The Canadian government of RB Bennett, seeking closer ties to the British Commonwealth, removes restrictions on child immigration and promises not to oppose a proposal for a Canadian farm school.[21]

Fairbridge, like Dr. Barnardo before him, had cultivated royal patronage. As early as 1924, the Prince of Wales (later Edward VIII) had spoken on behalf of Fairbridge at business luncheons held in the City of London.[22] Ten years later, with the onset of the Great Depression, child emigration to Canada has slowed considerably. Yet the economic impact on poor and working class British families makes the Fairbridge scheme newly attractive. The CES gets a major kick-start to its new fundraising drive on June 14, 1934, when Edward, Prince of Wales, addresses an influential audience at Grocer's Hall, London. Fairbridge is "the only completely successful form of migration at the present time," he tells his audience. It will be "a definite contribution to the solution of the problem, the great problem, of unemployment. This is not a charity, it is an Imperial investment." To kick off the campaign he offers £1,000 of his own money. Within a month he is met with a further £23,000 in donations toward the Society's £100,000 goal.[23] Together Edward and British Prime Minister Stanley Baldwin are able to raise $500,000 for the establishment of a Fairbridge Farm School in BC.[24] The CES uses the money to purchase the 400-hectare Pemberlea estate at Cowichan Station near Duncan, Vancouver Island, in March 1935. Appropriately, it is named the Prince of Wales Fairbridge Farm School. Another ardent Imperialist, author Rudyard Kipling, leaves $775,000 to the Society upon his death in 1936.[25]

September 25, 1935. The first 41 child immigrants arrive at Duncan — 27 boys and 14 girls, with the youngest, Ernie Todd, just four-and-a-half years old.[26] This first group has been taken from the tough streets of Birmingham, London, and Newcastle-on-Tyne. Most are from disadvantaged families, with only a few being orphans. One incident that becomes useful publicity is a poignant reminder of the children's urban origins. A Fairbridge matron, when meeting a party of children disembarking at Vancouver, speaks of the lovely fields, forests, and meadows they will find at Duncan. One of the children, confused, asks, "But please, ma'am, if there aren't any streets, where do we play?"[27]

At this early stage of the Prince of Wales Farm School, only four cottages — the Edith Attwood, Silver Jubilee, Queen Mary, and Lady Houston — had been completed. Todd would later recall the rest of the site consisting of an "old kitchen, a guesthouse, horse barn, sheep shed, bunkhouse and hayloft." The site is laid out in a broad crescent with plenty of room to roam for rambunctious youngsters. The cottages are designed to house up to 14 children with a bedroom and sitting room for the Cottage Mother. A further four cottages are added in 1936 — Liverpool, St. George's,

Richards, and Lord Riddell — and the magnificent Kenilworth dining hall with its high vaulted ceilings. The buildings are named after major contributors to the farm school, including the dining hall, named for wealthy industrialist Lord Kenilworth, who had donated $500,000 to the cause. The year's construction closes with the completion of the day school and Howard Mitchell Auditorium. "I recall some of my kindergarten," recalls Todd. "I saw the whole school being built. We would play in cardboard boxes beside the old cook stoves in the old kitchen."[28]

Former Coldstream guardsman Major Maurice F. Trew is hired as the first principal at the farm school. After his resignation in 1936, Kingsley Fairbridge's old friend Harry Logan, himself a Rhodes Scholar, is hired for the job. Logan is a veteran of WW I, returning to Canada after the war to teach classics at UBC.[29] Logan is an ideal choice — well educated, dedicated to the Fairbridge ideal, and gentle with children. Former Fairbridgian Ron Hancock recalls Logan with fondness. "Harry or HT was probably the greatest humanist I ever met. He was kind, gentle and understanding almost to a fault. He loved teaching and he loved young people, especially children." One staff member recalls him as "a charismatic idealist deeply convinced that potential delinquents from the most sordid of backgrounds could be transformed by love and kindness. He was the driving and inspirational force of the school though some of his views on child upbringing seemed more Utopian than realistic."[30]

October 9, 1936. *The Times* of London reports on the departure of the second party of children for the Prince of Wales Farm School. No less than the Lord Mayor and Lady Mayoress visit British Columbia House to help send off the 28 boys and girls who are to sail from Liverpool on the *Duchess of Atholl*. "The average age of the children, who looked healthy, well set up, and happy, was 11 years, and they included a number of brothers and sisters. Twenty-one of them came from the Tyneside, the Commissioner for Special Areas having given financial help towards their maintenance and traveling expenses in this country. In most cases the children had lost a parent or for some other reason the normal home life had been interrupted." The Lord Mayor had recently returned from a visit to the new farm school on Vancouver Island and felt they were "lucky indeed" to be headed there. The mayor is likely alluding to the fact that the areas from which these children had come are chronically disadvantaged. With unemployment levels entrenched in the double digits, their future prospects were not good. The British government had asked Fairbridge to give preference to children from these areas, providing the CES with grants for branch offices. Upon arrival in BC on October 22, the children are met by the mayors of both Vancouver and Victoria wishing them well in their new lives. Tellingly, "The Mayor of Victoria said that the Fairbridge Farm School was in the most English part of the whole Dominion of Canada."[31]

This group is quickly followed by a third party, which arrives in BC on November 6. The children are met by Principal Logan as they step off the CPR train in Vancouver. With one eye on Canadian fears of "importing British trash," the *Vancouver Sun* report focuses heavily on their fitness and general health. "This is the finest bunch of youngsters, the most intelligent, and possessing the finest personalities of any I've met in my many trips," CPR Colonization Agent E. Eisenberg had remarked when meeting the children in Quebec. "Their quick, native intelligence, glowing health and frolicsome spirits reflect the sound, hardy, robust British stock they represent." This group — also numbering 28 — comprises "eight boys and 11 girls from Newcastle-on-Tyne; six boys and two girls from London and a boy from Birmingham. [They] left Friday on the Nanaimo boat to live amid the wild beauty of a virgin landscape 40 miles from Victoria and 6,000 miles from the grimy industrial areas" from which they came. The youngest, Malcolm Macdonald, is just six years old and the eldest, Tom Turner, is 13. The Prince of Wales Farm School student population rises to 97.[32]

Life quickly settles down to a strict routine at the farm school. "Logan followed the daily routine that Kingsley had created almost from the beginning of Pinjarra in 1913. Early morning rises to undertake the "cottage duties," breakfast in the main hall, school during the day and then work on the farm in the afternoon. After the evening meal, eaten in the cottages, the children did errands for their Cottage Mother and finished their homework. On weekends there was sport and such activities as Boy Scouts and Girl Guides, with occasional school dances and parties."[33]

Development at the site progresses year by year, with four more cottages built in 1937 along with the principal's house and the office. A second wing is added to the day school in 1938 and an "industrial arts" building for training the boys. The final six cottages and a laundry are built between 1938 and '39. The children are fascinated by the flurry of construction activity as ground is cleared for the new chapel. The work is recorded by a film crew. Some of the old-growth timber is 90 metres tall and must be carefully brought down with guy wires. "Donkey" engines are used to pull out the stumps, with a little encouragement from dynamite.[34]

September 22, 1939. With the new Prince of Wales Fairbridge Farm School Chapel framed but still far from complete, a special ceremony is held for the laying of the cornerstone. The children are lined up along the road as the dignitaries arrive, preceded by a Scots honour guard. At a platform set up outside the unfinished chapel, officials speak to children and guests seated in neat rows. "A welcome to all attending the ceremony is extended by RW Mayhew, MP, Chairman of BC Fairbridge Committee and HT Logan, School Principal," reads the title card in the silent newsreel footage. "In a time of war it is wonderful that the society is able to find those who are still interested in what we are doing out here and in providing for the children," says Mayhew. Logan calls it "the most important day in the life of the school." "His Honour, Lieutenant-Governor Eric W. Hamber officiates at ceremony, assisted by the Right Reverend HE Sexton DD, the Bishop of Columbia," reads the next title card.[35]

April 20, 1940. A dedication ceremony is held at the completed chapel. The workmanship is stunning, with its distinctly Canadian wood paneling, soaring beams, and lath floors, all burnished to a shine. Light streams in through five stained glass windows of Norman design. In true British fashion, the clock tower standing tall over the entrance marks out the chapel as the spiritual focal point of the community. In the pews there is seating for 400. This time a full slate of church officials attends, representing parishes across the province. A choir of boys and girls fills the vaulted space with ethereal voices lifted heavenward by the new organ. The pipe organ, built in England by Harrison and Harrison of Durham with 4.5 tons of pipes, is itself a magnificent achievement. The same firm had built organs for Westminster Abbey and the cathedrals at Exeter, Worcester, Ely, and Wells, among others. It had been donated by Mrs. T. Mitchell as a memorial to her son John Howard, who had been killed in the First World War. Principal Logan notes that the $20,000 needed to build the chapel came from a stranger who had come to the farm school for an afternoon. After watching the children at work and play, he told Logan he wanted to make a gift but wished to remain anonymous. Other gifts came in from Fairbridge supporters across Canada and Britain.[36]

By 1940 construction at the Prince of Wales Farm School is complete, with the addition of a horse barn and hospital. A laundry had been built in 1939. Similar progress had been made in Australia, with the completion of farm schools at Molong, New South Wales, and at Bacchus Marsh, Victoria — later to be named Northcote Farm after its benefactor, Lady Northcote. Another first for the Prince of Wales Farm School is the establishment of the *Fairbridge Gazette*, produced entirely by resident boys and girls. Its first editor is Jim Lally, who had arrived with the first contingent in 1935. In its second edition published in August 1939, Lally reprints a letter from Edwin Lambert, a correspondent at the Molong farm. "The population here consists of 84 children, 70 boys and 14 girls and we are eagerly awaiting the arrival of 14 more children on 29th June. Our school was officially opened by the Governor-General of Australia last November; there were also many other notable personalities present. A village council has been formed to decide any matters concerning the welfare of our increasing village."[37]

2. SUMMER'S PARADISE: FINTRY FARM

MEANWHILE YET ANOTHER BENEFACTOR had his eyes on Fairbridge Farm Schools — wealthy Scottish aristocrat Captain James Cameron Dun-Waters, heir to a newspaper chain in Great Britain. Born in Torquay, England, on November 28, 1864, he grew up on the family estate in Fintry, Stirlingshire, Scotland. Dun-Waters had been an athlete and a hunter since his youth, with a high regard for outdoor pursuits. Upon entering studies at Cambridge in 1882 he soon distinguishes himself as an athlete. He marries in 1887 and soon after emigrates to British Columbia, where he purchases the 475-hectare property known as Short's Point on the north end of Okanagan Lake, near Vernon. From early on he demonstrates an even-handed spirit. When he sells his newspaper interests to move to Canada he gives employees a generous bonus. While serving as an officer in World War I, he provides funds for a soldier's hospital in Cairo.[38]

Dun-Waters becomes known to locals as "the Laird O' Fintry," a somewhat eccentric but respected figure. Among his many interests is the breeding of Ayrshire cattle, which he imports to the Okanagan Valley. Described as an "Ayrshire zealot," he set about spreading the breed throughout the province. In 1934 he donates four of his Ayrshire cattle to the East Kootenay Government Experimental Station at Windermere, BC. He becomes a fixture at the annual agricultural fairs held in Armstrong, BC, just north of Vernon. Dun-Waters "took an interest in the Fairbridge scheme quite early," notes historian David Dendy, "and in 1936 presented the Prince of Wales farm with a starter herd of Ayrshire cattle."[39]

But by 1936 Dun-Waters is terminally ill, with no heirs for his estate. Repeated efforts to sell the estate produce no buyers — there simply aren't enough people with that kind of money in BC during the Depression years. On July 6, 1938, he announces the donation of his Fintry estate — except for a small portion for his estate manager — to Fairbridge for the establishment of another farm school. The estate is valued at between $0.5 and 1 million. It's an incredible gift — 40 hectares of orchard, 70 hectares of hayfields, and 60 hectares of grounds with the Dun-Waters residence and the octagonal barn that will become synonymous with Fintry. His beloved Ayrshires provide the basis of a thriving dairy and there is a small sawmill. With irrigation, the Okanagan is a natural choice for fruit orchards. Fintry is ideally located on a gentle benchland extending a half-mile into Okanagan Lake, with seven varieties of apples plus pears, cherries, apricots, and peaches. A fruit packing plant is located on the lakeshore near the dock, shipping 23,000 boxes of fruit to markets over a 10-year period.[40]

Fairbridge management decides to use Fintry mainly as a "finishing school" for older boys, who will come for the last year or two of their training before leaving to go into full-time work. "This meant detachments of boys came up from Duncan for the summer and returned there in the fall after the apple crop was harvested," writes Dendy. Although a few boys and girls are sent to Fintry during the summer of 1938, the main contingent arrives in June 1939 — 28 boys and four girls, aged 12–16 — under the care of Logan's assistant William Garnett. *The Vernon News* sets the idyllic scene that will greet them: "It was a typical Okanagan summer day. On a broad verandah 28 black iron cots stood in rows, each meticulously made, the grey blankets folded and tucked with almost military precision. . . . Outside, the evening sun of a summer's day was within an hour of setting. Flowering and other shrubs made long shadows on the well-kept lawns. Myriads of bees droned away the sunny hours in masses of lavender planted around the sundial. Giant firs stood sentinel, and here and there the blue of the lake was visible. . . ."[41]

But this is no holiday camp. The boys are put to work in the Fintry orchard, spraying, thinning, picking, and packing fruit. The girls, under the direction of cottage mothers Mrs. Gray and Mrs.

Hanse, prepare the meals and do the housekeeping. "We started work today and have pretty well got on to it," notes one boy in a letter to the *Fairbridge Gazette*. "Our rising time is 6:30 a.m., we wash, get dressed and make our beds; there is a bed inspection at 7:05 and breakfast at 7:15. After breakfast we report to the packinghouse for regular duties and finish at 11:30. In the afternoon we work from one to four o'clock." McIntosh apples are packed for shipment using the distinctive blue Fintry label showing a boy holding up a crisp new apple. It's a respectable crop, totaling over 11,000 boxes of apples. "As a clever promotional move, part of the shipment was specially offered for sale to all subscribers to the Fairbridge Society," notes Dendy, with 5,000 boxes destined for Fairbridge patrons in England.[42]

"They chopped and carried wood; filled coal scuttles; swept verandahs; tidied the washroom; prepared vegetables and apples; weeded the gardens; and generally made themselves useful," reports the *Vernon News*. "They took turns in the barns, morning and evening, and one or two worked on the grader in the packinghouse. Mr. Garnett says their tasks are varied in the same way at Duncan."[43]

But Kingsley Fairbridge had recognized that children also need to play. For recreation, the lure of Okanagan Lake is irresistible. "Swimming seems to be the only word on everyone's lips after work at nights. The boys go in the lake three times a day, once in the morning before breakfast, again after work at four o'clock and finishing the day off with a swim after supper for about an hour." Sunday evenings are spent in the home of Fintry managers Angus and Ella Gray, with their daughter Isabel playing piano for church services.[44]

Art and Marie Harrop, who worked at Fintry as part of Angus Gray's regular crew, would later recall not so much the work as the social life. Dun-Waters' famous trophy room had been converted to a playroom, though still presided over by the fearsome grizzly bear he'd shot years ago. But now there's a ping-pong table and shelves of British children's magazines such as *Chatterbox* and *Boy's Own Paper* joining the Captain's hunting trophies. "There were cricket, lacrosse and baseball games. The boys lodged at Dun-Waters' house and slept on cots out on the screened-in verandah. Each night the people living at the ranch were invited down for applesauce and fresh homemade bread, which was a nightly treat. Bill Garnett instructed the boys in their prayers while the visitors were present. The boys then quietly disappeared to their cots out on the verandah."[45]

The *Vernon News* reporter sets a glowing scene, and takes time to interview the children:

> In charge of this huge family was the house-mother, Mrs. Ella Gray, herself the mother of a four-year-old boy. She had a capable assistant Mrs. Hanse, and four girls who help in their multitudinous duties. . . . Growing up under this roof and among these surroundings are the little chaps, who have been "born on the unlucky side of the street." From all corners of the Old Land they have come. Newcastle-on-Tyne, Glasgow, Hull, London were the respective birthplaces of a group of four intelligent lads to whom we spoke. While the charming house mother Mrs. Hanse and her two helpers put baked beans to heat in the large ovens of the coal stoves with which to appease the appetites of her hungry charges we talked with some of the lads around a blazing fire in the living room. There is the inevitable loquacious one, also the shy one; the fat one, the thin one; dark, fair; blue eyes and brown. . . . The lads are very polite.[46]

Already the spectre of war is looming over the children's lives. "The chatty one said that he has been here just a year, and hailed from Middlesboro in Yorkshire. The dialect of Yorkshire made it necessary to listen attentively. He told us that he had heard from 'me muther' during the previous week, and she had been telling him of the precautionary measures taken in the town which was his birthplace now the Empire is at war. 'And,' he continued, 'me bruther now, he is guarding the Suez Canal.'"[47]

Dun-Waters dies October 16, 1939, just as the boys and girls are about to return to Duncan for the winter. "Yet it may be a consoling thought for those many boys to realize that they, as the Fairbridge farm pupils, summed up in the old Laird's mind the most happy gesture of his life — the gift that brought British lads to learn of the Okanagan land," notes the *Vernon News*. "He expressed his pleasure, more than once, at the fact that he had been spared to see the first group of young lads come to the new school. . . ." Dun-Waters was generous to the end. One day during his last summer he'd taken the Fairbridge boys and girls to dinner at the National Hotel in Vernon, with the rare treat of ice cream for dessert. Under each ice cream dish was placed a silver dollar. The Fairbridge boys and girls will return to Fintry farm next April. But the summer of 1939 has left an indelible impression. "The best time of our lives," they declare.[48]

The highly successful Fairbridge Fintry apple exports could not be repeated the following year due to submarine warfare in the Atlantic. The August 1940 edition of the *Fairbridge Gazette* tries to downplay the threat. An editorial first notes the arrival of two parties of children and the departure of one of them to the farm school in Molong, Australia. It concludes that the shipment would never have been allowed either by Fairbridge officials or the British government "if there had been the slightest doubt as to their safety." This bravado is soon to be brutally shattered.

As the German bombing of Britain increases, British, Canadian, and American governments are eager to help remove British children from harm's way. The Children's Overseas Reception Board (CORB) is thus established by the British government in 1940 to send children to Canada and the US for the duration of the war. "Within five weeks of announcing its foundation, CORB had received around 32,000 applications for evacuation to the USA," write historians Roger Kershaw and Janet Sacks. "CORB estimated that some 6,000 British children might be admitted to the USA each month, but the official scheme never materialized and — in striking contrast to Canada — no CORB children were in the end evacuated there." More than 11,000 children had already been sent abroad through private means between 1939 and 1940, with Canada taking in 6,000 of them. But the CORB program is soon to become another casualty of war with the sinking of the *SS City of Benares*.[49] Fairbridge however — like Barnardo's — has cultivated a cozy relationship with aristocratic patrons and has the ears of top government officials on both sides of the Atlantic. It is allowed to continue shipping children to Canada during World War II. Fairbridge is also allowed exemption from the 1925 federal legislation limiting the age of unaccompanied minors to 14.[50]

3. Work, Discipline and Daily Life on a Fairbridge Farm

Meanwhile, back at Cowichan Station, life for the children and their adult minders goes on. For kids like Tom Isherwood, the Prince of Wales Farm School sometimes feels like a labour camp. He is just eight years old when he arrives in May 1947. "The regular chores might be running the tin dishes to the mess hall; it might be polishing the cottage floors 'til you could see your face in it. Everything to do with that complex, the kids did it," he recalls. "They didn't put anything heavy on you that your age couldn't handle. Little boys like me got to pull the weeds from endless rows of food stretching as far as the eye could see. If it was not weeding, we piled firewood for the cottage and other buildings after the older boys split the cords. Saturdays, we worked 'til noon, then we were free. We used to swim the Koksilah River; they'd dam it up every year for the kids." If there's cruelty on the farm, it isn't all coming from adults. On one occasion Tom is pinned under wet blankets by older boys almost to the point of suffocation. The smaller boys learn to work together to protect one another from older bullies.[51]

Arthur Sager's memories of his tenure as Duties Master during the summer of 1940 gives added insight into the work regime, and of the skill required to manage child labourers.

> For three hours every weekday morning and two hours every
> afternoon, in the sweltering fields of the farm, I acted as the
> slave driver of protesting bands of nine to 14-year-olds, ca-
> joling and browbeating them in their tasks of hoeing, raking,
> weeding, picking peas and digging potatoes. I assigned areas
> of work to groups of them, keeping the rowdiest apart, tried
> to persuade them it was a competitive game to be rewarded
> by 10 minute breaks, or got them singing roundels, and these
> tactics helped. . . . It was only when I shamed them by get-
> ting down on my knees and started weeding myself that the
> revolutionaries would go grumbling back to work.[52]

Work on the home site — cutting grass, tidying up, and piling
wood — was easier to handle, particularly the latter as singsongs
speeded up the time. And in the orchard, when the Games Mistress allowed some of her girls to join in the picking, baskets of
fruit were filled in record time in spite of some harmless dallying
in the branches of the plum trees. "The best part of the day started
at about three when play period began and when I doffed the role
of slave driver to become sports master." Before and after supper
the boys played soccer, rounders, or cricket, but with the arrival
of the hot weather swimming became the most popular form of
recreation.[53]

For most of the boys and girls, Fairbridge is a mixed blessing —
not quite the paradise they'd been promised nor the hell of some
English orphanages. As is often the case in life, it seems to depend
largely on the luck of the draw. For Fairbridge kids, that meant
whether or not you had a good Cottage Mother. As one boy later
recalled, "If you were not liked by your Cottage Mother, your life
was hell. She had complete control over us, she did not have to
answer to anybody; she was our keeper."[54] To a child this may have
seemed literally true, but in fact Cottage Mothers were answerable to the farm school administration. For one thing, they were

not allowed to use physical punishment, although teachers at the day school sometimes reserved this right. William Stoker recalls being called to the front of the class in day school and strapped for a minor infraction.[55] But among the Cottage Mothers' arsenal was the equally potent weapon of public humiliation and denial of privileges. They generally saw to the disciplining of girls while boys were sent to the Duties Master.[56]

Ernie Todd recalls the discipline he received as a toddler not yet five years old. "I wet my bed and as punishment I was made to stand in the middle of the supper table naked with all the other kids around it and I had to repeat these words: 'I am all wet. I am all wet.'"[57] One girl who arrived at Fairbridge's Molong farm in Australia during the 1930s recalled a more subtle but equally devastating punishment for wrongdoing. Describing the weekly "assault on the cottage . . . in the most scrupulous pursuit of dust-free floors, shining woodwork and sparkling windows," she noted what happened to anyone caught doing sub-standard work. "Cottage Mothers stood over them while they toiled, and if for any reason her wrathful eye was not appeased she would rain judgment on the offenders. . . . 'You boy!' she would snap. 'That floor's disgusting. You stay in this afternoon and polish it again.' This was agony for the poor kid because we lived for Saturday afternoon. . . ."[58]

But children are not without their own resources. One woman who lived at the Prince of Wales Farm School recalled a prank played on one of the Cottage Mothers. "One of my most vivid memories at Fairbridge was having to serve the matron her breakfast in bed on Sunday mornings. We hated that. Her eggs had to be boiled just right. I don't recall getting to eat boiled eggs, but I do recall the lumpy oatmeal. What we hated the most was going into her dark, scary room on early Sunday morning. It gave you the creeps going in there. We would tiptoe in, carrying her tray, hoping we didn't trip. We wanted to watch her drink it but she always dismissed us. We quickly left the room and huddled by her door — listening. But she knew we were there. 'Off you go girls, you have chores to do.' Every Sunday we made the matron's tea with the water we boiled the eggs in. Someone told us that the egg water was poisonous and if we made her tea with that water she would be poisoned. We waited nervously every Sunday afternoon to hear the bad news: The matron was dead. The wicked witch was gone! Just like the old witch in *The Wizard of Oz*. We felt justified. We thought she could be a mean old thing."[59]

Duties Master Arthur Sager was not one who relished the disciplinary aspect of his job. Yet keeping order amongst a gang of rambunctious boys meant enforcing some kind of discipline. Sager wisely chose the carrot rather than the stick wherever possible. "At the beginning they were obstreperous, sizing me up, and at table deliberately provocative, but after supper when I took them swimming they became more amenable and later when I read adventure stories aloud to them in the front room they simmered down completely." Sager also took them to movies on Saturday nights in nearby Duncan — another move sure to win the boys' favour. Often he had to help pay for their night out. "We walked the six miles there and back, the boys telling me about their lives in England or singing. They loved to sing — cowboy songs, negro spirituals and songs they'd made up and set to well-known tunes: '*Down on misery farm where you work all day and get no pay. Gone are the days when I was young and free, now are the days when I work in slavery. When I leave this blasted Fairbridge how happy I will be.*'"[60]

Sager recalls an incident where a freshly baked cake set out to cool had mysteriously shrunk by half. "Getting the children together and employing Sherlock Holmes tactics, I'd question each in turn, emphasizing that lying was worse than the crime. While only one admitted to the theft I knew by the size of the missing portion that more than one were guilty but having no option I gave the lad six strokes on the bottom, telling him he was the best of the lot." Within 10 minutes the other boys showed up to confess their part and asked to be punished. Wherever possible, Sager chose minor discipline such as giving boys extra duties, and used only a soft running shoe rather than a cane for spankings. One boy was repeatedly sent to him by Cottage Mothers for bedwetting — a common sign of stress amongst children in care. "In these and other recurring cases I suspected that the Cottage Mothers were more at fault than the boys, that sympathetic understanding was lacking. But moving children from one cottage to another was contrary to Fairbridge practice as it would have caused friction between 'mothers.'"[61]

But one woman recalls receiving "awful thrashings" from her Cottage Mother for being "the prankster, the arguer." She would later write that she felt "many members of the staff had little or no training in handling children. The popular housemothers had brought children of their own into the world and 'knew the ropes' already...."[62] This lack of experience surfaced particularly during the war when funds for hiring qualified staff became more and more difficult to obtain. Teacher Mary Schofield (later Nichols), who taught at the Prince of Wales Farm School from 1943–48, recalls that the Cottage Mothers were all widows. "Cottage Mothers are extremely varied," she writes in a letter to her family. She speaks of one as a "battle axe, madly strapping 10 boys in one day."[63]

Schofield had been hired in September 1943, moving from the West Kootenay mountain community of Revelstoke to accept the job. She teaches English, French, Health, and Social Studies, and occasionally music for Grades 7 through 10. She has a close relationship with her family in Vancouver and writes them lively, engaging letters. Her wit and humour shines through these letters, as does her gentleness with children. Mary's writing offers a unique insight into daily life and discipline at the farm school. She seems to get on well with her colleague, day school Principal Jock Gillatt.

"I have just had a gluttonous lunch in the riotous atmosphere of the dining-hall and am reclining until it is time to return and hold forth on *The Deserted Village*," she writes her parents on September 17, 1943. "Little figures are skipping joyously up and down the various paths, discussing life in their quite un-understandable accents. ... Their favourite sport [is] rushing out of their seats to kill flies. Mr. Gillatt pointed out the inadvisability of such activity to which the hunter replied, 'Whoy shouldn't Oi, Sir, Oi loikes killin' flois.' Mr. Gillatt and I had an entertaining talk after school today on the time he had when the first bunch of kids came out and they had school in the dining hall. He was at his wit's end because the kids were all most uncivilized so he told them to write on their trip over from England. 'Eee Sir,' came the reply, 'I was seasick all the way over.'"[64]

Mary — known to friends as "Mimi" or "Moppy" for her head of thick curly hair — soon becomes very popular with her students. "As usual, the kids all take a very active interest in me, especially the ones in my own class, who if not firmly squelched, call me 'Honeybunch' (Huneyboonch). Could God have meant me for a schoolmarm?" As Sager had done, she often spends her personal time taking the kids to movies. Mary seems to relish the social life at Cowichan Station. She writes of corn and wiener roasts by the Koksilah River, with swimming and sing-alongs by campfire. "Walking is quite a Fairbridge *piece de resistance*. Every evening after supp, Erica (Hunter) and I go on long tramps about the countryside, trying not to look too interested when we see Fairbridge love lives out walking in the autumn twilight." But at times the farm's isolation is oppressive. With wartime gasoline rationing, it can be difficult to get away. "The whole trouble about Fairbridge is that it takes an hour to walk into Duncan."[65]

Mary seems to find the children easier to get along with than most of the staff, though she expresses admiration for Logan and Gillatt. She must continually fend off the advances of various male staff members. She writes of one over-eager staff member that, "my BA rather stuns him. Great protection against prospective wolves, a BA and a school teaching degree." The peculiarities of Cottage Mothers crops up repeatedly in her letters. Writing in March 1944 she notes, "Usually, I don't visit cottage Ma's if I can help it because all the gossip you hear about everyone is too unnerving." Earlier in the year she had noted that Logan himself had been worrying about the state of Cottage Mother staff. Then in December she ends up in open conflict with them despite her best efforts. "There's this vulture cottage mother . . . who hates me with a PASSION, period. Mostly because of a bad case of green-eyed monster. . . . When she told her boys they were not to associate with me I burst!" She notes that the girls — and most of the staff — are united in their hatred of the senior Matron, a merciless tyrant.[66]

4. Crisis on the Farm, 1943–45

TROUBLE HAS BEEN BREWING among the Cottage Mothers themselves, who are growing increasingly dissatisfied with conditions at the farm. These conditions include deteriorating buildings, insufficient facilities for bathing and laundry, problems with hygiene amongst the girls, and a lack of contact with the outside world. The pay is poor for such a demanding job. They are given only a half-day off every two weeks and there is no transportation into Duncan. When they do take their vacations, they find that the relief staff has allowed chaos to rule in their absence. The crisis comes to a head with a mass resignation of Cottage Mothers in late 1943, protesting the conditions. The financial stresses of the wartime years leave Fairbridge strapped for cash to fund its operations. As yet there is no government regulation of staff working in childcare, though this is soon to change.[67]

But the Cottage Mothers may have been aware of a far darker shadow that had fallen over Prince of Wales Farm School — a pedophile in their midst. This may be why Mary Schofield had written in a puzzled tone that, "The older girls here are rather peculiar, refusing to take baths, wash their hair and they even sleep in their underwear. It's peculiar the boys are so clean, tidy, well mannered and clever, whereas the girls are just the opposite to a certain degree." If there had been incidents of sexual predation going on at the school, it's not surprising the girls would take steps to make themselves as unattractive as possible.[68]

Yet boys too have been at risk at the farm school. In July 1943 five boys are called to testify against Duties Master EE Rogers for gross indecency at a private trial held in Duncan. Rogers had worked at Prince of Wales in its early years but had been fired by Logan at the insistence of staff. He had gone to work for the Provincial Boys' Industrial School at Coquitlam, BC, and then was re-hired by Logan in autumn 1942, partly on the recommendation of provincial psychiatrist Dr. Crease. Dr. George Davidson, the former Director of Social Welfare for BC and now director of the Canadian Welfare Council, had written Logan of his misgivings about Rogers. A former student of Logan's, Davidson was one of the main contributors to the development of child welfare legislation in BC during the 1930s and '40s. He recalled interviewing Rogers with Logan in 1936 for the position of Duties Master and advising against hiring him. Logan insists in a 1943 report to the local Fairbridge committee that no proof could be found of Rogers' misdeeds. Finally one of the younger boys tells an older Fairbridgian living in Victoria, who then contacts the BC Provincial Police.[69]

Predators are often great charmers, and thus are able to hide their crimes for many years. Rogers seems to fit this profile, since he returned to Prince of Wales Farm School with glowing references from his co-workers at the Coquitlam institution and even from Dr. Crease. His trial is held in a closed court, likely to protect both the boys' reputations and that of Fairbridge Farm Schools, which would be wiped out if the scandal became public knowledge. Because the case had been prosecuted through the office of the Attorney-General, however, it had come to the attention of Premier John Hart. A Fairbridge supporter, Hart, too, keeps silent on the controversy. Rogers is convicted and sent to the provincial penitentiary.[70]

The scandal forces Logan to admit that the current system at Fairbridge is flawed. Rogers' trial results in a reorganization of the Duties Master department at the farm school. Former Principal's Assistant Major TM Wilson, formerly the day school caretaker, is given the position. Another staff member is assigned to oversee the children's recreational activities. Older boys in each cottage are assigned as "prefects" to assist Cottage Mothers in supervising the other boys. Unfortunately, it seems that Duties Master Wilson has a predilection for teenage girls. He is seen on occasion walking around the grounds with a girl on each arm. At staff meetings Logan warns him, but to little effect. The more careful girls learn to avoid Wilson's cottage.[71]

Complaints of "sexual delinquency" at Prince of Wales Farm School soon reach the BC government. Officials in the Child Welfare department had already been frustrated by Fairbridge's refusal to comply with the Provincial Act to Provide for the Protection of Children. The Act represents a bold departure in social policy, making the BC Superintendent of Child Welfare the guardian of children in care, using foster homes as its primary means of caring for children, and working with the Children's Aid Societies of Vancouver and Victoria. Until now Fairbridge has operated mostly on a "handshake agreement" with federal and provincial governments. Ottawa had given its approval for Fairbridge during the tenure of Prime Minister RB Bennett in March 1934, with BC Premier Thomas D. Patullo granting consent through BC Provincial Secretary Dr. GM Weir. The trouble begins with the passing of the Welfare Institutions Licensing Act, which comes into effect in April 1938. Dr. Weir, a Fairbridge supporter, assures Logan that he did not have the farm school in mind when he wrote the draft legislation.[72]

Meanwhile, Dr. Davidson writes Logan a very direct letter in July 1944, pointing out that Fairbridge had "consistently ignored the existence of the legislation ... and even went over the heads of departmental officials to obtain special political dispensation from Cabinet Ministers who, as a result of representations made by or on behalf of Fairbridge, instructed departmental officials to keep hands off and not apply the provisions of the Welfare Institutions Licensing Act in your case." This gave rise to deep resentment amongst Child Welfare officials at being prevented from doing their job. Fairbridge's London office had advised avoiding coming under the new legislation since it prohibited bringing children into BC from outside the province. Logan argues that, unlike other child emigration agencies, Fairbridge kids aren't "placed" with families but housed and educated at the farm school and then at age 16 provided with jobs in the community. He is convinced that children committed to the care of Fairbridge will be given far better care than they would if placed in foster homes.[73]

The field of social welfare is making great strides during the war years as a deeper understanding of child psychology is gained. No longer is it considered enough to merely ensure the physical necessities of life and a basic education are met. A child's unique emotional needs at different developmental stages are finally better understood. The Canadian Welfare Council had, under its long-time administrator social reformer Charlotte Whitton, begun to press for changes to the regulation of child immigration in the 1920s. The first child welfare legislation in BC, the Children's Protection Act, was passed in 1901 but it took until 1924 for a Superintendent of Neglected Children to be appointed. Under Whitton's direction the Council conducted province-by-province surveys of child welfare and made recommendations to government, starting with BC in 1927. Within a decade of that survey, while Dr. Davidson was Director of Social Welfare for BC, he questioned the Fairbridge policy of bringing children from English homes where both parents were still living. Fairbridge had been able to invoke special privilege to avoid compliance with the 1925 legislation banning child immigrants under age 14.[74]

Logan explains to his committee that the new generation of social workers — including BC Superintendent of Child Welfare Laura Holland — regards schemes like Fairbridge as retrograde. The Rogers affair and complaints filed by former Cottage Mothers has only tended to confirm this impression. Laura Holland has played a significant role in drafting the new social welfare policy in BC. Holland, who founded the Department of Social Work at UBC, started her career with reforming the Children's Aid Society of Vancouver during the 1920s, first improving its institutional care and then eliminating it altogether in favour of foster care. From there, she was hired by the Provincial Department of Child Welfare as Deputy Superintendent of Neglected Children, where she "completely reorganized the child welfare services of British Columbia." Holland had been recruited by Whitton herself to create a trained and competent childcare workforce in BC. Writing in the Canadian Welfare Council newsletter in 1951, Annie Angus noted, "To Miss Laura Holland the children of British Columbia owe an incalculable debt."[75]

Dr. Davidson had written Logan that he ranked Holland's "judgment, advice and fair-mindedness as second to none in all of Canada," and was puzzled at his resistance to her direction. Holland's colleague Isobel Harvey, another former student of Logan's at UBC, is the new Deputy Superintendent of Neglected Children. Logan writes to his committee that he suspects most of the opposition to the Prince of Wales Farm School is coming from Harvey. Like her colleagues, she believes the day for schemes such as Fairbridge is past. Harvey had expressed alarm at the rate of juvenile delinquency amongst Fairbridge kids, although this had mostly been confined to the petty misdemeanors typical of many young men undergoing a turbulent adolescence. Harvey first meets with Logan at the farm school on April 27, 1944. She is dismayed by Logan's casual attitude, especially toward the pedophile scandal, which "still persisted and was likely to contaminate new arrivals."[76]

At Holland's direction, the provincial government commissions an investigation of the Prince of Wales Farm School. Isobel Harvey arrives there on August 4, 1945 with other Child Welfare staff members, while provincial psychiatrist Dr. Crease arrives on the 7th. Harvey conducts private interviews with the girls while Dr. Crease gives psychological tests to both boys and girls. Some of the staff is also interviewed. About 35 of the 100 or more children are examined. Harvey notes that the girls' clothing, except for their Sunday dresses, is so poor-looking that "one might imagine they were residents of an orphanage in the last century." Cleanliness is a problem, with only one bathtub in each cottage. As Mary Schofield had noticed, adolescent girls especially are in need of someone to teach them how to groom themselves. Harvey wonders how their employers manage to put up with them in such a slovenly state. Somehow she fails to make the connection between this and the fact that the girls are probably trying to repel a molester.[77]

Harvey also reports negatively on the food served the children, "a dreadful sameness day after day," with the only well-balanced meal being served at dinner in the cottages. She cites a lack of fruit in their diet, though this is contradicted by Logan — the farm had produced its first surplus of fruit for canning during the past year. Harvey claims that Cottage Mothers enjoy bacon and eggs while watching children eat breakfasts of porridge, milk, and bread. This, too, is disputed by some staff.[78]

The health report by Dr. Crease cites cases of recurring tonsillitis with no attempt to seek medical treatment. Two boys are found to be wearing glasses they have outgrown. The problem of bedwetting is chronic. "Apparently enuresis has been accepted in a fatalistic manner," writes Harvey, "at least, one would judge so when a 16-year-old girl of average intelligence, who has been at Fairbridge eight years, still has a wet bed every night." She notes that the nurse lacks adequate qualification, her only previous experience being at a mental hospital. Dr. Crease orders medical treatment for some of the children and the hiring of a special nurse for the worst enuresis cases. He further orders that four children requiring special care be removed from Fairbridge care and placed in foster homes.[79]

Discipline continues to be administered according to an outdated British parochial school model, Harvey observes. This actually contradicts founder Kingsley Fairbridge, who disdained physical punishment.

This is not the form of discipline known to Canadians, where we endeavour at least to teach self-discipline. The children are harried over every mistake that most mothers would wisely overlook. Corporal punishment is said to be very rare, but according to the children, that statement is untrue. Girls of 12 and over are sent to a man for strapping, often for merely high spirits such as a pillow fight. . . . Then the necessity for regimentation of the children makes any child who is different liable to punishment. Over and over in the records you find that the ability to take punishment is emphasized, while the ability to discipline oneself is scarcely mentioned.[80]

The farm's approach to discipline takes no account of the traumatic histories of some children:

One 12-year-old with the stature of an eight-year-old came out in 1941; he was through the Blitz in England and was emotionally affected so that he dawdled over everything, even coming home from school. His Cottage Mother knew he had come from a home where he was physically abused. To cure him of dawdling home from school she took a stick and gave him a whipping. She was a bit scared afterwards because he turned grey and shook for the rest of the day. "But," said she, "he never dawdled again, and now he has learned to take his punishment like a little man." Yet she wonders why he does not grow.[81]

This startling lack of sensitivity to children's needs, particularly amongst the Cottage Mothers — what Harvey calls the "foundation stone of a cottage system" — exposes a critical weakness. As she explains, they are the children's substitute for their own mothers. But with the chronic staffing problems at the farm school, it's impossible for children to get any sense of stability in their home environment. Harvey notes the case of one boy who had already had nine different Cottage Mothers. She further cites a complete breakdown in communication between them and senior staff. "No conferences are held where all those who are working with a child meet together. The half-yearly reports reveal this very clearly where the school, the cottage and the medical service all give opposing reports on the child. The Principal apparently makes all decisions regardless of staff opinion."[82]

Regarding the training placements for senior boys and girls outside the farm school, Harvey commends the Aftercare Officer for doing the best she can for the girls. However, for the boys, letter communication from Logan seems to be the only follow-up, a method she regards as "next to useless." The usual problems apply — not the least being a child's fear of punishment from an employer he has complained about. First impressions of a work placement can suddenly change when the true nature of an abusive employer is revealed. The agreement with employers stipulates that half of a Fairbridge child's wages are paid to the school. This leaves young men and women struggling to support themselves. "One old Fairbridgian with whom I talked said she earned $15 a month and had only $7.50 to dress herself on, buy car fare, drugs and essentials," Harvey writes. "Another old Fairbridgian said she had to live for two years on $12.50 a month, and that none of the clothes that were given her were even wearable outside Fairbridge."[83]

As to the sexual misconduct that had led to the investigation, Harvey records that the farm school has made no attempt to manage the problem. The Child Welfare Branch was disturbed by the high incidence of out-of-wedlock pregnancies among Fairbridge girls. "Between 1938 and 1944, one-third of the girls (19 out of 57) who left for outside employment at the age of 16 became illegitimately pregnant. Their illegitimacy rate was three times higher than that among single girls of a similar age in the province," writes historian Patrick Dunae.[84] There are also reports of abortions, though Principal Logan is unaware of the details. When Harvey discusses with Logan "the homosexual activities which had so alarmed others," he brushes it off by saying, "the British people are over-sexed." Harvey reports that in the Rogers pedophilia case, two other staff members had been implicated. "Experiences such as these have a terrific effect on a child, and should be taken into account when dealing with the child. Mr. Logan feels that a psychiatrist does very little for a child, he only needs a friend to show him the right way."[85]

"Gossip swirls around with its usual carefree abandon due to the visit of the Social Service saggy-bags and what the government will recommend should be done for Fairbridge,"writes Mary Schofield in September.[86] Fairbridge by this time has been receiving an annual subsidy of $12,500 from the BC government, plus $3,520 a year toward teacher's salaries.[87] On Dr. Davidson's recommendation, provincial authorities suspend the grant pending the results of the investigation. Logan advises the London executive not to send any more children from England until the crisis is resolved. At a government conference with the farm school committee in September, it's agreed that Harvey's report "warrants immediate action by the Society." Should Fairbridge decide to close the farm school, the government stands ready to place its children in foster homes within six months.[88]

As testimony to the caring and competent work of teachers like Mary Schofield, Dr. Crease reports that Fairbridge children are in excellent mental condition and that the teaching is right up to their capacity. Among the recommendations he makes are that staff salaries be increased. When the new Duncan school district salary schedules are released in 1946, Mary reports to her family that her rate will go from $1,580 per year to $1,650, with a bonus of $90 for teachers who have taught in the district for three years. Sadly, she is forced to resign in May 1948 due to a family illness — her father dies shortly afterward. Day school Principal Gillatt, obviously impressed by her work, urges her to consider returning once she's had sufficient leave.[89]

Newspaper reports of the provincial investigation surface in January and February 1945, although the public is spared the gory details. Once again, Fairbridge's cozy relationship with officials as high as the premier's office seems to be paying off. Privately, Deputy Provincial Secretary Walker assures Fairbridge he has no desire "to bring forward the Rogers affair." But the unwelcome attention on the Prince of Wales Farm School has attracted the attention of federal immigration officials, who "are under the impression that some of the children sent to the school are below Canadian standards and would not be admitted to this country under any other auspices," due to major physical or mental deficiencies.[90]

Logan feels compelled to explain the situation to his staff, who until now have been kept out of the loop. Mary Schofield writes a letter to her family breaking the news, skewed heavily by Logan's interpretation of the facts. He focuses on Fairbridge's refusal to register under the Welfare Institutions Licensing Act, and seems intent on continued resistance.

> He doesn't want the Social Service people putting their finger in his little pie because of their wild enthusiasm for foster homes. If they had much power in the place, they'd put some of the kids in these homes which would enrage the people in England who have sent their kids out here because they want them to grow up at Fairbridge, not in someone else's home. And the subscribers in England ... who pay the piper, naturally want to call their own tune without interference from the BC Social Service. So they have now reached a great impasse — they insist on minding Fairbridge's business and Mr. Logan insists on minding his own and until some agreement is reached, no more kids can come. But Gordon Green, a member of the London committee has providentially arrived in Victoria and presumably is arranging a way out. It makes me burn tho' to think of a lot of old busybodies keeping over 100 poor little characters waiting in England just because they think they should run everything.[91]

Provincial Secretary Pearson had warned in October 1944 that unless Fairbridge was prepared to cooperate, he would consider opening up the investigation to a public enquiry. Gordon Green arrives in Canada early in January 1945, meeting first in Ottawa with AL Jolliffe, Deputy Minister of Mines and Resources, Immigration Branch, and his assistant in charge of juvenile immigration MJ Scobie. "I found a clear understanding of the trouble and an unmistakable will to help me solve it," Green notes in a report to the Fairbridge executive. "It was apparent that the Principal was open to attacks because he upheld a feeble staff and lacked decision in his command." Scobie sets out for BC with Green to meet with Deputy Provincial Secretary Walker. Green negotiates an amendment to the Welfare Institutions Licensing Act, having it changed to allow Fairbridge continued emigration of children into British Columbia.[92]

Not content with that, Green and Scobie propose a special amendment to the Protection of Children Act, removing guardianship powers from the Superintendent of Child Welfare in the case of Fairbridge children. Scobie concedes Green's point that the Society "could not yield its responsibilities in such a way over the lives of the children entrusted to it nor could it send $60,000 annually to Canada for their care and maintenance whilst having no voice in the nature and extent of the custody, training, placing and after-care of the children." Green writes the Fairbridge board that they can expect "complete cooperation" from the Child Welfare department — in exchange for certain concessions. The management at Prince of Wales Farm School will be required to "keep in touch with the Welfare officials, use their help and conform to their standards."[93]

Green meets with Provincial Secretary George Pearson on January 23. Pearson agrees to the amendments provided certain conditions are met. Decision-making authority for the Prince of Wales Farm School must be transferred from Fairbridge's London executive to a local board of governors and be answerable to the Minister for Child Welfare. More careful screening of applicant children in England must be done to avoid sending out those lacking the capacity to adjust to their new situation in Canada. Following a brief visit to the farm school by Deputy High Commissioner Stephen Holmes later that week, Green is advised to invite two women to join the local board of governors — Laura Holland and Annie Angus, a social worker with the Children's Aid Society of Vancouver. Holland's appointment to the board had been recommended in February 1944 but was deferred pending the results of the investigation.[94]

Certain staff changes must also be made, starting with the hiring of a trained social worker as the new Matron at the farm school. Green reports to the High Commissioner in Ottawa that Logan will be asked to resign as principal of the Prince of Wales Farm School in June. Provincial Secretary Pearson had pressed this point as early as November 1943, commending the principal's "character and integrity," but concluding that his management skills were inadequate.[95] Green, too, cites Logan's "personal qualities and high reputation," noting that Fairbridge will retain his services for public relations and fundraising.

Logan's assistant, William Garnett, is appointed principal in July 1944 by the newly re-organized board. Garnett is released from his duties with the Royal Canadian Navy to accept the job. He is described by the Fairbridge board as someone who "lives and breathes Fairbridge." Amended Fairbridge policy requires the board to employ staff trained in childcare and special training in farm school methods before the postwar influx of children arrive. Inevitably, this will mean that the less satisfactory Cottage Mothers will lose their jobs. Fairbridge agrees to work with the provincial government in student aftercare and job placements. Most placements so far have been confined to the Vancouver Island and Lower Mainland area. Some trainees will now be sent as far afield as Kelowna and Vernon.[96]

No less than Sir Charles Hambro, a member of the London executive, visits the farm school in May 1945 to boost morale. "Sir Charles made a speech in the dining hall," writes Mary Schofield. "He told us there was a little band of brothers who would be with us as soon as transportation could be arranged. Hurrah!"[97] The flow of children resumes with a party of 17 boys and 10 girls arriving at the farm on July 29 — the first to arrive at Cowichan Station since 1941. They had traversed the Atlantic separately — the boys on the *SS Bayano* and the girls on the *SS Erria*. As if to mark the occasion, they had been accompanied on the train from London by Gordon Green. Although rationing is still in effect, Fairbridge spares no expense for the first postwar emigration party. "We were accommodated three to a cabin. During the day we played games of shuffleboard and spent some of our time filling up on ice cream, sweets and fruit. The meals were very good; we often had chicken, which is something not very often seen in England these days," writes one of the boys in the *Fairbridge Gazette*.[98]

But their exhilaration will be short-lived — the writing is on the wall for the Prince of Wales Farm School. Within five years, the dream of Kingsley Fairbridge will die a quiet death in Canada. The last six children arrive at Cowichan Station on May 25, 1948. Their signatures in chalk can be seen to this day preserved in the boiler room of the Chapel.[99]

5. SUNSET OVER BC's NEW EDEN

DURING WORLD WAR II, 70 "Old Fairbridgian" boys and 12 girls served in various branches of the military and merchant marine. Two were killed in action and one — Jim Lally — was made a prisoner of war when his RCAF plane was shot down over Germany. One of the dead sacrificed to the Allied cause is Harry Logan's son John Elmo Logan.[100] But the casualties of war number far more than the killed and wounded. They include cherished values and institutions, however wrong-headed or well intentioned. Hopes remain bright following the provincial investigation and subsequent reorganization of the Prince of Wales Farm School, but postwar conditions continue to pose a serious challenge. With the British Isles financially exhausted after six years of war, restrictions are put on the flow of cash outside the country. Qualified staff is as difficult to find as during the war years.

By January 1945 the farm school has only 100 residents — half the total capacity of the cottages. The effect is even more pronounced at Fintry Farm. In 1940 there were 18 boys and two girls there from June to October; by 1943 only seven boys aged 15–18 are there. "Now that we are allowed to expand once more I hope before long that Fintry will become more and more active as a centre for teaching boys the more advanced agricultural methods and a post-graduate school for Old Fairbridgians," Sir Charles had written in 1945. A proposal to use Fintry as a resettlement location for persons displaced by the war fails to materialize.[101]

And in fact Fintry is the first Fairbridge asset to be put on the chopping block. Already in November 1943, RW Mayhew, a member of the local farm school committee, had written Sir Charles advising that Fintry be disposed of as soon as possible. Mayhew argued that it provided training for too few children to make its expense worthwhile. Although British contributions to Fairbridge remained strong during 1946–47, a report filed by Fintry's subcommittee in 1948 made it clear that it was still far from enough: total losses from 1938–48 were nearly $43,000. The board of governors turns down an offer of $55,000 for Fintry in the fall of 1947 (the land had been valued at between $0.5–1 million when Dun-Waters bequeathed the estate in 1938). In October 1948 a realty firm finally sells the estate for $65,000 to a private owner.[102]

Even with the resumption of emigration parties from the UK after the war, the parties are smaller. With two parties in 1946, the first arriving at Cowichan Station November 29 and the second on December 9, only 15 boys are added to the farm school's population. This makes it impossible to qualify for government grants to hire teachers of domestic science or manual training — key components of the farm school's curriculum. A return to pre-war numbers is seen in the emigration party of May 31, 1947, comprising 27 boys and one girl, but it's a short-lived surge. Although the Fairbridge Society in London plans to send 84 new children in 1948, the deepening financial crisis forces them to send only six. Likely at Laura Holland's urging, problem cases at the farm school are referred to the Child Welfare department for placing in foster homes. A few of the most difficult cases are repatriated to England.[103]

The Fairbridge executive in London explains that although

there's no lack of funds in England, the difficulty of transferring British Sterling remains. An effort will have to be made to make up for the shortfall by raising funds in Canada, with the goal of $100,000 per year. Harry Logan offers to spearhead the fundraising drive in Eastern Canada. But despite the new board's optimism, the May 1948 party of children proves to be the last. In May 1949 Provincial Secretary George Pearson tells visiting officials of the Fairbridge Society that the Prince of Wales Farm School must be brought fully under the jurisdiction of the BC Department of Education. "Finally, in July 1949, the British Columbia directors resolved to disband their board and to close the facility. Since the provincial government effectively controlled the board, the London executive had little choice but to accept the decision," writes Dunae. In March 1950 the Prince of Wales Farm School lands are rented by the dairy firm Stevenson and McBryde, inheriting 70 head of purebred Ayrshire cattle — the final legacy of Captain Dun-Waters. The last children at the farm school leave in December. During its 15 years of operation a total of 329 children lived and worked at the Prince of Wales Farm School — 97 girls and 232 boys.[104]

But the legacy of Kingsley Fairbridge — both the good and the bad — lives on.

6. Outside Eden: Picking Up the Pieces

The book was closed at last on child emigration to Canada. Partly Fairbridge was the victim of changing times. Advances in the field of child welfare had put an end to the emigration of children overseas without their families. Child welfare had made major strides during the war years, culminating in the Curtis Commission in the UK in 1947. The Commission re-evaluated the condition of all children's homes and facilities throughout Britain based on new criteria, such as the need for affection and a more homelike atmosphere. The Curtis Report was directly responsible for Britain's 1948 Child Act, laying the foundations of a social welfare system that was badly needed in the aftermath of war. "Less than two years after publication of the Curtis Report, the Poor Law had been repealed and replaced by a series of statutes making separate provision for children and for the elderly and disabled people, with another statute for hospitals," writes Kenneth Henry Brill. The report would revolutionize childcare in Britain, calling for a shift to a foster care system and doing away with orphanages entirely. The commission was not, however, opposed to private children's homes and cottage-based systems or farm schools. But the days of Fairbridge and Barnardo's operating with a free hand were over — they would now be answerable to social welfare agencies and required to conform to their standards.[105]

In BC the counterpart to the Curtis Report was the Marsh Report prepared in 1948 by Leonard C. Marsh, a PhD with the Department of Social Work at the University of British Columbia. Marsh studied conditions at the Prince of Wales Farm School and made recommendations for improvements. His assessment was considerably more positive than the Harvey Report, while acknowledging that "there has been a radically changed appreciation of the critical problems of institutional care. The fact must be faced that to bring very young children to a new country, simple though it sounds, is to tackle immigration the hard way." Marsh advised that by far the preferred approach to emigrating children to Canada is to do so when they are already of school-leaving age or accompanied by their parents. Harvey had essentially concluded that Fairbridge was obsolete and should be replaced by the foster care system advocated by the Curtis Commission.[106]

With the massive societal and economic upheavals brought on by the First World War and then the Great Depression, Kingsley Fairbridge's original vision had become untenable in barely more than 20 years. As historian David Dendy points out, already by the 1930s, its training scheme "meant that the boys were being trained to be farm labourers and the girls to be farm domestics or farmer's wives, at a time when mechanization and the Depression were sending unprecedented numbers of rural Canadians to the cities." But Dendy's conclusion that the Fairbridge Farm Schools "did much more good than harm" is debatable. Despite the "stiff upper lip" presented by "Old Fairbridgians" in the decades since the closures at Cowichan Station and Fintry, not all former residents of the farms recall their experiences with pleasure.[107]

Patricia Skidmore, daughter of "Fairbridge girl" Marjorie Arnison, and the current editor of the *Fairbridge Gazette,* puts it this way: "Of the 329 children sent to the school there are 329 different stories — and yes, they range where some state that being sent to Fairbridge was the very best of luck; but there are many, many stories of neglect and abuse and emotional trauma." Skidmore explains that although 95 percent of Fairbridge boys and girls were *not* orphans, many were *told* they were. "Being an orphan was used as a very derogatory term and confusing to my young mother, because she was not an orphan. Thus, many children such as my mother never really got over losing their families. And to be treated horribly at the school, and to be told over and over by your cottage 'mother' that you were 'British trash,' and an orphan was a difficult way to grow up."[108]

British Prime Minister Gordon Brown's apology in February 2010 was thus a watershed moment for thousands of Home Children scattered around the globe. Skidmore says the apology was the catalyst for her mother's healing. "It wasn't until my mother and I were invited to British PM Gordon Brown's apology that she was able to finally shed the shame of being removed from her mother's care in 1937. Possibly it was the first time in her life where she felt she had nothing to fear, and it took her years to speak out against her treatment at the farm school."[109]

Neither was the Australian experience at the Pinjarra Farm School what Kingsley Fairbridge intended. Author Sanchia Berg, writing of one woman's recollections of growing up there, relates a tale of abuse. "Some children seem to have been fond of their substitute parents, and have good memories of the Farm, but Jackie's Cottage Mother was cruel. Lonely and scared, Jackie started wetting her bed at night. The Cottage Mother would force her head into the toilet and then flush it or lock her into a dark cupboard under the stairs. Jackie tried to run away but she was always brought back. 'There was no-one to turn to,' she told me. Jackie was disgusted to learn that the Home Office had been specifically warned about the Farm three years before she arrived but had still sent children there."[110]

As is often the case, once a founder either dies or becomes too absorbed with corporate duties, the original intent can become corrupted. Kingsley Fairbridge — like Dr. Barnardo, Annie Macpherson, and others in the child emigration movement — seems to have had a genuine concern for children. While he was present at the farm school in Australia, children were indeed treated with fairness and compassion. "With an average age of about 10 on arrival, most of the young emigrants of 1912–13 spent up to five or six years on the Pinjarra farm working alongside Fairbridge but also extending their formal education," writes Fairbridge historian Geoffrey Sherington. "Still only in his thirties, he undoubtedly developed a strong rapport with these first parties of children. As his wife and a later commentator have suggested, it was during the First World War that a community almost like an extended family developed at Pinjarra, albeit governed by Fairbridge's own values and sense of imperial mission."[111]

The work of British social worker Margaret Humphreys in reuniting Australian child migrants with their families was initially met with a spate of denials from former Fairbridge residents, who loudly defended the institution. Humphreys was told emphatically by one man at a Fairbridge reunion near Sydney, "It might have happened to Catholic migrants, but not to us. We're Fairbridgians!" However, this soon gave way to Fairbridgians who began to tell stories of deprivation, mental cruelty, and brutality. When Flo Hickson, a former resident of an Australian Fairbridge Farm School, visited the site in her 60s in 1987, a flood of traumatic memories caused a breakdown. She was sent to the farm at age five, living and working there between 1928 and 1941. Hickson was moved to write a memoir of her experiences. "Always, somewhere in a cottage, somebody was being thrashed with a strap on the bare bottom, as if life wasn't punishing enough with the deprivation of home, family and country," she recalls.[112]

The Australian newspaper *The Daily Mail* reported on June 14, 2011 that 69 former residents of Fairbridge Farm School at Molong in New South Wales are seeking compensation for physical and sexual abuse they allegedly suffered there. About 890 children were sent to Molong between 1936 and 1974. Lawyer Peter Semmler "outlined a number of inquiries and reports from governmental bodies throughout the decades regarding allegations of abuse at the school," including reports of sadistic beatings. "'There was evidence British authorities blacklisted Fairbridge Farm School for a short time and recommended no more children should be sent there,' Mr. Semmler said." Former managing director of the Australian Broadcasting Corporation David Hill, another former resident of Molong, said, "some of the Cottage Mothers were brutally sadistic." Others who managed to escape the abuse recalled life at Molong as "tough but fair."[113]

The same horrific scenario had been going on at the Fairbridge Pinjarra farm. An investigation by reporter Joe Catanzaro during 2012 revealed that 205 children sent there between 1930 and 1981 have been awarded more than $1.1 million in payments for abuses suffered at the farm. "The staggering number of payouts came to light after child migrants broke decades of silence to expose incidences of pedophilia, pack rape, brutal beatings and slave labour-like conditions that have scarred them for life," Catanzaro reported in *The West Australian*. Six of these victims spoke to the newspaper, shattering the long-held belief that Fairbridge was better than other child migrant institutions. Formerly sealed documents in Britain show that authorities turned a blind eye despite warnings of the abuse. As early as 1949, former Fairbridge Pinjarra Principal Dallas Patterson had warned the British Home Office with detailed accounts of exploitation, slavery, and sexual abuse dating back to the 1930s. The case was bolstered by the discovery in 2012 of a 99-year-old Fairbridge registry book, previously thought to be lost. A complete record of children's histories since coming into the care of Fairbridge, the book also lists out-of-court settlements paid to victims of abuse. "Child migrant and former Labour MP Mike Barnett said he believed Fairbridge had dodged the same level of scrutiny and subsequent infamy applied to other child migrant institutions because of its patronage from British royalty and a WA (Western Australia) board that was stacked with local movers and shakers."[114]

To its credit, almost from the beginning, the Australian government supported Margaret Humphreys' work by providing her with an office and a paid staff member. Then on November 16, 2009 the historic moment for generations of Australian child immigrants finally came. Prime Minister Kevin Rudd became the first head of state from a former British colony to offer a public apology and reparations funds to its "forgotten children." "We come together today to deal with an ugly chapter in our nation's history," Rudd said to a packed audience in the Great Hall of Australia's Parliament House, Canberra:

> And we come together today to offer our nation's apology. To say to you, the Forgotten Australians, and those who were sent to our shores as children without your consent, that we are sorry. . . . We acknowledge the particular pain of children shipped to Australia as child migrants — robbed of your families, robbed of your homeland, *regarded not as innocent children but regarded instead as a source of child labour.* For these failures to offer proper care to the powerless, the voiceless and the most vulnerable, we say sorry. We reflect too today on the families who were ripped apart simply because they had fallen on hard times. And let us also resolve this day that this national apology becomes a turning point in our nation's story. The truth is this is an ugly story. And its ugliness must be told without fear or favour if we are to confront fully the demons of our past.[115]

The problem with well-intentioned philanthropists seems to be one of scale. Once the operation expands beyond a certain point, there's simply no way to ensure that everyone in the firm will be as purely motivated. As child migration expert Dr. Barry M. Coldrey notes, professional standards for childcare staff didn't exist in Australia before the 1960s. "Often the staff were almost as deprived as the young people for whom they were caring. In fact, some had been raised in institutions themselves. They had a sparse, sometimes miserable life and projected their frustrations on to the children."[116] The sheer scale of the farm schools — and the separation from real family — made Fairbridge's vision of a true home atmosphere nearly impossible. Journalist Janet Wainwright, who reviewed Flo Hickson's memoir, concluded, "In retrospect, Kingsley Fairbridge's philanthropic dream to give the British children a better life was no more successful than Australia's separating Aboriginal children from their parents."[117]

Although the 1940s had seen a giant leap forward in the understanding of childhood emotional needs, the proposed solution — foster care — has since proven nearly as problematic as the solutions employed by 19th century philanthropists like Dr. Barnardo. A November 25, 2012 report in *The Telegraph* by Roger Graef noted that in Britain's modern foster care system, there are plenty of victims. "On average, a child in care moves 'home' every 11 months — think what damage that does to their chances of building the trust vital to creating successful relationships," Graef writes. "And after the age of five, a child's chances of being adopted successfully go down exponentially." One of the girls who arrived with the last party of children at the Prince of Wales Farm School would later recall that the abuses there "fade in comparison to abuses some of us faced in different foster homes."[118]

The sad experience of Tom Isherwood reinforces the failure of foster care. As with many families who sent children to Fairbridge Farm Schools, Tom's mother may have been lured by recruiting posters put up by the organization. His father had been killed during the war and Tom's earliest memories are of the bombing raids over Britain. For families living in deep poverty, struggling to feed hungry mouths, Fairbridge seemed like the perfect solution. Not unlike the "oranges and sunshine" promised child migrants to Australia, Fairbridge children sent to Canada were promised a land of golden opportunity. And with war raging over Britain, many parents were desperate to get their children to safety. "There wasn't much could frighten you more than the sound of bombs falling," Isherwood recalls. "When the air raid sirens go you just do what you're trained to do. School started in England when you were five years old, and we went every day during the bombing."[119]

His experience at the Prince of Wales Farm School was fair, if tightly disciplined and filled with hard work. Thankfully, both boys and girls were allowed time to explore the ample acreage and the nearby Koksilah River with its swimming and fishing hole. Occasionally the boys would head to nearby Duncan without permission for a visit to town. "We were disciplined severely the time we did get caught out of bounds, but it was worth it," he recalls. "When we did speak, I believe the people loved our English accent but were for the most part glad to see us head back out of town. If they had only known, we were not Fagin's vagrants, pickpockets or thieves."[120]

It was when the farm was forced to close in 1949–50 that things really went off the rails for Isherwood. He was shuffled from foster home to foster home over a dozen times in five years. A brief stint in a strict Catholic school in Vancouver did its best to crush his spirit. He recalls thinking of one of his foster mothers, "How could Mum know what we did at Fairbridge where we were growing up with little hearts of stone and feelings that were stretched like elastic bands, ready to snap at any time. I was to be seen and not heard, and harsh loveless discipline was normal to my way of life." Separated from his sister at age eight, he would later learn — too late — that she had gone to Australia. By the time he discovered her whereabouts she had already died. He could only stand at her gravesite and weep for a lost sister.[121]

As with so many of the British Home Children, it was the utter lack of love and affection that scarred Isherwood for life. "My young life would hear of no more tears and for a while my heart turned to stone," he recalls. "Nothing came in and nothing went out. I was on a journey to become a survivor — happy outside but very sad inside. Whoever said the past could come back to haunt you was dead on the money."[122]

If you happened to be one of the tough kids, you may have come through the experience relatively unscathed. Former Fairbridgian William Stoker, who came out to the Prince of Wales Farm School in 1937, found the regimented lifestyle suited him well. Coming from the rough streets of Newcastle, by age 11 he was already a member of a local street gang. His father had died when he was an infant, leaving his mother with several children to support, living in gritty public housing tenements. Stoker recalls seeing Fairbridge posters in the Newcastle market and telling his mother he wanted to sign up for a new life in Canada. Later, at age 17, he signed up for the Canadian military during World War II, claiming his age as 18 due to a mistake in his birth certificate. He would go on to a postwar career in the military and in civilian security services for Canadian airports. "I didn't find army life difficult. It was easy to accept. But you know, Fairbridge instilled a work ethic, a daily routine."[123]

Patricia Skidmore recalls growing up as the daughter of a child migrant as a "shameful and often worrying experience for me. As a schoolgirl, I used to tell my classmates that I was from Mars. They seemed to think it was funny, and quite likely some thought I was peculiar. For me, it gave a moniker for my feeling of difference." Patricia as a child never felt she fit in, even though she grew up with a family of her own. "I felt apart from the rest. I didn't belong. I had no sense of family. No roots to ground me to my place of birth. My mother's background, her past, her childhood, her family, was missing. She would not tell me why. It worried me deeply. She rarely spoke of her five years at the Prince of Wales Fairbridge Farm School or why she was sent there as a little girl. All she offered to me was a bleak image . . . a gravel pit, stark, denuded, stripped, and frightening in its lack of detail. She rarely spoke of her family in England. The little she told me left me with more questions than answers."[124]

Once again, we see how a public apology by a head of state can often unlock feelings that have been kept in a vault for decades. When Patricia and her mother attended Prime Minister Brown's apology in London, a reporter asked Marjorie where she felt she belonged. In recent years she had become close to her English relatives, rebuilding family ties that had been lost. "She had to think about it, and with determination said, 'I belong in Canada with my children.' It took her 73 years to be able to say that and it was Brown's apology I believe that allowed her to move forward in this way, and accept her past."[125]

Acceptance is at least a step toward healing. But to those traumatized at an early age, a hole is opened in their psyche that may never fully heal. "I have struggled over 50 years with no help or understanding from the people that did this to me," says Isherwood. He has had to carry a lifelong sense of "being robbed of my childhood and family." A poem he wrote, "First Christmas in Canada, 1947," captures the angst of a child torn from his moorings: "Man is born equal so it's said; / Tell that to the orphan in the iron bed."[126]

Fairbridge boys and girls at Prince of Wales Farm School, near Duncan, BC, 1936. Ron Smith collection/Fairbridge Chapel Society Archives.

Captain James Cameron Dun-Waters, the benefactor who donated his Fintry farm estate near Vernon, BC to Fairbridge. Vernon and District Museum and Archives.

The lovely acres of Fintry farm in the Okanagan where Fairbridge boys and girls were sent to finish their agricultural training. Photo circa 1938. Vernon and District Museum and Archives.

A sketch of Kingsley Fairbridge in working clothes; artist unknown. Ron Smith collection/Fairbridge Chapel Society Archives.

The octagonal barn at Fintry farm. Vernon and District Museum and Archives.

CHAPTER 9

Aftermath —
Troubled Childhood, Troubled Future

If you look deeply into the palm of your hand, you will see your parents and all generations of your ancestors. All of them are alive in this moment. Each is present in your body. You are the continuation of each of these people.
— Thich Nhat Hanh, *The Sun* magazine, November 2011

The ragman is fate, but you bring him to pass.
There's never a rag, but you make it, alas!
— Edwin Leibfreed, 1913

THE SAD TRUTH IS THAT, as the philosopher Hegel says, people and governments never learn anything from history. A strange thing for a historian to admit, I know. But we seem to be moving backward to the mentality of the times when the idea of child slavery and export was born. Since the 1980s, there has been a corporate-driven movement away from the Commons and the social contract. Social services departments everywhere have been eviscerated, their staff's role changed from one of helping the disadvantaged to policing them. It's the very ideal of Victorian morality: wealth and class equal power, those without either are powerless, therefore they are innately weak and deserving of their fate. The classic blame-the-victim rationale. It's a particularly vicious mélange of Malthusian doctrine, social Darwinism, and monopoly capitalism on steroids. No nation nourished on such a bitter root can expect to do anything but repeat history and collapse in on itself.

And how far have we really come in the past 100 years? The lessons learned from the 19th and early 20th centuries about poverty seem to have been lost in the oligarchy's new push for dominance. A series of special BBC News reports in 2005 noted that more than one in four British children today suffer from the disadvantages of poverty. "Poverty is the single greatest threat to the well-being of children in the UK," wrote Neera Sharma, Policy Officer with Barnardo's. In "inner London," including the East End where so many "child savers" got their start in the 1860s, the poverty rate today is still as high as 54 percent. In British Columbia it's somewhat better, but not compared to Canadian national averages. BC has the second-highest rate of childhood poverty in Canada at over 14 percent, or about 1 in 7 children. In a modern Western democracy this is shocking.[1]

The ultra conservative worldview that is sliding us backward is driven as much by ideology as the actions of 19th century Christian philanthropists. It's an ideology that doesn't stoop to consider evidence — but then ideology seldom does. The Occupy movement has done much to promote awareness of the "One Percent" who control the majority of the world's wealth. And the data strongly indicates that societies with the largest gaps in income tend to do worse across a broad range of indicators — education, health, crime, addiction, etc. *The Spirit Level: Why Greater Equality Makes Societies Stronger* by British epidemiologists Richard Wilkinson and Kate Pickett, makes this point. Lynsey Hanley, reviewing the book in *The Guardian*, sums it up well: "On almost every index of quality of life, or wellness, or deprivation, there is a gradient showing a strong correlation between a country's level of economic inequality and its social outcomes." Certainly 21st century poverty in Western countries isn't anywhere near as abject as it was in a 19th century British slum — yet. But at the rate we're going, it won't be long.[2]

Don't get me wrong. I thank whatever God or gods are out there that I was born a Canadian. Growing up during the Trudeau era, I was nourished on his great vision of "The Just Society." To me that ranks right up there with the humanitarian genius of Gandhi. Before we were forced to swallow the bitter pill of "fiscal conservatism" we built a country that had actually learned from its history. Men like Tommy Douglas, the father of Canadian medicare, worked with people in small prairie farming towns. For these people one bad crop was a threat, two was a dangerous downward slide, and three would wipe you out completely. For some it would take considerably less than that. A sickly child and a hopeless burden of medical bills could finish you off just as quickly. Life for the majority was lived on the thin line between home and homeless. For a brief period we learned from our history and saw to it that homelessness was — for most Canadians — a thing of the past, unless you were one of Canada's First Nations. We learned from our British heritage what happens to a society where a few ultra-wealthy live in health and comfort while the masses ride the razor's edge between solvency and destitution. Child slavery was just one social consequence.

We learned that treating everything as a commodity results in human beings becoming expendable, that social Darwinism is nothing more than a fancy rationale for greed — a sociopathic Gospel of Wealth that cares nothing for its millions of victims. Listen to Andrew Carnegie, the elder statesman of industrial capitalists: "We accept and welcome therefore, as conditions to which we must accommodate ourselves, great inequality of environment, the concentration of business, industrial and commercial, in the hands of a few, and the law of competition between these, as being not only beneficial, but essential for the future progress of the race." Competition? Today's captains of industry would likely argue that monopolies and corporate welfare are a far better approach. Progress? For the One Percent, yes. But for the rest of us?

Or any kind of future for our kids and grandkids? Not looking good. In the UK alone, income inequality increased by 32 percent between 1960 and 2005. Since the 1980s income inequality in the US and UK has increased exponentially to levels not seen since the 1920s.[3]

It was 19th century capitalists who perverted Darwin's theory of natural selection to over-emphasize that "only the fittest survive," or as TH Huxley put it, the "nature red in tooth and claw" model of cutthroat competition. Students of Darwin like Peter Kropotkin — better known for his anarchist writings — discovered a very different side to nature in his field studies: cooperation. His book *Mutual Aid* extended this observation to human societies as well. Kropotkin as an evolutionary thinker remains virtually unknown, and until recently the model of humans as innately competitive rather than cooperative was accepted as a given. The feminist thinkers of the 1960s and '70s were the first since Kropotkin to question this hierarchical view. Sadly, such critical thinking has been submerged in the monopoly capitalism tsunami of the past 30 years.

What about the argument that if these children had remained in Britain instead of being emigrated to Canada their lives would have been far worse? It's a rhetorical question that's impossible to answer, and therefore moot. Every individual case would have been different. Still, as I've said at my public presentations on the Home Children, if economic conditions in Britain couldn't create enough jobs for everyone, why not emigrate whole families together? And in fact, by the 1920s, when pressure to reform child immigration was mounting, the Church of England's Empire Settlement Program did just that, for some families. But sadly, for agencies like Barnardo's it was a profitable business as well as a social service. It was obviously cheaper to emigrate children than adults, and cheaper to emigrate than to keep them in an orphanage or workhouse. In fact, when Maria Rye began emigrating children, her primary argument was a fiscal, not a social one, along just those lines.

And what is it that can induce decent, well-intentioned individuals to close ranks and cover up a crime? It happened with Dr. Barnardo's organization in the case of his Canadian superintendent Alfred Owen, who impregnated some of the adolescent girls in his charge. And it happened again at the Prince of Wales Fairbridge Farm School, where both boys and girls were sexually exploited, though managerial incompetence rather than collaboration seems to have been the case here. In Australia a case is being made that collaboration with sexual predators was endemic within child emigration agencies. Sociologists might argue that we are dealing with the fundamentally tribal nature of humans. Even the elite and the social organizations of which they are a part are just another "tribe," or as sociologists describe them, "small groups." "No matter how large, impersonal, and bureaucratic an organization may appear to be from the outside, careful examination usually reveals the existence of whole networks of small, informal social groups within the larger structure. Often these can prove decisive to the success of the large organization," writes Robert Nisbet in *The Social Bond*. Or, arguably, of its failure, when things go wrong.[4]

And of course it has much to do with power dynamics — in the case of child migration, children without recourse to fundamental rights were at the mercy of those who were placed in a position of absolute authority over their lives. "A person who has control of services that others need or desire [*the child emigration agencies and their officers*] and cannot get on their own . . . [*the families of most child migrants*] is plainly in a position of power."[5]

The process of social interaction that goes into the formation of society's constituent groups includes an exchange of conformity or loyalty to the group that requires a closing of ranks during crisis. Although this can explain sociologically the reasons for cover-ups of criminal or merely despicable behaviour, to the ethical observer it remains deeply disturbing. Yet the Alfred Owen scandal was kept quiet until the publishing of June Rose's book *For the Sake of the Children* in 1987. In the Prince of Wales Farm School case,

Principal Logan's incompetence in rooting out sexual offenders from his staff was met with a quiet resignation and a transfer to a lower profile job. It's the moral choice that can face each one of us: how far am I willing to go on behalf of a cause I believe to be right and good? And when does that "good" turn into its own shadow? At what point should the good of society replace the good of the group to whom I feel I owe my loyalty?

> It is easier to build strong children than to repair broken men.
>
> — Frederick Douglass[6]

WHAT ABOUT THE IDEA that all this digging up the past is just a neurotic fixation, something that's best left alone? That assumes we *can* leave life-altering moments in the past, whether they happened to us or one of our ancestors. My wife had a grandfather who was wiped out in the Great Depression and even though, like me, she grew up in the prosperous era of the '60s, she still saves every plastic bag and scrap of leftovers. Was this learned behaviour? Or was some element of this passed down, "in the bones," as it were? Despite Dr. Barnardo's optimism about new beginnings and children as a *tabula rasa*, nothing could fully replace blood ties. The nature vs. nurture debate may go on forever with no resolution. But we know enough about the emergent field of epigenetics to know that environment leaves a distinct, heritable impression on DNA. "Developmental, behavioral, educational, and family problems in childhood can have both lifelong and intergenerational effects," states one study.[7]

The field of Early Childhood Education is thus proving to be a critical component of childcare in the 21st century. The good news is that the brain's plasticity allows for a great deal of healing in the first 3–6 years of life. If, on the other hand, the child's environment those first critical years is badly compromised, he or she can expect to spend a lifetime trying to cope with the fallout. In 1999, Canadian scientist Dr. Fraser Mustard and Margaret Norrie McCain co-authored the groundbreaking *Early Years Study: Reversing the Real Brain Drain* for the Ontario government. "We consider . . . that the period of early child development is equal to or, in some cases, greater in importance *for the quality of the next generation* than the periods children and youth spend in education or post secondary education," they concluded[8] (emphasis added).

Epigenetics also supplies the missing link to physical health, as a predictor of heart disease, asthma, diabetes, and other chronic diseases. But most importantly, it's proof positive that — as the old adage goes — investment in our children is an investment in our future. "If you want a highly competent population with limited behaviour problems and no violence, then you don't have any choice but to invest in early childhood development," said Dr. Mustard. "We know now that development of the brain in the early years of life, particularly the first three years, sets the base of competence and coping skills for the later stages of life. . . . Brain development in the period from conception to six years sets a base for learning, behaviour and health over the life cycle. Ensuring that all our future citizens are able to develop their full potential has to be a high priority for everyone."[9] Another study on early childhood adversity and toxic stress comes to the same conclusion: "the boundaries of pediatric concern must move beyond the acute medical care of children and expand into the larger ecology of the community, state, and society."[10]

Building on the work done by Mustard and McCain, another recent study pointed out a close link between childhood abuse and a high risk during adulthood for various forms of addiction and general dysfunction. "Persons who had experienced four or more categories of childhood exposure, compared to those who had experienced none, had 4–12-fold increased health risks for alcoholism, drug abuse, depression, and suicide attempt; a 2–4-fold increase in smoking, poor self-rated health . . . and sexually transmitted disease; and a 1.4–1.6-fold increase in physical inactivity and severe obesity." The study concluded a strong relationship between childhood abuse factors and a high risk for several of the leading causes of death in adulthood.[11]

Our historians and news media thus have a vital role to play by not playing into the elite's social Darwinist view of human existence. "Although life as it's lived on the ground, close to home, is peppered with suffering, stresses, injustices, and foul play, it is, for the most part, lived out in hundreds of small acts of kindness and generosity," writes Jeremy Rifkin in *The Empathic Civilization*. "Comfort and compassion between people creates goodwill, establishes the bonds of sociality, and gives joy to peoples' lives. Much of our daily interaction with our fellow human beings is empathic because that is our core nature. Empathy is the very means by which we create social life and advance civilization."[12] Dr. Mustard seems to agree with this prescription: "The new evidence is a celebration of what good 'mothering' has done for centuries. Parents have always known that babies and young children need good nutrition, stimulation, love and responsive care."[13]

Sadly for the majority of British Home Children, this was precisely what they did *not* get. Although the brain has far more flexibility than was once believed, the decline of plasticity with age seems a given. Once the critical threshold of birth to age six is passed, it becomes progressively harder to undo the damage. The amazing thing is that people like Elizabeth Thompson, Walter Roberts, and Gladys Martin can call upon a deep reserve of strength they never knew they had, a strength that keeps them going. But there are others who are simply not born with the equipment to cope. These ones we will lose. They are the casualties of civilization.

As if to demonstrate that industrial capitalists still have not learned the lessons of the past 400 years of poverty in Western societies, it took an economic argument to sway current business leaders into funding Dr. Mustard's research. Charles Coffey, retired vice-president of RBC Financial Group and Chair of the Early Child Development Council, has become one of Mustard's biggest supporters. "Like many business people, my first reaction was, 'What's this got to do with banking?' [Mustard] makes the case that this is as much an economic issue as it is a social issue."[14]

It's hardly surprising that Coffey and others like him approach the issue from a purely fiscal, pragmatic point of view. This mindset has been there all along in social efforts to deal with poverty. Here's what Scottish magistrate Patrick Colquhoun had to say in 1806: "Poverty . . . is a most necessary and indispensable ingredient in society, without which nations and communities could not exist in a state of civilization. It is the lot of man — *it is the source of wealth, since without poverty there would be no labour, and without labour there could be no riches, no refinement, no comfort, and no benefit to those who may be possessed of wealth*" (emphasis added). Colquhoun was in step with Robert Malthus and other 19th century economics theorists. Historian Simon Fowler noted that, although British workhouses were "largely designed for a pool of able-bodied idlers and shirkers," such a class of people "hardly existed outside the imagination of a generation of political economists."[15]

For years before discovering Dr. Mustard's work I put it like this: *We are walking history*, by virtue of the fact we carry DNA. Like it or not, we carry its burdens. And as psychologist Carl Jung revealed, DNA is far more than the sum of our physical parts — with it we inherit ancestral memory, culture, and the unresolved traumas of the past. The responsible thing to do personally is to uncover the secrets and do our own healing work. The responsible thing for a nation to do is to make amends to the victims wherever possible.

SO PUT YOURSELF IN A HOMEBOY'S PLACE: dragging furrows into a Manitoba horizon behind a team of horses, day after day. Wondering when you'll see anyone or anything else. Expected to shoulder the workload of a full-grown man while you're still a child. And completely at the mercy of whatever farmer you happen to be sent to. Put yourself in a homegirl's place: up before dawn, cooking, cleaning, pumping water from the well in freezing temperatures.

Constantly on the alert for the lascivious advances of the men in the household. And sometimes losing that battle, ending up with an unwanted pregnancy. If the farmer has children, they will go to school; you likely won't. When there's time you'll get to go to Sunday school. Socializing with the neighbouring kids is frowned on, so you won't be getting many dance invitations. Forced to work to a contract you had no part in framing. And when you're 11 or 12 or 16 years old, an indenture contract lasting three or four years feels like a lifetime. Never knowing if the family you had to leave behind in Britain has forgotten you. And then, once dispatched to a remote farm in the Canadian outback, wondering when you'll see your visiting agent, if ever.

Those overstretched men and women — the visiting agents — played a unique role: the chance to bring a sense of worth, security, and protection to boys and girls who had never imagined anyone would care. Many of these inspectors seem to have been easily fooled by farmers like Charles Lakey who abused their charges. Then there were the simple daily folk: the deliverymen, the country parsons, the neighbours. The minute they realized something was wrong they did something about it. They came to the child's aid. It's a part of human nature as innate as the savagery the social Darwinists like to bleat about — the willingness to put oneself in harm's way to help a suffering fellow human, or any creature in distress. Like the New York bus driver who picked a blind dog up off the street and took him to a shelter, and the veterinarian who never gave up on him. Illustrating beautifully that what we do, however small, makes a huge difference — to someone. And equally, what we do to hurt leaves a lasting mark.

Then there's the old equation of power. Under a patriarchal system — or any system of hierarchy — there's bound to be abuse of authority. It's inevitable. Absolute power corrupts absolutely. Dr. Barnardo to some extent illustrates this point. Starting off as an eager missionary in the East End, he demonstrated real compassion for destitute children and he set about doing something about it while others were content to let the poor rot. But there's a wide blind spot to Christian altruism — or maybe any altruism. It assumes that if one does good works then all will be right with the world, if not now, then at some promised future time. It certainly can't be wrong to "feed the good wolf" instead of the "bad wolf," as First Nations people say. But fundamentalist altruism reveals a naïveté about human nature. By insisting upon total control of his organization, Dr. Barnardo allowed his "bad wolf" too much room, so that the desire to help sometimes became a possessive demon, ready to snatch children forcibly away from their parents. Meanwhile, the feminists may have been right to say that what we need is not "power over" but "power with." Sadly, few working models seem to be in the offing at the moment.

So do we simply not bother to embark upon humanitarian ventures, knowing that the element of human corruption will inevitably creep in? Knowing that, along with the sincere, caring individuals in an organization like Barnardo's or Fairbridge, there will be some who are sociopaths or sexual predators? Hardly. I have little doubt that the volunteers who first went out into London's beleaguered East End in the 1860s to help with the devastating fallout of the cholera epidemics were sincere. You don't walk into an inferno like that unless you're powerfully motivated by some form of altruism.

The problem seems partly to be one of scale — beyond a certain size, an organization too easily goes off the tracks originally laid out for it. Like any other organism, organizations have a lifecycle, despite being artificial constructs. They begin in spirit, as the dream of their founders — as so often Dr. Barnardo claimed his best ideas arose from dreams. But to cross the choppy seas of reality, a ship must be built. To keep crossing ever-larger oceans we must build ever-larger vessels. As the hull grows larger it requires more time, more energy, more money. The spirit grows gradually more distant, more remote. We become so lost we mistake the vessel for the goal.

But we have too much invested in the vessel to stop now. We have so displaced our own personhood we have *become* the vessel. To deny it now, we think, would be to deny ourselves. If we've lost the spirit utterly, it's just possible we would deceive, defraud, and even kill to keep the vessel afloat. At this point, short of an epiphany from God, we truly are lost souls. We have become The Corporation. I think this is what happened to Dr. Barnardo. In his early years working as an unpaid missionary in London's East End, he was moved by a powerful religious faith and a genuine love for children. But somewhere along the line he became the *vessel* instead of the dream it contains, ready to do almost anything to keep it afloat. The needs of the children themselves and their parents were strangely absent. If Kingsley Fairbridge had lived long enough it's possible he too would have gradually succumbed to this process of attrition. For many of the "child savers" it may have been the same.

Therefore, I would argue that it is *not* a country's institutions that make it great. They are mostly the remaindered husks of past greatness — at best, monuments to human ingenuity that no longer serve their purpose. True greatness lies with the people who make a country without ever knowing they are doing so. These are not the empire builders, the propagandists, the government functionaries. They are the humble, the poor, the wretched — the Home Children. Not some glorified notion of the "proletariat" or the "noble" poor. There is *nothing* noble about poverty. They are the hapless pawns of industry, the slaves without whom no empire of any kind could be built. I keep hoping — probably naïvely — that humanity will one day get beyond the need for slaves and empires.

But once again, is it the shining City on the Hill they sweat and die to build that is great? In our secular, consumerist age we forget that Blake's New Jerusalem is a City of Spirit. The city of roads, bridges, subways, skyscrapers, and technology is a monument, not to their wealthy masters, but to these lowly workers. Because they persisted, they endured, they suffered the tortures of the damned to build some rich maniac's obsession while their children had barely enough to eat, wore rotten clothes, and had only a dirty hovel to sleep in. They were the lost and lonely children, the boys and girls often sent against their will to a land distant enough to be the moon. Before they could comprehend what was happening to them, they endured fear, loneliness, and the battering of both body and spirit. They slept in freezing attics and barns with the animals, they carved furrows from rocky soil and calved in the cold dawn when most of them had never even seen a plough or a cow before in their short, sharp lives.

Out of all that, they somehow survived. Out of rejection, taunts, filthy names, lives wiped blank of meaning and all identity, they endured. If indeed there is such a thing as a hero — and I mistrust the very idea — then these children deserve the name. Institutions and corporations are merely the shell of human courage and dignity, ever at risk of becoming dangerous, repressive idols. "Heroes" come in all sizes and shapes. Often it's their capacity to endure ordinary trials, not die in battle, that mark people as heroes. The Home Children may not have discovered a new medicine or saved someone from drowning but they entered the burning house of spirit and — mostly — emerged alive.

But perhaps even more than those Home Children who survived, we must honour the spirits of those who did *not* make it. The George Everett Greens and Arnold Walshs — the ones not gifted with a spirit resilient enough to be bent and twisted continually without snapping. The ones who looked into the night sky and saw only blackness and more blackness that no stars could penetrate. The ones whose light went out like snuffed candles behind eyes that had known only neglect, pain, and a complete absence of love.

Yet here is the miracle — that somehow these infant spirits now reach across time to tap us on the shoulder and say, *Remember me, so that I didn't die for nothing.* There is great justice in this — that some small soul whose light guttered out a hundred miles from any sign of help now speaks to us from the realm of the ancestors, a century or more later. It's proof, as English songwriter and social activist Roy Harper sings, that "the spirit lives" and cannot be forever silenced.

May their great-hearted ghosts at last be laid to rest.

Home Children — How Would I Know?

IT'S IMPORTANT TO REMEMBER that because British child immigrants in Canada faced prejudice and the all-too-human "fear of the other," many of these Home Children tried to hide their identities. The misnomer Home Children (few ended up with permanent childhood homes) applied to poor children and orphans who lived in Britain's various children's homes, orphanages, and Poor Law institutions. The term derives from the epithet "homeboy" or "homegirl," used by Canadians in a derogatory sense with the same implications as the term "gutter trash."

In Canada the trade unions feared that the child immigrants would take away jobs, particularly during tough economic times. It was a groundless fear, since many Home Children were never paid their wages upon coming of age, as their contracts of indenture had promised. And in any case, those who were compensated often received far below going rates for labour.

The net result was that many Home Children in Canada did their best to lose any association with their British past for fear of ridicule or worse. My grandfather Cyril William Joyce lost all trace of his British accent even though he was 16 when he was emigrated. And as with survivors of trauma such as war veterans, many such as Cyril simply chose not to speak of their experiences at all. (It's likely that the worst-treated children became victims of Post Traumatic Stress Disorder.) Consequently, in many families there may have been little or no transmission of these immigrants' stories to their descendants. The unfortunate loss of family — and by extension national — history is incalculable.

Some Clues

- If your ancestor ever mentioned the terms "homeboy," "home-girl," or "the old boys club." These clubs were associations of grown child immigrants who met to celebrate the organizations that brought them to Canada, and included the Old Fairbridgians and Barnardo's Old Boys and Old Girls clubs.
- If any mention was made of Barnardo's, Waifs and Strays, or other child emigration agencies. (See Marjorie Kohli's *The Golden Bridge* for a complete list.)
- If a grandparent or other ancestor was "sponsored" for emigration from the UK but was still a child at the time of their arrival, particularly if they were sent without their parents.
- If you had an American ancestor who was sent to a farm on the "orphan train."
- If a male ancestor worked on a Canadian farm as a child with a family not his own.
- If a female ancestor worked as a house servant as a child or adolescent.
- If you have ancestors who were vague about how they emigrated to Canada.

Home Children Research Resources

Many historical records are now available on the Internet; however, don't stop there if you don't find anything — an email enquiry can be helpful since so many records have yet to be digitized and uploaded. This list is not comprehensive but will give you a good start.

- Library and Archives Canada: this online archive includes a searchable database of Canadian immigration records. (Keep in mind some records have been lost or destroyed over the years.) http://www.collectionscanada.gc.ca/databases/home-children/index-e.html.

- British Isles Family History Society of Greater Ottawa: while BIFHSGO does not conduct family research on behalf of its members or the public, it does provide useful research links on its website. http://www.bifhsgo.ca/index.php.

- British Home Children in Canada: this website operated by Lori Oschefsky, a Home Child descendant, is loaded with useful historical information. As founder of the British Home Children Advocacy and Research Association, Ms. Oschefsky is also a first-class researcher for families seeking documentation. http://canadianbritishhomechildren.weebly.com/; http://britishhomechildrenadvocacy.weebly.com/.

- Young Immigrants to Canada: this webpage by Marjorie Kohli has some useful links: http://jubilation.uwaterloo.ca/~marj/genealogy/homeadd.html.

- The National Archives, UK: has a searchable online database for 1,000 years of British government records. http://www.nationalarchives.gov.uk/default.htm.

- Barnardo's: go to the "What We Do" page and check out the "Making Connections" program, which will help you gain access to records of former child migrants. They also offer a Family History Service for those researching child immigrant ancestors but will charge a £100 fee for retrieval of family records. http://www.barnardos.org.uk.

- Ivy Sucee: families with Home Child ancestors who passed through Barnardo's Hazelbrae distributing home in Peterborough, Ontario should contact Ivy Sucee, who has a large archive of artifacts and information relating to this Home and will arrange tours of Peterborough sites significant to Barnardo's history. Her work is supported by donations so please be generous. Contact Ivy at: 705-742-7523.

- Fairbridge Canada: primarily useful for those families with a family member who was a resident of Fairbridge Farm Schools in British Columbia. Includes a regular newsletter, the *Fairbridge Gazette*, some copies of which are posted at the website. http://fairbridgecanada.com/.

- Middlemore Homes database, UK: primarily useful for those families in Canada's Maritime provinces with Home Child ancestors. http://www.connectinghistories.org.uk/links.asp.

- Child Migrants Trust: Nottingham-based organization established by Margaret Humphreys. Primarily focused on helping reunite Australian child immigrants with their families. Also administers the Family Restorations Fund for child immigrants seeking to reunite with family. Will in some cases help locate family records in Britain. http://www.childmigrantstrust.com/.

Notes to Chapter 1

1. Child Migration Timeline, http://otoweb.cloudapp.net/timeline/interactive.html, March 5, 2012.

2. Interestingly, pressure to reform Britain's educational system was already mounting. William Edward Forster drafted the first legislation providing for partially state-funded public schools, the Elementary Education Act 1870. In the past, school attendance had been discretionary, administered by local school boards. Forster's Act brought school attendance under national scrutiny, requiring attendance between the ages of five and 10, with some discretion allowed in agricultural areas. Source: Wikipedia, History of Education in England, March 5, 2012.

3. Kenneth Bagnell, *The Little Immigrants* (Toronto: General Paperbacks, 1980, 1991), pp. 21, 22; Child Migration Timeline, http://otoweb.cloudapp.net/timeline/interactive.html, March 5, 2012.

4. Charles Dickens, *Oliver Twist*, with Introduction by Irving Howe (New York: Bantam Classics edition, 1982), pp. 11, 12.

5. Ibid., p. 59.

6. Peter Higginbotham, Introduction, www.workhouses.org.uk, Feb. 10, 2012.

7. Ibid. The government survey was released in a report titled *Abstract of Returns Made by the Overseers of the Poor*. The SPCK inventory was published as *An Account of Several Work-houses for Employing and Maintaining the Poor*.

8. Wikipedia, workhouse, Feb. 10, 2012. Source: Colin Gibson, *Dissolving Wedlock* (NY: Routledge, 1993).

9. Charles Dickens, *Oliver Twist*, pp. 11, 12.

10. Wikipedia, workhouse, Feb. 10, 2012. Sources: Simon Fowler, *Workhouse: The People: The Places: The Life Behind Closed Doors* (The National Archives, 2007); Eric Hopkins, *Childhood Transformed* (Manchester: Manchester University Press, 1994).

11. Andrew Mearns, *The Bitter Cry of Outcast London: An Inquiry into the Condition of the Abject Poor* (London: James Clarke & Co., 1883).

12. Ibid.

13. Spartacus Educational, re: Seebohm Rowntree and Charles Booth, http://www.spartacus.schoolnet.co.uk/RErowntreeS.htm, http://www.spartacus.schoolnet.co.uk/PHbooth.htm, Jan. 28, 2013.

14. Kenneth Bagnell, *The Little Immigrants*, pp. 20, 21.

15. Ibid., p. 105. The story has been recounted endlessly in histories of Barnardo and his work.

16. Ibid., p. 111.

17. Child Migration Timeline, http://otoweb.cloudapp.net/timeline/interactive.html, March 5, 2012.

18. Kenneth Bagnell, *The Little Immigrants*, pp. 24–25, 31.

19. For a complete list and details of organizations emigrating poor children, see Marjorie Kohli, *The Golden Bridge: Young Immigrants to Canada, 1833–1939* (Toronto: Natural Heritage Books, 2003).

20. Kenneth Bagnell, *The Little Immigrants*, p. 24.

21. *The Guild Messenger, Memoirs of the Late Dr. Barnardo*, by Mrs. Barnardo and James Marchant (source: Leslie Drew fonds, Shawn Lamb Archives, Touchstones Museum of Art and History, Nelson, BC), p. 18.

22. Norman Wymer, *Father of Nobody's Children, A Portrait of Dr. Barnardo* (London: Hutchinson, 1954), p. 157.

23. *The Guild Messenger, Memoirs of the Late Dr. Barnardo*, by Mrs. Barnardo and James Marchant (source: Leslie Drew fonds, Shawn Lamb Archives, Touchstones Museum of Art and History, Nelson, BC), p. 18.

24. See Bagnell re: veracity of Jim Jarvis story, pp. 105–8, 140. However, Ivy Sucee, who represents Barnardo's in Canada from her Peterborough, Ontario home, says Jarvis was real but that she is unable to say more about him due to confidentiality issues.

25. *The Guild Messenger, Memoirs of the Late Dr. Barnardo*, p. 18.

26. Roy Parker, *Uprooted: The Shipment of Poor Children to Canada, 1867–1917* (Vancouver: UBC Press, 2008), pp. 71, 72.

27. Ibid., pp. 45, 50.

28. Kenneth Bagnell, *The Little Immigrants*, p. 141.

29. Roy Parker, *Uprooted: The Shipment of Poor Children to Canada, 1867–1917*, ibid., p. 120.

30. Ibid., p. 236.

31. Ibid., pp. 41, 238–39.

32. Gail Corbett, *Barnardo Children in Canada* (Toronto: Dundurn Press, 1997, 2002), p. 31.

33. Roy Parker, *Uprooted: The Shipment of Poor Children to Canada 1867–1917*, pp. 238–40.

34. Perry Snow, *Neither Waif Nor Stray: The Search For a Stolen Identity* (Calgary: Universal U-Publish, 2000), p. 12.

35. Margaret Humphreys, *Empty Cradles* (London: Corgi Books, 1995, 1997). See pp. 277–280 where Humphreys shows evidence that the Catholic Church actively sought child immigrants for use as labourers.

36. Roy Parker, *Uprooted: The Shipment of Poor Children to Canada 1867–1917*, pp. 46, 47.

37. Kenneth Bagnell, *The Little Immigrants*, p. 39.

38. Roy Parker, *Uprooted: The Shipment of Poor Children to Canada 1867–1917*, pp. 47, 49. The italics are in Doyle's original report.

39. Kenneth Bagnell, *The Little Immigrants*, p. 45.

40. Ibid., pp. 45, 46; Roy Parker, *Uprooted: The Shipment of Poor Children to Canada 1867–1917*, p. 50. For more on LV Rogers see Chapter 7, "Leslie Vivian Rogers — A Scholar and a Gentleman."

41. Kenneth Bagnell, *The Little Immigrants*, pp. 60, 61; Roy Parker, *Uprooted: The Shipment of Poor Children to Canada 1867–1917*, p. 51.

42. Kenneth Bagnell, *The Little Immigrants*, pp. 84, 85.

43. Joy Parr, *Labouring Children: British Immigrant Apprentices to Canada, 1869–1924* (Toronto: University of Toronto Press, (1980) 1994 ed., pp. 149–50. According to Kohli (p. 30), George Bogue Smart, born in Brockville, Ontario on May 13, 1864, was "the first and only one to hold this office."

44. Report of George Bogue Smart, undated; Immigration Branch microfiche records, reel 4746, RG76, Volume 79, file 6648, part 8, held at the National Archives, Ottawa; author's files Waifs & Strays 12/13 reel C4746. From the context of the letter, it appears the new home had only received two parties of immigrant children by the time of his first inspection. He notes the recent official opening of the Home on Oct. 7, 1924 at 665 Huron Street.

45. Marjorie Kohli, *The Golden Bridge: Young Immigrants to Canada, 1833–1939* (Toronto: Natural Heritage Books, 2003), p. 31.

46. Letter to Bogue Smart dated Feb. 3, 1924, signature illegible; Immigration Branch microfiche records, reel 4746, RG76, Volume 79, file 6648, part 8, held at the National Archives, Ottawa; author's files Waifs & Strays 3/4 reel C4746.

47. Marjorie Kohli, *The Golden Bridge: Young Immigrants to Canada, 1833–1939*, ibid., p. 30.

48. Joy Parr, *Labouring Children: British Immigrant Apprentices to Canada, 1869–1924*, ibid., p. 149.

49. Roy Parker, *Uprooted: The Shipment of Poor Children to Canada 1867–1917*, p. 241. The Act required that the Secretary of State be satisfied "that their consent had been obtained before justices as well as their parents having been consulted, or it being shown that it was impracticable to do so."

50. Roger Kershaw and Janet Sacks, *New Lives for Old: The Story of Britain's Child Migrants* (London: National Archives, 2008), p. 118; Kenneth Bagnell, *The Little Immigrants*, ibid., p. 225.

51. Kenneth Bagnell, *The Little Immigrants*, pp. 223, 224.

52. Letter of George Bogue Smart, Sept. 30, 1925; Immigration Branch microfiche records, reel 4746, RG76, Volume 79, file 6648, part 8, held at the National Archives, Ottawa; author's files Waifs & Strays 17/18 reel C4746.

53. Phyllis Harrison, *The Home Children* (Winnipeg: Watson & Dwyer Publishing, 1979), pp. 242, 243.

54. Ibid., p. 238.

55. Ibid, pp. 78, 79.

56. Ibid, p. 236.

57. Ibid, p. 245.

58. Jane Cole Hamilton, "Of Lost and Lonely and Little Children," *Toronto Star*, Nov. 3, 1984.

59. Phyllis Harrison, *The Home Children*, pp. 162, 245–47.

60. Perry Snow, *Neither Waif Nor Stray*, p. 10.

61. Margaret Humphreys, *Empty Cradles*, p. 165.

62. John Bradshaw, *Family Secrets* (New York: Bantam Books, 1995), p. 49.

63. Perry Snow, *Neither Waif Nor Stray*, p. 9.

64. Sean Arthur Joyce, "Conversations with Crow: Healer," from *The Charlatans of Paradise* (Nelson, BC: New Orphic Publishers, 2005), p. 42.

65. A Brief Look at the History of White Mill, www.whitemill.org, March 28, 2012. White Mill is currently a National Trust historic site managed by retired professor Colin Cope, who is the likely author of the website text.

66. Based on genealogical research by Brian Charles Joyce, *A History of White Mill and the Joyce Family*, privately published booklet, Wheathampstead, Hertfordshire, UK, 2005.

67. George Orwell, *The Penguin Complete Novels of George Orwell* (Harmondsworth, UK: Penguin Books Ltd., 1983), p. 505.

68. Ibid.

69. A Brief History of the Waifs and Strays Society, http://www.hiddenlives. org.uk/articles/history.html, March 12, 2012. "The Archbishop of Canterbury, Dr. Archibald Tait, was asked to become the President of the Society," the website further notes. "He formally agreed to this on 24 Aug. 1881. From this date on the Society became an officially recognised organisation of the Church of England. It was known as the Church of England Central Home for Waifs and Strays. In Jan. 1882 a house in Clapton, London was rented and set up as the first boy's home. The first children were received into the Society's care on 14 Feb. 1882."

70. Marjorie Kohli, *The Golden Bridge: Young Immigrants to Canada, 1833–1939*, pp. 157–58.

71. Ibid., pp. 158–161. "In Dec. 1899, the position of Inspector of British Immigrant Children and Receiving Homes was created by the Department of the Interior, which by then was responsible for immigration," explains Kohli. (p. 30)

72. Encyclopedia of Immigration, Empire Settlement Act (1922), http://immigration-online.org/96-empire-settlement-act-canada-1922.html, March 12, 2012.

73. Church of England Council of Empire Settlement Report and Foreword, Aug. 29, 1929; source: Lambeth Palace archives. Recommendations for a Council of Overseas Settlement were made at a church conference on Jan. 24, 1925; the name was subsequently changed to the Church of England Council of Empire Settlement. Wyndham Deedes was a distinguished WW I veteran who had fought at Gallipoli. His family were aristocratic landowners from Kent. Deedes had served as secretary to British High Commissioner Sir Herbert Samuel in Palestine from 1920–22. Rather than return to his country manor in Kent, he chose to stay in London during his retirement years doing unpaid social work. (Source: Wikipedia.)

74. Ibid.

75. "Opposition critics, fearful that British settlers would be drawn into cities, called for a more comprehensive settlement plan for immigrants. In Feb. 1926, Conservative Simon F. Tolmie offered faint praise for the government's involvement in the settlement schemes, but criticized the fact that once here, many immigrants were left on their own. An "aftercare" program was established for British settlers, but when farming became a hardship, some returned home, others moved on to the United States and many migrated to Canada's cities and towns." — Canada, *Debates of the House of Commons*, Feb. 15, 1926, pp. 999–1000. Source: Library and Archives Canada online article (pamphlet describing Empire Settlement Act), Former

archival reference no. RG76-I-A-1.

76. Church of England Council of Empire Settlement Migrants' Expenses statement, April 26, 1930; source: Lambeth Palace archives. These expenses were to be met equally by the Council and the Secretary of State.

77. Church of England Council of Empire Settlement annual report, 1934; source: Lambeth Palace archives. Author's research files.

78. Ibid.

79. Kenneth Bagnell, *The Little Immigrants*, p. 216.

80. Letter of George Evans to Barnardo's, Sept. 22, 1929. Author's research files.

81. Church of England Council of Empire Settlement annual report, 1934; source: Lambeth Palace archives. Author's research files.

82. For the full text of Rudd's apology see: http://pmrudd.archive.dpmc.gov.au/node/6321.

83. For the full text see the official British Parliamentary web archive: http://www.parliament.uk/business/news/2010/02/prime-ministers-statement-child-migration/. See also: *UK Offers Apology for Children Sent Overseas to Lives of Abuse*, Feb. 25, 2010, http://www.digitaljournal.com/article/288091; *UK Apology to Former Child Migrants First Anniversary*, 24/02/2011, http://www.childmigrantstrust.com/news/uk-apology-to-former-child-migrants--1st-anniversary--24022011.

84. McKay made a similar statement in the *Fairbridge Gazette*, Spring 2010 issue, pp. 4, 5. "I personally felt that the formal apology by the Prime Minister Gordon Brown was very sincere and straight from the heart. He recounted the terrible mistakes committed by the government-sponsored agencies, which resulted in far too much abuse and suffering of Child Migrants and their families."

85. *Canada Doesn't Plan Child Migrant Apology*, CBC News, Nov. 16, 2009, http://www.cbc.ca/news/canada/story/2009/11/16/child-migrant-canada.html.

86. Roy Parker, *Uprooted: The Shipment of Poor Children to Canada, 1867–1917* (Vancouver, UBC Press, 2008), pp. 140, 154.

87. Ibid., pp. 288-90. For the British Hansard records on this report see: http://www.publications.parliament.uk/pa/cm200001/cmselect/cm-health/152/15206.htm.

88. Lori Oschefsky, British Home Children Canada, BHC Stories: George Everett Green, http://canadianbritishhomechildren.weebly.com/george-everett-green.html, Nov. 7, 2012.

89. Ibid.: Arnold Walsh, http://canadianbritishhomechildren.weebly.com/arnold-walsh.html, Nov. 7, 2012.

90. *Winnipeg Free Press*, Nov. 29, 1895, posted at: British Home Children Canada, http://canadianbritishhomechildren.weebly.com/george-everett-green.html, Nov. 7, 2012. The *Free Press* here was actually quoting the *London Advertiser* of London, Ontario.

91. Roy Parker, *Uprooted: The Shipment of Poor Children to Canada 1867–1917*, p. 25.

92. Kenneth Bagnell, *The Little Immigrants*, p. 242.

93. Roy Parker, *Uprooted: The Shipment of Poor Children to Canada 1867–1917*, pp. 288–89.

94. Ibid., p. 282.

95. Sean Arthur Joyce, "Crow Drops in for Coffee," from *Star Seeds* (Nelson, BC: New Orphic Publishers), 2009.

Notes to Chapter 2

1. Letter to Helen Dickey from Barnardo's Aftercare by LF Clargo, July 14, 1988. When the Macpherson Homes were shut down in Canada in 1925, all records were transferred to Barnardo's. The birth certificate for Elizabeth Emma Thompson shows her birthdate as Nov. 12, 1891, in Hoxton Old Town, London.

2. Lilian Birt, *The Children's Home-Finder* (London, James Nisbet & Col. Ltd., 1913); reprinted from the McMaster University Library Digital Commons. Lilian Birt, Macpherson's niece, writes in her biographical sketch of her aunt: "That [James Macpherson] was an attractive and interesting speaker to children is borne witness to by an old lady still living, who remembers Mr. Macpherson, accompanied by his daughter Annie, coming to the public school at Kettering, Northampton, which this lady attended as a child, and speaking to the children in a way she had never heard before. Up to that time she had never heard or thought of God but as a dreadful all-powerful Being, waiting to punish naughty people, but Mr. Macpherson spoke to them of God as the Friend of little children who loved them and liked to see them at play as well as at prayer. This presentation of God as a Father, more loving than any earthly one, she never forgot." — pp. 4, 5.

3. Letter to Helen Dickey from Barnardo's Aftercare by Marjorie Stoner, Oct. 10, 1988. According to Stoner the address of the Thompsons would later be known as Rushmore Road, Clapton Park, East London.

4. I'm using a certain amount of poetic license here. It's debatable whether Annie Macpherson would have been personally overseeing new admissions to her homes at this late date in her career. Her work ethic was very strong, so it's not altogether implausible. According to Lilian Birt in *The Children's Home-Finder*, Macpherson's health began to decline in 1902 with a case of double pneumonia. She died Nov. 27, 1904.

5. Lilian Birt, *The Children's Home-Finder*, pp. 53, 54. *The Revival*, an evangelist periodical, by this time was known as *The Christian*.

6. The term used by Lilian Birt in *The Children's Home-Finder*, pp. 32–35.

7. Lilian Birt, *The Children's Home-Finder*, pp. 32–35.

8. Coprolite, Wikipedia, June 20, 2012: "Coprolites are classified as trace fossils as opposed to body fossils, as they give evidence for the animal's behaviour (in this case, diet) rather than morphology. They serve a valuable purpose in paleontology because they provide direct evidence of the predation and diet of extinct organisms."

9. Lilian Birt, *The Children's Home-Finder*, p. 4. "Born in Campsie, by Milton, Stirlingshire, Annie Parlane Macpherson was the eldest, Rachel Stuart the second, and Louisa Caroline Stirling the youngest of a family of seven. Their father, James Macpherson, came of the Highland clan of that name. His forbears had been farmers and small landowners in Stirlingshire.

   "Their mother, Helen Edwards, belonged to a family of Norse descent, who settled like so many other Scandinavians on the east coast of Scotland near Stonehaven. John Edwards, her brother, was a college friend of James Macpherson's in Glasgow, and the intimacy resulted in Helen Edwards' marriage to her brother's friend.

   "Both young men were seriously-minded, but while John Edwards entered the ministry of the Presbyterian Church, James Macpherson, who was a member of the Society of Friends, became a teacher, a calling in which he displayed peculiar gifts and originality of mind. [He]... was invited by Ada, Lady Lovelace (daughter of Lord Byron), to come to England to establish schools in the neighbourhood of her estate. In these schools nature study and industrial training in manual and outdoor pursuits were combined with the usual school routine."

10. Ibid., pp. 10–15.

11. Ibid., pp. 5–7.

12. Ibid., pp. 26–28.

13. Ibid., pp. 24, 25.

14. Ibid., pp. 30, 31.

15. W. Luckin, *The Final Catastrophe — Cholera in London*, 1866, pp.32–34; The Wellcome Trust Centre for the History of Medicine at UCL webpage, http://www.ncbi.nlm.nih.gov/pmc/articles/PMC1081893/?page=1, June 20, 2012.

16. Lilian Birt, *The Children's Home-Finder*, pp. 31, 32.

17. Ibid. pp. 38, 49.

18. Marjorie Kohli, *The Golden Bridge: Young Immigrants to Canada, 1833-1939* (Toronto: Natural Heritage Books, 2003), p. 90.

19. Lilian Birt, *The Children's Home-Finder*, pp. 25, 26.

20. Ibid., pp. 53, 54.

21. Ibid., p. 38.

22. Ibid., p. 56.

23. Ibid., pp. 59, 60.

24. Ibid., pp. 60, 61.

25. Ibid.

26. *The Guild Messenger, Memoirs of the Late Dr. Barnardo*, by Mrs. Barnardo and James Marchant, p. 18; (source: Leslie Drew fonds, Shawn Lamb Archives, Touchstones Museum of Art and History, Nelson, BC).

27. Roger Kershaw & Janet Sacks, *New Lives for Old: The Story of Britain's Child Migrants* (London: The National Archives, Kew, 2008), pp. 25, 26. Initially Rye as a social reformer was interested in improving the lot of British middle-class working women; as early as 1862 she helped a group of young women emigrate to New Zealand. (*New Lives for Old*, ibid., p. 21.)

28. Ibid., p. 24.

29. Ibid., p. 22.

30. Andrew Simpson, *Who Spoke for the Children Sent to Canada?*, blog article, June 20, 2012, http://chorltonhistory.blogspot.ca/2012/06/who-spoke-for-children-sent-to-canada.html.

31. Andrew Simpson, *They Spoke for the Children Sent to Canada*, blog article, June 21, 2012, from sources in the *Manchester Guardian* 1907–1910, http://chorltonhistory.blogspot.ca/2012/06/they-spoke-for-children-sent-to-canada.html. According to Simpson the criticism voiced against child emigration came from the emerging socialist movement, of which Garrett and

Skivington were adherents.

32. According to www.greatships.net: "Launched in 1900, the Allan Line's *Tunisian* was built by Alex Stephen & Son of Glasgow. She took her maiden voyage on 5 April 1900, from Liverpool to Halifax and Portland, Maine. A month later, she made her first trip to Québec and Montréal." According to the Immigrant Ships Transcribers Guild, "The *Tunisian* seemed to be the primary carrier of British Home Children making as many as 8 to 10 trips per year."

    "Refrigeration on board ship first appeared in 1899 on the *Bavarian*, the first of the 20th century fleet of the Allan Line," writes historian Marjorie Kohli. "She was followed in 1900 by the *Tunisian*, which boasted good heating and ventilation. It also had hot and cold, fresh and salt, water on tap and four-berth emigrant cabins with spring mattresses. Many parties of young emigrants arrived on this vessel."

    "Alfred Owen related the experience of a Barnardo party on board the *Tunisian*," Kohli relates. "They sailed on Sept. 19, 1901, with a stop in Moville, Ireland, then headed out into the Atlantic. The weather was so bad on this voyage that the children were dreadfully ill — lifeless, as Owen described them. All of the children were undressed and put to bed and sawdust was spread on the floor with, as Owen said, there being nothing more they could do." — Marjorie Kohli, *The Golden Bridge: Young Immigrants to Canada, 1833-1939* (Toronto: Natural Heritage Books, 2003), p. 52. Sources: http://www.greatships.net/tunisian.html June 15, 2012; http://www.immigrantships.net/v4/1900v4/tunisian19080430.html, June 14, 2012; http://www.norwayheritage.com/p_ship.asp?sh=tuni2, June 15, 2012.

33. At the time of writing it's not known whether this number of child immigrants on this voyage of the *Tunisian* is accurate. It is based on Marjorie Kohli's web database Immigrants to Canada: Ships They Sailed On, http://jubilation.uwaterloo.ca/~marj/genealogy/ships3.html, June 21, 2012.

34. Alfred Owen, *Ups and Downs*, Vol. V, No. 4, July 2, 1900, p. 4.

35. Ibid.

36. Marjorie Kohli, *The Golden Bridge: Young Immigrants to Canada, 1833–1939*, p. 97; James S. Gilchrist, *Marchmont Distributing Home, Belleville, Ontario 1870–1925* (Belleville: Epic Press, 2003), Timeline, p. 215.

37. Residential Walk brochure, www.visitstratford.ca, July 16, 2012.

38. Ellen Agnes Bilbrough, *Home of Industry, Miss Macpherson's Work Among the Little Ones, on Both Sides of the Atlantic* (London: Shum & Bonnet, 1873), as quoted by Gilchrist (see 36), pp. 69, 70.

39. Lilian Birt, *The Children's Home-Finder*, pp. 134–35.

40. Ellen Agnes Bilbrough, *British Children in Canadian Homes* (Kirkaldy, Scotland: A. Beveridge, 1879), as quoted by Gilchrist (see 36), pp. 32, 33.

41. Letter to Helen Dickey from Barnardo's Aftercare by Marjorie Stoner, Oct. 10, 1988.

42. Ibid.

43. Ibid.

44. Ibid.

45. Ellen Agnes Bilbrough, *British Children in Canadian Homes*, as quoted by Gilchrist (see 36), p. 31.

46. James S. Gilchrist, *Marchmont Distributing Home, Belleville, Ontario 1870–1925*, ibid., pp. 100–01.

47. Kenneth Bagnell, *The Little Immigrants: The Orphans Who Came to Canada* (Toronto: General Paperbacks, 1991), pp. 45, 46, 60.

48. Letter to Helen Dickey from Barnardo's Aftercare by Marjorie Stoner, Oct. 10, 1988; email from Helen Dickey to author, Nov. 8, 2011.

49. Letter to Helen Dickey from Barnardo's Aftercare by Marjorie Stoner, Oct. 10, 1988.

50. Obituary, George Frederick Deptford, *Revelstoke Review*, Dec. 1956; Letter/memoir of Helen McLuhan, aunt of Helen May Dickey, dated Feb. 1987.

51. Letter to Helen Dickey from Barnardo's Aftercare by Marjorie Stoner, Oct. 10, 1988; email from Helen Dickey to author, Nov. 8, 2011; letter to author from Helen Dickey, July 30, 2012.

52. Obituary, *Revelstoke Review*, July 16, 1924; emails from Helen Dickey to author, Nov. 8, Nov. 30, 2011; letter from Helen Dickey to author, Dec. 10, 2011.

53. Letter/memoir of Helen Edwards-McLuhan, mother of Helen May Dickey, dated Feb. 1987.

54. Ibid.

55. George Frederick Deptford obituary, *Revelstoke Times*, Dec. 1956.

56. Letter/memoir of Helen Edwards-McLuhan, mother of Helen May Dickey, dated Feb. 1987.

57. Ibid.

58. Letter of Helen Dickey to the author, June 11, 2012.

59. Letter/memoir of Helen Edwards-McLuhan, mother of Helen May Dickey, dated Feb. 1987.

60. Ibid.

61. Obituary, George Frederick Deptford, *Revelstoke Review*, Dec. 1956.

62. Obituary, Elizabeth Emma (Thompson) Deptford, *Revelstoke Review*, Aug. 15, 1984; letter from Helen Dickey to author, March 15, 2012; letter from Helen Dickey, July 30, 2012; author's files.

63. Letter from Helen Dickey to author, June 11, 2012.

64. Letter from Helen Dickey to author, July 30, 2012.

65. Lilian Birt, *The Children's Home-Finder*, pp. 184–86.

66. Letter to author from Helen Dickey, July 30, 2012.

67. Roy Parker, *Uprooted: The Shipment of Poor Children to Canada, 1867–1917* (Vancouver: UBC Press, 2008), p. 287.

68. Letter to author from Helen Dickey, July 30, 2012.

69. Lilian Birt, *The Children's Home-Finder*, pp. 200, 201.

70. Ibid., pp. 252–53.

71. Ibid., pp. 256–57.

72. Andrew Simpson, *They Spoke for the Children Sent to Canada*, blog article, June 21, 2012, from sources in the *Manchester Guardian* 1907–1910, http://chorltonhistory.blogspot.ca/2012/06/they-spoke-for-children-sent-to-canada.html.

Notes to Chapter 3

1. Inferred from Barnardo's admission records for Walter and William Roberts, as per May 14, 2009 letter to FW Roberts from Barnardo's Making Connections service. Fred's full name was Frederick George Roberts. Fred and Ruth Roberts family files.

2. Gillian Wagner, *Barnardo* (London: Weidenfeld & Nicolson, 1979), p. 179.

3. Barnardo's records show "William Frank Duddridge (21), tailor's cutter; Charles J. Duddridge (18), apprentice; Henry Duddridge (16), and Albert Duddridge (14), printer's boy, all living with their parents."

4. At the time of the Roberts' brothers' admission to Barnardo's Homes on June 27, 1893, Florence Minnie is listed as two years old, "boarded-out at 65 Richmond Street, Barton Hill, Bristol."

5. Barnardo's admission records for Walter and William Roberts, Fred and Ruth Roberts files.

6. "The parish of Toxteth Park originally formed part of the West Derby Union which came into existence in 1837. However, on 24th June 1857 it became an independent Poor Law Parish. In 1859, the parish built a new workhouse on Smithdown Road in Toxteth. It could accommodate 700 inmates." See also period poster, "Extracts from the Order of the Poor Law Board; Punishments for the Misbehaviour of the Paupers in the Workhouse." The Workhouse: The Story of an Institution, http://www.workhouses.org.uk/ Liverpool/; Toxteth Park Poor Law and Parish, Liverpool, http://www. workhouses.org.uk/ToxtethPark/; Dec. 7, 2012.

7. Joy Parr, *Labouring Children: British Immigrant Apprentices to Canada, 1869– 1924* (Toronto: University of Toronto Press, 1980, 1994), p. 71. "Neither admission nor emigration was made conditional upon parental consent, and children were rarely allowed to return to their parents," writes Parr. "But with so many children constantly entering the home they were obliged to maintain a steady emigrant stream. There was always the chance that embarking youngsters who saw their relations might be dissuaded from the carefully instilled conviction that they would enjoy life in Canada.. . . The home therefore developed a selective notification policy for kin. Some parents were informed well in advance of their children's departure and invited for a farewell visit to the home. . . . Before-sailing notices were sent for one-third of the girls at Barnardo's and to almost two-thirds of the parents described in the admission reports as respectable."

8. June Rose, *For the Sake of the Children — Inside Dr. Barnardo's: 120 Years of Caring for Children* (London: Hodder & Stoughton, 1987), p. 126. Wagner notes that by the time of his death in 1905, Dr. Barnardo's organization was caring for 1,300 disabled children. Wagner, *Barnardo*, ibid., pp. 289, 310.

9. Barnardo's admission records for Walter and William Roberts, Fred and Ruth Roberts family files.

10. Barnardo's admission records for Walter and William Roberts, May 14, 2009 letter to FW Roberts from Barnardo's Making Connections service, Karen Fletcher, Archives and Administration Officer. Sheppard House was likely named after Samuel Gurney Sheppard, an early benefactor of Barnardo's and later board member.

11. June Rose, *For the Sake of the Children*, p. 174

12. Gillian Wagner, *Barnardo*, p. 177; *The Goldonian*, http://www.goldonian. org/photos/photo_archive_homes/pages/teighmore.htm; Dec. 11, 2012. According to Lori Oschefsky at British Home Children in Canada: "Al-

though often referred to as being at Gorey, it was actually on La Rue d'Aval, midway between St. Saviour's Hospital and Ransoms Garden Centre. It closed in April 1938. Teighmore still exists as Teighmore House, but Tudor House is long gone. Both properties are remembered today by the place names Tudor Close and Teighmore Park." http://canadianbritishhomechildren.weebly.com/teighmore-channel-islands.html; Dec. 11, 2012.

13. *The Star*, May 11, 1880, quoting Dr. Barnardo in *Night and Day*; British Home Children in Canada, http://canadianbritishhomechildren.weebly.com/teighmore-channel-islands.html; Dec. 11, 2012.

14. Ibid.

15. Ibid.

16. June Rose, *For the Sake of the Children*, pp. 175–76.

17. Ibid., p. 175.

18. Ruth Roberts memoir, privately published; author's files.

19. May 14, 2009 letter to FW Roberts from Barnardo's Making Connections service, Karen Fletcher, Archives and Administration Officer.

20. The SS *Cambroman* was launched Oct. 6, 1892 at Birkenhead for the British & North Atlantic Company as a cargo steamer and was fitted for passenger accommodation in 1899 by its new owners the Dominion Line. It held 1,275 passengers, all in third class, serving the Liverpool to Portland route until Nov. 1901. In 1907 it was acquired by the Red Star Line and served the Antwerp to New York route until being scrapped in 1910. http://www.norwayheritage.com/p_ship.asp?sh=cambm, June 21, 2012; Ancestry.com, http://freepages.genealogy.rootsweb.ancestry.com/~thoma/ThomaGene/Ships/Cambroman.html, June 14, 2012. Owen's comment on the *Cambroman* appears in *Ups and Downs*, July 2, 1900.

21. As reported in *Ups & Downs*, April 1, 1900, p. 11; July 2, 1900, p. 1.

22. Alfred Owen, *Ups and Downs*, Vol. V, No. 4, July 2, 1900, p. 4.

23. Gail Corbett, *Nation Builders: Barnardo Children in Canada* (Toronto: Dundurn Press, 2002), pp. 75, 76. Corbett notes that the distribution home on Pacific Avenue was opened in 1896, making it the one in use when the Roberts brothers arrived. By 1908 it had moved to 75 Bannerman Avenue and the Farm Home had been shut down due to almost continuous financial losses.

24. Memorable Manitobans, an online resource provided by the Manitoba Historical Society, has this to say of Edmund Amos Struthers: "Born near St. Johns, Quebec on 22 Jan. 1855, he moved as a child to Wisconsin where he

was educated at Fort Atkinson. In 1872 he accompanied his uncle, a Dominion Land Surveyor, to Manitoba to help him in laying out the Hudson's Bay Company Reserve in the Red River Settlement. Two years later he took up a homestead at the present site of Winnipeg Beach, but he spent the bulk of his time doing government surveys around Lake Winnipeg and the Lake of the Woods. In the spring of 1882, he joined the Canadian Pacific Railway in charge of topographical surveys of potential routes between Winnipeg and Moose Jaw. He later took charge of the railway immigration bureau.

"During his employment with the CPR, he became acquainted with TJ Barnardo who was attempting to establish a training farm for destitute children in Manitoba. In the late 1880s, Struthers moved to Russell, Manitoba where he purchased 10,000 acres for Dr. Barnardo's Home and also constructed an office and distributing home at Winnipeg. Thousands of girls and boys were processed through the facility during the years that Struthers was affiliated with it."

In 1884 he married Mary Ellen Vaughan, daughter of surveyor Amos Hawley Vaughan. They had six children. After the closure of the Russell Farm Home in 1909 he retired and returned to Winnipeg, where he managed the new Barnardo's distribution home at 75 Bannerman Avenue. He died there on Oct. 10, 1935 and was buried in St. John's Cemetery. http://www.mhs.mb.ca/docs/people/struthers_ea.shtml; Dec. 12, 2012.

25. *Ups & Downs*, July 2, 1900, p. 1. "Leaving Liverpool on March 31st we reached Halifax on April 9th. The Manitoba contingent, 35 for the Farm Home, and the same number for the Winnipeg Home, landed at Halifax and proceeded for the West under the very efficient charge of Mr. Struthers. The remainder, forming the Ontario contingent, went on in the ship to Portland, where they first set foot on American shores on the morning of the 11th."

26. Saskatchewan did not become a province until 1905.

27. Ruth Roberts memoir, privately published; author's files.

28. Ibid.

29. Barnardo's records for Walter and William Roberts, Fred and Ruth Roberts family files; Ruth Roberts memoir, privately published; author's files. To my transcription of the Barnardo's documents, Ruth added: "Walter's second daughter, Lavinia and his oldest son, Lorne, told Fred and me several times each that Walter was forced to write these two favourable letters by Charles Lakey who mistreated Walter from the first day."

30. Barnardo's records for Walter and William Roberts, Fred and Ruth Roberts family files; Ruth Roberts memoir, privately published; author's files.

31. Barnardo's records for Walter and William Roberts, Feb. 12, 1901 report; Fred and Ruth Roberts family files.

32. Barnardo's records for Walter and William Roberts, March 1901 report; Fred and Ruth Roberts family files; Ruth Roberts memoir, privately published; author's files.

33. Ibid.

34. Ibid.

35. Ibid.

36. *Ups & Downs*, "Reading Between the Lines," Feb. 1902, p. 6.

37. Barnardo's records for Walter and William Roberts, March 1901 report.

38. Ruth Roberts memoir, privately published; author's files.

39. Barnardo's records for Walter and William Roberts, April and May 1901 reports.

40. Barnardo's records for Walter and William Roberts, March 1901 report.

41. Barnardo's records for Walter and William Roberts, May 1901 report; Ruth Roberts memoir, privately published; author's files. Barnardo's records show that they paid Walter's hotel and medical bills.

42. Barnardo's records for Walter and William Roberts, June, Nov. and Dec. 1901 reports; Fred and Ruth Roberts files.

43. *Ups & Downs*, July 2, 1900, "Visits and Visitors," p. 6; author's files. The two visiting agents named are "Messrs. Newman and Mitchell" while a Mr. Griffith and Mr. Gaunt cover Ontario. In the Feb. 1902 *Ups and Downs*, the editor speaks of Bogue Smart as the "recently appointed" inspector.

44. Ruth Roberts memoir, privately published; author's files.

45. *Ups & Downs,* March 1902, p. 9.

46. Ibid., April–May 1902.

47. Barnardo's records for Walter and William Roberts, Dec. 31, 1902 report; Ruth Roberts memoir, privately published; author's files.

48. *Ups & Downs,* "Our Young Colonists in the West," April 1903, pp. 16, 17.

49. Barnardo's records for Walter and William Roberts, Jan. 1904 reports; Ruth Roberts memoir, privately published; author's files.

50. *Ups & Downs*, July 2, 1900, "Values and Bargains," p. 5; author's files.

51. Barnardo's records for William Roberts, Nov. 24, 1904 report; Fred and Ruth Roberts files.

52. *Ups & Downs*, "Merit and Reward," June 1902, p. 6; Barnardo's records for

Walter and William Roberts, Jan. 1905 reports; Fred and Ruth Roberts files.

53. Barnardo's records for Walter and William Roberts, Jan. 1905 reports; Fred and Ruth Roberts files.

54. Barnardo's records for Walter and William Roberts, Jan.–June 1905 reports; Fred and Ruth Roberts files.

55. Barnardo's records for Walter and William Roberts, Sept.–Dec. 1905 reports; Fred and Ruth Roberts files.

56. Barnardo's records for William Roberts, Nov. 24, 1904 report; Fred and Ruth Roberts files.

57. Barnardo's records for William Roberts, Jan. 29, 1906 report; Fred and Ruth Roberts files.

58. Ibid.

59. Barnardo's records for William Roberts, Jan. 29, 1906 report; Fred and Ruth Roberts files.

60. Barnardo's records for William Roberts, Sept. 12, 1906 report; Barnardo's records for Walter Roberts, 1907 report; Fred and Ruth Roberts files. The 1907 report notes that Walter has hired on with Charles Buckle at Yorkton.

61. *Ups & Downs*, July 2, 1900, "Westward Ho!," p. 7; author's files.

62. Joy Parr, *Labouring Children: British Immigrant Apprentices to Canada, 1869–1924*, p. 132.

63. Barnardo's records for William Roberts, Feb. 21, 1908, Nov. 5, 1909 reports; Barnardo's records for Walter Roberts, 1909 report; Fred and Ruth Roberts files.

64. Ruth Roberts memoir, privately published; author's files. Edith Yeatman was born Jan. 24, 1899 at Ebrington, England. She came to Canada with her parents in 1908. They settled in Springside, Saskatchewan. Walter and Edith's children were Violet, born Jan. 24, 1918; Lavinia (Vin), born April 24, 1919; Lorne, born May 13, 1922; Fred, born July 12, 1924; and Phillip, born March 21, 1927.

65. The Influenza Pandemic of 1918, http://virus.stanford.edu/uda/, Dec. 21, 2012. The Wikipedia entry for "Spanish Flu" notes that the first cases were actually reported in the US and the rest of Europe before arriving in Spain. "Spain was a neutral country in World War I and had no censorship of news regarding the disease and its consequences. Germany, the United States, Britain and France all had media blackouts on news that might lower morale, and did not want to disclose information about the disease and the number of deaths to their enemies."

66. Ruth Roberts memoir, privately published; author's files.

67. City of Rossland, Rossland history, http://www.rossland.ca/history, Dec. 21, 2012.

68. Ruth Roberts memoir, privately published; interview notes with author, Dec. 2012.

69. Art Joyce, *A Perfect Childhood — 100 Years of Heritage Homes in Nelson* (Nelson, BC: Kootenay Museum Association and Historical Society, 1997), pp. 125, 130–31.

70. Ruth Roberts memoir, privately published, author's files; emails from Ruth Roberts with information from Fred Roberts. Walter was buried in the Rossland-Trail cemetery. His sister Minnie was later buried beside him. The author's Great Uncle Arthur "Bud" Maynard worked at Cominco during this period and was also "leaded" but managed to survive, subsisting on a disability pension and part-time jobs thereafter.

71. Ruth Roberts memoir, privately published; author's files.

72. Phyllis Harrison, *The Home Children* (Winnipeg: Watson & Dwyer Publishing Ltd., 1979), p. 238.

73. Email communication with Ruth Roberts, Dec. 23, 2012.

74. Ibid.

75. Ibid.

76. Ibid. "By that time many of the Trail suburbs had formed their own co-operative transportation system to transport workers to and from the Trail smelter to work," she explains. "This enabled families to live in the healthier suburbs where the air was cleaner and where land was cheaper, and where gardens could be grown and, in some cases small farms could be had where chickens, cows, pigs, etc. could be raised thus contributing to the families' food supply. Not until several years after WW II could ordinary workmen afford to purchase their own vehicle."

77. Ibid.

78. Many of the children were also given a copy of *The Traveller's Guide from Life to Death*, a compendium of wisdom no doubt based on scriptural teachings. Artifact copies of this book are extant in the Ivy Sucee collection, Peterborough, Ontario. See also Phyllis Harrison, *The Home Children*, p. 177, where a woman recalls receiving one of these books for her trunk.

79. Joy Parr, *Labouring Children: British Emigrant Apprentices to Canada: 1869–1924*, p. 106.

80. Phyllis Harrison, *The Home Children*, p. 239.

Notes to Chapter 4

1. Based on the timeline at http://www.firstworldwar.com/timeline/1915.htm, Nov. 8, 2012.

2. Gladys Irene Martin was born March 27, 1908 at Bristol, Louisa was born July 29, 1910 and Enid Ruby on April 19, 1921. Source: Barnardo's Aftercare letter to Irene Campbell, daughter of Gladys Irene, June 30, 2000.

3. *The Bristol Miracle,* George Müller Charitable Trust, http://www.mullers.org/heritage/the-work-of-mullers, pp. 5, 6; Nov. 8, 2012. The first annual report was published Oct. 7, 1834.

4. George Müller Charitable Trust, http://www.mullers.org/heritage/muellers-family, Nov. 8, 2012.

5. *The Bristol Miracle,* George Müller Charitable Trust, http://www.mullers.org/heritage/the-work-of-mullers, pp. 6–8; Nov. 8, 2012.

6. Bristol Home Children, http://emigrated.bafhs.org.uk/emig.htm, Nov. 8, 2012.

7. Mary Carpenter, http://en.wikipedia.org/wiki/Mary_Carpenter, Nov. 8, 2012.

8. Tim Lambert, *A Brief History of Bristol, England: Bristol in the 19ᵗʰ Century,* http://www.localhistories.org/bristol, Nov. 8, 2012.

9. Michael O'Kelly, "Pioneer Social Reformer Mary Carpenter (1807–1877): Love AND Statistics," *Significance Magazine: Statistics Making Sense,* http://www.significancemagazine.org/details/wcbcxclusivc/974561/Pioneer-social-reformer-Mary-Carpenter-1807-1877-Love-AND-statistics.html, Nov. 8, 2012.

10. Marjorie Kohli, *The Golden Bridge: Young Immigrants to Canada, 1833–1939* (Toronto: Natural Heritage Books, 2003), pp. 291–93; Mary Carpenter, Wikipedia, http://en.wikipedia.org/wiki/Mary_Carpenter, Nov. 8, 2012.

11. Marjorie Kohli, *The Golden Bridge,* pp. 191–92.

12. Bristol Home Children, http://emigrated.bafhs.org.uk/emig.htm, Nov. 8, 2012.

13. Ibid.

14. A Unique Record of Life in the Village Home Barkingside from 1876–1986, http://www.goldonian.org/barkingside/index.htm, Nov. 7, 2012. The author bases his information on *Barnardo,* by Gillian Wagner; *Memoirs of the Late Dr. Barnardo* by Mrs. Barnardo and James Marchant; *Father of Nobody's Children* by Norman Wymer; and Barnardo's *Guild Messenger* magazine.

15. Ibid., Nov. 9, 2012. The website's author credits Dr. Barnardo as the father of foster care. Barnardo in 1882 had written: "I must declare most emphatically that even the Village Home, with all its advantages, is not so good as boarding-out; and my only regret is that from the nature of the case, the system of boarding-out is not applicable to every girl. If it were, I would empty the Girls' Village Home to-morrow, and scatter the inmates throughout the length and breadth of the land, boarding them out in ordinary homes, amid natural surroundings, among respectable working-class people in rural districts."

16. A Unique Record of Life in the Village Home Barkingside from 1876–1986: The Early Years, http://www.goldonian.org/barkingside/subpage/the_%20early_years.htm, Nov. 9, 2012.

17. Ibid.

18. Ibid.

19. Girls' Village Home Barkingside 1927, Rules to be observed, http://www.goldonian.org/barkingside/subpage/village_life_the_rules.htm, Nov. 9, 2012. Although these rules are from a slightly later era, I have used them for the 1916 year on the assumption that they would have been similar.

20. A Unique Record of Life in the Village Home Barkingside from 1876–1986, http://www.goldonian.org/barkingside/index.htm, Nov. 9, 2012; re: Dr. Barnardo's 1886 manifesto.

21. A Unique Record of Life in the Village Home Barkingside from 1876–1986, http://www.goldonian.org/barkingside/subpage/village_life_the_rules.htm, Nov. 9, 2012.

22. Author interview of Jean Alexander, May 7, 2012, author's files; *The Story of My Mother, Gladys Irene Martin, A Barnardo Home Child*, by Irene (Fudge) Campbell. Jean (Jeanette) is one of the children of Gladys Irene Martin-Fudge.

23. Founder's Day evolved from Dr. Barnardo's early habit of giving some of his "family" of children small gifts on his birthday. As adults these children returned the favour, sending gifts or money to Barnardo's Homes on that day. With his typical shrewdness for fundraising, Dr. Barnardo began to use it as a means of boosting donations during the traditionally slow fundraising months of summer. Founder's Day continued to be celebrated at the Village until 1954.

24. Based on the June 26, 1920 Founder's Day program found at: http://www.goldonian.org/barkingside/images/open_day_1920/front_page.htm, Nov. 9, 2012. Once again, Barnardo's is patronized by royalty, with the presence of the Duke and Duchess of Somerset at the 1920 celebrations.

25. BC Archives file MSS.2469, box 1, file 1: Annie Margaret Angus fonds.

26. A Unique Record of Life in the Village Home Barkingside from 1876–1986: 1873–1929; Barkingside Village Life 1927; http://www.goldonian.org/barkingside/tvh_1873_20.htm; http://www.goldonian.org/barkingside/subpage/village_life_the_rules.htm, Nov. 9, 2012.

27. Joy Parr, *Labouring Children: British Emigrant Apprentices to Canada: 1869–1924* (Toronto: University of Toronto Press, 1980, 1994), p. 71. "In 42 percent of the cases of Barnardo girls, kin received only a printed after-sailing form posted a day after their daughter, niece or granddaughter left for Canada."

28. Letter from Alice Whiteman, 54 Green Lane, Ilford, Feb. 23, 1920 to Girls Village Home Barkingside, addressed to "The Governor," a Mr. Godfrey. The new governors seem to have arrived later in the year. Source: Barnardo's documents, files of Irene Campbell.

29. Letter from Barnardo's Aftercare worker Karen Fletcher to Irene Campbell, June 30, 2000.

30. Letter from Alice Whiteman, March 9, 1920 to Girls Village Home Barkingside. Source: Barnardo's documents, files of Irene Campbell.

31. June Rose, *For the Sake of the Children*, 1987, p. 101. ". . . according to the Governor of the Village Mr. Godfrey, for some years before the war the girls disliked the prospect of going to Canada. He tried to put their case to the Executive Committee. The minutes record that Mr. Godfrey attached considerable importance to the 'amount of respect paid to objections to emigration from a) relations b) guardians and c) children.'"

32. *Ups & Downs*, Barnardo's newsletter, May 1920, p. 11.

33. Ibid.

34. Ibid.

35. Ibid.

36. Ibid.

37. Ibid., pp. 11, 12.

38. Ibid., p. 12.

39. Ibid.

40. Ibid. April 1, 1900, p. 8.

41. Sadleir House Timeline and History, www.sadleirhouse.ca, Nov. 14, 2012. Kendry's mansion underwent several name changes as it changed ownership; at present it is a student and community centre for Trent University

known as Sadleir House. According to Trent Valley historian Elwood Jones, "Their train stopped as it crossed the laneway from George Street to the front of Hazelbrae on the hill overlooking the Midland railway line that is now part of the Rotary trail. The children...had only a short walk to their new Canadian home."

42. June Rose, *For the Sake of the Children*, 1987, pp. 102, 103; Roy Parker, *Uprooted: The Shipment of Poor Children to Canada, 1867–1917 (Vancouver:* UBC Press, 2008), pp. 72, 73. As Parker notes, "Indeed until Rose published her book in 1987 this chapter in the account of Barnardo's Canadian activities remained largely closed." The May 1920 issue of *Ups and Downs* noted that the Hobdays had been in charge of Canadian operations for six months.

43. Dawn Crofts, genealogical sketch of Mafey Skelton; research notes of Lori Oschefsky, email Nov. 11, 2012; author's files. Ms. Crofts is a great niece of Skelton who resides in Adelaide, South Australia. According to genealogical researcher Lori Oschefsky, an obituary for Owen at Kelowna has been found, dated Nov. 13, 1944. "Kelowna, BC is where Mafey's incoming passenger list says she's headed after returning to Canada after the birth of her child Mary Minnie Owen," notes Ms. Oschefsky.

44. Dawn Crofts, genealogical sketch of Mafey Skelton; research notes of Lori Oschefsky, email Nov. 11, 2012; author's files. "Our family never had any contact with her again or any descendants," writes Crofts. "We have been unsuccessfully searching for 20 years."

45. Letter from Alice Whiteman, 54 Green Lane, Ilford, April 7, 1920 to Girls Village Home Barkingside; letter to Alice Whiteman from Barnardo's, April 8, 1920. Source: Barnardo's documents, files of Irene Campbell.

46. Elwood Jones, *Barnardo Children, Heritage Gazette* Volume 3, nos. 2, 3; Nov. 1999. There seems to be some confusion amongst historians as to the precise date when Hazelbrae was built. Jones writes: "Edward Caddy sketched the house at the top of Conger's Hill in 1839, and it was a fine house by any standard even then. The property passed to John R. Benson, the town's first merchant, in a public auction in 1837 and remained in the family until 1872, when this particular property was purchased by Alexander Smith.

"Sheriff Conger appears to have built the first grand home on this site. Conger was Peterborough's first sheriff, 1841–56, and was a sometime MPP and mayor. He died of tuberculosis in 1864, at the age of 60. He offered the house for sale in 1861, and the advertisement was still running in July 1863. His home, "Terrace Hill Cottage," was occupied by the Hon. Sidney Smith, the Postmaster General of Canada.... Alexander Smith built Hazelbrae on the top of the hill, perhaps in 1871 and 1872; perhaps earlier."

In Gail Corbett's *Nation Builders: Barnardo Children in Canada* (Toronto: Dundurn, 1997, 2002, p. 40), she notes that "Hazelbrae was 'an elegant brick mansion' three stories high, standing on five acres of land at the junction of the Cobourg-Peterborough line and the Grand Trunk rail line. The house dated to as early as 1840. . ."

47. Barnardo's visitation records for Gladys Irene Martin; files of Irene (Fudge) Campbell.

48. Barnardo's visitor's report of G. Gillan (?), July 24, 1920, files of Irene (Fudge) Campbell.

49. A recent paper from Laval University states that "Most children who have enuresis have no psychological disorder. The dated concept that enuresis frequently is due to anxiety or stress is unproven." This does not explain, however, why enuresis was so common amongst children in orphanages and rescue homes. See Joy Parr, p. 103, where she notes that while the Barnardo's sample she checked produced an estimate of 10 percent of the children suffering enuresis, "the problem does appear repeatedly in the Quarrier, Birt and Macpherson files, and the trait was believed to be widespread among child immigrants." Most references on enuresis do list stress as a possible cause. http://www.fmed.ulaval.ca/pediatrie/fileadmin/docs/serveur_ pediatrie/Acces_reserve/Medecins/Articles_scientifiques/recueil/Enuresis. pdf

50. Barnardo's visitation records for Gladys Irene Martin; files of Irene Campbell.

51. Ibid.

52. Letter from Barnardo's Aftercare worker Karen Fletcher to Irene Campbell, June 30, 2000.

53. Barnardo's visitation records for Gladys Irene Martin; files of Irene Campbell.

54. Ibid.

55. Ibid.

56. *The Canadian Encyclopedia*, Charlotte Whitton, http://www.thecanadian-encyclopedia.com/articles/charlotte-whitton, Nov. 12, 2012; http:// en.wikipedia.org/wiki/Charlotte_Whitton, Nov. 16, 2012.

57. Barnardo's visitation report, Nov. 21, 1925; files of Irene Campbell. There is a sudden gap in visitation records during her final two-year period with the Thornes.

58. Email from Irene Campbell to author, Nov. 17, 2012.

59. Barnardo's visitation report, Dec. 3, 1928; files of Irene Campbell; email dated Dec. 5, 2012 with photo attachment showing family Bible frontispiece showing Hobdays as witnesses.

60. Letter from Lady Superintendent Rose Hobday, mis-dated Jan. 2, 1928; letter from Gladys Fudge, undated; letter from Gladys Fudge, Dec. 17, 1928; files of Irene Campbell. Gladys misspells Moira Street as "Moria Street."

61. Letters from Rose Hobday to Gladys Fudge, Dec. 18, 1928; files of Irene Campbell.

62. Letter from Gladys Fudge to Rose Hobday, Dec. 19, 1928; letter from Canadian Bank of Commerce, Belleville, May 1, 1929; files of Irene Campbell.

63. *Ups & Downs*, Aug. 5, 1930 and April 5, 1932; Library and Archives Canada microfiche files.

64. See *Ups & Downs*, Jan. 2, 1933; March 1934; March 1935; July 1935; June 1936; Dec. 1938; Dec. 1941; Library and Archives Canada microfiche files. The Dec. 1938 issue notes that the Barnardo's facilities affected by the evacuation drill were Boys' Garden City, Woodford; Stepney Causeway; the Folkestone Hospital; and "our ever-open doors in southern and eastern England were cleared of children."

65. Correspondence: letter from Rose Hobday to Kirkpatrick, April 24, 1935; Immigration Department letter to Bristol Public Assistance Officer, May 18, 1935; letter from City of Bristol to Kirkpatrick, June 4, 1935; files of Irene Campbell.

66. Correspondence: letter from Migration Department to JH Roberts, June 7, 1935; letter from James Sullivan, Sutcliffe Boys' Home, Bath, June 28, 1935; letter from JH Roberts, Barnardo's Homes, Clifton, Bristol, June 28, 1935; files of Irene Campbell. The Sutcliffe Industrial School, later the Sutcliffe Boys' School, had been established in Jan. 1848 as a reformatory for boys already in trouble with the law or at risk of becoming so. Named for its founder William Sutcliffe, the institution housed up to 30 boys and provided training in various trades. The boys were given an annual summer holiday at the beach.

67. Correspondence: letter from Migration Department to Rose Hobday, Toronto, July 1, 1935.

68. Correspondence: letter from Migration Department to Rose Hobday, Toronto, July 15, 1935; letter from Migration Department to JH Roberts, Bristol, July 26, 1935; letter from JH Roberts, Bristol, to PT Kirkpatrick, Stepney Causeway, Oct. 18, 1935; letter from James Sullivan, Sutcliffe Boys'

Home, Nov. 2, 1935; files of Irene Martin.

69. Irene (Fudge) Campbell, *The Story of My Mother, Gladys Irene Martin, A Barnardo Home Child*, published in *Canadian Stories*, Ed Jensen, 2012.

70. Joy Parr, *Labouring Children: British Emigrant Apprentices to Canada: 1869–1924*, p. 91.

71. Interview with Jeanette (Fudge) Alexander by author, May 7, 2012.

72. Irene (Fudge) Campbell, *The Story of My Mother, Gladys Irene Martin, A Barnardo Home Child*.

73. Joy Parr, *Labouring Children: British Emigrant Apprentices to Canada: 1869–1924*, ibid., p. 55. "Visits were usually undertaken in winter when personnel could be spared and sleighing was easy, but when farm work was too slack and the conditions of children's employment could not accurately be judged . . . pauper children were often left in unsuitable homes for a year or more after their removal was recommended."

74. Phyllis Harrison, *The Home Children* (Winnipeg: Watson & Dwyer Publishing Ltd., 1979), p. 165.

75. Joy Parr, *Labouring Children: British Emigrant Apprentices to Canada: 1869–1924*, p. 105.

76. Email from Irene Campbell, April 26, 2012.

77. Interview with Jeanette (Fudge) Alexander, May 7, 2012.

78. Email from Irene Campbell, April 26, 2012.

79. Email from Irene Campbell, April 12, 2012.

80. Interview with Jeanette (Fudge) Alexander, May 7, 2012.

81. Interview with Irene (Fudge) Campbell, Feb. 17, 2012.

82. Letter from Barnardo's Aftercare Officer Karen Fletcher to Irene Campbell, June 30, 2000; files of Irene Campbell.

83. Interview with Jeanette (Fudge) Alexander, May 7, 2012.

84. Jodie Duffy, "Cousins together to ease the pain," *Illawarra Mercury*, Aug. 7, 2002.

85. Interview with Jeanette (Fudge) Alexander, May 7, 2012.

86. Interview with Irene (Fudge) Campbell, Feb. 17, 2012.

87. Interview with Irene (Fudge) Campbell, Feb. 17, 2012.

NOTES TO CHAPTER 5

1. Kenneth Bagnell, *The Little Immigrants* (Toronto: General Paperbacks, 1980), p. 158. Barnardo made his first visit to Canada in July, 1884, partly to inspect the distribution home that had been gifted to his organization the year before and also to prospect for new centres from which to disperse his child migrants.

2. Barnardo's records, George Evans, courtesy Ron and Dave Evans. The record states that George Evans was admitted into Barnardo's care on July 23, 1909 at the age of 1 year, 1 month; born May 31, 1908 in Evesham Workhouse. The religious denomination of his mother was noted as Church of England and the child had been baptized. The earnings noted, 2s/6d (2 shillings, 6 pence), would have amounted to about 30 cents per week.

3. Ibid. George's mother Emily was earning about 84 cents a week (7 shillings), quite a bit more than her grandfather but still clearly not enough to support a family. The "union" referred to was the Evesham Union Workhouse.

4. Wikipedia entry, Evesham, http://en.wikipedia.org/wiki/Evesham.

5. Barnardo's records, George Evans, courtesy Ron and Dave Evans.

6. Sir Frederic Morton Eden, *The State of the Poor: A History of the Labouring Classes in England, with Parochial Reports*, 1797, cited at http://www.workhouses.org.uk. According to the Wikipedia entry "workhouse," "The earliest known use of the term dates from 1631, in an account by the mayor of Abingdon reporting that 'wee haue erected wthn our borough a workehouse to sett poore people to worke.'"

7. From http://www.workhouses.org.uk/Evesham/.

8. Wikipedia, "workhouse," and "New Poor Law"; Charles Dickens, *Oliver Twist*, Bantam Classics edition, Introduction by Irving Howe, p. xiii. Howe explains: "Inspired by Malthusian economists who believed there must always be a segment of the population in destitute condition, the Poor Law had as its purpose to prevent or minimize breeding among paupers. The poorhouse was made as repulsive a place as possible; the sexes, including husbands and wives, were separated; the meals were wretched; uniforms were required. Dickens writes in *Oliver Twist* of 'three meals of thin gruel a day, with an onion twice a week, and half a roll on Sundays' — a caricature, but not an outrageous or unwarranted one."

9. Charles Dickens, *Oliver Twist*, Bantam Classics edition, Introduction by Irving Howe, pp. 11, 12; Wikipedia, "workhouse," re: Sampson Kempthorne

design. According to the Wikipedia entry "workhouse," "In 1836 the Poor Law Commission distributed six diets for workhouse inmates, one of which was to be chosen by each Poor Law Union depending on its local circumstances. . . . For instance, a breakfast of bread and gruel was followed by dinner, which might consist of cooked meats, pickled pork or bacon with vegetables, potatoes, yeast dumpling, soup and suet, or rice pudding. Supper was normally bread, cheese and broth, and sometimes butter or potatoes." Dickens clearly had no experience of such a sumptuous menu in the workhouse.

10. Trevor May, *An Economic and Social History of Britain 1760–1970*, Longman Group, 1987; Felix Driver, *Power and Pauperism* (Cambridge: Cambridge University Press, 2004).

11. Gail H. Corbett, *Barnardo Children in Canada* (Woodview, Ontario: Homestead Studios, 1981), p. 17; Babies' Castle history, Goldings Web Photo Gallery by Frank Cooke, Feb. 2, 2012, http://www.goldonian.org/photos/photo_archive_homes/pages/babies_castle_england_.htm; *Every Woman's Encyclopedia*, 1910 edition, article on Dr. Barnardo's Homes by Bridey M. O'Reilly, found at http://chestofbooks.com/food/household/Woman-Encyclopaedia-1/Dr-Barnardo-s-Homes.html, Feb. 2, 2012.

12. Barnardo's file card record for George Evans, courtesy Ron and Dave Evans.

13. Wikipedia, Thomas John Barnardo; *Barnardo's Children*, official history, Barnardo's, www.barnardos.org.uk.

14. Woodford Bridge history, Goldings Web Photo Gallery by Frank Cooke, Feb. 2, 2012, http://www.goldonian.org/photos/photo_archive_homes/pages/woodford_bridge.htm.

15. M.K. Smith, Thomas John Barnardo ("the Doctor"), *the encyclopedia of informal education*, 2002, updated Dec. 1, 2011. Among the clauses in Barnardo's "boarding out" agreement was that they "restore the said child to any person sent by the Director to receive it, on getting one fortnight's notice of removal or equivalent payment." Even visits from relatives or friends of the child had to be approved by Barnardo's.

16. Barnardo's file card record for George Evans, courtesy Ron and Dave Evans. According to one source (http://www.goldonian.org, Feb. 3, 2012), WBTS — or Goldings, as it was also known — was purchased by Barnardo's in Sept. 1921 and received the first contingent of boys from Stepney Causeway on April 19, 1922. "The then Prince of Wales who was to become Edward VIII opened the school officially on 17th Nov. 1922."

17. Report from William Baker Technical School Governor's Office, Oct. 13,

1927; Letter, July 5, 1928, from Barnardo's records, courtesy Ron and Dave Evans.

18. Based on Frank Norman, *Banana Boy, A Childhood Autobiography* (London: Secker & Warburg, 1969), found at http://www.goldonian.org/mem_sub_pages/frank_norman_ex.htm, Feb. 3, 2012. Norman writes of his experience there in the 1940s: "Though the Governor was a mild clergyman named MacDonald, the institution was run with a rod of iron. Drill, marching, physical training and cold showers were the order of the day. The PT instructor was the most important man in the place for they adhered insanely to the idiotic adage about healthy bodies having healthy minds. You had to be tough or you went under. Indeed one boy died whilst I was there; it was said to have been from natural causes, but then, some causes are more natural than others.

   "I think Barnardo's worst crime was their blatant under-estimation of the intelligence of just about every boy and girl in their care as a result of which they set their sights low. The only trades that could be learnt at Goldings were carpentry, cobbling, gardening, tinsmithing and printing, the latter being intellectually the most advanced. A boy with a creative streak in his make-up was a dead pigeon from the start. Artistic expression and individuality were squashed as soon as they reared their ugly heads. Certainly the country needed people with these kind of trades, and it may well be that the majority of the boys at Goldings were better suited to a trade than a profession. But certainly it was not true of all and absolutely it was not true of me."

19. Based on Frank Norman, *Banana Boy, A Childhood Autobiography*, http://www.goldonian.org/mem_sub_pages/frank_norman_ex.htm, Feb. 3, 2012. I have adapted Norman's experience almost word for word to the fictional "Tommy."

20. *The Guild Messenger* was a newsletter produced for "Barnardo Old Boys and Girls." Some of the recollections found at http://www.goldonian.org are positive, even tinged with nostalgia for their stay at Golding and other Barnardo institutions. The six "houses" that comprised WBTS were Somerset, Cairns, Aberdeen, Mount Stephen, Buxton and McCall.

21. Barnardo's file card record for George Evans, courtesy Ron and Dave Evans.

22. Letter from Canadian Pacific Railway Company, Department of Colonization and Development from TE Roberts, British Superintendent, to P. Roberts, Migration Department, Barnardo's Homes, Stepney Causeway; *SS Duchess of Bedford* information from http://www.duchessofbedford.com/, Feb. 3, 2012.

23. From evening programs for the *SS Duchess of Bedford* Main Lounge, dated

March 4 and March 10, 1929, found at http://www.duchessofbedford.com/, Feb. 3, 2012.

24. Kenneth Bagnell, *The Little Immigrants*, pp. 215–17; Gail H. Corbett, *Barnardo Children in Canada*, pp. 97, 102. The Jarvis Street receiving home opens in 1923. "It had been for many years the residence of Sir William Mulock," writes Bagnell, "a former minister in the Laurier Cabinet, and a justice of the Ontario Supreme Court. Mulock was also an Anglican, and through the church became not only a friend of Hobday's but a sympathetic supporter of the work of child immigration, particularly Barnardo's. When Mulock found his mansion too much to care for in his declining years, Hobday — through the contributions of supporters, some assistance from London, and above all the several thousands of dollars donated by former Barnardo boys and girls then working in Canada — was able to buy it." (p. 217)

25. Letter to EA Struthers from Thomas Nicholls, Canadian Manager for Hudson's Bay Company Overseas Settlement Ltd., Jan. 15, 1929, advising Struthers of George's placement in Ribstone, and referring to its earlier letter dated Oct. 16, 1928. Document courtesy Ron and Dave Evans.

26. Letter from George Evans to John Hobday written from Ribstone, Alberta, Sept. 22, 1929. Document courtesy Ron and Dave Evans.

27. Kenneth Bagnell, *The Little Immigrants*, pp. 214–15.

28. Letter from Mrs. Clapp date stamped at Winnipeg as received on Jan. 16, 1929. She seems to have got George's age wrong by one year. Document courtesy Ron and Dave Evans.

29. Letter from Barnardo's Winnipeg distribution home dated Jan. 18, 1929; letter from Hudson's Bay Overseas Settlement Ltd. dated Jan. 15, 1929. Documents courtesy Ron and Dave Evans.

30. Letters dated July 24, 1935 to Postmaster and Mr. Kinney; Evans family photographs. Documents courtesy Ron and Dave Evans.

31. Letter, signed but signature illegible, Aug. 2, 1935, to Mr. and Mrs. Clapp, 38 Nansen Road, Ipswich. Document courtesy Ron and Dave Evans.

32. Email from Dave Evans, Jan. 28, 2012; letter from Dave Evans to the author, envelope date stamped Feb. 10, 2012.

33. Marjorie Kohli, *The Golden Bridge: Young Immigrants to Canada, 1833–1939* (Toronto: Natural Heritage Books, 2003), p. 156. George writes Barnardo's in March 1941.

34. Roger Kershaw and Janet Sacks, *New Lives for Old*, p. 187.

35. Marjorie Kohli, *The Golden Bridge*, p. 156.

36. Letter to George Evans dated March 21, 1941, signed but signature illegible. Document courtesy Ron and Dave Evans.

37. Statement of Service in the Canadian Armed Forces for George Evans, Public Archives Canada document dated May 9, 1975; letter by George Evans, May 25, 1943. George's war records make no mention of his recruitment to such a unit, but he may have served alongside them in Scotland.

38. Newfoundland and Labrador Heritage website, Newfoundland Overseas Forestry Unit, http://www.heritage.nf.ca/law/forestry_unit.html, Feb. 15, 2012. "Recruiters reported an abundance of applicants eager to assist in the war effort overseas — aside from a previous call from the British Royal Navy for 625 recruits, this was the first opportunity Newfoundlanders had to serve abroad. As a result, the problem quickly shifted from finding enough men to determining which were most suitable for the job. . . . Within two months, they had selected some 2,150 volunteers, all between the ages of 18 and 55. Upon acceptance, recruits agreed to six months' labour in the United Kingdom and signed a contract outlining the terms of employment. They would earn $2 per day (the then minimum wage local paper companies paid), but had to send half of that home to relatives in Newfoundland. Wages were further reduced to $1 per day for any work missed due to illness or accident. The first draft of 350 men sailed from St. John's to Liverpool on Dec. 13, 1939. By mid-Feb., the entire unit had arrived in Britain and started to work in forests extending from southern England to the Scottish Highlands."

39. Ballater Historic Forestry Project Association, via http://www.mgl. ca/~cpike/balllaterhistory.html; http://www.ballaterforestry.org.uk/, Feb. 15, 2012. I'm taking some poetic license here, assuming George's pay rate was the same as the Newfoundland Overseas Forestry Unit men.

40. Letter from George Evans, May 25, 1943, Ballater, Aberdeenshire, Scotland. Document courtesy Ron and Dave Evans.

41. Letter from TF Tucker, Barnardo's, May 26, 1943; courtesy Ron and Dave Evans.

42. Letter to Barnardo's written by George Evans, June 6, 1943; courtesy Ron and Dave Evans.

43. Letter to George Evans from Barnardo's dated June 10, 1943; author's files. The letter mentions an uncle George, a collier aged 30 living at Hincley (sic) Leicester; Aaron, also a collier, aged 26, address unknown; Jack, 20, a carriers assistant, Blackwell, Worcestershire; Joseph, 14, "farm lad with grandfather";

Elizabeth, aged 29 (?) with grandfather; Rhoda Evans, 16, domestic servant, Newington nr. Evesham; Annie, 10, with grandfather.

44. Letter to George Evans from Barnardo's dated Nov. 12, 1943; courtesy Ron and Dave Evans.

45. Letter from Dave Evans to the author, envelope date stamped Feb. 10, 2012; email from Dave Evans, Jan. 28, 2012; *Calgary Herald* article, May 14, 1951. Dorothy's two children were Allan Peter and Christina. In an email from Dave Evans dated Feb. 15, 2012, he writes: "After talking to my brother, Jack, who was 15 years old when Dad died, he said that Dad was not married to the second wife, her name was Dorothy Vincheenie (may be spelt wrong) and she came over from England as she was married to another fellow from Hillcrest, also a soldier and those children were not Dad's."

46. Extrapolated from details reported in the *Calgary Herald*, May 14, 1951.

47. Extrapolated from details reported in the *Calgary Herald*, May 14, 1951. Interestingly, the family mythology to this day maintains that George died in a hunting accident. "My father died in a hunting accident when he was 39 years old," Dave Evans wrote me in an email on Jan. 28, 2012. He later corrected George's age at the time of death and conceded that it may in fact have been a suicide.

48. Jane Cole Hamilton, "Of Lost and Lonely and Little Children," *Toronto Star*, Nov. 3, 1984.

49. Letter from Dave Evans to the author, envelope date stamped Feb. 10, 2012; email from Dave Evans, Jan. 28, 2012.

50. Andrew N. Morrison, *Thy Children Own Their Birth, Diasporic Genealogies and the Descendants of Canada's Home Children*, thesis submitted to the University of Nottingham, June 2006, p. 225; Margaret Norrie McCain and J. Fraser Mustard , *Early Years Study: Reversing the Real Brain Drain* (Toronto: Government of Ontario,1999), http://www.familyindex.net/Categories/ Children/Health/00173.htm. See Chapter 9: *Aftermath — Troubled Childhood, Troubled Future*.

51. Andrew N. Morrison, *Thy Children Own Their Birth*, pp. 208–09.

Notes to Chapter 6

1. Barnardo's admission records for Joseph Harwood, Jan. 5, 1889, courtesy of Barnardo's After Care Services; files of Bev Harwood and the author.

2. Ibid.

3. Bev Harwood, emails to author Feb. 24 & 25, 2013, Harwood family census data from 1851, 1861, 1871, 1881, 1891, 1901, 1911. The Harwood family is firmly of Hertfordshire stock, with Joe's father John born in Broxbourne in 1841 and his mother Ann Valentine born at Westmill in 1847. John was the son of a miller who held various jobs throughout his working life — grocer's carman (probably a deliveryman), footman and gardener. His sons would mostly follow in his footsteps, holding jobs such as porter, coachman, draper's assistant, carpet salesman, and shopkeeper for a confectionary store. Two of them — Frederick and Henry — would become hairdressers, an unusual job for men in Victorian England. The 1881 census shows Joe at age 12 as second oldest of eight children, his siblings Frederick, John, Frank, Emma, Annie, Charles, and the youngest child Kate, just born that year. Four more children would be added to the family in the coming years — Henry, Ada, Robert, and the youngest, Edward, known as Ted. The Harwood siblings' birthdates were: Frederick, 1867, Joe, 1869, Annie Edith, 1870, John Valentine, 1872 or 73, Frank, 1874, Emma, 1876, Charles, 1877, Kate, 1880, Henry, 1882, Ada, 1884, Robert Valentine, 1886, Edward "Ted" Gilbert, 1890.

4. Based on Barnardo's admission records for Joseph Harwood, Jan. 5, 1889.

5. Ibid.

6. Ibid.

7. Ibid.

8. Ibid.

9. Based on Struthers' report dated Aug. 30, 1894, admission records for Joseph Harwood, courtesy of Barnardo's After Care Services; files of Bev Harwood and the author. I've taken poetic liberty in setting the event two weeks after Joe's birthday; the record states that Mrs. Fleming wrote Barnardo's in Nov. 1890.

10. The author is paraphrasing from many actual reports sent in by Barnardo boys to *Ups and Downs*, some of which are directly quoted in the text.

11. http://en.wikipedia.org/wiki/Calgary, July 3, 2013; based on these references: Tom Ward, *Cowtown: An Album of Early Calgary*, 1975; *Calgary: City of Calgary Electric System*, McClelland and Stewart West, p. 255; *The Great Fire of 1886*, retrieved 2013-03-06; *The Sandstone City*, 2002-11-21, retrieved 2013-03-06.

12. Based on Barnardo's records for Joseph Harwood, log entries summarizing letters to and from Harwood, courtesy of Barnardo's After Care Services; files of Bev Harwood and the author.

13. Ibid., April 3, 1894 entry.

14. Ibid., May 25, 1896 entry. I've allowed for two days delivery time for the letter.

15. City of Vernon website, http://www.vernon.ca/lifestyles/history/, July 3, 2013.

16. British Home Children in Canada, http://canadianbritishhomechildren. weebly.com/russell-manitoba-barnardos.html, Jan. 29, 2013.

17. Ibid., Feb. 20, 2013; Marjorie Kohli, *The Golden Bridge — Young Immigrants to Canada, 1833–1939* (Toronto: Natural Heritage Books, 2003), p. 145; June Rose, *For the Sake of the Children* (London: Hodder & Stoughton, 1987), pp. 88, 89. Kohli estimates the Russell Farm Home was 8,000 acres (3,240 hectares) while Rose puts it at about 10,000 (4,045 hectares). From Dr. Barnardo himself, writing in May 1889, we have the figure I've noted in the text: "The area of the Farm now acquired is in all 8,960 acres or fourteen square miles. This has been acquired by grant and by purchase in several distinct sections. 1,000 acres were added during the year under review."

18. British Home Children in Canada, http://canadianbritishhomechildren. weebly.com/russell-manitoba---barnardos.html, Feb. 20, 2013.

19. *Ups and Downs*, Vol. 5, No. 4, July 2, 1900.

20. Ibid.

21. "Final Tribute to Popular Pioneer Joe Harwood, 83," *Vernon News*, May 25, 1950; Vernon Archives and author's files; Transcript of an interview with the late Fred Harwood by Terry Hurst, Feb. 18, 1974, Vernon Archives.

22. *Ups and Downs*, Vol. 5, No. 3, April 1900.

23. Ibid..

24. Ibid., Vol. 4, No. 2, Jan. 1899.

25. Ibid..

26. Ibid., Vol. 4, No. 2, Jan. 1899.

27. Ibid., Vol. 5, No. 3, April 1900.

28. Ibid., Vol. 8, No. 1, April–May 1902.

29. Ibid.

30. Barnardo's records for Joseph Harwood, Dec. 4 and 30, 1903 entries, courtesy of Barnardo's After Care Services, files of Bev Harwood and the author.

31. "Final Tribute to Popular Pioneer Joe Harwood, 83," *Vernon News*, May 25, 1950; Vernon Archives and author's files; interview by author with Vic Harwood, son of Ted Harwood, Jan. 28, 2013; email from Bev Harwood, May

12, 2012, author's files. Ted Harwood was born in 1890 so his career with the Royal Navy was brief as he would only have been 22 in 1912. According to the Wikipedia entry for HMS *Bulwark* (1899), "In 1908, Captain Robert Falcon Scott of Antarctic fame became *Bulwark's* commander, becoming the youngest junior battleship commander at that time."

32. "Joe Harwood's Plea — Bring Out More Well Trained British Boys," *Vernon News,* July 1, 1937, p. 4; "Final Tribute to Popular Pioneer Joe Harwood, 83," *Vernon News,* May 25, 1950; Vernon Archives and author's files. Among Joe's last civic duties is to organize a reunion banquet for Okanagan valley pioneers in 1938, as President of the North Okanagan Old Timers' Association; he had been present at its establishment in 1913. Similar associations had been established by pioneer residents of the Okanagan and Kootenay regions both as fraternal organizations and as a means of recording early settler history. — *Vernon News,* Feb. 13, 1913; Nov. 3, 1938; *Ups and Downs* July 1939, Vol. 61, No.1.

33. Mabel Johnson, 24th Report of the Okanagan Historical Society, 1960, p. 38.

34. "Final Tribute to Popular Pioneer Joe Harwood, 83," *Vernon News,* May 25, 1950; "Joe Harwood's Plea — Bring Out More Well Trained British Boys," *Vernon News,* July 1, 1937, p. 4; Vernon Archives and author's files.

35. "Joe Harwood's Plea — Bring Out More Well Trained British Boys."

36. *Vernon News,* June 24, 1937; Vernon Museum Archives.

37. "Joe Harwood's Plea — Bring Out More Well Trained British Boys."

38. *Vernon News,* June 24, 1937; Vernon Museum Archives; Wikipedia: Harry Snell, 1st Baron Snell, http://en.wikipedia.org/wiki/Lord_Snell, Feb. 12, 2013.

39. "Joe Harwood's Plea — Bring Out More Well Trained British Boys"; Barnardo's official history, http://www.barnardos.org.uk/what_we_do/who_we_are/history.htm, Feb. 11, 2013. According to Barnardo's, "The homes ran along strictly disciplined lines and children were instilled with a sense of responsibility and self-sufficiency. They were expected to rise early and spent hours cleaning and tidying their rooms, digging and planting in the garden and carrying out maintenance work. All children received elementary education and some form of job training. Residential care emphasized children's physical and moral welfare rather than their emotional wellbeing."

40. Ibid.

41. Ibid.

42. Letter from Barnardo's Canadian Superintendent John Hobday to *Maclean's* Magazine editor, Oct. 26, 1937; letter from Hobday to GJ (Greville

Jackson) Rowland, Dec. 11, 1937; letter from London Superintendent PT Kirkpatrick to Hobday, Dec. 24, 1937. When Joe and Mary celebrate their 50th anniversary in 1943, his fame as a Barnardo boy makes their special event provincial news. He writes to thank the Hobdays for their anniversary greetings, noting that, "Both the *Vancouver Sun* and the *Vancouver Daily Province* gave us lovely write-ups. Also the local radio station for the Okanagan gave us a fifteen-minute program." — Letter from Joe Harwood thanking the Hobdays for their anniversary greetings, July 8, 1943.

43. Letter from Joe Harwood to John Hobday, Dec. 6, 1937; letter from Hobday to Joe Harwood, Nov. 29, 1937. In a letter from Hobday to Harwood dated Dec. 11, 1937, Hobday asks if he can remember the details of Dr. Barnardo's speech given that day in 1889 on the *SS Vancouver*, as "I have for a long time been trying to collect the sayings of Dr. Barnardo which have been remembered by our old boys." The Hobdays would retire in 1945 to be replaced by long-time Toronto staffer George Black. — letter from new Superintendent to Joe Harwood, Dec. 26, 1945.

44. "Final Tribute to Popular Pioneer Joe Harwood, 83," *Vernon News*, May 25, 1950; Mabel Johnson, 24th Report of the Okanagan Historical Society, 1960, pp. 39, 40.

45. Mabel Johnson, 24th Report of the Okanagan Historical Society, 1960, p. 42.

46. Ibid., pp. 39, 40.

47. "This Will Be My Last Public Duty Says Joe," *Vernon News*, Nov. 3, 1938.

48. Interview with Vic Harwood by author, Jan. 28, 2013; interview with Bev Harwood, Feb. 25, 2013.

49. Mabel Johnson, 24th Report of the Okanagan Historical Society, 1960, pp. 39, 40.

50. As quoted by Mabel Johnson, 24th Report of the Okanagan Historical Society, 1960, pp. 42.

Notes to Chapter 7

1. Leslie Drew, *LVR–The Wit and Wisdom of Leslie Vivian Rogers* (Duncan, BC: Chiss Gu Jat Publishing, 1985), p. 7.

2. Shirley D. Stainton, letter to Leslie Drew, March 4, 1985, Leslie Drew fonds, Shawn Lamb Archives, Touchstones Museum of Art and History, Nelson, BC.

3. Leslie Drew, *LVR–The Wit and Wisdom of Leslie Vivian Rogers*, p. 7.

4. Kenneth Bagnell, *The Little Immigrants* (Toronto: General Paperbacks, 1980), p. 123 (see also photo plates).

5. Jane Cole Hamilton, "Of Lost and Lonely and Little Children," *Toronto Star*, Nov. 3, 1984.

6. Roy Parker, *Uprooted — The Shipment of Poor Children to Canada, 1867–1917* (Vancouver: UBC Press, 2008), p. 284. As cited by Parker, Parr was analyzing accounts given by Home Children in Phyllis Harrison's book, *The Home Children* (Winnipeg: Watson & Dwyer Publishing Ltd., 1979).

7. LF Clargo, Barnardo's Aftercare Services, letter to Leslie Drew, Sept. 27, 1984, Leslie Drew fonds, Shawn Lamb Archives, Touchstones Museum of Art and History, Nelson, BC.

8. Leslie Drew, *LVR–The Wit and Wisdom of Leslie Vivian Rogers*, p. 9.

9. Jane Cole Hamilton, letter, Feb. 5, 1985, Leslie Drew fonds, Shawn Lamb Archives, Touchstones Museum of Art and History, Nelson, BC. Drew had written Hamilton upon reading her article in the Nov. 3, 1984 *Toronto Star*.

10. Leslie Drew, letter to Bob Marshall, Township of Haldimand (Alnwick) Ontario, March 19, 1985, Leslie Drew fonds, Shawn Lamb Archives, Touchstones Museum of Art and History, Nelson, BC.

11. James Marchant and Syrie Barnardo, *The Guild Messenger, Memoirs of the Late Dr. Barnardo*, p. 18, Leslie Drew fonds, Shawn Lamb Archives, Touchstones Museum of Art and History, Nelson, BC.

12. Ibid. estimates between 600–700, while Norman Wymer, author of *Father of Nobody's Children, A Portrait of Dr. Barnardo* (London: Hutchinson, 1954, p. 157) puts the pre-1882 figure at 900.

13. Roger Kershaw and Janet Sacks, *New Lives for Old* (London: National Archives, 2008), p. 187. "Between 21 July and 20 Sept. 1940, 18 voyages were made carrying 2,664 children to new lives in Canada, Australia, New Zealand and South Africa. Many more than 14,000 would have traveled overseas had it not been for the disastrous events on 17 Sept. . . . "

14. AE Williams, *Barnardo of Stepney*, The British Publishers, 1953, p. 130; June Rose, *For the Sake of the Children* (London: Hodder & Stoughton, 1987), p. 112.

15. Gillian Wagner, *Barnardo* (London: Weidenfeld and Nicolson, 1979), p. 191.

16. June Rose, *For the Sake of the Children*, p. 113.

17. Ibid., pp. 114, 116.

18. AE Williams, *Barnardo of Stepney*, p. 130.

19. Leslie Drew, *LVR–The Wit and Wisdom of Leslie Vivian Rogers*, p. 11.

20. KLS Gunn, letter to Leslie Drew from Office of the Registrar, Queen's University, Feb. 8, 1985, Leslie Drew fonds, Shawn Lamb Archives, Touchstones Museum of Art and History, Nelson, BC.

21. Joy Parr, *Labouring Children: British Immigrant Apprentices to Canada, 1869–1924* (Toronto: University of Toronto Press, 1980, 1994), pp. 108–09.

22. *The Kelowna Courier and Okanagan Orchardist*, Aug. 3, 1916.

23. Derek Tye, letter to Leslie Drew, Nov. 24, 1984, Leslie Drew fonds, Shawn Lamb Archives, Touchstones Museum of Art and History, Nelson, BC.

24. Leslie Drew, letters to Bob Marshall, Corporation of the Township of Haldimand, Feb. 25 & March 19, 1985, Leslie Drew fonds, Shawn Lamb Archives, Touchstones Museum of Art and History, Nelson, BC.

25. Clarence Thackeray, letter to Leslie Drew, March 4, 1985, Leslie Drew fonds, Shawn Lamb Archives, Touchstones Museum of Art and History, Nelson, BC. This fact had also been confirmed by clerk Bob Marshall of the Township of Haldimand (Alnwick), though without specifying the Village of Roseneath. (Bob Marshall, letter to Leslie Drew, Feb. 25, 1985, ibid.)

26. Clarence Thackeray, letter to Leslie Drew, March 4, 1985; Derek Tye, letter to Leslie Drew, Nov. 24, 1984; Leslie Drew fonds, Shawn Lamb Archives, Touchstones Museum of Art and History, Nelson, BC.

27. KLS Gunn, letter to Leslie Drew from Office of the Registrar, Queen's University, Feb. 8, 1985, Leslie Drew fonds, Shawn Lamb Archives, Touchstones Museum of Art and History, Nelson, BC. Gunn does not mention the honours in political science but it is noted in the *Kelowna Courier* article cited.

28. A biographical outline of LVR found in the Leslie Drew fonds of the Shawn Lamb Archives, so far uncorroborated, lists his teaching career in this chronological sequence: "taught public school Osaca, Hope Township, 1906; Alnwick Township 1907–08; Elbow, Saskatchewan, 1909–11."

29. Clarence Thackeray, letter to Leslie Drew, March 4, 1985, Leslie Drew fonds, Shawn Lamb Archives, Touchstones Museum of Art and History, Nelson, BC. Thackeray noted that Woodvale School at the time of writing had been converted to a summer residence.

30. *The Mountaineer*, 1956 Nelson High School yearbook excerpt, Leslie Drew fonds, Shawn Lamb Archives, Touchstones Museum of Art and History, Nelson, BC.

31. *The Kelowna Courier and Okanagan Orchardist*, Aug. 3, 1916; Leslie Drew,

LVR — *The Wit and Wisdom of Leslie Vivian Rogers*, ibid., p. 11.

32. *The Kelowna Courier and Okanagan Orchardist*, Aug. 3, 1916.

33. Derek Tye, letter to Leslie Drew, Nov. 24, 1984, Leslie Drew fonds, Shawn Lamb Archives, Touchstones Museum of Art and History, Nelson, BC.

34. Gerald Priest, letter to Leslie Drew, undated; Leslie Drew fonds, Shawn Lamb Archives, Touchstones Museum of Art and History, Nelson, BC.

35. Janet EV Graham, letter to Leslie Drew, Jan. 16, 1985, Leslie Drew fonds, Shawn Lamb Archives, Touchstones Museum of Art and History, Nelson, BC.

36. Leslie Drew, *LVR–The Wit and Wisdom of Leslie Vivian Rogers*, ibid., p. 15; re: history of women's vote in Canada, see the Nellie McClung Foundation, http://www.ournellie.com/womens-suffrage/history-of-womens-rights, Feb. 1, 2013; Marianopolis College, Quebec, The History of Women Suffrage in Canada, http://faculty.marianopolis.edu/c.belanger/quebechistory/encyclopedia/Canada-WomensVote-WomenSuffrage.htm, Feb. 1, 2013.

37. Derek Tye, letters to Leslie Drew, Nov. 24, 1984 & April 11, 1985, Leslie Drew fonds, Shawn Lamb Archives, Touchstones Museum of Art and History, Nelson, BC.

38. *The Mountaineer*, 1956 Nelson High School yearbook excerpt, Leslie Drew fonds, Shawn Lamb Archives, Touchstones Museum of Art and History, Nelson, BC.

39. Leslie Drew, *LVR–The Wit and Wisdom of Leslie Vivian Rogers*, pp. 21, 22.

40. Ibid., p. 17.

41. Ibid., p. 15.

42. Ibid., p. 8.

43. Ibid., pp. 29, 30.

44. Ibid., pp. 7, 27–28; biographical outline, Leslie Drew fonds, Shawn Lamb Archives, Touchstones Museum of Art and History, Nelson, BC.

45. Ibid., pp. 7, 27; biographical outline, Leslie Drew fonds, Shawn Lamb Archives, Touchstones Museum of Art and History, Nelson, BC. According to a letter from Leslie Drew to LVR High School Principal Neil W. McDonald dated Jan. 23, 1985, Rogers' will named Mrs. CW "Jessie" Appleyard of Nelson as his sole beneficiary.

46. Gordon Fleming, letter to Leslie Drew, March 28, 1985, Leslie Drew fonds, Shawn Lamb Archives, Touchstones Museum of Art and History, Nelson, BC.

47. Leslie Drew, *LVR–The Wit and Wisdom of Leslie Vivian Rogers*, pp. 9–11.

Notes to Chapter 8

1. From transcription of archival film footage, with a title card that reads: "The ceremony of laying the cornerstone at the New Chapel, Prince of Wales Fairbridge Farm School, Vancouver Island, BC. Sept. 22, 1939." Author's files.

2. Geoffrey Sherington and Chris Jeffery, *Fairbridge: Empire and Child Migration* (London: Woburn Press, 1998), p. 15. Kingsley Fairbridge was born May 2, 1885 in Grahamstown, South Africa. His parents were Rhys Seymour Fairbridge and Rosalie Helen (Ogilvie) Fairbridge.

3. Ibid., pp. 5, 17–19. Fairbridge cultivates the patronage of Earl Grey, contacting him again in 1908 to outline his scheme for child emigration (p. 20).

4. Ibid., pp. 25–26.

5. Stan Sauerwein with Arthur Bailey, *Fintry: Lives, Loves and Dreams* (Victoria: Trafford/Central Okanagan Heritage Society, 2000), p. 144; *Vernon News*, Jan. 29, 1942.

6. Geoffrey Sherington and Chris Jeffery, *Fairbridge: Empire and Child Migration*, p. 12.

7. Kingsley Fairbridge, *The Times*, May 1910; Prince of Wales Fairbridge Farm School fonds, BC Provincial Archives, file MS.2045, box 1.

8. Ibid.; Stan Sauerwein with Arthur Bailey, *Fintry: Lives, Loves and Dreams*, p. 144; Geoffrey Sherington and Chris Jeffery, *Fairbridge: Empire and Child Migration*, pp. 16, 25.

9. Geoffrey Sherington and Chris Jeffery, *Fairbridge: Empire and Child Migration*, p. 1; *The Operative*, May 5, 1839, partially reproduced and quoted in the *Fairbridge Gazette*, Spring 2010, p. 17, article by Pat Skidmore.

10. *Ups &°Downs*, Vol. 9, No. 2, April 1903, p. 1.

11. Joy Parr, *Labouring Children: British Immigrant Apprentices to Canada, 1869–1924* (Toronto: University of Toronto Press, 1980, 1994), p. 143.

12. Geoffrey Sherington and Chris Jeffery, *Fairbridge: Empire and Child Migration*, pp. 13, 15, 25–26.

13. Ibid., p. 21, notes that Fairbridge conceived his child emigration plan "within a much wider strategy of consolidating the British Empire through settlement and specifically settlement in Southern Africa. As such he was fulfilling the legacy of Cecil Rhodes."

14. Stan Sauerwein with Arthur Bailey, *Fintry: Lives, Loves and Dreams*, p. 144, re: Society mandates; Geoffrey Sherington and Chris Jeffery, *Fairbridge:*

Empire and Child Migration, ibid., p. 25, re: "unifying Anglo-Saxon people throughout the Empire."

15. Stan Sauerwein with Arthur Bailey, *Fintry: Lives, Loves and Dreams*, p. 144.

16. *Vernon News*, Vernon, BC, Jan. 29, 1942.

17. Geoffrey Sherington and Chris Jeffery, *Fairbridge: Empire and Child Migration*, pp. 46–47.

18. *Vernon News*, Vernon, BC, Jan. 29, 1942.

19. Helen Borrell, "The Fairbridge Farm School," *BC Historical News*, Winter 1995/96, pp. 17–23.

20. Geoffrey Sherington and Chris Jeffery, *Fairbridge: Empire and Child Migration*, pp. 110–14, 166.

21. Ibid., p. 160.

22. Ibid., p. 156.

23. Ibid., pp. 160–61; "Story of Founding of Fairbridge," *The Vernon News*, Jan. 29, 1942.

24. Helen Borrell, "The Fairbridge Farm School," *BC Historical News*, Winter 1995/96, p. 18.

25. Stan Sauerwein with Arthur Bailey, *Fintry: Lives, Loves and Dreams*, p. 146.

26. *Fairbridge Gazette*, Christmas 2006, p. 18; transcription of archival film footage for ceremony of laying the cornerstone at the new Chapel, Prince of Wales Fairbridge Farm School, Sept. 22, 1939.

27. David RB Dendy, monograph, Kelowna, BC public archives, Sept. 1983, p. 119; *Fairbridge Gazette*, Christmas 2006, p. 4; Geoffrey Sherington and Chris Jeffery, *Fairbridge: Empire and Child Migration*, ibid., pp. 177–78. Sherington and Jeffery cite Patrick Dunae's analysis of the total 329 Fairbridge children sent to the Prince of Wales Farm School, showing that "only five percent were now orphans with no known living parents."

28. *Fairbridge Gazette*, Christmas 2006, pp. 5, 18; *Some Fairbridge Milestones*, BC Archives document, file MS.2045, box 1. The cottages built in 1937 are: Lumley, Strathcona, Douglas and Pennant; in 1938, the Dulverton, MacMillan, Hill and Molyneux cottages are added. The last two, Leybourne and Davidson, are built in 1939.

29. Geoffrey Sherington and Chris Jeffery, *Fairbridge: Empire and Child Migration*, ibid., pp. 172–74.

30. *Fairbridge Gazette*, Christmas 2006, pp. 5, 12 re: Hancock and Arthur Sager memories of Logan; *Fairbridge Gazette*, Spring 2010, p. 8 (source: UBC ar-

chives Logan fonds) notes in a biography of Logan that he was born March 5, 1887 in Londonderry, Nova Scotia and educated at Vancouver High School, McGill University, Oxford University (as Rhodes Scholar for BC 1908–11), Presbyterian College (McGill 1911–12), and New College Edinburgh (1912–13) where he studied theology. "Harry Logan and Gwyneth Murray met in Oxford in 1909 and were engaged to be married in 1911, when Logan returned to Canada. . . . Logan taught Classics at McGill University College of BC from 1913–15 until his career was interrupted by war service." He died in 1971.

31. *Fairbridge Gazette*, Christmas 2008, pp. 14, 15; reproduction of *The Times*, Oct. 9, 1936. In the *Fairbridge Gazette*, Summer 2007, p. 6, editor Pat Skidmore notes that, "in the distressed areas — the old industrial heartlands of South Wales, the West of Scotland, Lancashire, Tyneside and West Yorkshire," unemployment "never fell below a million in the 1920s and remained at shockingly high levels of between 40% and 60% (even 80% in some of the most blighted regions) during the 1930s." Sheringon and Jeffery note, "Following the creation in 1934 of the Commissioner for Special Areas the British Government urged the Society to take more children from the "distressed areas" in the north of England, Wales and Scotland, providing grants to open offices of the Society in those areas. By 1939, Fairbridge branch offices had opened in Newcastle-on-Tyne, Cardiff and Glasgow." (*Fairbridge: Empire and Child Migration*, p. 176.)

32. Ibid., p. 15; reproduction of *Vancouver Sun*, Nov. 7, 1936; Fairbridge Milestones, original document from Prince of Wales Farm School, BC Archives file MS.2045, box 1.

33. Geoffrey Sherington and Chris Jeffery, *Fairbridge: Empire and Child Migration*, pp. 175–76.

34. *Some Fairbridge Milestones*, BC Archives document, file MS.2045, box 1; transcription of archival film footage.

35. Transcription of archival film footage, author's notes; *Fairbridge Gazette*, Vol. 1, No. 8, Aug. 1940; Ron Smith, *Fairbridge Chapel Dedication* (source: *Cowichan Leader*, April 25, 1940), author's files. Included among the dignitaries officiating were Right Rev. Harold E. Sexton, Bishop of British Columbia; Right Rev. Walter R. Adams, Bishop of the Kootenays; Rev. Hugh A. McLeod, Minister of First United Church, Victoria; Rev. HT Archbold, Duncan; and Rev. Canon TM Hughes.

36. Ron Smith, *Fairbridge Chapel Dedication* (source: *Cowichan Leader*, April 25, 1940), author's files; *Fairbridge Gazette*, Summer 2009, p. 21, letter dated Aug. 1, 1990 from Somerset regarding history of chapel organ; letter of D.

Stuart Kennedy to Prince of Wales Farm School, Oct. 5, 1959, BC Archives file MS.2045. When the Prince of Wales Farm School closed in 1950, the organ was donated to the University of Victoria and later installed in Victoria's Christchurch Cathedral in 1975.

37. *Some Fairbridge Milestones*, BC Archives, file MS.2045, box 1; *Fairbridge Gazette*, Vol. 1, No. 5, Aug. 1939, BC Archives, file MS.2045, box 1. Geoffrey Sherington and Chris Jeffery, *Fairbridge: Empire and Child Migration*, p. 171.

38. "Laird of Fintry is Called by Death," *The Vernon News*, Oct. 16, 1939, pp. 1, 9.

39. Report for 1930 of Government Experimental Station, Windermere, BC by Superintendent RG Newton, BSA, Minister of Agriculture, Ottawa, 1932, Windermere Valley Archives; *A History of Fintry*, by David RB Dendy, monograph, 1983, Kelowna Public Archives; "Laird of Fintry is Called by Death," *The Vernon News*, Oct. 16, 1939, pp. 1, 9.

40. "Fintry Estate Presented to Fairbridge Schools," *Vernon News*, July 7, 1938; the Jan. 29, 1942 issue estimates Fintry's value at $1 million.

41. "Fintry Fairbridge Boys Learn to Pick 'Macs,'" *Vernon News*, Oct. 5, 1939; *A History of Fintry*, by David RB Dendy, monograph, 1983, Kelowna Public Archives.

42. *Fairbridge Gazette*, Vol. 1, No. 5, Aug. 1939; *A History of Fintry*, by David RB Dendy, monograph, 1983, p. 120, Kelowna Public Archives; *Rambling in Paradise*, from *The Western Recorder*, Vancouver, BC, Sept. 1943, pp. 4–5, Vernon Archives.

43. "Fintry Fairbridge School Closes Until Next April," *Vernon News*, Oct. 19, 1939.

44. *Fairbridge Gazette*, Vol. 1, No. 5, Aug. 1939.

45. 56th Report of the Okanagan Historical Society, 1992, p. 64.

46. "Fintry Fairbridge School Closes Until Next April," *Vernon News*, Oct. 19, 1939; "Fintry Fairbridge Boys Learn to Pick 'Macs,'" *Vernon News*, Oct. 5, 1939.

47. "Fintry Fairbridge School Closes Until Next April," *Vernon News*, Oct. 19, 1939; "Fintry Fairbridge Boys Learn to Pick 'Macs,'" *Vernon News*, Oct. 5, 1939.

48. 38th Report of the Okanagan Historical Society, Nov. 1, 1974; "Fintry Fairbridge School Closes Until Next April," *Vernon News*, Oct. 19, 1939.

49. Roger Kershaw and Janet Sacks, *New Lives for Old* (London: National Archives, 2008), pp. 171–72.

50. Roger Kershaw and Janet Sacks, *New Lives for Old*, p. 171.

51. Interview with Tom Isherwood, Jan. 30, 2012.

52. *Fairbridge Gazette*, Summer 2007, p. 14; excerpt from Arthur Sager's memoir, *It's in the Book: Notes of a Naïve Young Man* (Victoria, BC: Trafford, 2003), pp. 167–7.

53. *Fairbridge Gazette*, Summer 2007, p. 14; excerpt from Arthur Sager's memoir, *It's in the Book: Notes of a Naïve Young Man.*

54. Philip Bean and Joy Melville, *Lost Children of the Empire* (London: Unwin Hyman, 1989), cited in the *Fairbridge Gazette*, Summer 2007, p. 13.

55. Interview with William Stoker, Aug. 23, 2012.

56. *Fairbridge Gazette*, Spring 2007, p. 21, excerpt from Arthur Sager's memoir, *It's in the Book: Notes of a Naïve Young Man*, ibid., where he notes that "Cottage mothers were not permitted to use corporal punishment. . . ."

57. *Fairbridge Gazette*, Christmas 2006, p. 18.

58. Geoffrey Sherington and Chris Jeffery, *Fairbridge: Empire and Child Migration*, pp. 175–76.

59. *Fairbridge Gazette*, Christmas 2006, p. 15.

60. Ibid., p. 15; excerpt from Arthur Sager's memoir, *It's in the Book: Notes of a Naïve Young Man.*

61. *Fairbridge Gazette*, Christmas 2006, p. 15; Spring 2007, pp. 20–21; excerpt from Arthur Sager's memoir, *It's in the Book: Notes of a Naïve Young Man*, ibid. In Ben Wicks' memoir, *No Time to Wave Goodbye* (Toronto: General Paperbacks, 1989, p. 91) he notes a similar problem with children removed from their families from the cities of Britain during the bombing raids of WW II. "The fear and anxiety of children who had been separated from their parents for the first time resulted in the most common complaint — bedwetting."

62. *Fairbridge Gazette*, Summer 2006, p. 12; re: experience of Joan Vallentin.

63. Correspondence of Mary (Schofield) Nichols, BC Archives file MSS.2459, letter excerpts Sept. 17, 1943 and Oct. 3, 1943.

64. Ibid. Sept. 17, 1943.

65. Ibid. Sept. 17, 1943 and Oct. 3, 1943.

66. Correspondence of Mary (Schofield) Nichols, BC Archives file MSS.2459, letter excerpts Jan. 16, 1944, Mar. 5, 1944 and Dec. 4, 1944.

67. Administrative records held in files designated MS.2045 by BC Archives have been sealed by the donor, Fairbridge, until 2035. Corroborating ma-

terial has been graciously provided by Oliver Cosgrove through the Australian Joint Copying Project, National Library of Australia, Canberra, 1991; Australian Joint Copying Project handbook. Part 10, Dominions Office, class, piece and file list / compiled by Margaret E. Phillips, http://books.google.ca/books?printsec=frontcover&vid=ISBN0642105170&red ir_esc=y#v=onepage&q&f=false.

68. Correspondence of Mary (Schofield) Nichols, BC Archives file MSS.2459, letter excerpts Nov. 15, 1943.

69. See note 67; provincial government report, Oct. 10, 1944; a Dominion Office file microfilmed as part of the Australian Joint Copying Project, National Library of Australia, Canberra, 1991.

70. See note 67.

71. See note 67.

72. Provincial government report, Oct. 10, 1944; a Dominion Office file microfilmed as part of the Australian Joint Copying Project, National Library of Australia, Canberra, 1991.

73. Dr. Davidson's report of "political interference" is cited in a provincial government report dated Oct. 10, 1944; a Dominion Office file microfilmed as part of the Australian Joint Copying Project, National Library of Australia, Canberra, 1991.

74. K. Phyllis Burns, Vancouver Children's Aid Society, 1901–1951, *Canadian Welfare*, Apr. 15, 1951, Vol. XXVII, no. 1, re: work of Canadian Council on Child Welfare and history of reform. As noted in *People, Politics and Child Welfare in British Columbia*, edited by Leslie T. Foster and Brian Wharf (Vancouver: UBC Press, 2007, p. 17), similar surveys of child welfare were conducted in eight other provinces between 1927 and 1949. See also note 67.

75. K. Phyllis Burns, Vancouver Children's Aid Society, 1901–1951, *Canadian Welfare*, Apr. 15, 1951, Vol. XXVII, no. 1; Annie Margaret Angus, Canadian Welfare Council newsletter, Feb. 1951, p. 6. As noted in *People, Politics and Child Welfare in British Columbia*, edited by Leslie T. Foster and Brian Wharf (Vancouver: UBC Press, 2007, p. 16) other social workers instrumental in laying down a new approach to child welfare in BC were Zella Collins and Mary MacPhedran. Collectively with Holland they were dubbed "the three wise women from the east."

76. Provincial government report, Oct. 10, 1944; a Dominion Office file microfilmed as part of the Australian Joint Copying Project, National Library of Australia, Canberra, 1991. Historian Patrick Dunae noted that the first

scrutiny of the Prince of Wales Farm School came in 1943, when Edith Pringle, Deputy Inspector of Provincial Welfare Institutions, "carried out a preliminary assessment of the farm school's policies. She was distressed to find that the Fairbridge infirmary did not comply with the provincial Hospitals Act and that its medical staff were not properly qualified." (*Child Welfare and Social Action in the 19th and 20th Centuries: International Perspectives*, essays by various authors, edited by Jon Lawrence and Pat Starkey, Liverpool University Press, 2001; *Gender, Generations and Social Class: The Fairbridge Society and British Child Migration to Canada, 1930–1960*, Patrick Dunae, pp. 91, 92.)

77. Report of Isobel Harvey for the BC Child Welfare department, Aug. 1944, pp. 2, 3; a Dominion Office file microfilmed as part of the Australian Joint Copying Project, National Library of Australia, Canberra, 1991.

78. Ibid.; Interview of Mary Nichols by author, Oct. 16, 2012.

79. Report of Isobel Harvey for Provincial Child Welfare department, Aug. 1944, pp. 2, 3; a Dominion Office file microfilmed as part of the Australian Joint Copying Project, National Library of Australia, Canberra, 1991.

80. Ibid. pp. 4, 5.

81. Ibid.

82. Ibid., p. 6.

83. Ibid. p. 7.

84. Patrick Dunae, *Gender, Generations and Social Class: The Fairbridge Society and British Child Migration to Canada, 1930—960, Child Welfare and Social Action in the 19th and 20th Centuries: International Perspectives* (essays by various authors) edited by Jon Lawrence and Pat Starkey, Liverpool University Press, 2001, p. 93.

85. Report of Isobel Harvey for Provincial Child Welfare department, Aug. 1944, p. 8.

86. Correspondence of Mary (Schofield) Nichols, BC Archives file MSS.2459, letter excerpts Sept. 14, 1944.

87. *Victoria Daily Times*, Jan. 9, 1945.

88. *Victoria Daily Times*, Jan. 8 & 9, 1945; provincial government report, Oct. 10, 1944, noting minutes of Sept. 11, 1944 meeting; a Dominion Office file microfilmed as part of the Australian Joint Copying Project, National Library of Australia, Canberra, 1991.

89. Correspondence of Mary (Schofield) Nichols, BC Archives file MSS.2459, letter excerpts Sept. 20, 1946; May 18, 1948; letters from Jock Gillatt dated

July 29, 1947 and May 13, 1948.

90. *Victoria Daily Times,* Jan. 9, 1945; provincial government report, Oct. 10, 1944; a Dominion Office file microfilmed as part of the Australian Joint Copying Project, National Library of Australia, Canberra, 1991.

91. Correspondence of Mary (Schofield) Nichols, BC Archives file MSS.2459, letter excerpts Jan. 17, 1945.

92. Report of Gordon Green to London executive of Fairbridge Society, March 5, 1945; provincial government report, Oct. 10, 1944; a Dominion Office file microfilmed as part of the Australian Joint Copying Project, National Library of Australia, Canberra, 1991.

93. Report of Gordon Green to London executive of Fairbridge Society, March 5, 1945; a Dominion Office file microfilmed as part of the Australian Joint Copying Project, National Library of Australia, Canberra, 1991.

94. Report of Gordon Green to London executive of Fairbridge Society, March 5, 1945; provincial government report, Oct. 10, 1944; a Dominion Office file microfilmed as part of the Australian Joint Copying Project, National Library of Australia, Canberra, 1991; BC Archives: Annie Margaret Angus fonds, MSS.2469. The new Fairbridge BC board of governors included MP RW Mayhew, chairman; PB Fowler and AJ Hendry, vice-chairmen; with an executive comprised of Mayhew, Hendry, Fowler, LF Solly, LA Grogan (secretary), and Logan. Appointment of a Fintry advisory committee was pending. As of Sept. 1946 the board was comprised of Logan, Mayhew (Chairman), LF Solly (Deputy Chairman), Colonel FT Fairey, Laura Holland, WC Mainwaring, P. Walker, AJ Watson, WL Woodhouse, HA Beckwith, Colonel HW Laws, and Annie Angus.

95. Provincial government report, Oct. 10, 1944; Dominion Office file microfilmed as part of the Australian Joint Copying Project, National Library of Australia, Canberra, 1991.

96. Report of Gordon Green to London executive of Fairbridge Society, March 5, 1945; a Dominion Office file microfilmed as part of the Australian Joint Copying Project, National Library of Australia, Canberra, 1991.

97. Correspondence of Mary (Schofield) Nichols, BC Archives file MSS.2459, letter excerpts May 22, 1945. The Sir Charles she refers to here is likely Charles Jocelyn Hambro of the wealthy Hambro banking family (3 Oct. 1897–1963). Hambro worked in British intelligence during the war as a member of the Special Operations Executive (SOE). http://en.wikipedia.org/wiki/Charles_Jocelyn_Hambro, Jan. 17, 2013.

98. Prince of Wales Fairbridge Farm School list of children sent to the farm

school between Sept. 25, 1935 and May 25, 1948, http://fairbridgecanada. com/farmschoolrollcall.pdf, Jan. 17, 2013; *Fairbridge Gazette*, Vol. 6, No. 2, Fall–Nov. 1945, p. 1.

99. Prince of Wales Fairbridge Farm School list of children sent to the farm school between Sept. 25, 1935 and May 25, 1948, http://fairbridgecanada. com/farmschoolrollcall.pdf, Jan. 17, 2013.

100. Among those killed in action were Harold Thomas Kemp, killed in Normandy in 1944 and Norman Alsop, killed in 1944.

101. David RB Dendy, *A History of Fintry*, monograph, Kelowna, BC public archives, Sept. 1983, p. 121; Stan Sauerwein with Arthur Bailey, *Fintry: Lives, Loves and Dreams*, p. 147.

102. Stan Sauerwein with Arthur Bailey, *Fintry: Lives, Loves and Dreams*, p. 148.

103. Prince of Wales Fairbridge Farm School list of children sent to the farm school between Sept. 25, 1935 and May 25, 1948; www.fairbridgecanada. com; notes from meeting minutes of Fairbridge's BC Board of Governors, Nov. 8, 1947, BC Archives MS.2045.

104. Patrick Dunae, *Gender, Generations and Social Class: The Fairbridge Society and British Child Migration to Canada, 1930–1960, Child Welfare and Social Action in the 19th and 20th Centuries: International Perspectives* ibid., p. 95; Stan Sauerwein with Arthur Bailey, *Fintry: Lives, Loves and Dreams*, pp. 148–49.

105. Kenneth Henry Brill, *The Curtis Experiment* (thesis), Faculty of Commerce and Social Science, University of Birmingham, UK, e-thesis repository, http://etheses.bham.ac.uk/1315/1/Brill91PhD1.pdf, synopsis, Jan. 22, 2013. "Their extensive list of recommendations was broadly put into effect by the Children Act 1948, which remained in force until 1 April 1971 when social services for children were taken over by the social services committees under the Local Authority Social Services Act of 1970."

106. Report of Leonard C. Marsh, BSc (Econ.), M.A., PhD, Department of Social Work, University of British Columbia; formerly Director of Social Research, McGill University; Research Advisor, Dominion Committee on Reconstruction, etc., March 1948; BC Archives MS.2045.

107. David RB Dendy, *A History of Fintry*, monograph, 1983, Kelowna Public Archives.

108. Interview with Patricia Skidmore via email, Jan. 9, 2012.

109. Ibid; text of PM Brown's apology is available at: http://www.parliament.uk/ business/news/2010/02/prime-ministers-statement-child-migration/, Jan. 22, 2013.

110. *Farm of Fear,* http://poundpuplegacy.org/node/38272, Jan. 22, 2013.

111. Geoffrey Sherington, Fairbridge Child Migrants, *Child Welfare and Social Action in the 19ᵗʰ and 20ᵗʰ Centuries: International Perspectives* (essays by various authors), p. 67.

112. Margaret Humphreys, *Empty Cradles* (London: Corgi Books, 1994/1997), p. 132; Flo Hickson, *Child Migrant from Liverpool,* Plowright Press, PO Box 66, Warwick, UK CV34 4XE, http://www.plowrightpress.co.uk/Flo.htm, Jan. 22, 2013.

113. "British Child Migrants Launch Legal Action Against Australian Government," Frank Thorne, *The Daily Mail,* June 14, 2011; "Working on a Farm Where Love Never Bloomed," *The Western Mail* (Australia), Aug. 8–9, 1987.

114. "Fairbridge Sex Abuse Scandal Revealed," *The West Australian,* May 26, 2012; "Fairbridge Child Abuse Investigated in WA," Sharon Kennedy, May 29, 2012.

115. "Australian Apology to British Child Migrants: Speech in Full," *The Telegraph,* Nov. 16, 2009; British Home Children in Canada (video of full apology), http://canadianbritishhomechildren.weebly.com/australian-apology.html, Jan. 22, 2013.

116. Barry M. Coldrey, "A Mixture of Caring and Corruption," *Studies: An Irish Quarterly Review,* March 2000, cited at Pound Pup Legacy website, http://poundpuplegacy.org/node/22643, Jan. 22, 2013.

117. Flo Hickson, *Child Migrant from Liverpool,* Jan. 22, 2013.

118. "When Love Alone Isn't Enough," Roger Graef, *The Telegraph,* Nov. 25, 2012; http://www.telegraph.co.uk/news/politics/ukip/9702249/When-love-aloneisnt-enough.html, Jan. 22, 2013; *Fairbridge Gazette,* Spring 2007, p. 10.

119. Interview with Tom Isherwood by author, Jan. 30, 2012.

120. Interview with Tom Isherwood, Jan. 30, 2012; *Tom Isherwood, Child Migrant, Aquitania, May 25, 1947,* Pier 21: Canada's Immigration Museum, http://www.pier21.ca/research/collections/online-story-collection/child-migrants, Jan. 22, 2013.

121. Ibid.

122. *Tom Isherwood, Child Migrant, Aquitania, May 25, 1947,* ibid., Jan. 22, 2013.

123. Interview with William Stoker, Aug. 23, 2012.

124. Interview with Patricia Skidmore via email, Jan. 9, 2012.

125. *Ibid.*

126. Tom Isherwood, "First Christmas in Canada 1947" (poem), email Jan. 29, 2012; *Tom Isherwood, Child Migrant, Aquitania, May 25, 1947*, ibid., Jan. 22, 2013.

Notes to Chapter 9

1. *The Changing Face of Poverty*, Julian Knight, BBC News, July 26, 2005; "Breaking the Cycle of Child Poverty," Neera Sharma, BBC News, July 25, 2005; "BC's 14.3 percent Child Poverty Rate Ranks Second Worst in Canada Says Report," Dirk Meissner, Canadian Press, Nov. 21, 2012; http://www.vancouversun.com/business/cent+child+poverty+rate+ranks+second+worst+Canada+says+report/7588641/story.html#ixzz2FUgzq6KF, Jan. 22, 2013.

2. "The Way We Live Now," Lynsey Hanley, *The Guardian*, March 14, 2009, http://www.guardian.co.uk/books/2009/mar/13/the-spirit-level, Jan. 23, 2013, review of Richard Wilkinson & Kate Pickett, *The Spirit Level: Why Greater Equality Makes Societies Stronger* (London: Bloomsbury Publishing PLC, 2009).

3. The Equality Trust Research Digest, Income Inequality: Trends and Measures 2011; available for download at http://www.equalitytrust.org.uk/resources/publications; Jan. 23, 2013.

4. Robert A. Nisbet, *The Social Bond: An Introduction to the Study of Society* (New York: Alfred A. Knopf, 1970), p. 89.

5. Ibid., p. 66.

6. "Frederick Douglass (born Frederick Augustus Washington Bailey, c. Feb. 1818–Feb. 20, 1895) was an American social reformer, orator, writer and statesman. After escaping from slavery, he became a leader of the abolitionist movement, gaining note for his dazzling oratory and incisive antislavery writing. He stood as a living counter-example to slaveholders' arguments that slaves did not have the intellectual capacity to function as independent American citizens. Many Northerners also found it hard to believe that such a great orator had been a slave." Source: Wikipedia.

7. Andrew S. Garner, MD, PhD; Jack P. Shonkoff, MD; Benjamin S. Siegel, MD; et al., *Early Childhood Adversity, Toxic Stress, and the Role of the Pediatrician: Translating Developmental Science into Lifelong Health*, Pediatrics Vol. 129 No. 1, Jan. 1, 2012, pp. e224 -e231, http://pediatrics.aappublications.org/content/129/1/e224.full.html.

8. *Remembering Dr. Fraser Mustard (1927–2011)*, Jennifer Lanthier, University

of Toronto News, Nov. 17, 2011; http://news.utoronto.ca/remembering-dr-fraser-mustard-1927—-2011; Jan. 23, 2013; Margaret McCain and J. Fraser Mustard, *Early Years Study: Reversing the Real Brain Drain* (Toronto: Government of Ontario,1999), http://www.familyindex.net/Categories/Children/Health/00173.htm.

9. Kristin Rushowy, "Canada is Failing its Kids, MD says," *Toronto Star*, April 30, 2007, http://www.thestar.com/News/article/208734, Jan. 23, 2013; Margaret McCain and J. Fraser Mustard, *Early Years Study: Reversing the Real Brain Drain.*

10. Andrew S. Garner, MD, PhD; Jack P. Shonkoff, MD; Benjamin S. Siegel, MD; et al., *Early Childhood Adversity, Toxic Stress, and the Role of the Pediatrician: Translating Developmental Science into Lifelong Health.*

11. Vincent J. Felitti, Robert F. Anda, Dale Nordenberg, et al., "Relationship of Childhood Abuse and Household Dysfunction to Many of the Leading Causes of Death in Adults." *American Journal of Preventative Medicine*, Vol. 14, No. 4.

12. Jeremy Rifkin, *The Empathic Civilization* (NY: Tarcher/Penguin, 2010), pp. 9, 10.

13. Margaret McCain and J. Fraser Mustard, *Early Years Study: Reversing the Real Brain Drain.*

14. Kristin Rushowy, "Canada is Failing its Kids, MD says," *Toronto Star*, April 30, 2007.

15. Wikipedia, "workhouse," Feb. 10, 2012. Sources: Trevor May, *An Economic and Social History of Britain 1760–1970*, Longman Group, 1987, pp. 120, 122; Simon Fowler, *Workhouse: The People: The Places: The Life Behind Closed Doors*, The National Archives, 2007, pp. 10, 14.

Index

Tarbox, Mr., 114–117

Teighmore Home, Jersey Islands, 99–102, 307*, 308*

Thackeray, Clarence, 218, 331*

Theodore, SK, 104, 106, 109, 116, 119

Thompson family, 57–90; Elizabeth Emma (Deptford), 57–61, 72–87, 89 (photo), 284, 301*, 306*; Caroline Maud, 57–61, 72–74, 76–79, 81, 86; James Jr., 81; James Sr., 57, 59, 60, 86

Tibbotts, Richard, 109, 113, 114

Todd, Ernie, 234, 246

Toxteth Park Workhouse, 94, 307*

Trail, BC, 45, 117, 119, 312*

Trew, Major Maurice F., 235

Tucker, TF, 178, 324*

Turner, Tom, 236

Tye, Derek, 218, 219, 221, 331*, 332*

University of British Columbia, Department of Social Work, 265

Ups & Downs, 72, 107, 110–113, 138, 139, 142, 151, 154, 192, 194, 197, 198, 200, 207, 208

Vernon, BC, 79, 84, 86, 194, 201, 202, 207–211, 239, 243, 261

Vernon News, 202, 206–209, 231, 232, 240, 241–243

Vancouver, BC, 80, 236, 254, 271

Vancouver Sun, 236, 329*, 335*, 343*

Wagner, Gillian, 215, 307*, 313*

Waifs & Strays Society, 17, 25, 31, 38, 39, 299*; Elizabeth Rye Home, 25, 28

Walker, Dr. Jane, 215, 216

Wallace, Rev. Robert, 77

Walsh, Arnold, 51, 289, 301*

Watson, EH, 105, 106

Weir, Dr. GM, 252

Welfare Institutions Licensing Act, BC, 252, 259, 260

White, David, 105, 196

Whiteman, Alice, 136, 137, 143, 148, 315*, 316*

Whitton, Charlotte, 27, 136, 147, 148, 253, 317*

Whitwell, Mark, 130

William Baker Technical School, 168–170, 205, 321*, 322*

Williams, AE, 215, 330*

Wilson, Major TM, 251

Windermere, BC, 239, 336*

Winnipeg, MB, 84, 103, 106–110, 148, 172, 195, 196, 309*

Wood, Rev. HW, 163, 165

World War I, 39, 80, 81, 84, 117, 127, 132, 136, 138, 147, 172, 223, 232, 238, 239, 265, 267, 311*

World War II, 45, 49, 151, 154, 176, 209, 212, 213, 215, 216, 221–223, 243, 244, 248, 250, 262, 272

YMCA, 83, 141, 172

Yorkshire, 242

Yorkton, SK, 103, 105, 107–109, 112, 115, 190

Sean Arthur Joyce is better known in the West Kootenay region of British Columbia as Art Joyce for his newspaper columns and books on local history. Joyce has been a freelance journalist for 25 years.

Born in the East Kootenay community of Kimberley, BC, in 1959, Joyce grew up in a family steeped in the love of history. He estimates having published 250,000 words in his "Heritage Beat" column for the *Nelson Daily News* from 1996–2000. While doing genealogical research on the Joyce family, he discovered his grandfather Cyril Joyce was a Home Child, and began researching Canada's Home Children.

Joyce's poems and essays have appeared in Canadian and international literary journals, including *Canadian Author*, *Fiddlehead*, *Whetstone* and *Acumen* (UK). In 2001, with funding from BRAVO TV, he wrote and directed a poetry video, *The Muse: Chameleon Fire*. In 2006 he appeared in an international anthology, *The Book of Hopes and Dreams* (bluechrome press, UK), featuring work by Lawrence Ferlinghetti and Margaret Atwood. New Orphic Publishers of Nelson, BC, published his first two major collections of poetry, *The Charlatans of Paradise* (2005), and *Star Seeds* (2009).